Lately coffee has been upsetting my stomach, so I've switched to tea instead. Turns out, I really love it! When I was a child, I wasn't the least bit interested in the taste or fragrance of tea, but now I'm really enjoying savoring the different flavors. I guess I'm a grown-up now. I was drinking Earl Grey because I like it, but one of my assistants pointed out, "That's actually Darjeeling." Hmm.

Naoshi Komi

Don't you have anyone else to draw?

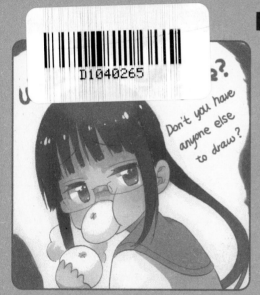

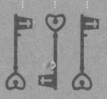

NAOSHI KOMI was born in Kochi Prefecture, Japan, on March 28, 1986. His first serialized work in *Weekly Shonen Jump* was the series *Double Arts*. His current series, *Nisekoi*, is serialized in *Weekly Shonen Jump*.

NISEKOI: False Love

VOLUME 21

SHONEN JUMP Manga Edition

Story and Art by
NAOSHI KOMI

Translation — Camellia Nieh
Touch-Up Art & Lettering — Stephen Dutro
Design — Izumi Evers
Shonen Jump Series Editor — John Bae
Graphic Novel Editor — Amy Yu

First published in Japan in 2011
by SHUEISHA Inc., Tokyo.
English translation rights arranged
by SHUEISHA Inc.

Printed in the U.S.A.

Published by VIZ Media, LLC
P.O. Box 77010
San Francisco, CA 94107

10 9 8 7 6 5 4 3 2 1
First printing, May 2017

Story and Art by
NAOSHI KOMI

NISEKOI
False Love
vol. 21: To Mari

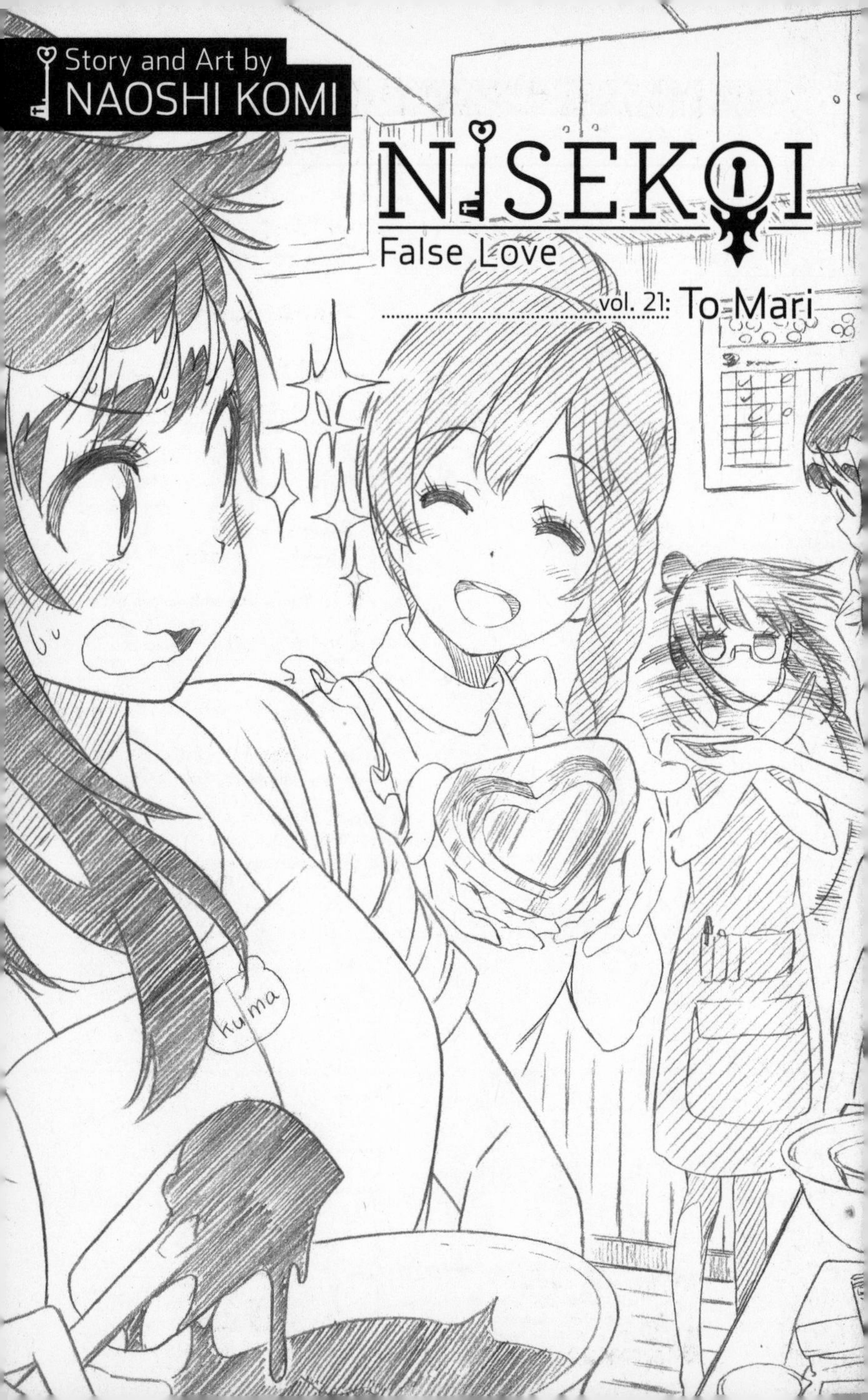
kuma

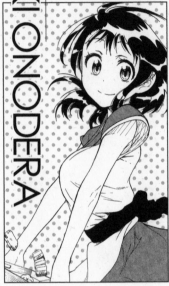

CHITOGE KIRISAKI

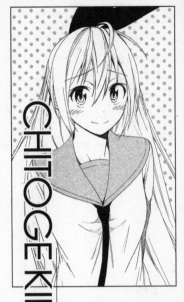

A half-Japanese bombshell with stellar athletic abilities. Short-tempered and violent. Comes from a family of gangsters.

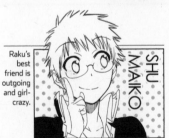

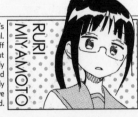

RAKU ICHIJO

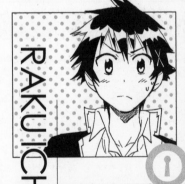

A normal teen whose family happens to be yakuza. Cherishes a pendant given to him by a girl he met ten years ago.

KOSAKI ONODERA

A girl Raku has a crush on. Beautiful and sweet, Kosaki has no shortage of admirers. She's a terrible cook but makes food that *looks* amazing.

SHU MAIKO

Raku's best friend is outgoing and girl-crazy.

RURI MIYAMOTO

Kosaki's best gal pal. Comes off as aloof, but is actually a devoted and highly intuitive friend.

MARIKA TACHIBANA

Daughter of the chief of police, Marika is Raku's fiancée, according to an agreement made by their fathers—an agreement Marika takes very seriously! Also has a key and remembers making a promise with Raku ten years ago.

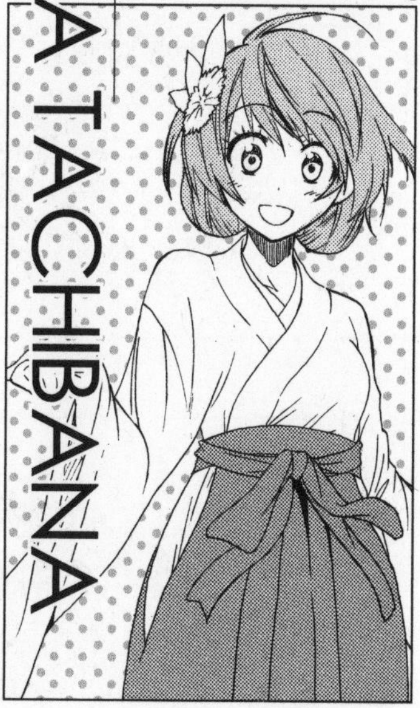

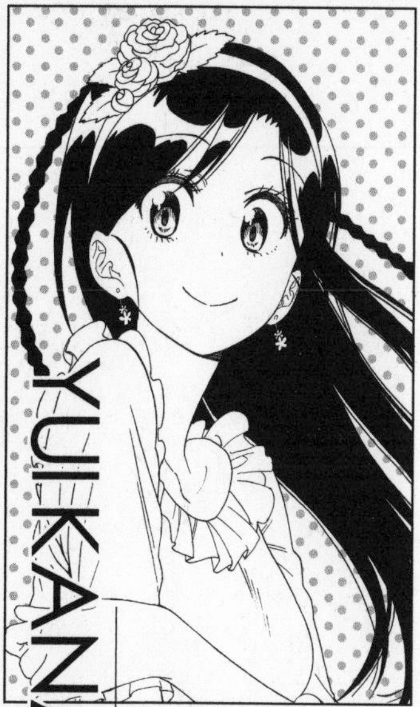

YUI KANAKURA

A childhood friend of Raku's, Yui is the head of a Chinese mafia gang and the homeroom teacher of Raku's class at his school. She is currently staying at Raku's house and also has a special key linked to some kind of promise...

CHARACTERS & STORY

Ten years ago, Raku Ichijo made a promise with a girl he loved that they would get married when they met again...and he still treasures the pendant she gave him to seal their pledge.

Thanks to his family's circumstances, Raku has to pretend he's dating Chitoge Kirisaki, the daughter of a rival gangster. Despite their constant spats, Raku and Chitoge manage to fool everyone. Chitoge also has a token from her first love ten years ago—an old key. Meanwhile, Raku's crush, Kosaki, also has a key, as do Marika, the girl Raku's father has arranged for him to marry, and Yui, a childhood friend who's their homeroom teacher. When Yui's gang pressures her to get married, she confesses her love to Raku. Raku struggles with how to respond, but he finally turns Yui down. As a result, he begins to take a good look at how he really feels...

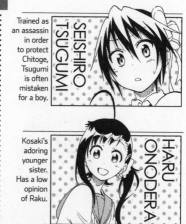

SEISHIRO TSUGUMI

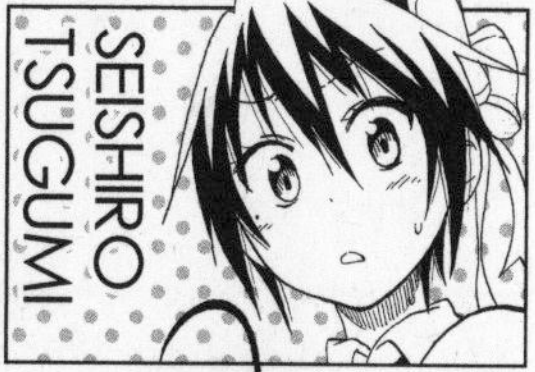

Trained as an assassin in order to protect Chitoge, Tsugumi is often mistaken for a boy.

HARU ONODERA

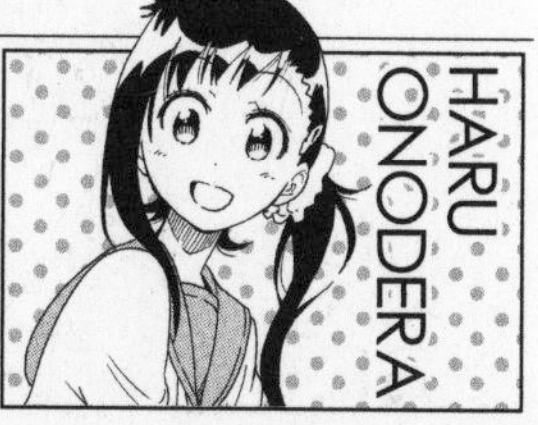

Kosaki's adoring younger sister. Has a low opinion of Raku.

NISEKOI
False Love

vol. 21: To Mari

TABLE OF CONTENTS

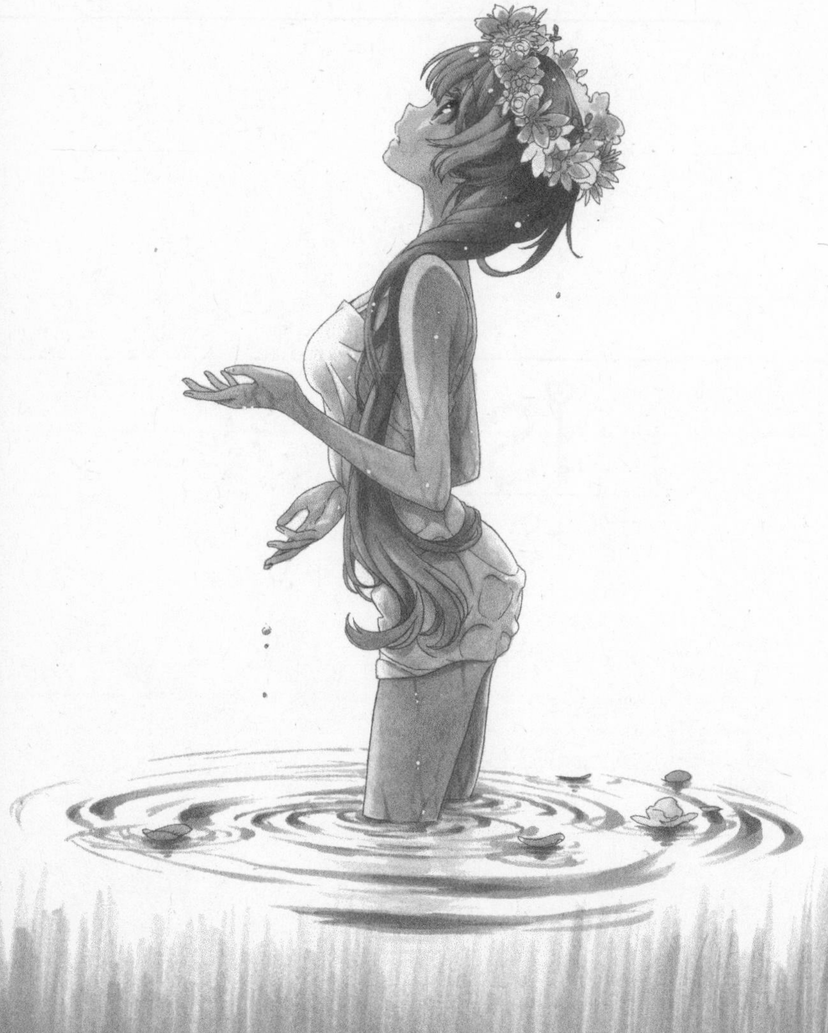

Chapter 180: Seen

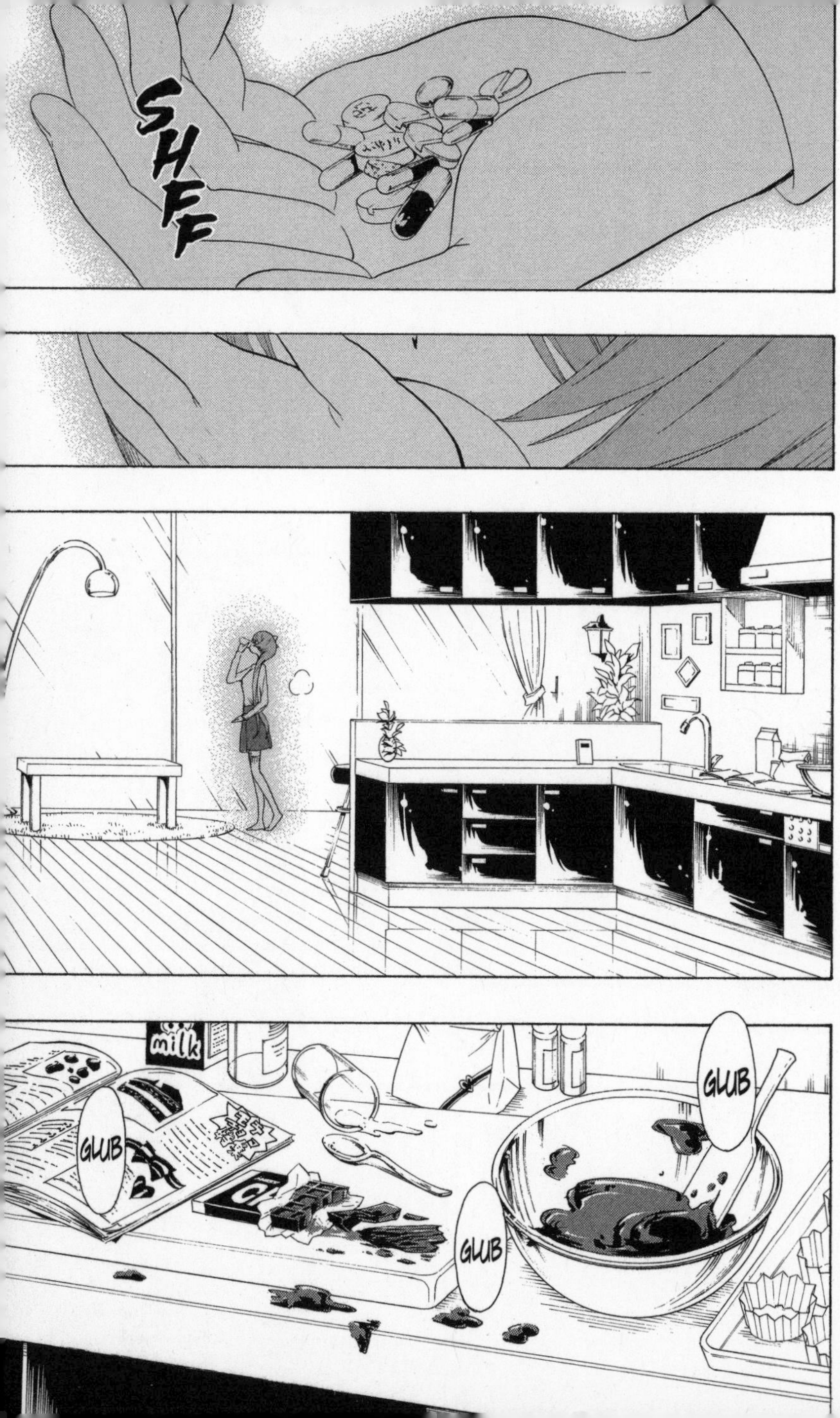
SHFF
milk
GLUB
GLUB
GLUB

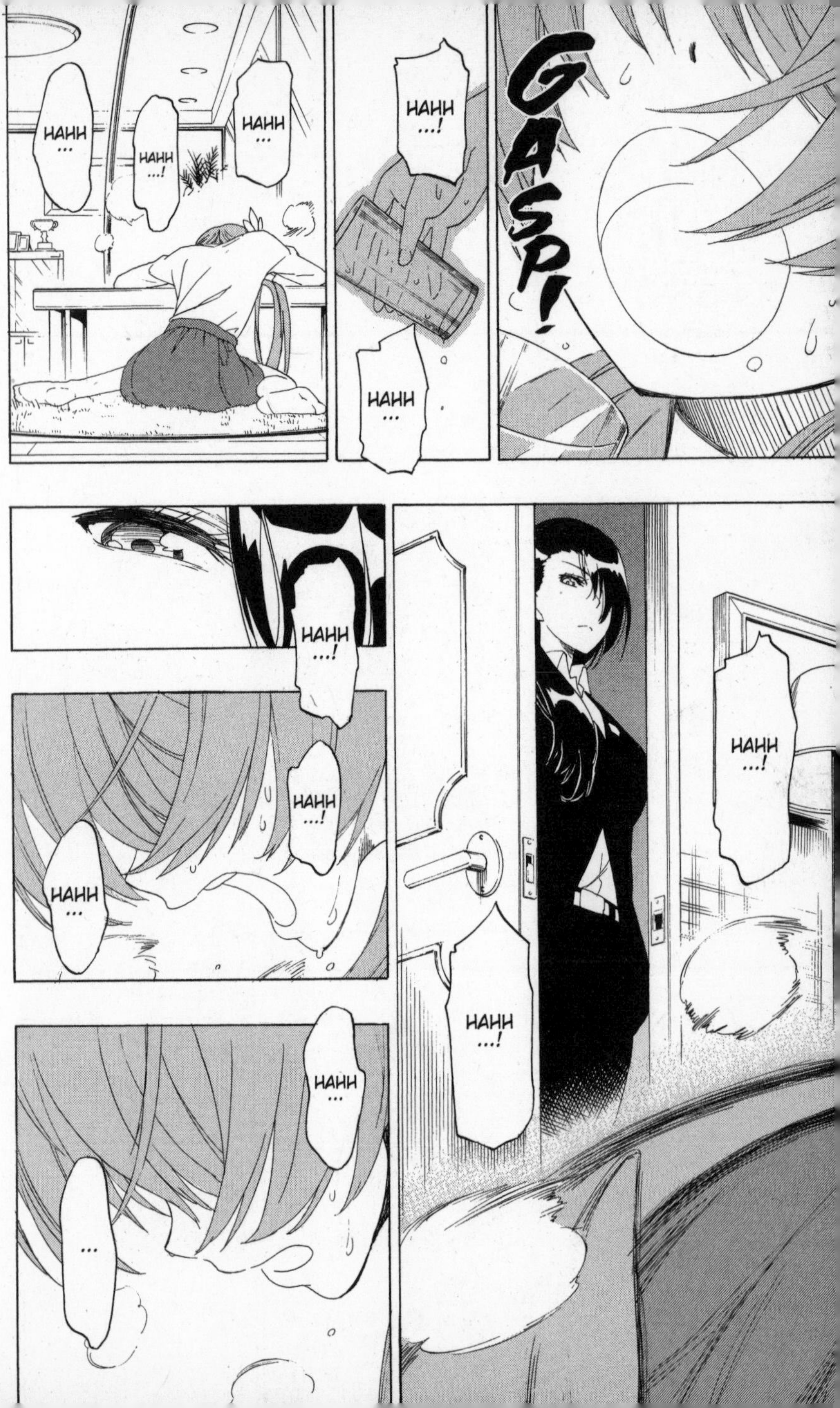
GASP!
HAHH...!
HAHH...
HAHH...
HAHH...!
HAHH...
HAHH...!
HAHH...!
HAHH...!
HAHH...!
HAHH...
HAHH...
...

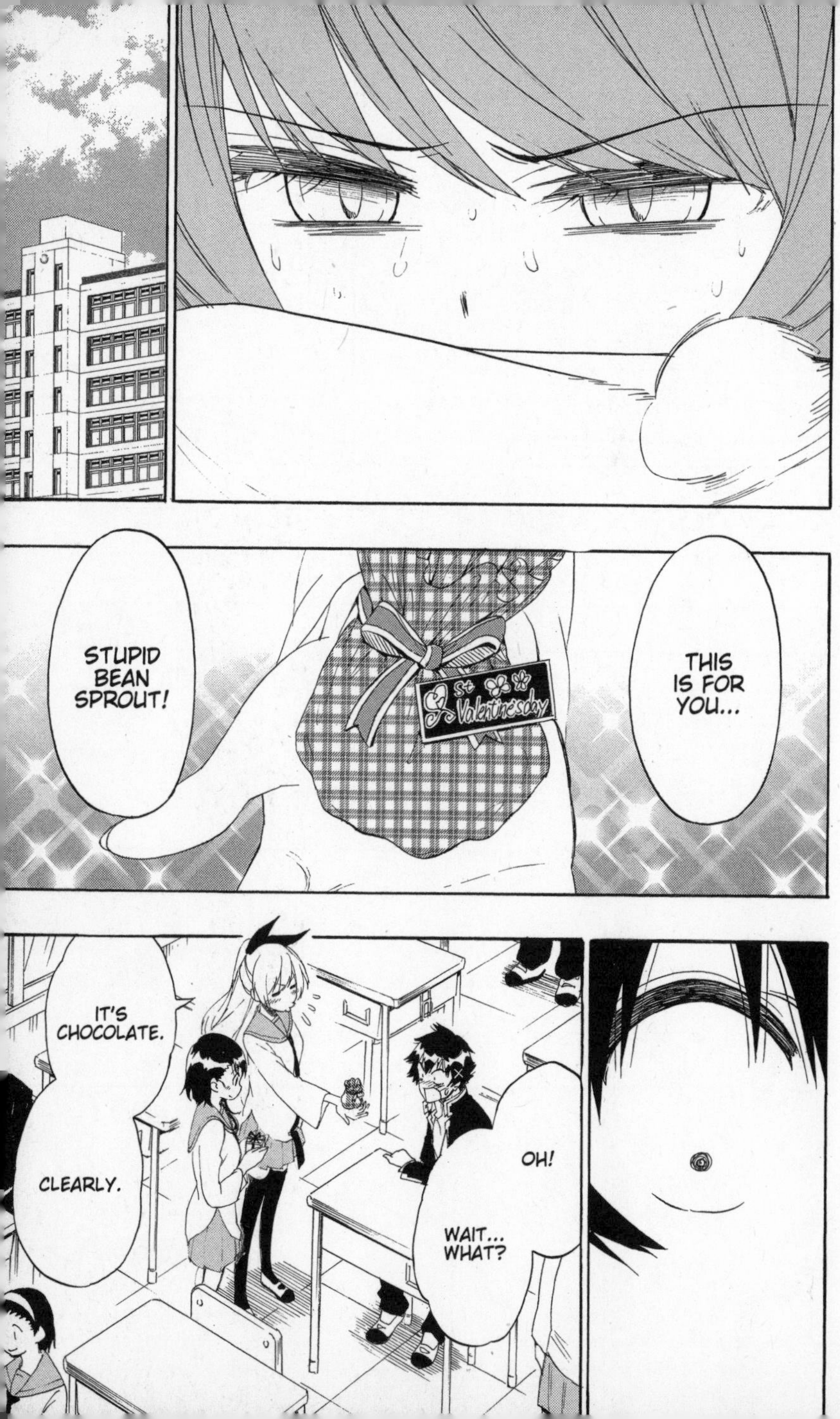
THIS IS FOR YOU...
St Valentine's day
STUPID BEAN SPROUT!
IT'S CHOCOLATE.
OH!
WAIT... WHAT?
CLEARLY.

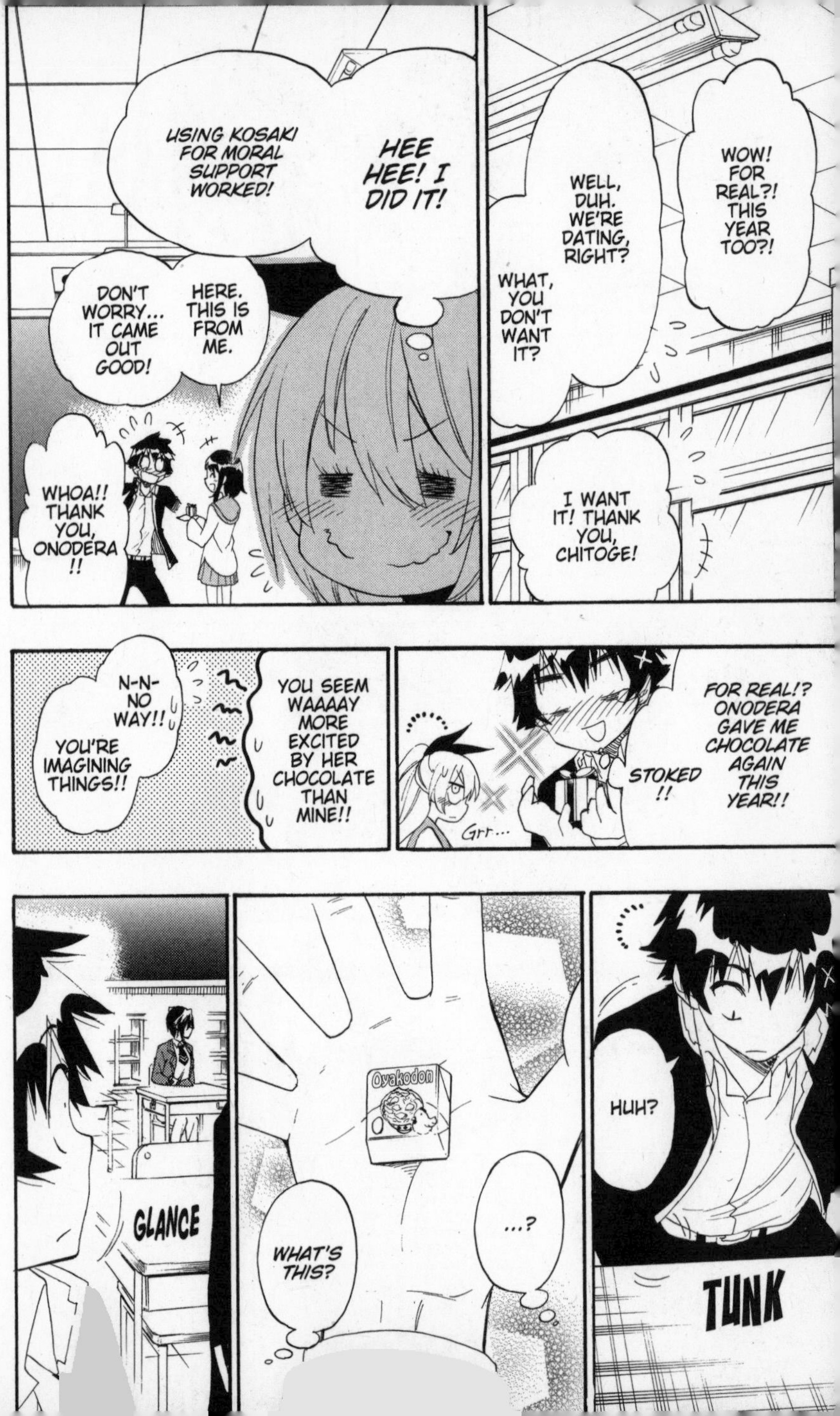
WOW! FOR REAL?! THIS YEAR TOO?!
WELL, DUH. WE'RE DATING, RIGHT?
WHAT, YOU DON'T WANT IT?
I WANT IT! THANK YOU, CHITOGE!
HEE HEE! I DID IT!
USING KOSAKI FOR MORAL SUPPORT WORKED!
HERE. THIS IS FROM ME.
DON'T WORRY... IT CAME OUT GOOD!
WHOA!! THANK YOU, ONODERA!!
FOR REAL!? ONODERA GAVE ME CHOCOLATE AGAIN THIS YEAR!!
STOKED!!
Grr...
YOU SEEM WAAAAY MORE EXCITED BY HER CHOCOLATE THAN MINE!!
N-N-NO WAY!!
YOU'RE IMAGINING THINGS!!
HUH?
TUNK
Oyakodon
...?
WHAT'S THIS?
GLANCE

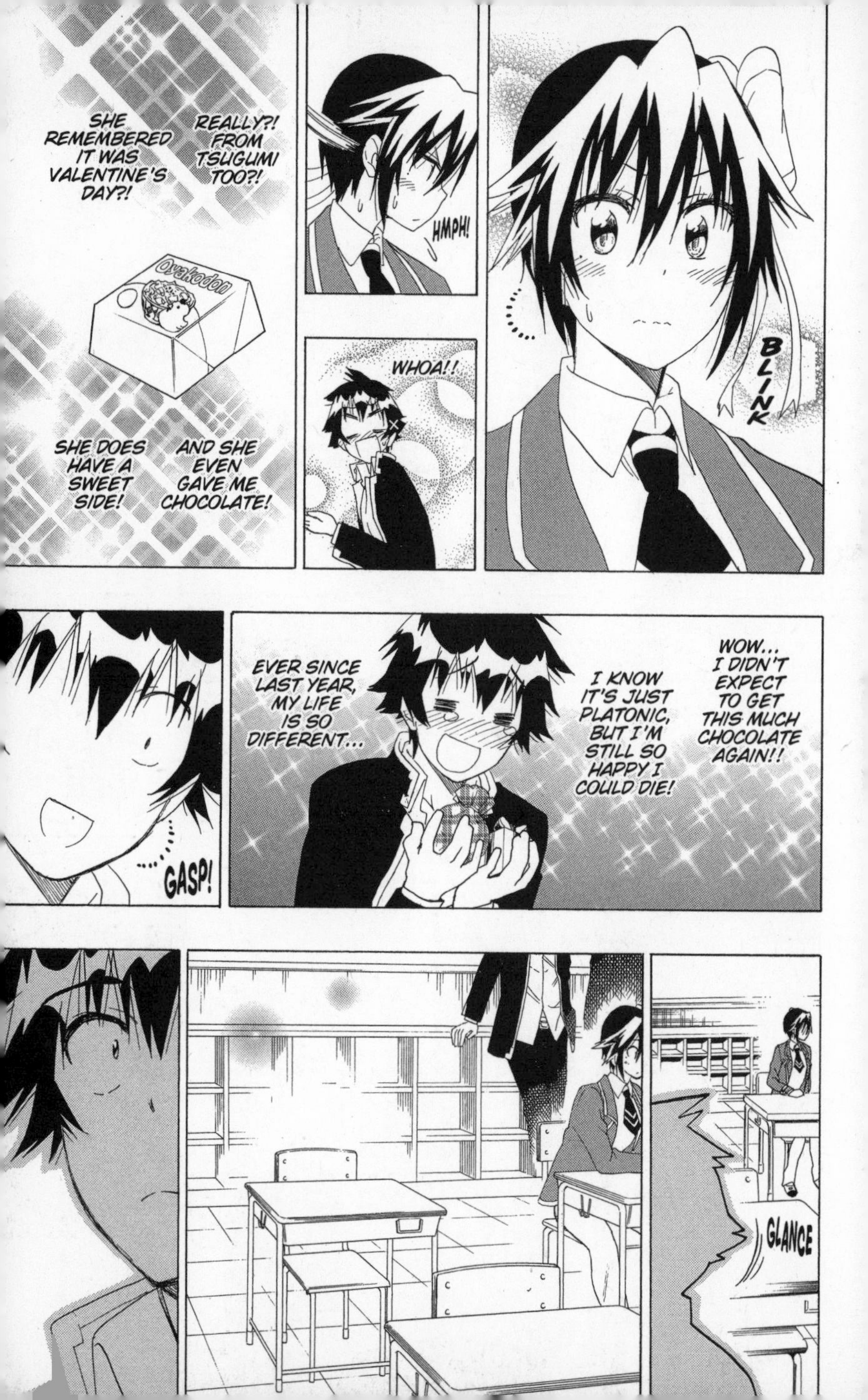
BLINK
HMPH!
WHOA!!
REALLY?! FROM TSUGUMI TOO?!
SHE REMEMBERED IT WAS VALENTINE'S DAY?!
Oyakodon
AND SHE EVEN GAVE ME CHOCOLATE!
SHE DOES HAVE A SWEET SIDE!
WOW... I DIDN'T EXPECT TO GET THIS MUCH CHOCOLATE AGAIN!!
I KNOW IT'S JUST PLATONIC, BUT I'M STILL SO HAPPY I COULD DIE!
EVER SINCE LAST YEAR, MY LIFE IS SO DIFFERENT...
GASP!
GLANCE

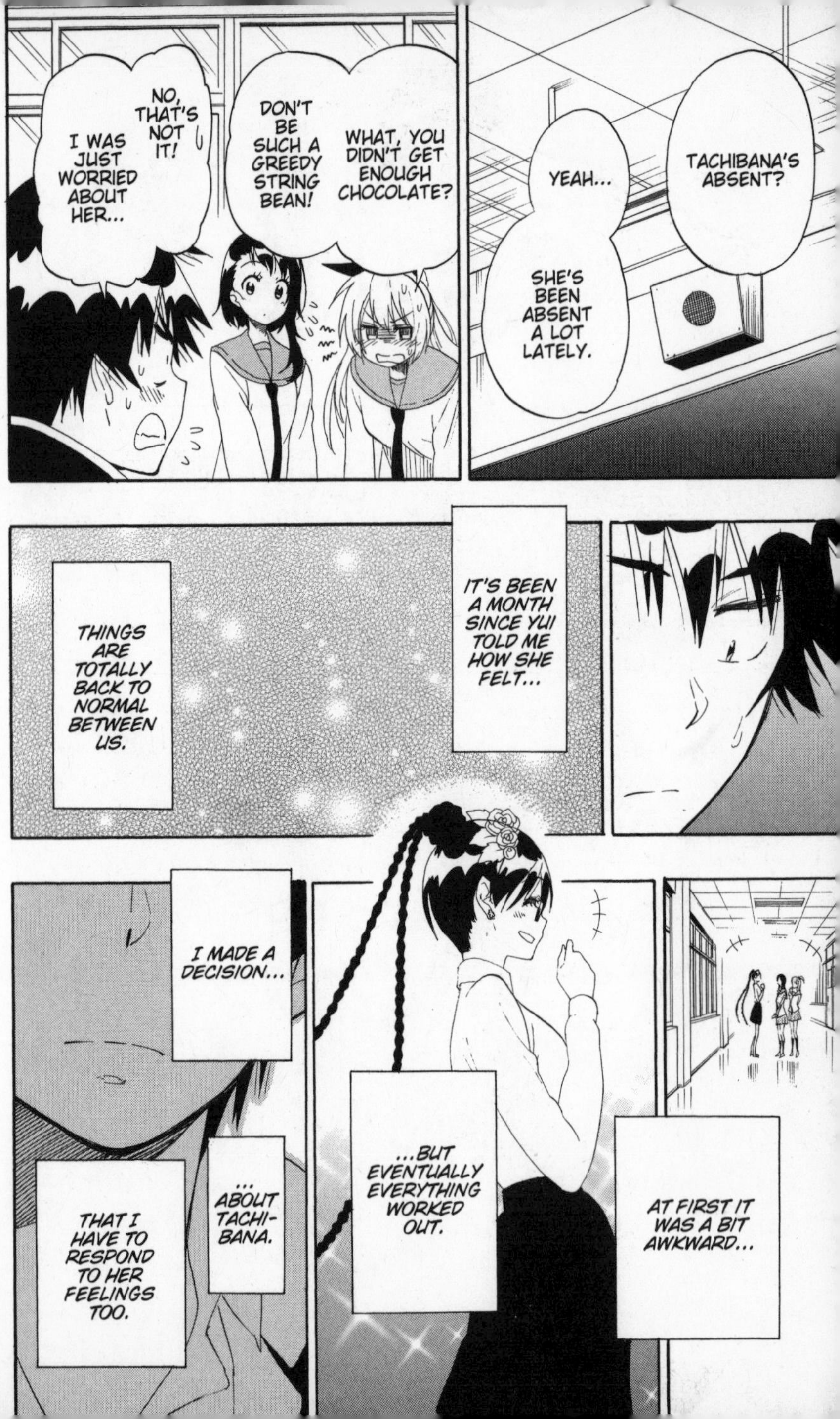
TACHIBANA'S ABSENT?
YEAH...
SHE'S BEEN ABSENT A LOT LATELY.
WHAT, YOU DIDN'T GET ENOUGH CHOCOLATE?
DON'T BE SUCH A GREEDY STRING BEAN!
NO, THAT'S NOT IT!
I WAS JUST WORRIED ABOUT HER...
IT'S BEEN A MONTH SINCE YUI TOLD ME HOW SHE FELT...
THINGS ARE TOTALLY BACK TO NORMAL BETWEEN US.
AT FIRST IT WAS A BIT AWKWARD...
...BUT EVENTUALLY EVERYTHING WORKED OUT.
I MADE A DECISION...
...ABOUT TACHI-BANA.
THAT I HAVE TO RESPOND TO HER FEELINGS TOO.

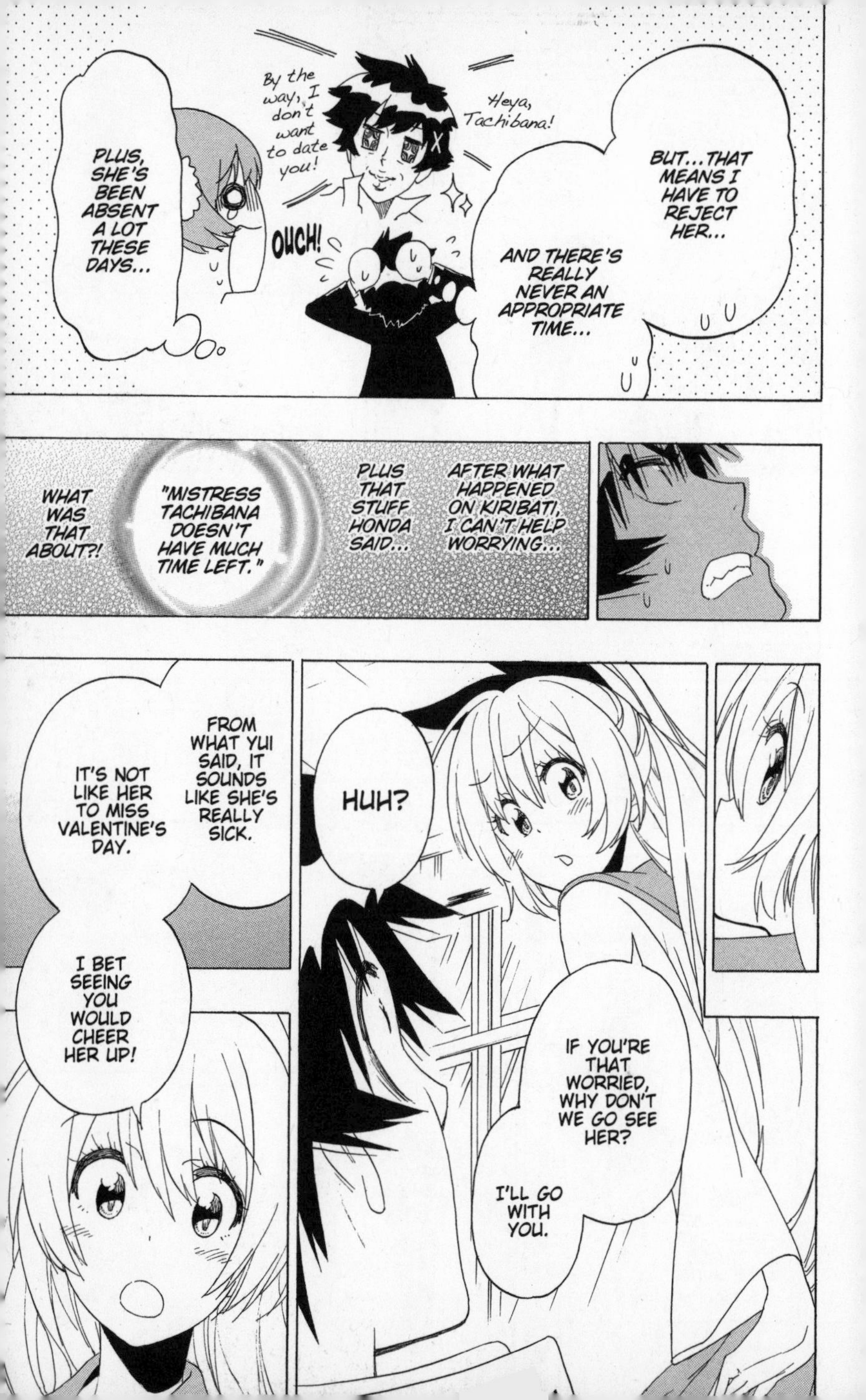
BUT...THAT MEANS I HAVE TO REJECT HER...
AND THERE'S REALLY NEVER AN APPROPRIATE TIME...
Heya, Tachibana!
By the way, I don't want to date you!
OUCH!
PLUS, SHE'S BEEN ABSENT A LOT THESE DAYS...
AFTER WHAT HAPPENED ON KIRIBATI, I CAN'T HELP WORRYING...
PLUS THAT STUFF HONDA SAID...
"MISTRESS TACHIBANA DOESN'T HAVE MUCH TIME LEFT."
WHAT WAS THAT ABOUT?!
HUH?
IF YOU'RE THAT WORRIED, WHY DON'T WE GO SEE HER?
I'LL GO WITH YOU.
FROM WHAT YUI SAID, IT SOUNDS LIKE SHE'S REALLY SICK.
IT'S NOT LIKE HER TO MISS VALENTINE'S DAY.
I BET SEEING YOU WOULD CHEER HER UP!

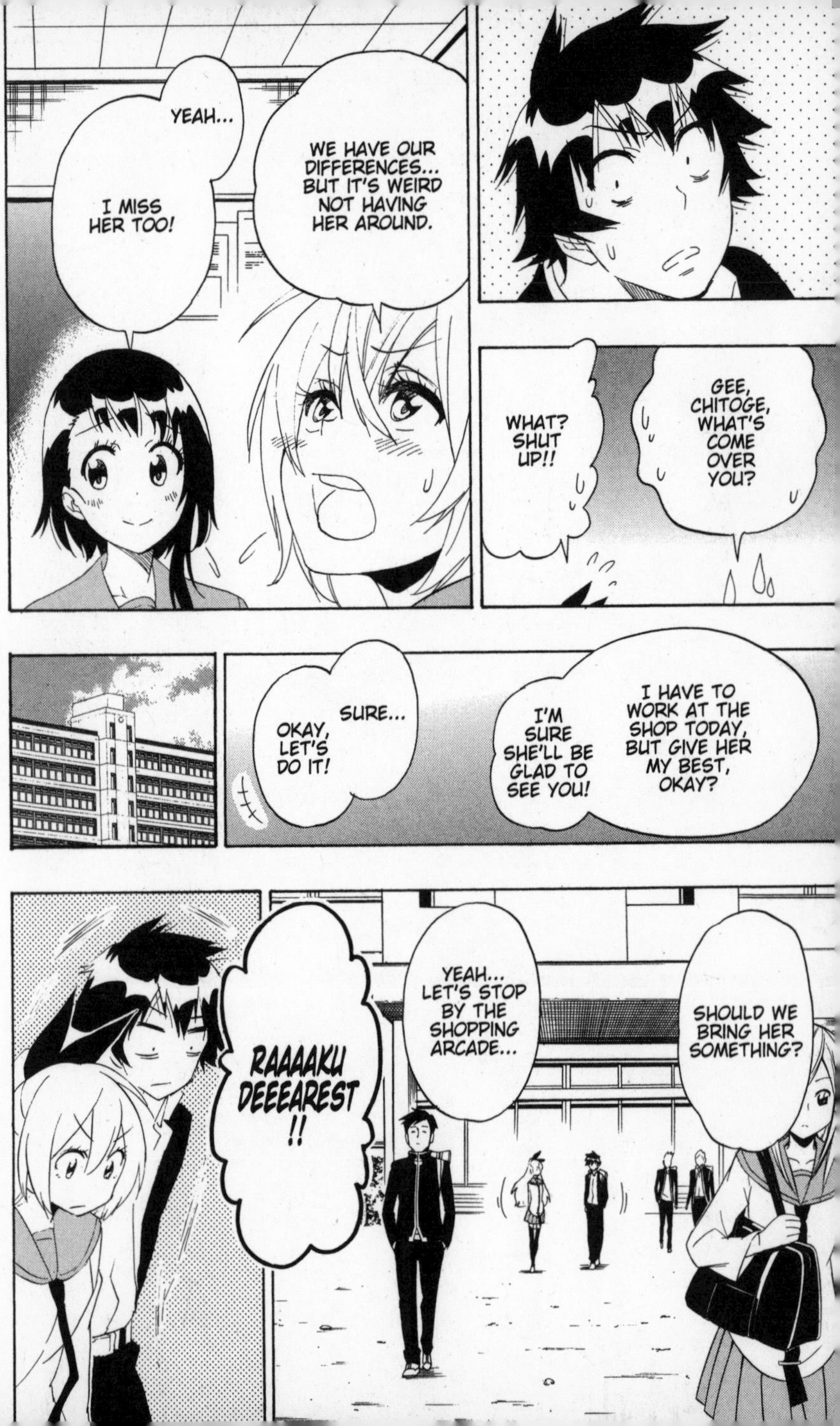
GEE, CHITOGE, WHAT'S COME OVER YOU?
WHAT? SHUT UP!!
WE HAVE OUR DIFFERENCES... BUT IT'S WEIRD NOT HAVING HER AROUND.
YEAH... I MISS HER TOO!
I HAVE TO WORK AT THE SHOP TODAY, BUT GIVE HER MY BEST, OKAY?
I'M SURE SHE'LL BE GLAD TO SEE YOU!
SURE... OKAY, LET'S DO IT!
SHOULD WE BRING HER SOMETHING?
YEAH... LET'S STOP BY THE SHOPPING ARCADE...
RAAAAKU DEEEEAREST!!

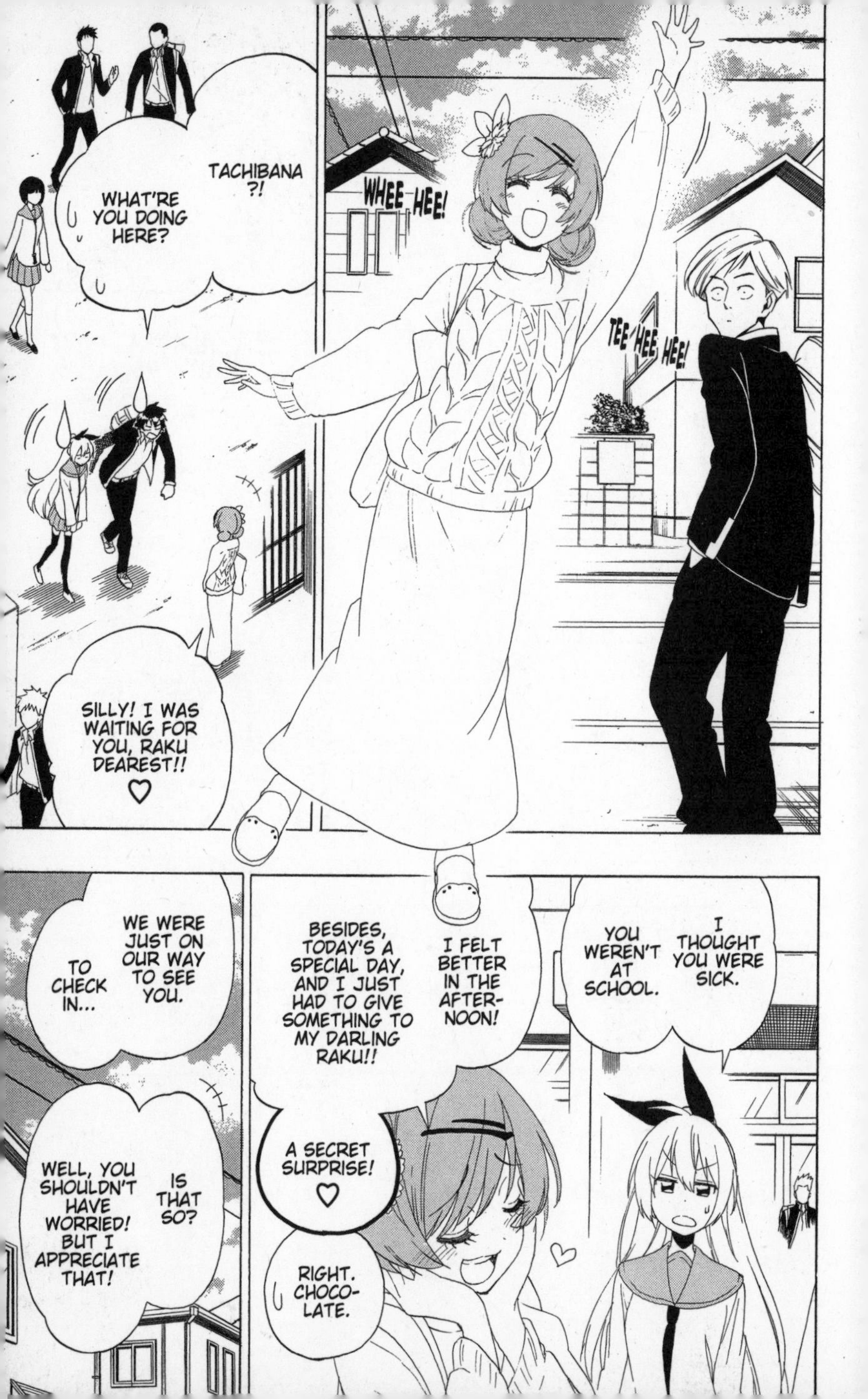
WHEE HEE!
TEE HEE HEE!
TACHIBANA?!
WHAT'RE YOU DOING HERE?
SILLY! I WAS WAITING FOR YOU, RAKU DEAREST!! ♥
I THOUGHT YOU WERE SICK.
YOU WEREN'T AT SCHOOL.
I FELT BETTER IN THE AFTERNOON!
BESIDES, TODAY'S A SPECIAL DAY, AND I JUST HAD TO GIVE SOMETHING TO MY DARLING RAKU!!
A SECRET SURPRISE! ♥
RIGHT. CHOCOLATE.
WE WERE JUST ON OUR WAY TO SEE YOU.
TO CHECK IN...
IS THAT SO?
WELL, YOU SHOULDN'T HAVE WORRIED! BUT I APPRECIATE THAT!

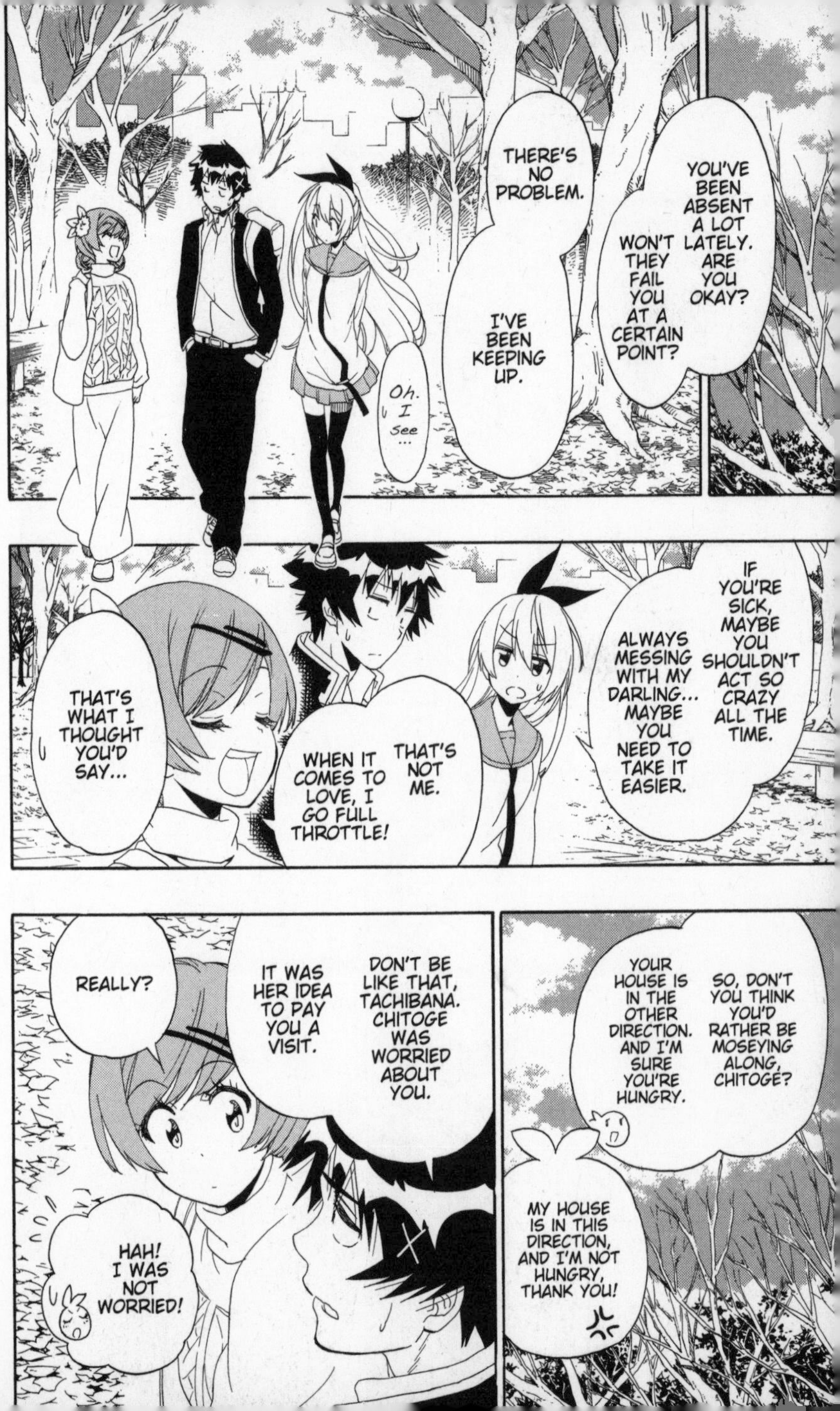
YOU'VE BEEN ABSENT A LOT LATELY. ARE YOU OKAY?
WON'T THEY FAIL YOU AT A CERTAIN POINT?
THERE'S NO PROBLEM.
I'VE BEEN KEEPING UP.
Oh. I see...
IF YOU'RE SICK, MAYBE YOU SHOULDN'T ACT SO CRAZY ALL THE TIME.
ALWAYS MESSING WITH MY DARLING... MAYBE YOU NEED TO TAKE IT EASIER.
THAT'S NOT ME.
WHEN IT COMES TO LOVE, I GO FULL THROTTLE!
THAT'S WHAT I THOUGHT YOU'D SAY...
SO, DON'T YOU THINK YOU'D RATHER BE MOSEYING ALONG, CHITOGE?
YOUR HOUSE IS IN THE OTHER DIRECTION. AND I'M SURE YOU'RE HUNGRY.
MY HOUSE IS IN THIS DIRECTION, AND I'M NOT HUNGRY, THANK YOU!
DON'T BE LIKE THAT, TACHIBANA. CHITOGE WAS WORRIED ABOUT YOU.
IT WAS HER IDEA TO PAY YOU A VISIT.
REALLY?
HAH! I WAS NOT WORRIED!

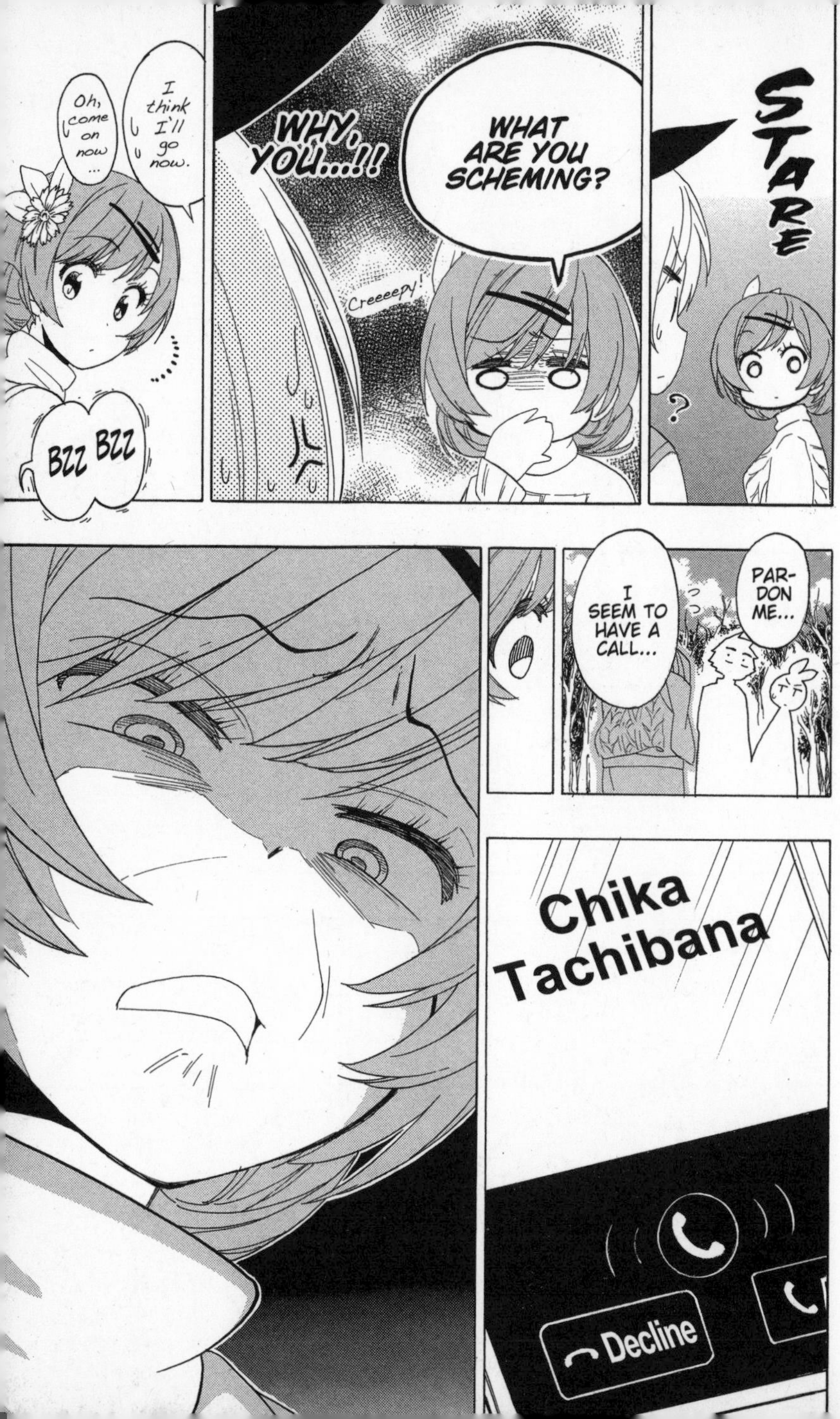
STARE
?
WHAT ARE YOU SCHEMING?
WHY, YOU...!!
Creeeepy!
I think I'll go now.
Oh, come on now...
BZZ BZZ
PARDON ME...
I SEEM TO HAVE A CALL...
Chika Tachibana
Decline

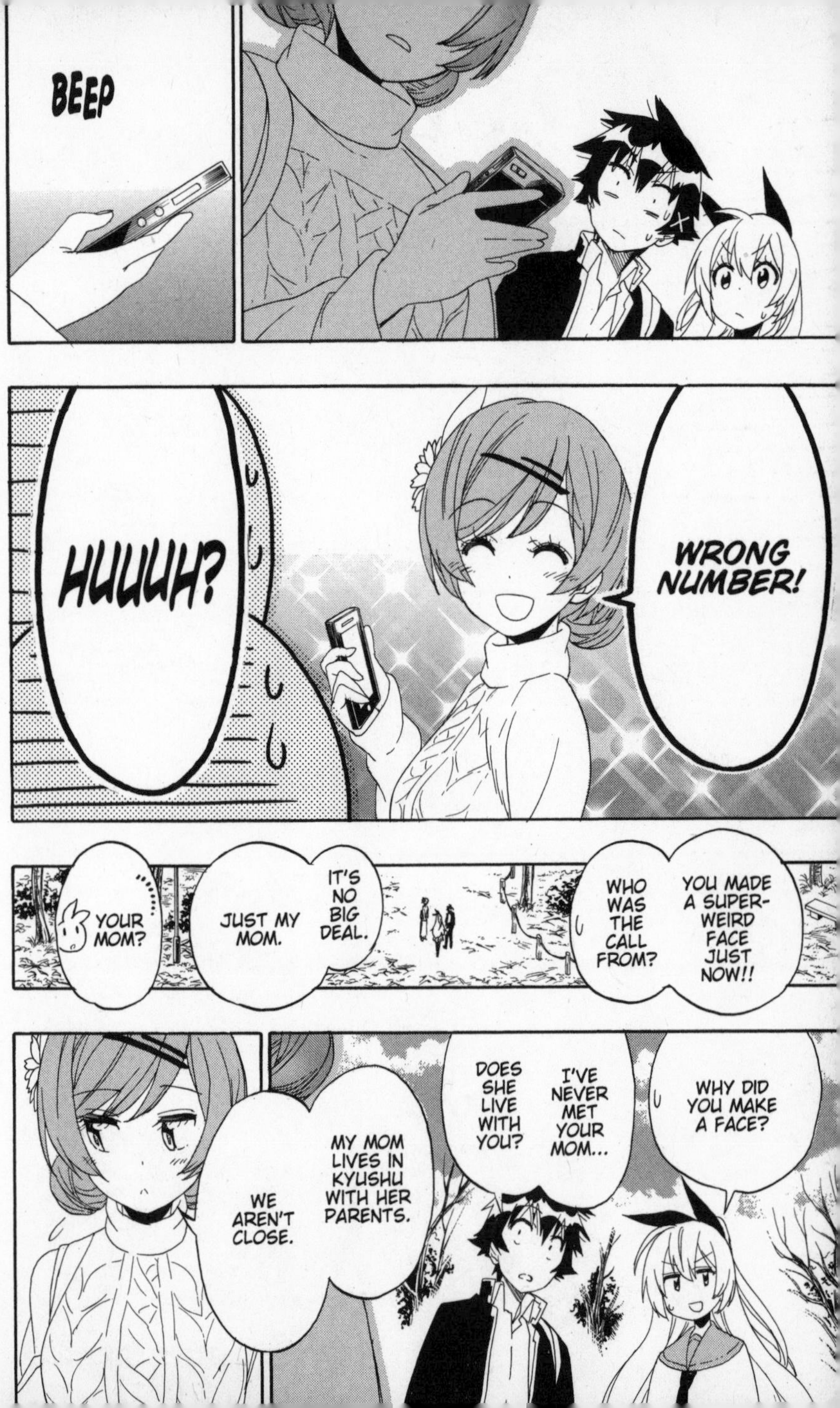
BEEP
WRONG NUMBER!
HUUUH?
YOU MADE A SUPER-WEIRD FACE JUST NOW!!
WHO WAS THE CALL FROM?
IT'S NO BIG DEAL.
JUST MY MOM.
...YOUR MOM?
WHY DID YOU MAKE A FACE?
I'VE NEVER MET YOUR MOM...
DOES SHE LIVE WITH YOU?
MY MOM LIVES IN KYUSHU WITH HER PARENTS.
WE AREN'T CLOSE.

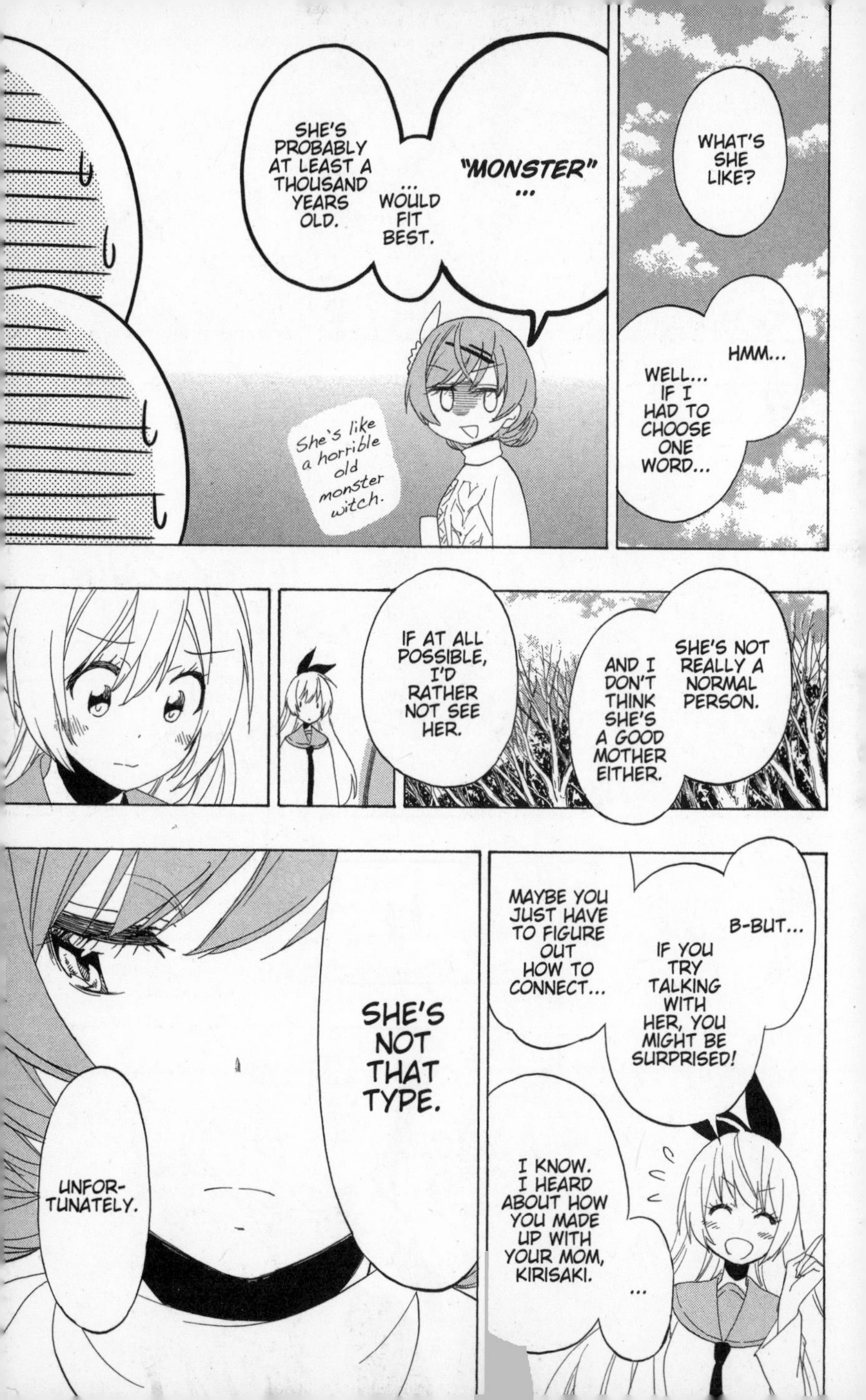
WHAT'S SHE LIKE?
HMM...
WELL... IF I HAD TO CHOOSE ONE WORD...
"MONSTER"...
... WOULD FIT BEST.
SHE'S PROBABLY AT LEAST A THOUSAND YEARS OLD.
She's like a horrible old monster witch.
SHE'S NOT REALLY A NORMAL PERSON.
AND I DON'T THINK SHE'S A GOOD MOTHER EITHER.
IF AT ALL POSSIBLE, I'D RATHER NOT SEE HER.
B-BUT...
IF YOU TRY TALKING WITH HER, YOU MIGHT BE SURPRISED!
MAYBE YOU JUST HAVE TO FIGURE OUT HOW TO CONNECT...
I KNOW. I HEARD ABOUT HOW YOU MADE UP WITH YOUR MOM, KIRISAKI.
...
SHE'S NOT THAT TYPE.
UNFORTUNATELY.

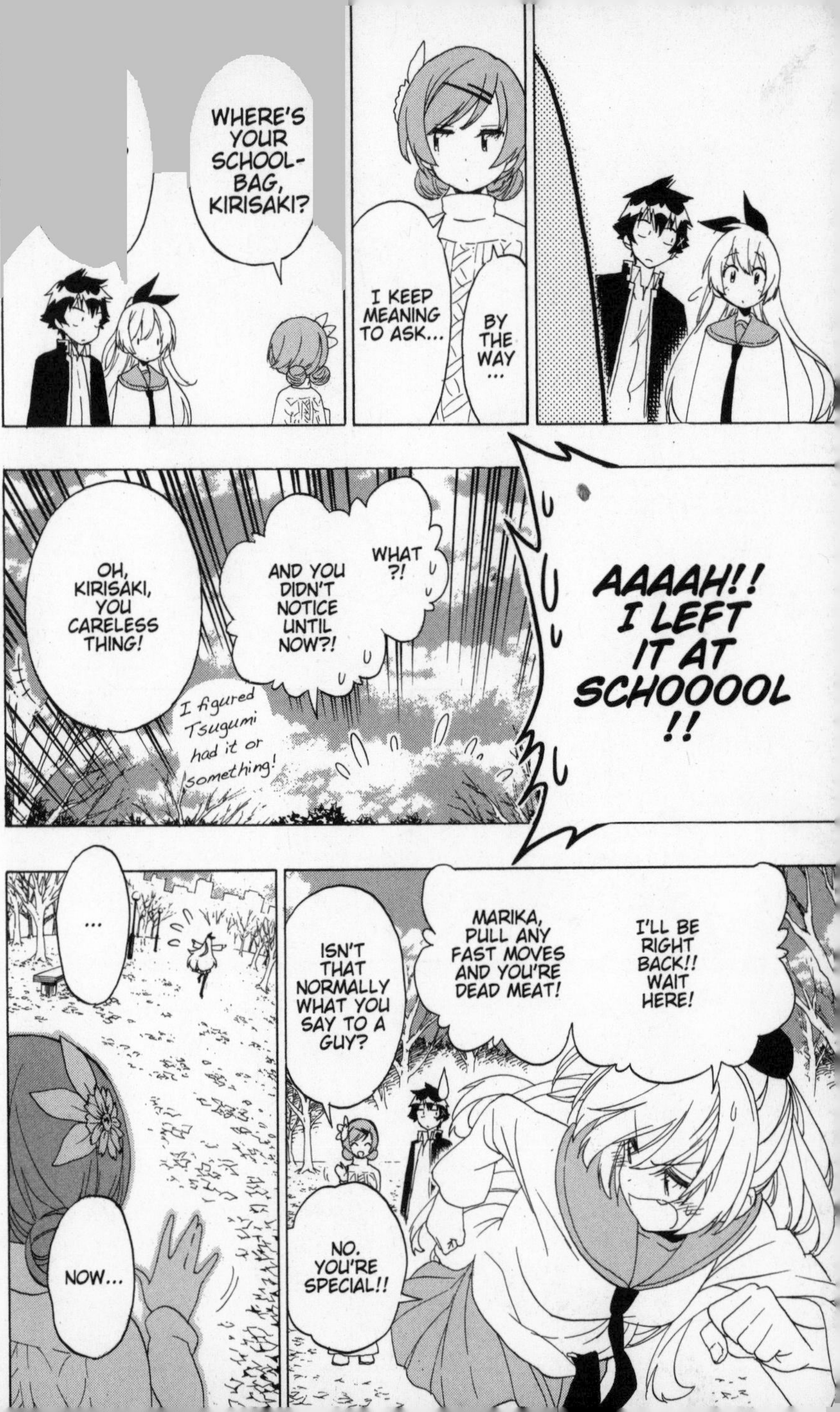
BY THE WAY...
I KEEP MEANING TO ASK...
WHERE'S YOUR SCHOOL-BAG, KIRISAKI?
AAAAH!! I LEFT IT AT SCHOOOOL!!
WHAT?!
AND YOU DIDN'T NOTICE UNTIL NOW?!
OH, KIRISAKI, YOU CARELESS THING!
I figured Tsugumi had it or something!
I'LL BE RIGHT BACK!! WAIT HERE!
MARIKA, PULL ANY FAST MOVES AND YOU'RE DEAD MEAT!
ISN'T THAT NORMALLY WHAT YOU SAY TO A GUY?
NO. YOU'RE SPECIAL!!
...
NOW...

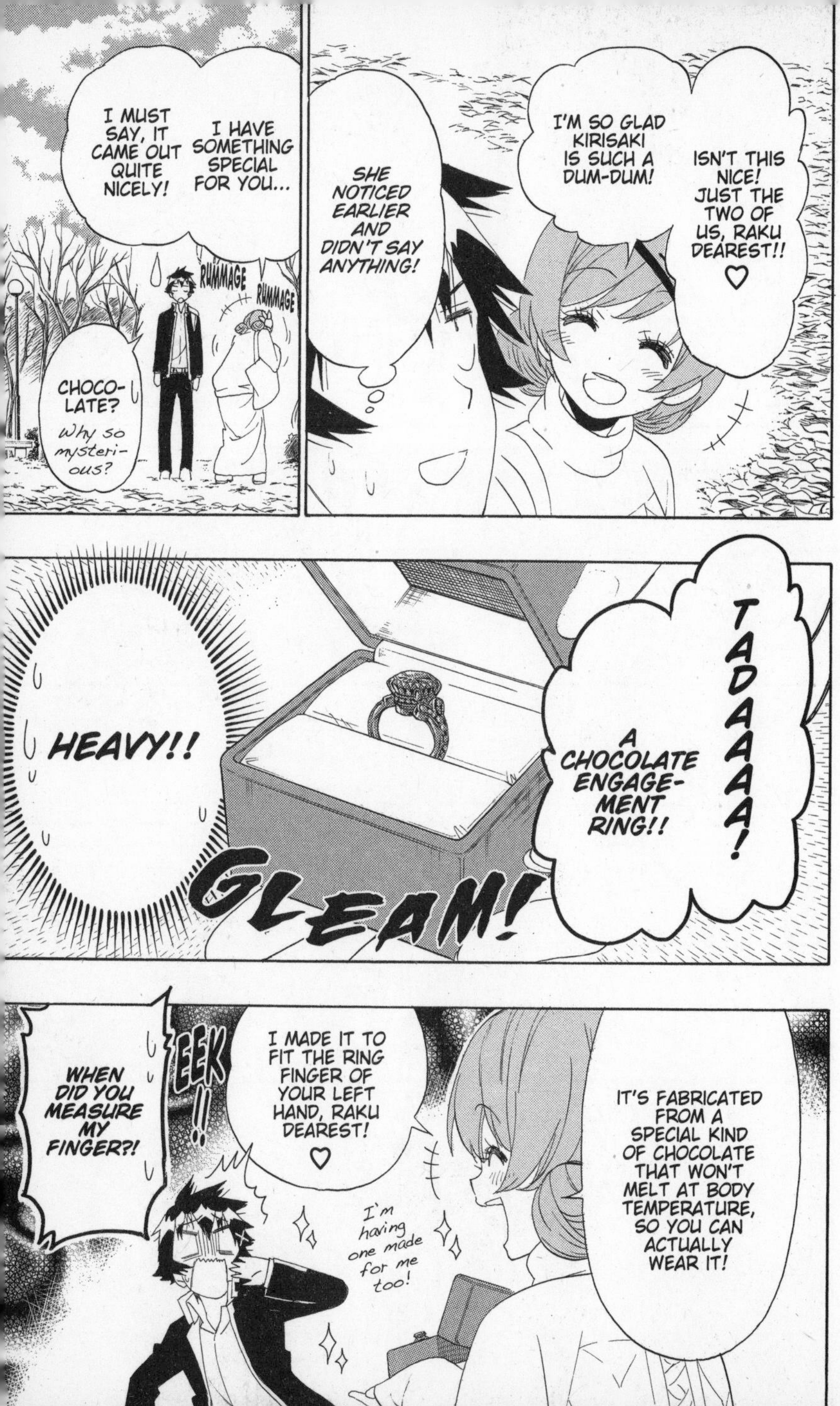
ISN'T THIS NICE! JUST THE TWO OF US, RAKU DEAREST!! ♡
I'M SO GLAD KIRISAKI IS SUCH A DUM-DUM!
SHE NOTICED EARLIER AND DIDN'T SAY ANYTHING!
I HAVE SOMETHING SPECIAL FOR YOU...
I MUST SAY, IT CAME OUT QUITE NICELY!
RUMMAGE
RUMMAGE
CHOCOLATE?
Why so mysterious?
TADAAAAA!
A CHOCOLATE ENGAGEMENT RING!!
GLEAM!
HEAVY!!
IT'S FABRICATED FROM A SPECIAL KIND OF CHOCOLATE THAT WON'T MELT AT BODY TEMPERATURE, SO YOU CAN ACTUALLY WEAR IT!
I MADE IT TO FIT THE RING FINGER OF YOUR LEFT HAND, RAKU DEAREST! ♡
I'm having one made for me too!
EEK!!
WHEN DID YOU MEASURE MY FINGER?!

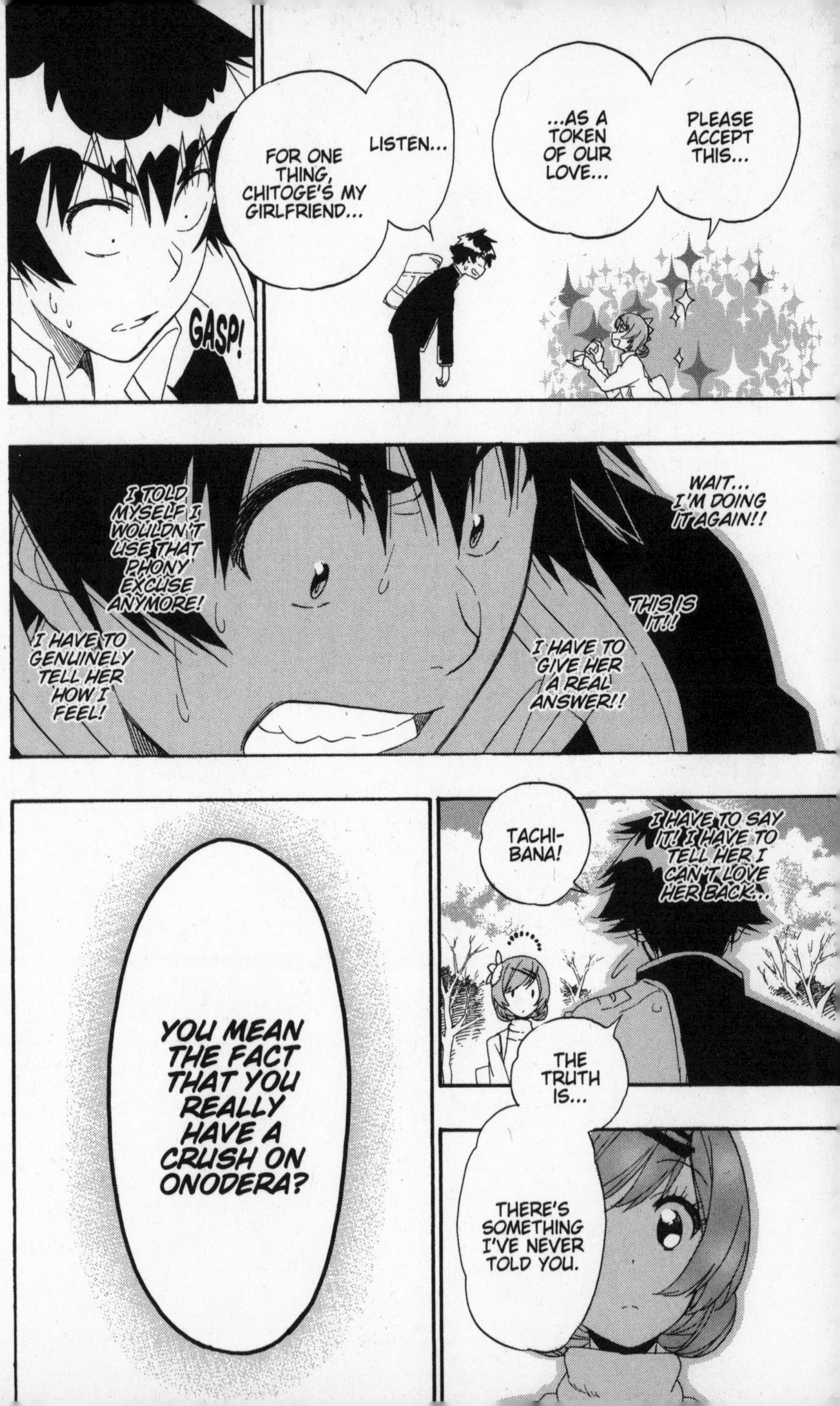
PLEASE ACCEPT THIS...
...AS A TOKEN OF OUR LOVE...
LISTEN...
FOR ONE THING, CHITOGE'S MY GIRLFRIEND...
GASP!
WAIT... I'M DOING IT AGAIN!!
THIS IS IT!!
I HAVE TO GIVE HER A REAL ANSWER!!
I TOLD MYSELF I WOULDN'T USE THAT PHONY EXCUSE ANYMORE!
I HAVE TO GENUINELY TELL HER HOW I FEEL!
I HAVE TO SAY IT! I HAVE TO TELL HER I CAN'T LOVE HER BACK...
TACHIBANA!
THE TRUTH IS...
THERE'S SOMETHING I'VE NEVER TOLD YOU.
YOU MEAN THE FACT THAT YOU REALLY HAVE A CRUSH ON ONODERA?

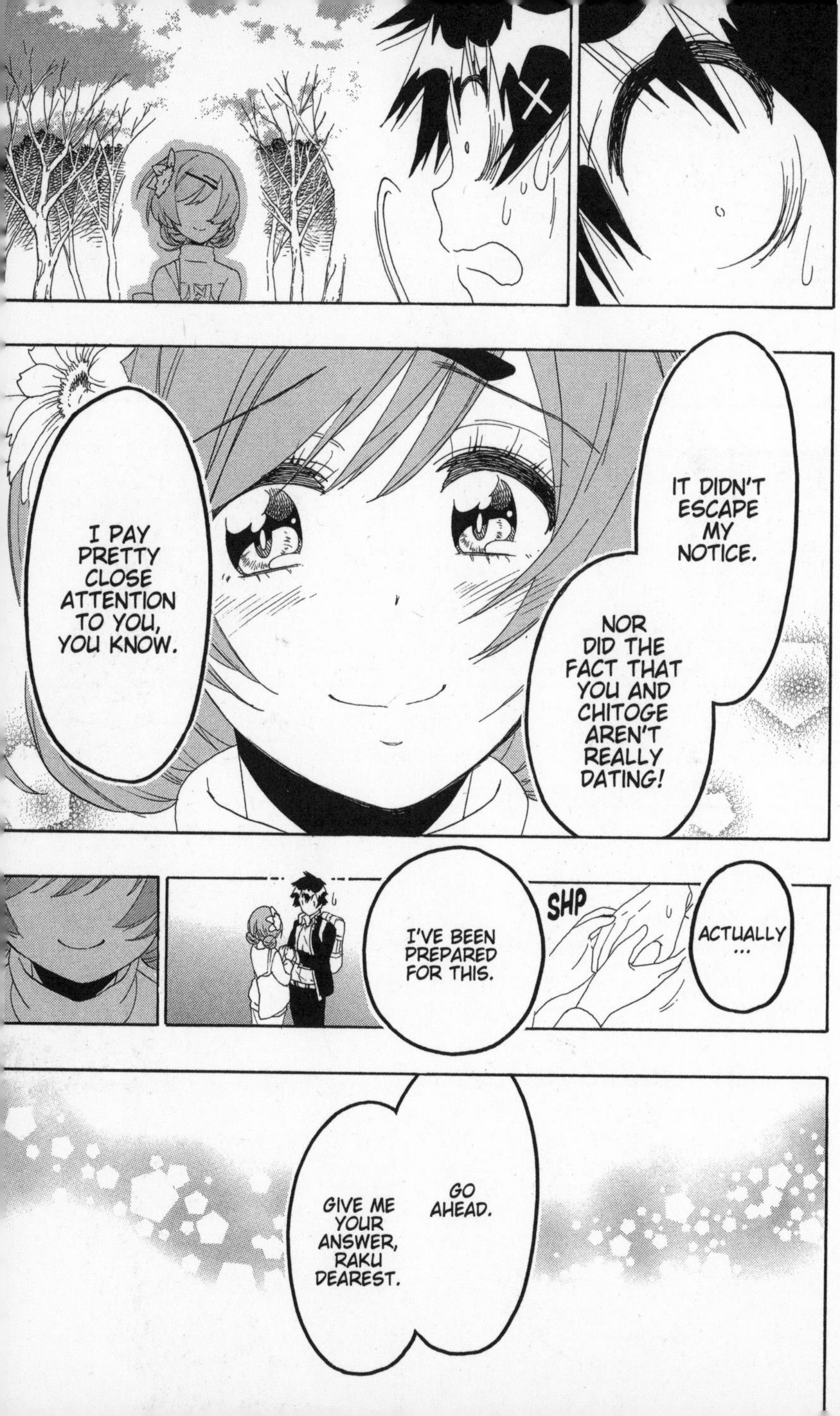
IT DIDN'T ESCAPE MY NOTICE.
NOR DID THE FACT THAT YOU AND CHITOGE AREN'T REALLY DATING!
I PAY PRETTY CLOSE ATTENTION TO YOU, YOU KNOW.
ACTUALLY...
SHP
I'VE BEEN PREPARED FOR THIS.
GO AHEAD.
GIVE ME YOUR ANSWER, RAKU DEAREST.

At least
she
seems to
be feeling
okay.

Well...

Sheesh...

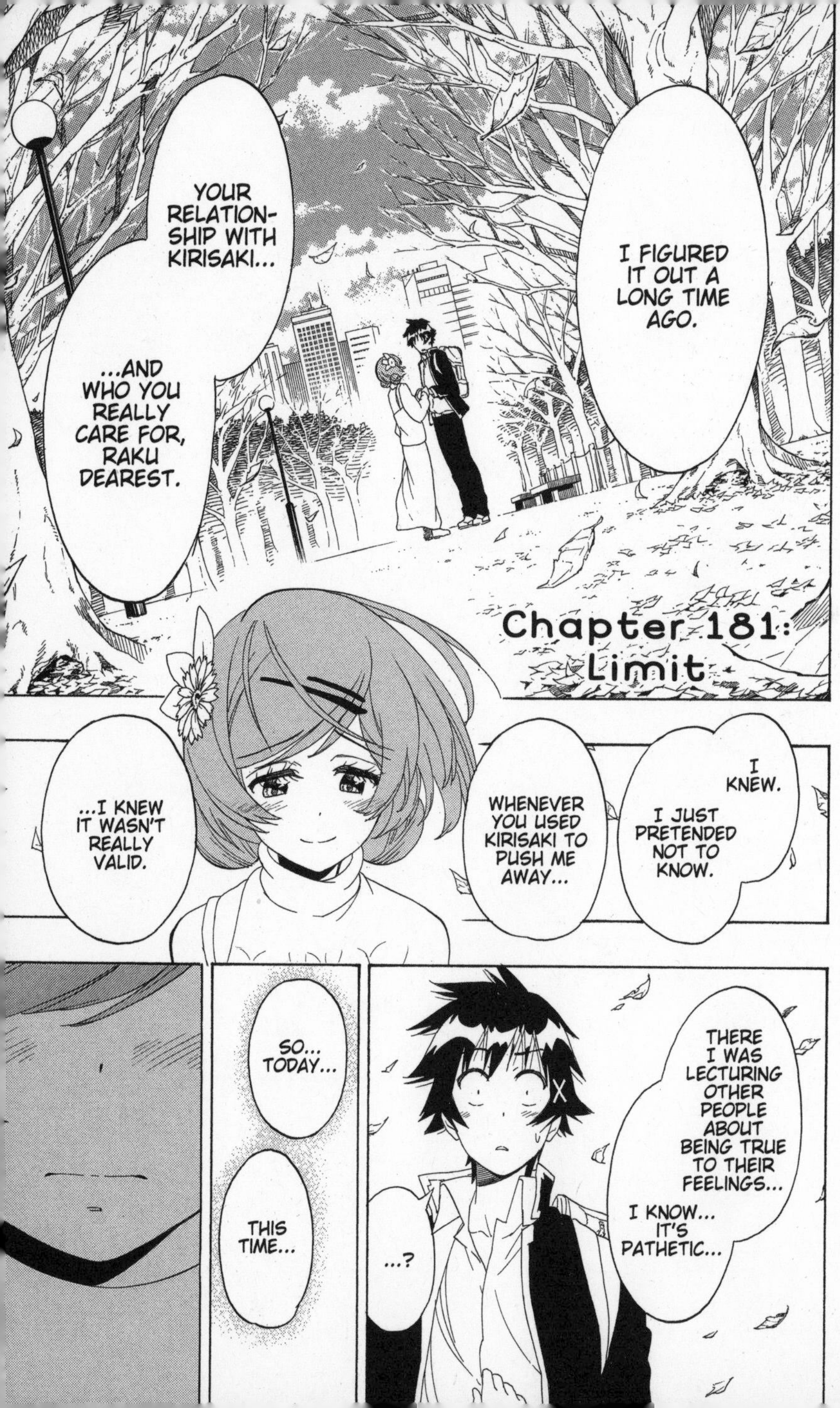
I FIGURED IT OUT A LONG TIME AGO.
YOUR RELATIONSHIP WITH KIRISAKI...
...AND WHO YOU REALLY CARE FOR, RAKU DEAREST.
Chapter 181: Limit
I KNEW.
I JUST PRETENDED NOT TO KNOW.
WHENEVER YOU USED KIRISAKI TO PUSH ME AWAY...
...I KNEW IT WASN'T REALLY VALID.
THERE I WAS LECTURING OTHER PEOPLE ABOUT BEING TRUE TO THEIR FEELINGS...
I KNOW... IT'S PATHETIC...
...?
SO... TODAY...
THIS TIME...

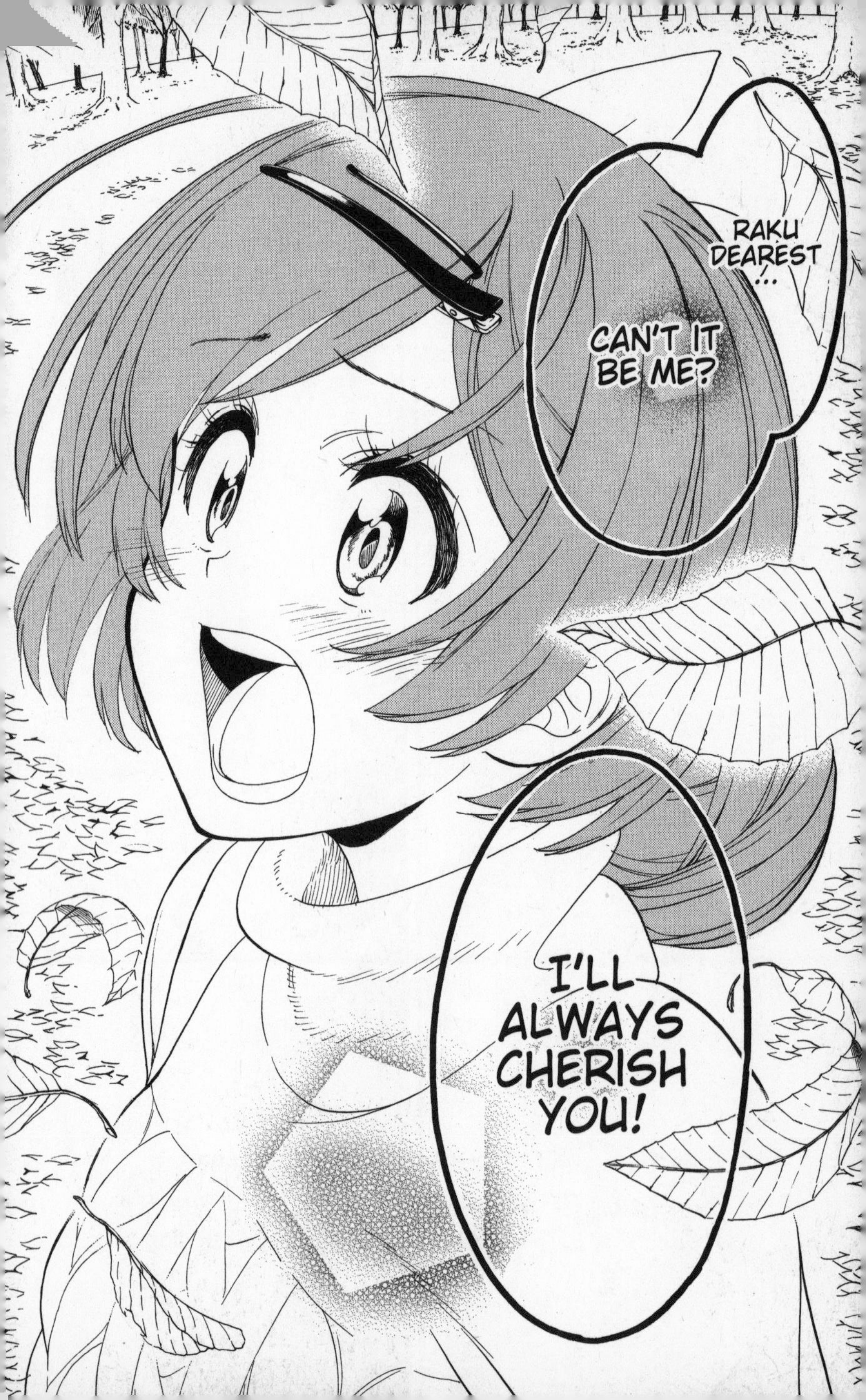
RAKU DEAREST...
CAN'T IT BE ME?
I'LL ALWAYS CHERISH YOU!

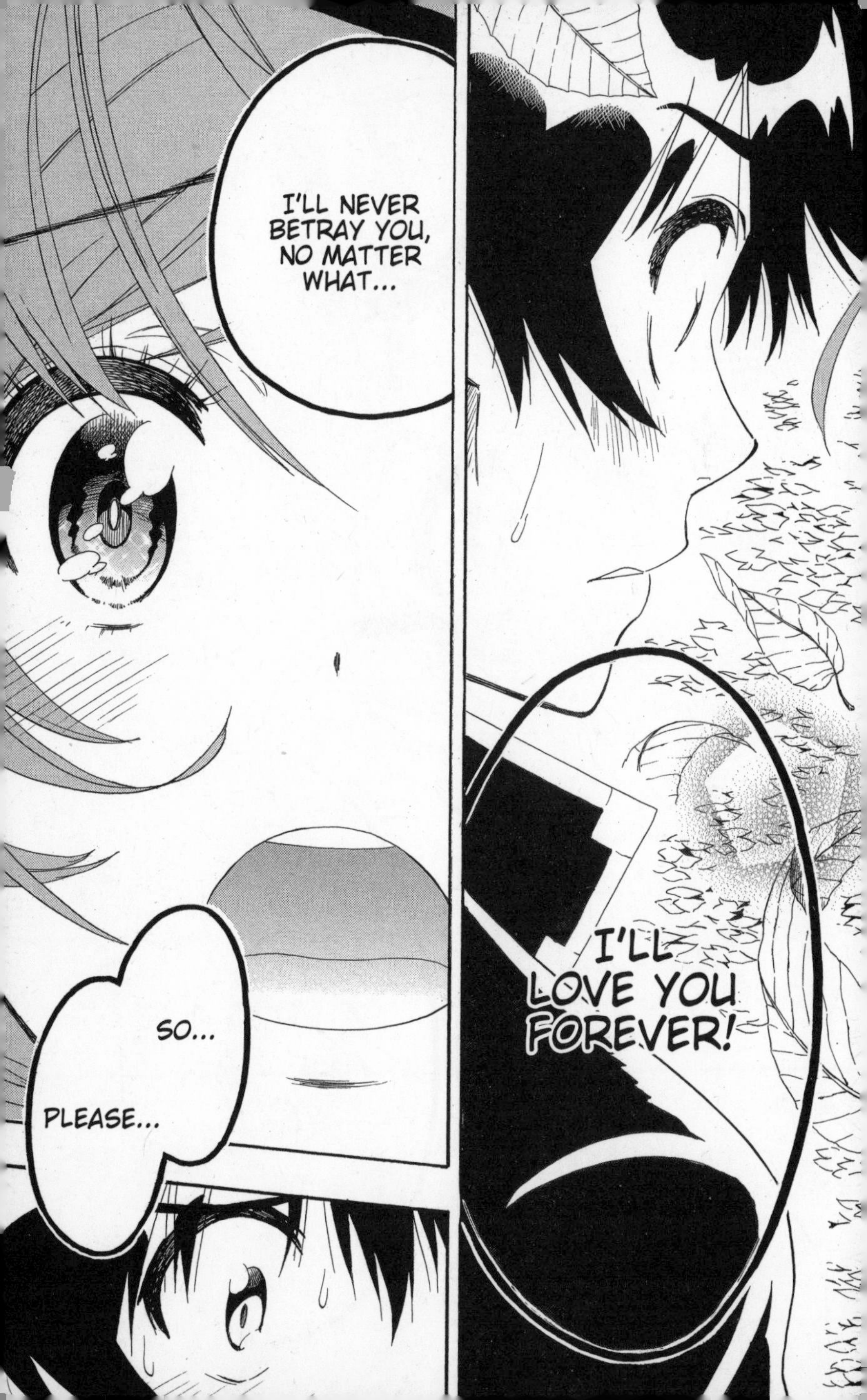
I'LL LOVE YOU FOREVER!
I'LL NEVER BETRAY YOU, NO MATTER WHAT...
SO...
PLEASE...

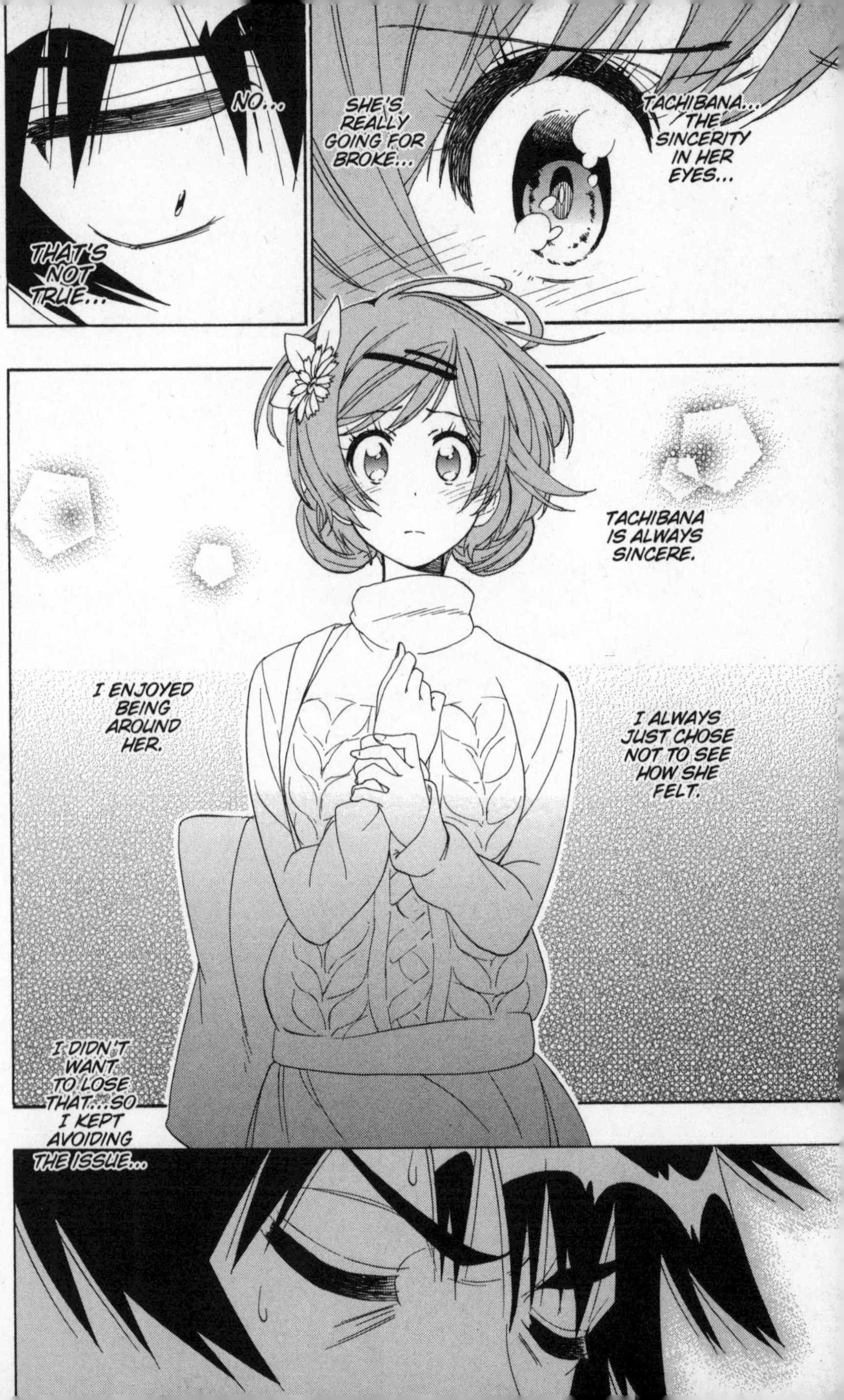
TACHIBANA... THE SINCERITY IN HER EYES...
SHE'S REALLY GOING FOR BROKE...
NO...
THAT'S NOT TRUE...
TACHIBANA IS ALWAYS SINCERE.
I ALWAYS JUST CHOSE NOT TO SEE HOW SHE FELT.
I ENJOYED BEING AROUND HER.
I DIDN'T WANT TO LOSE THAT...SO I KEPT AVOIDING THE ISSUE...

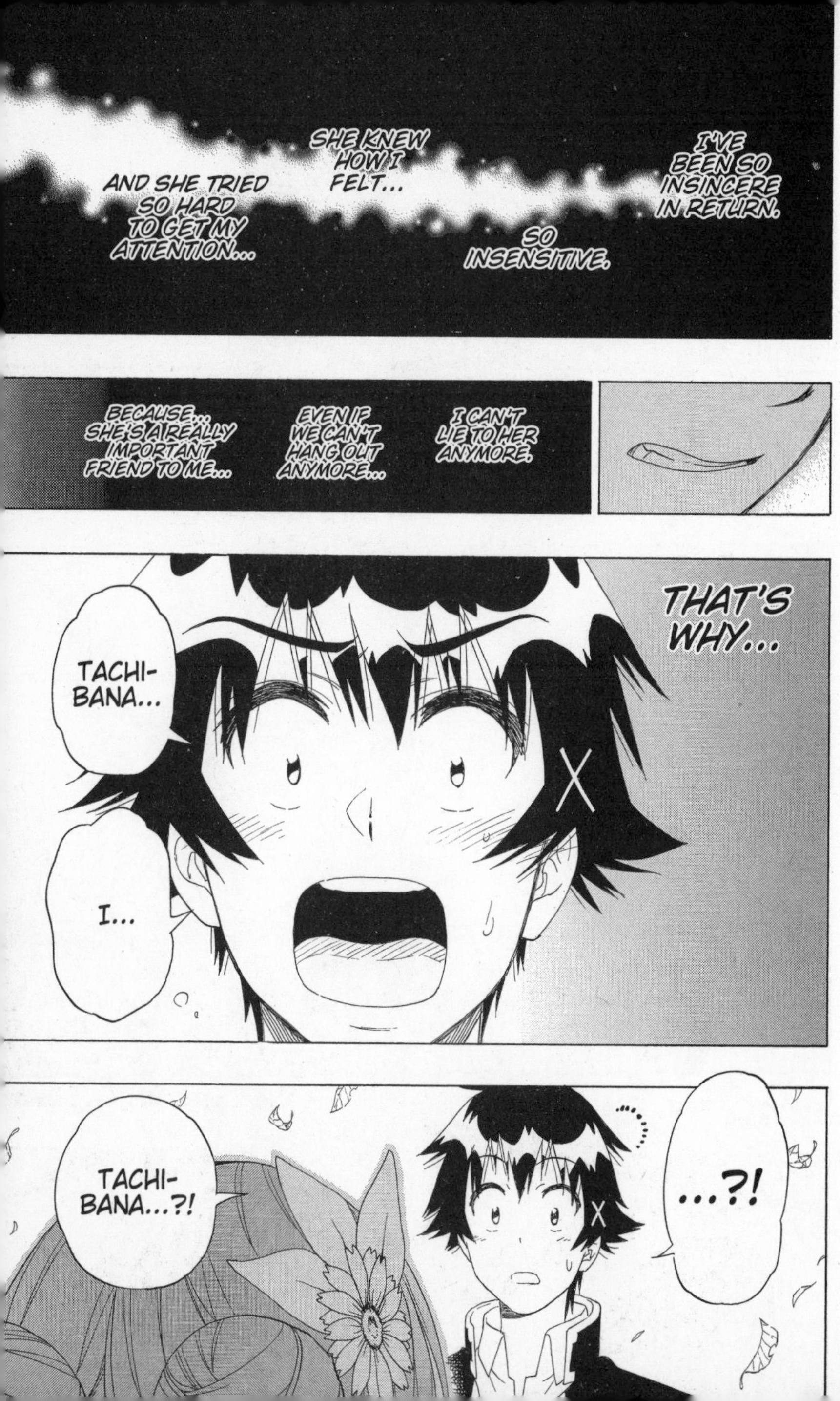
I'VE BEEN SO INSINCERE IN RETURN.
SO INSENSITIVE.
SHE KNEW HOW I FELT...
AND SHE TRIED SO HARD TO GET MY ATTENTION...
I CAN'T LIE TO HER ANYMORE.
EVEN IF WE CAN'T HANG OUT ANYMORE...
BECAUSE... SHE'S A REALLY IMPORTANT FRIEND TO ME...
THAT'S WHY...
TACHIBANA...
I...
...?!
TACHIBANA...?!

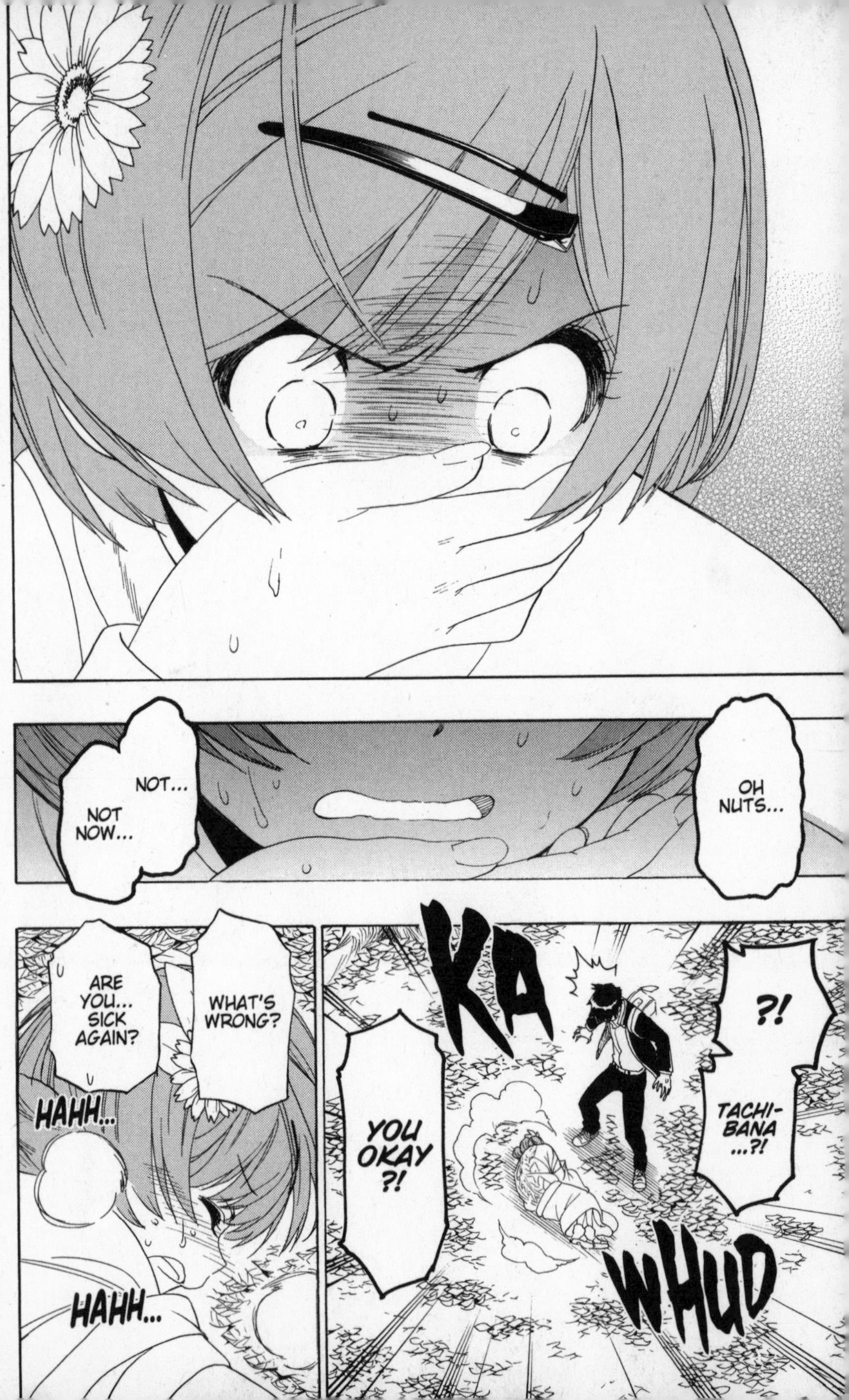
OH NUTS...
NOT... NOT NOW...
?!
KA
TACHI-BANA ...?!
YOU OKAY ?!
WHUD
WHAT'S WRONG?
ARE YOU... SICK AGAIN?
HAHH...
HAHH...

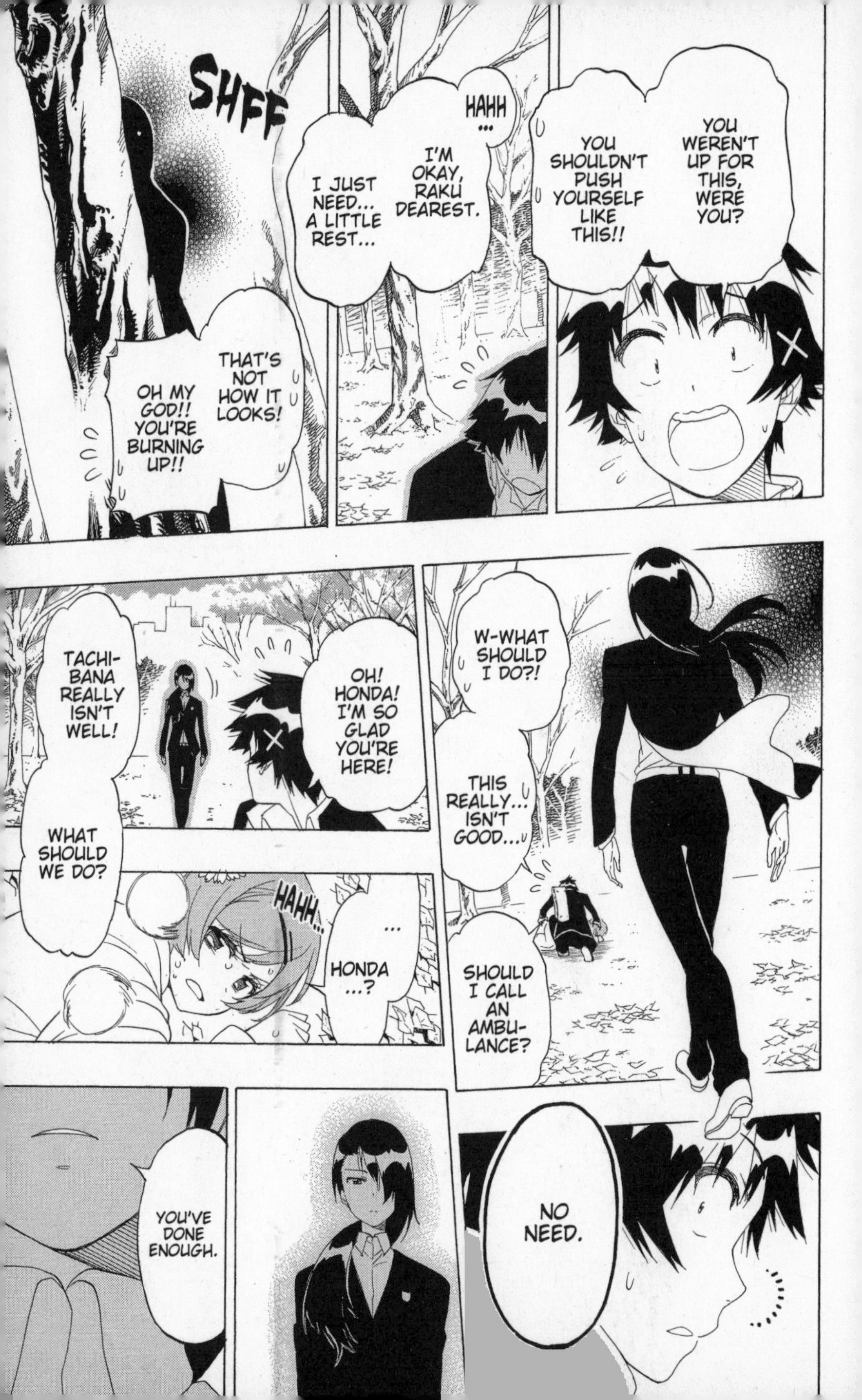
YOU WEREN'T UP FOR THIS, WERE YOU?
YOU SHOULDN'T PUSH YOURSELF LIKE THIS!!
HAHH...
I'M OKAY, RAKU DEAREST.
I JUST NEED... A LITTLE REST...
SHFF
THAT'S NOT HOW IT LOOKS!
OH MY GOD!! YOU'RE BURNING UP!!
W-WHAT SHOULD I DO?!
THIS REALLY... ISN'T GOOD...
SHOULD I CALL AN AMBU-LANCE?
OH! HONDA! I'M SO GLAD YOU'RE HERE!
TACHI-BANA REALLY ISN'T WELL!
WHAT SHOULD WE DO?
HAHH...
...
HONDA ...?
NO NEED.
...
YOU'VE DONE ENOUGH.

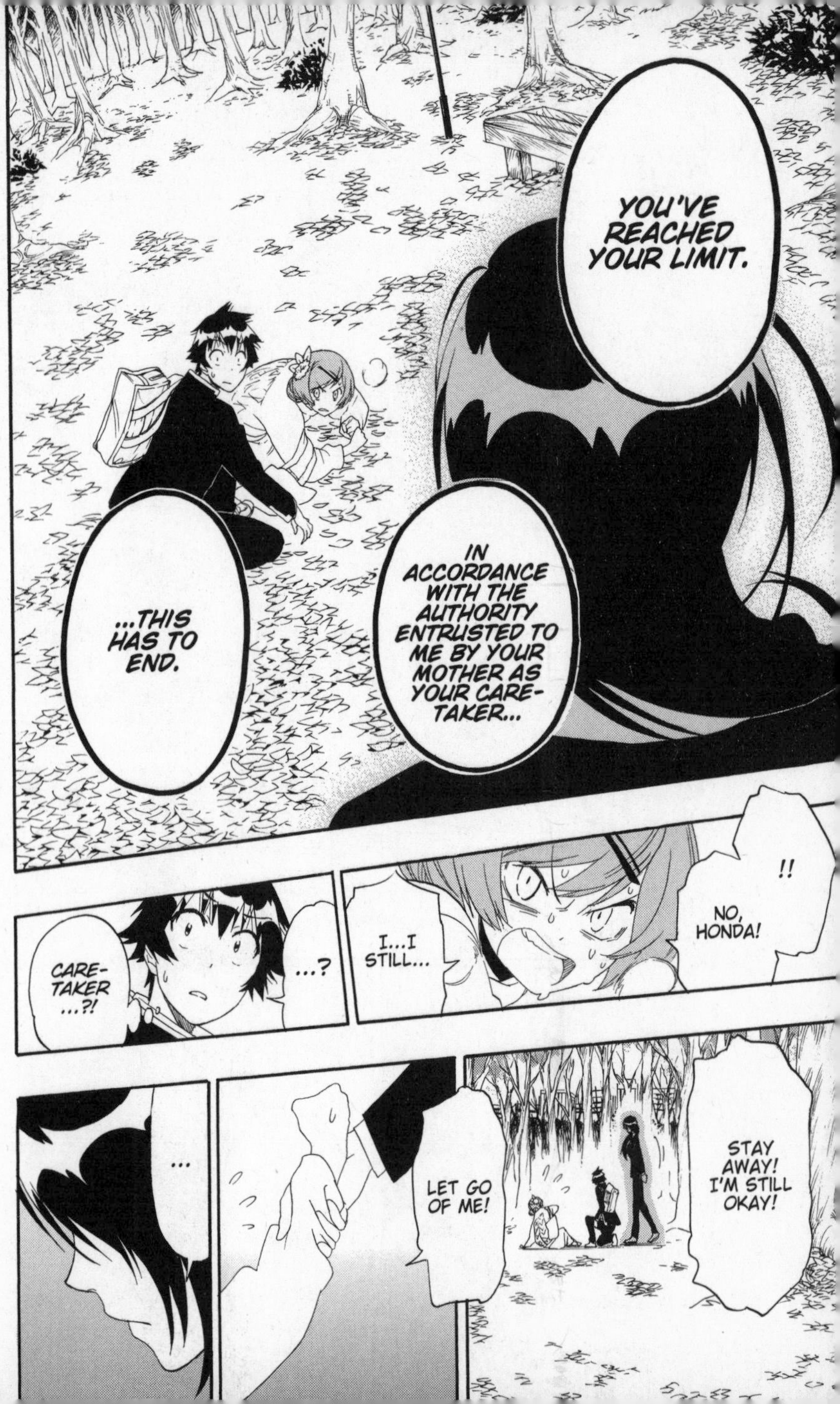
YOU'VE REACHED YOUR LIMIT.
IN ACCORDANCE WITH THE AUTHORITY ENTRUSTED TO ME BY YOUR MOTHER AS YOUR CARE-TAKER...
...THIS HAS TO END.
!!
NO, HONDA!
I...I STILL...
...?
CARE-TAKER...?!
STAY AWAY! I'M STILL OKAY!
LET GO OF ME!
...

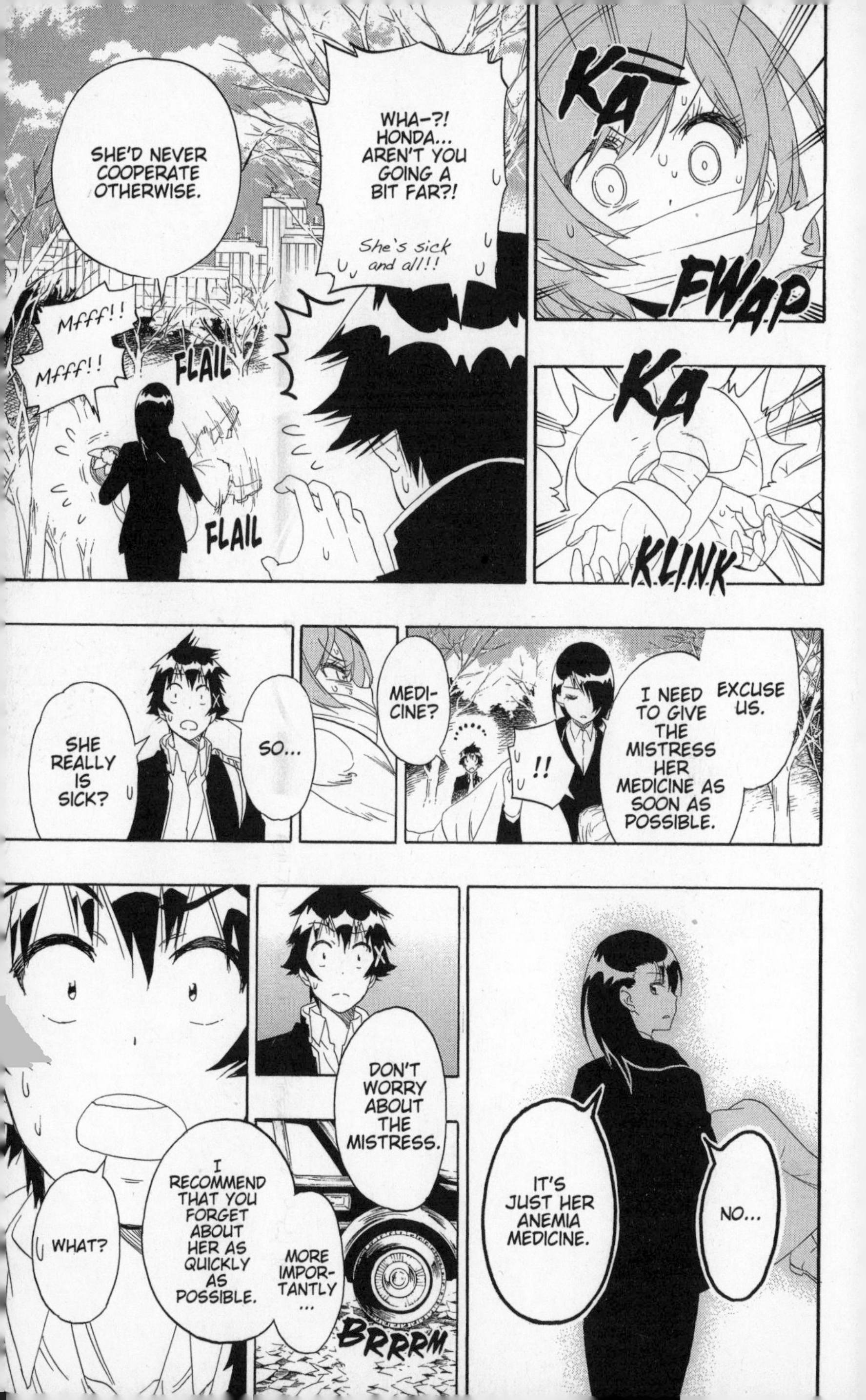
KA
FWAP
KA
KLINK
WHA-?! HONDA... AREN'T YOU GOING A BIT FAR?!
She's sick and all!!
SHE'D NEVER COOPERATE OTHERWISE.
Mfff!!
Mfff!!
FLAIL
FLAIL
EXCUSE US.
I NEED TO GIVE THE MISTRESS HER MEDICINE AS SOON AS POSSIBLE.
!!
MEDI-CINE?
SO...
SHE REALLY IS SICK?
NO...
IT'S JUST HER ANEMIA MEDICINE.
DON'T WORRY ABOUT THE MISTRESS.
MORE IMPOR-TANTLY...
I RECOMMEND THAT YOU FORGET ABOUT HER AS QUICKLY AS POSSIBLE.
BRRRM
WHAT?

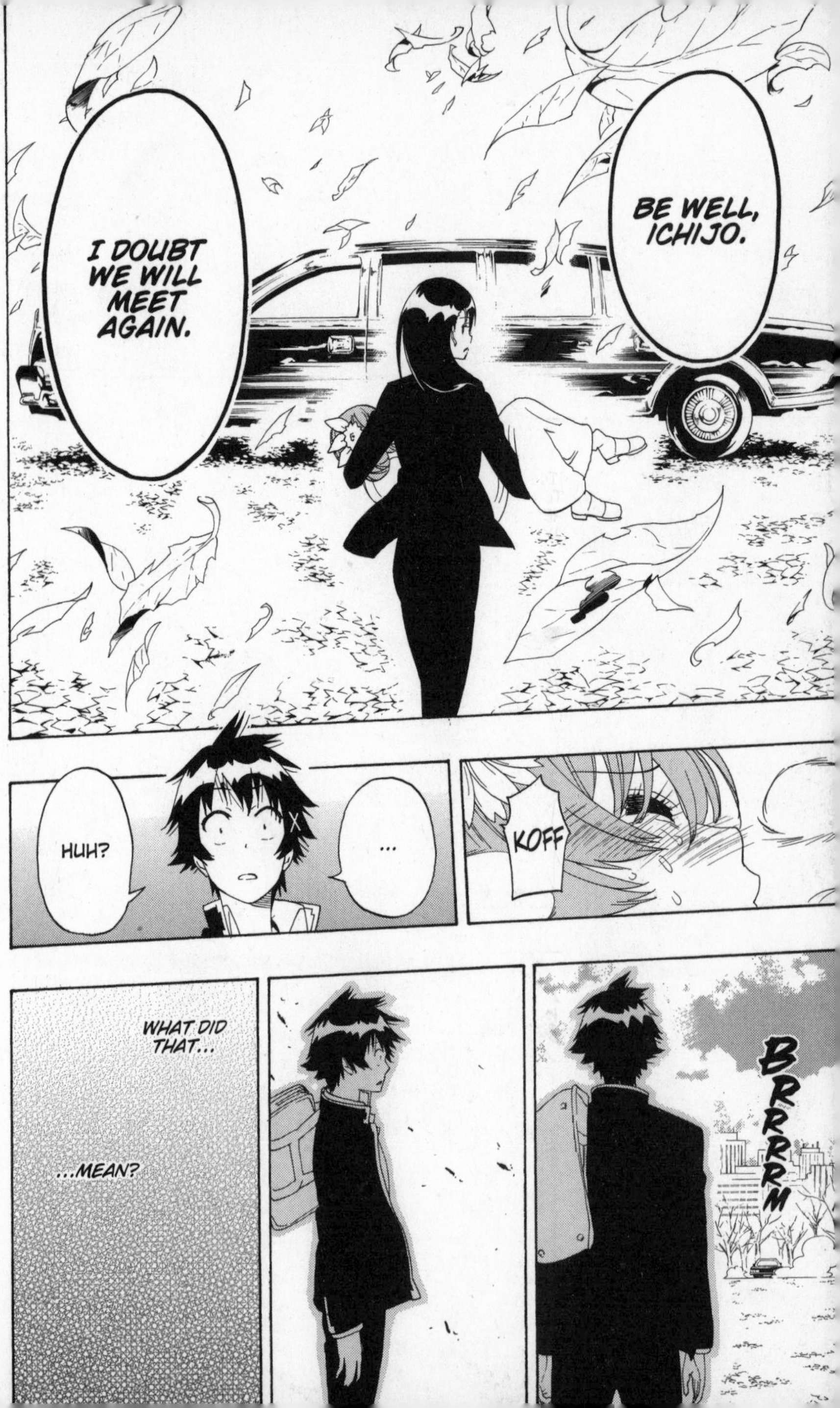
BE WELL, ICHIJO.
I DOUBT WE WILL MEET AGAIN.
KOFF
...
HUH?
BRRRRM
WHAT DID THAT...
...MEAN?

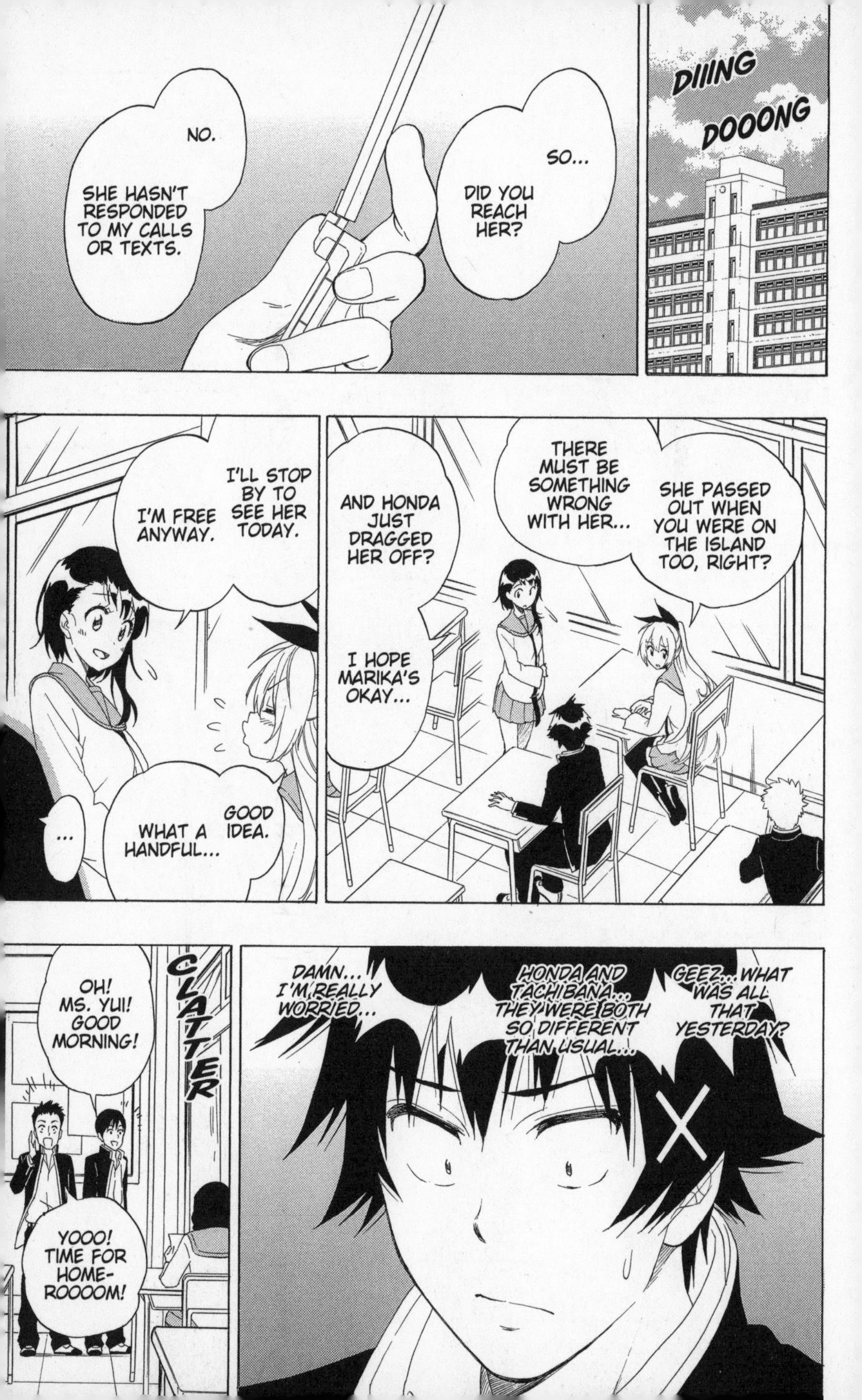
DIIING
DOOONG
SO...
DID YOU REACH HER?
NO.
SHE HASN'T RESPONDED TO MY CALLS OR TEXTS.
SHE PASSED OUT WHEN YOU WERE ON THE ISLAND TOO, RIGHT?
THERE MUST BE SOMETHING WRONG WITH HER...
AND HONDA JUST DRAGGED HER OFF?
I HOPE MARIKA'S OKAY...
I'LL STOP BY TO SEE HER TODAY.
I'M FREE ANYWAY.
GOOD IDEA.
WHAT A HANDFUL...
...
GEEZ... WHAT WAS ALL THAT YESTERDAY?
HONDA AND TACHIBANA... THEY WERE BOTH SO DIFFERENT THAN USUAL...
DAMN... I'M REALLY WORRIED...
CLATTER
OH! MS. YUI! GOOD MORNING!
YOOO! TIME FOR HOME-ROOOOM!

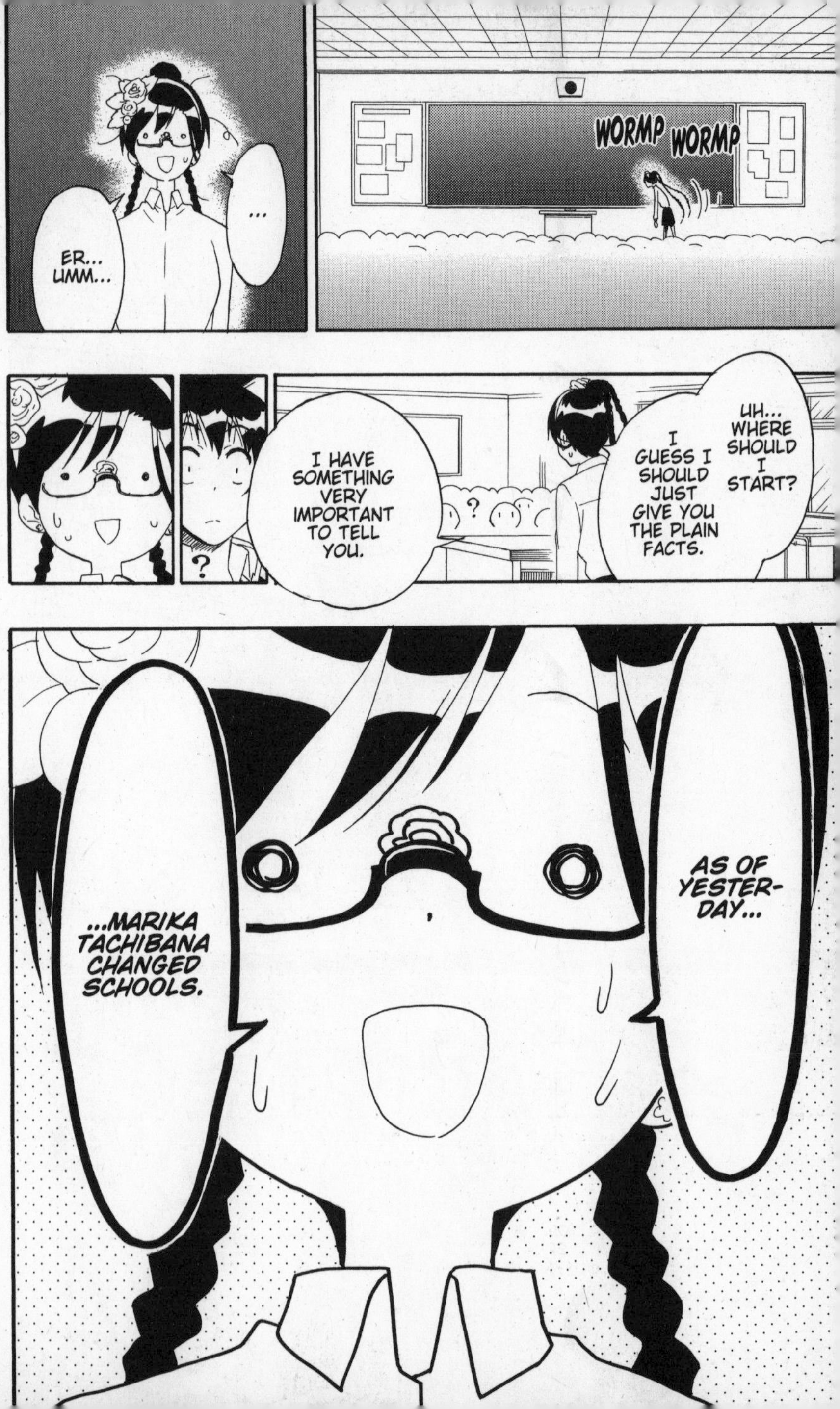
WORMP WORMP
...
ER... UMM...
UH... WHERE SHOULD I START?
I GUESS I SHOULD JUST GIVE YOU THE PLAIN FACTS.
?
I HAVE SOMETHING VERY IMPORTANT TO TELL YOU.
?
AS OF YESTER-DAY...
...MARIKA TACHIBANA CHANGED SCHOOLS.

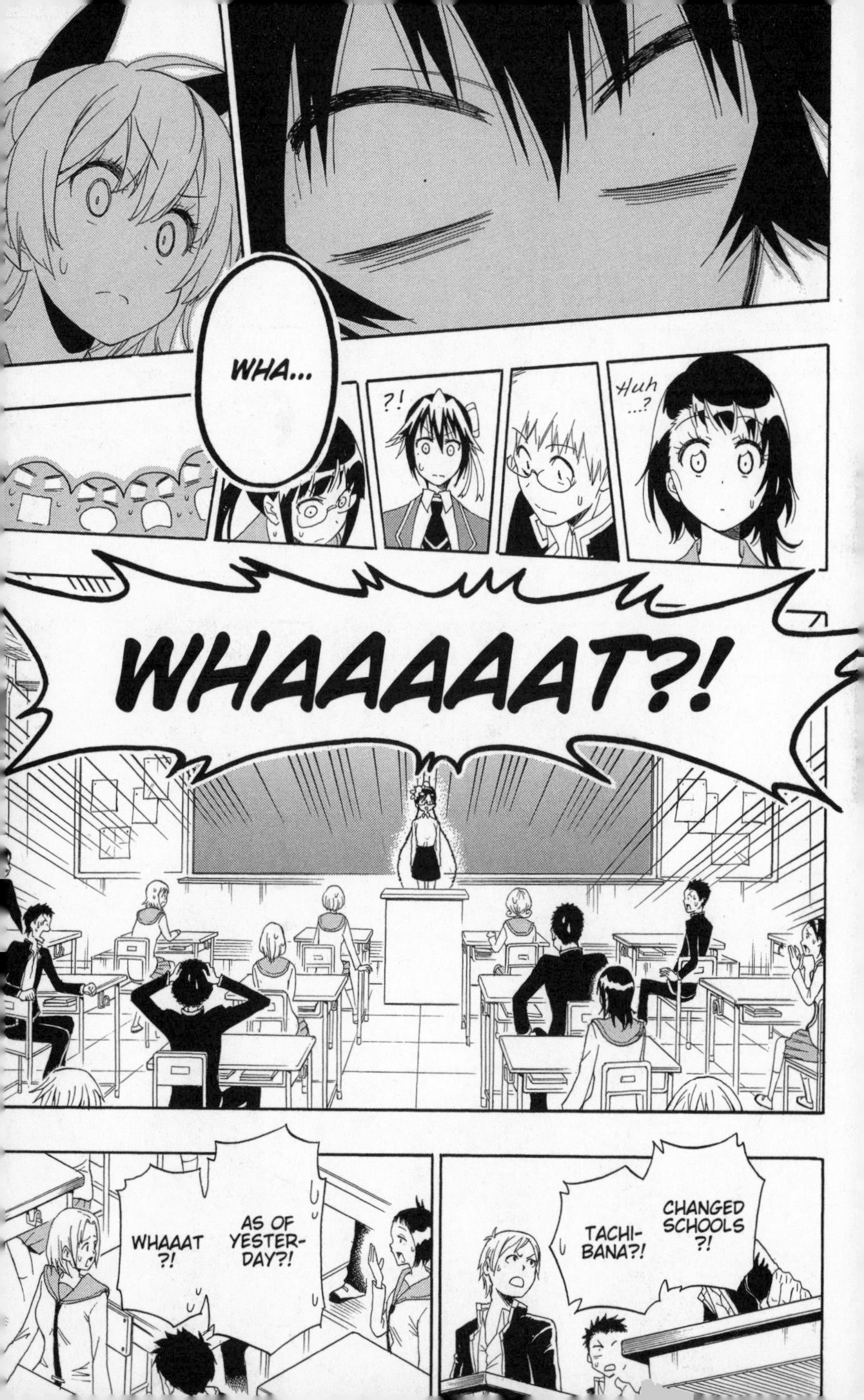
Huh ...?
?!
WHA...
WHAAAAAT?!
CHANGED SCHOOLS ?!
TACHI-BANA?!
AS OF YESTER-DAY?!
WHAAAT ?!

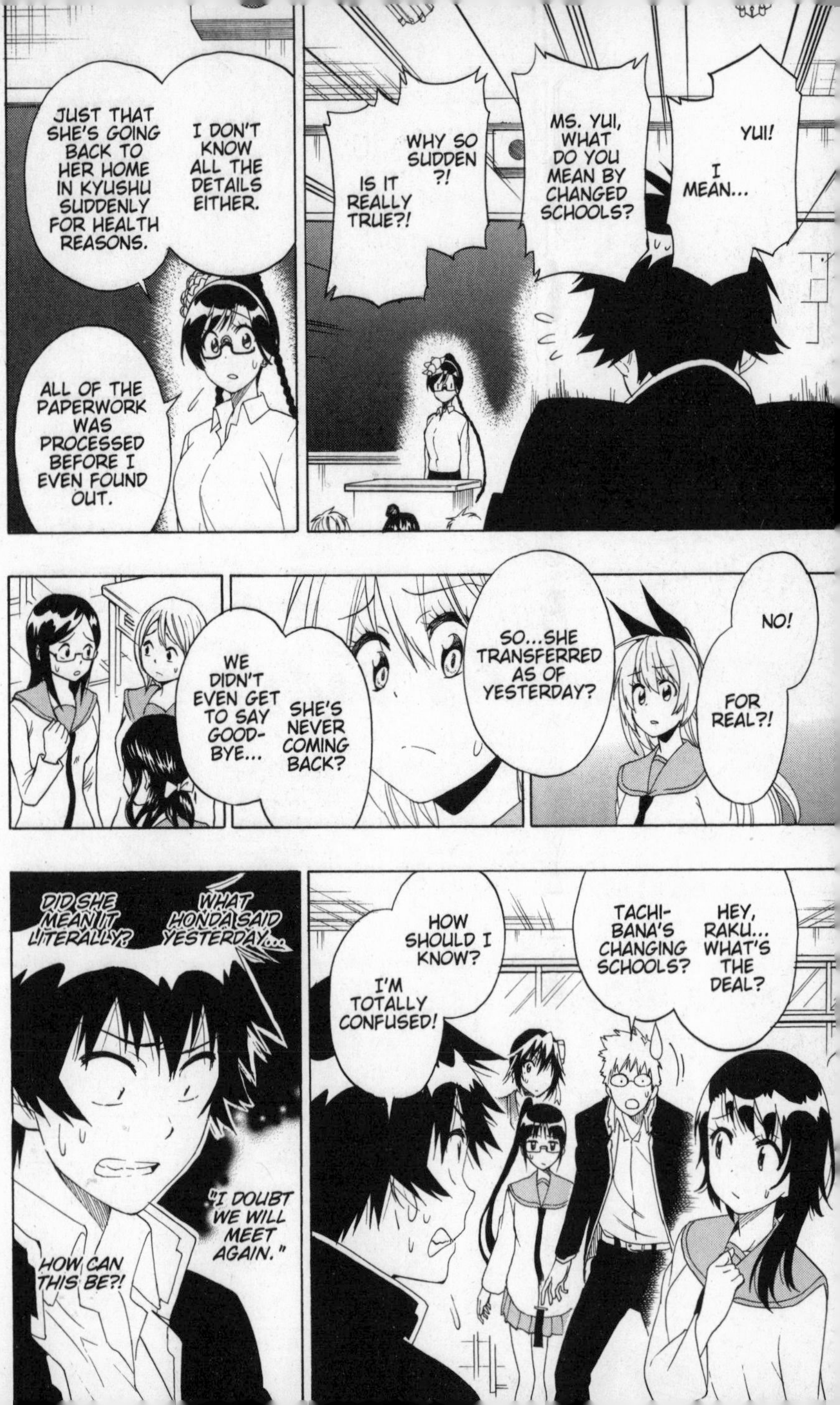
YUI!
I MEAN...
MS. YUI, WHAT DO YOU MEAN BY CHANGED SCHOOLS?
WHY SO SUDDEN?!
IS IT REALLY TRUE?!
I DON'T KNOW ALL THE DETAILS EITHER.
JUST THAT SHE'S GOING BACK TO HER HOME IN KYUSHU SUDDENLY FOR HEALTH REASONS.
ALL OF THE PAPERWORK WAS PROCESSED BEFORE I EVEN FOUND OUT.
NO!
FOR REAL?!
SO...SHE TRANSFERRED AS OF YESTERDAY?
SHE'S NEVER COMING BACK?
WE DIDN'T EVEN GET TO SAY GOOD-BYE...
HEY, RAKU... WHAT'S THE DEAL?
TACHI-BANA'S CHANGING SCHOOLS?
HOW SHOULD I KNOW?
I'M TOTALLY CONFUSED!
WHAT HONDA SAID YESTERDAY...
DID SHE MEAN IT LITERALLY?
"I DOUBT WE WILL MEET AGAIN."
HOW CAN THIS BE?!

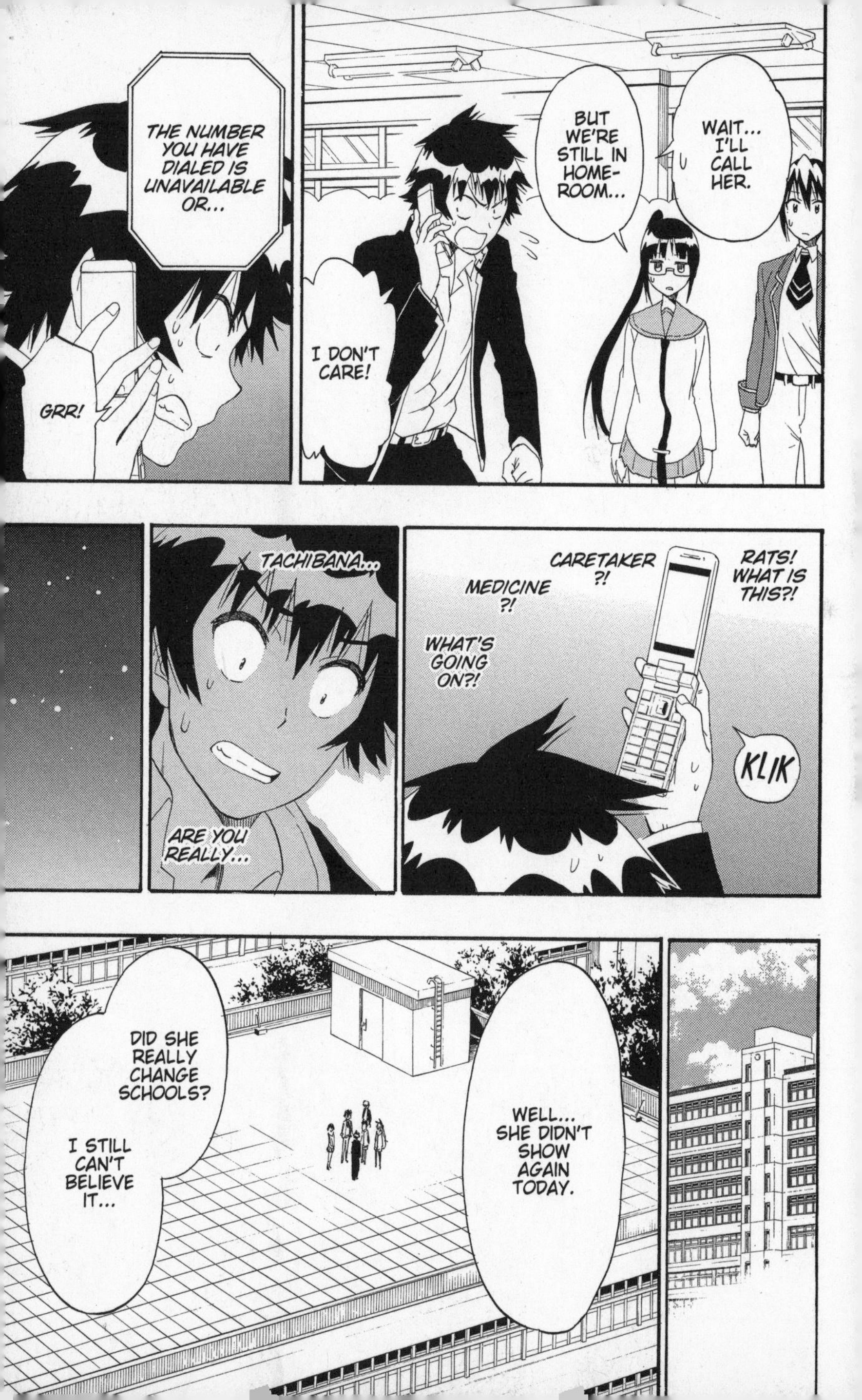
WAIT... I'LL CALL HER.
BUT WE'RE STILL IN HOME-ROOM...
I DON'T CARE!
THE NUMBER YOU HAVE DIALED IS UNAVAILABLE OR...
GRR!
RATS! WHAT IS THIS?!
CARETAKER?!
MEDICINE?!
WHAT'S GOING ON?!
KLIK
TACHIBANA...
ARE YOU REALLY...
WELL... SHE DIDN'T SHOW AGAIN TODAY.
DID SHE REALLY CHANGE SCHOOLS?
I STILL CAN'T BELIEVE IT...

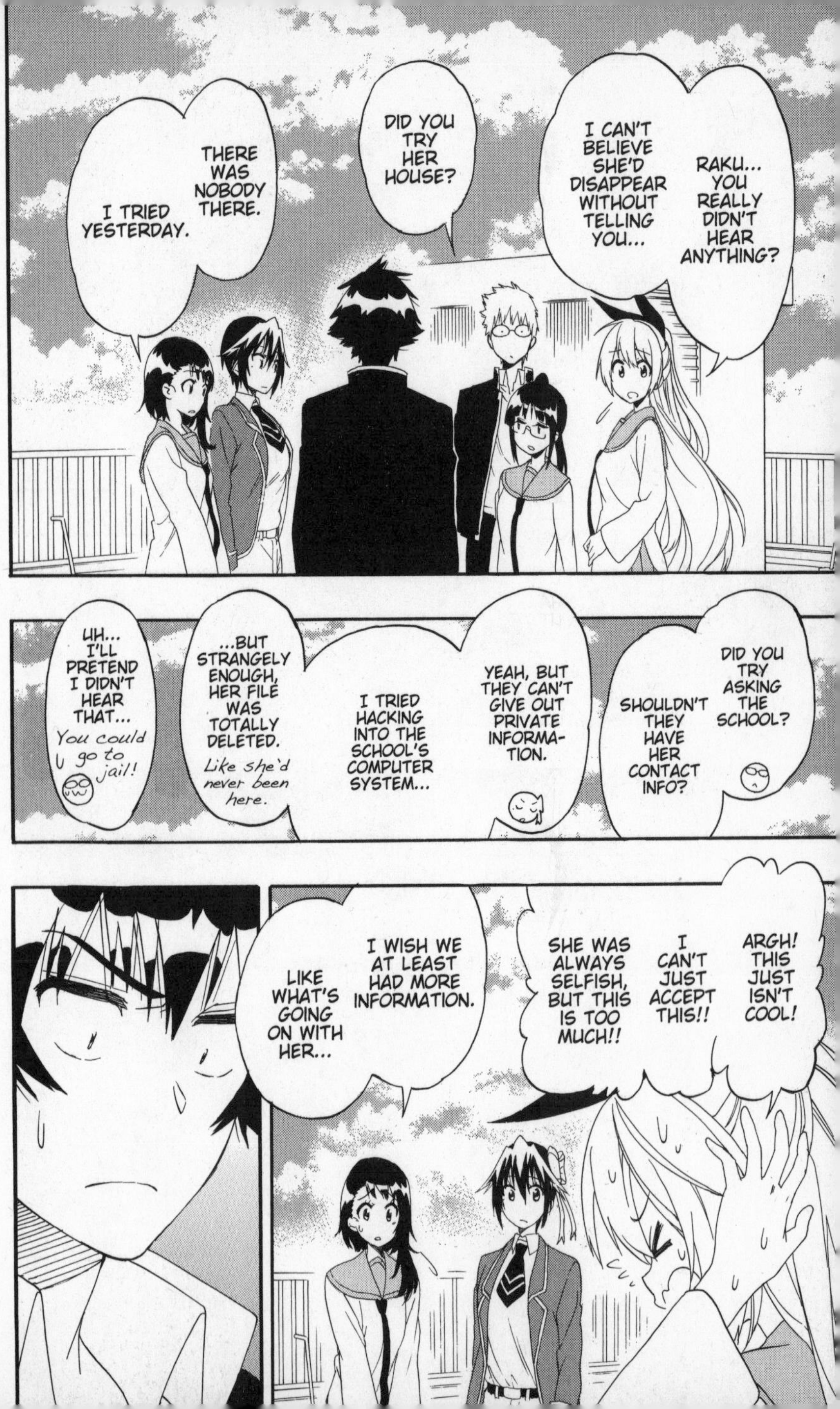
RAKU... YOU REALLY DIDN'T HEAR ANYTHING?
I CAN'T BELIEVE SHE'D DISAPPEAR WITHOUT TELLING YOU...
DID YOU TRY HER HOUSE?
THERE WAS NOBODY THERE.
I TRIED YESTERDAY.
DID YOU TRY ASKING THE SCHOOL?
SHOULDN'T THEY HAVE HER CONTACT INFO?
YEAH, BUT THEY CAN'T GIVE OUT PRIVATE INFORMATION.
I TRIED HACKING INTO THE SCHOOL'S COMPUTER SYSTEM...
...BUT STRANGELY ENOUGH, HER FILE WAS TOTALLY DELETED.
Like she'd never been here.
UH... I'LL PRETEND I DIDN'T HEAR THAT...
You could go to jail!
ARGH! THIS JUST ISN'T COOL!
I CAN'T JUST ACCEPT THIS!!
SHE WAS ALWAYS SELFISH, BUT THIS IS TOO MUCH!!
I WISH WE AT LEAST HAD MORE INFORMATION.
LIKE WHAT'S GOING ON WITH HER...

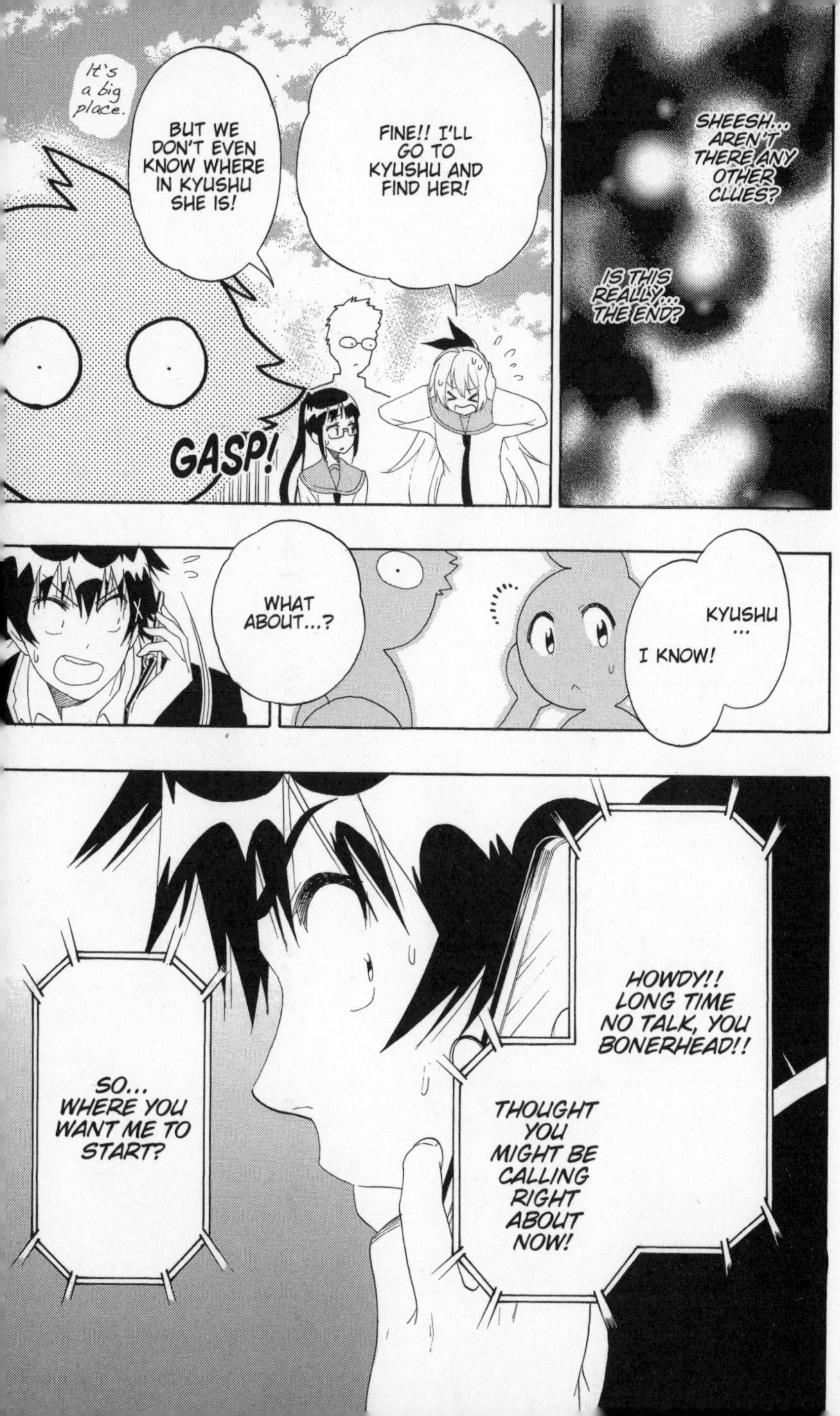
SHEESH... AREN'T THERE ANY OTHER CLUES?
IS THIS REALLY... THE END?
FINE!! I'LL GO TO KYUSHU AND FIND HER!
BUT WE DON'T EVEN KNOW WHERE IN KYUSHU SHE IS!
It's a big place.
GASP!
KYUSHU...
I KNOW!
WHAT ABOUT...?
HOWDY!! LONG TIME NO TALK, YOU BONERHEAD!!
THOUGHT YOU MIGHT BE CALLING RIGHT ABOUT NOW!
SO... WHERE YOU WANT ME TO START?

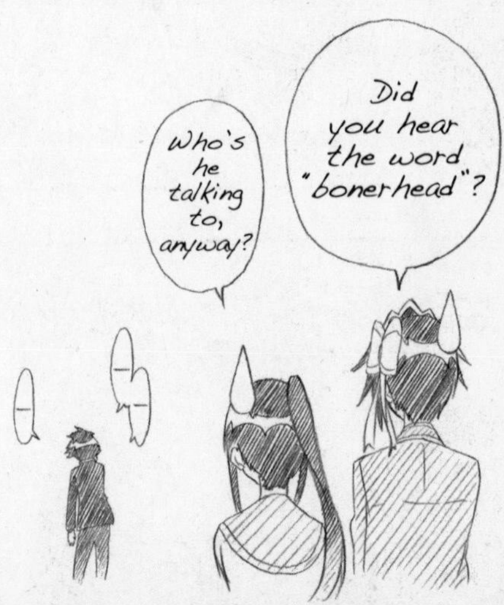
Did you hear the word "bonerhead"?
Who's he talking to, anyway?
—
—
—

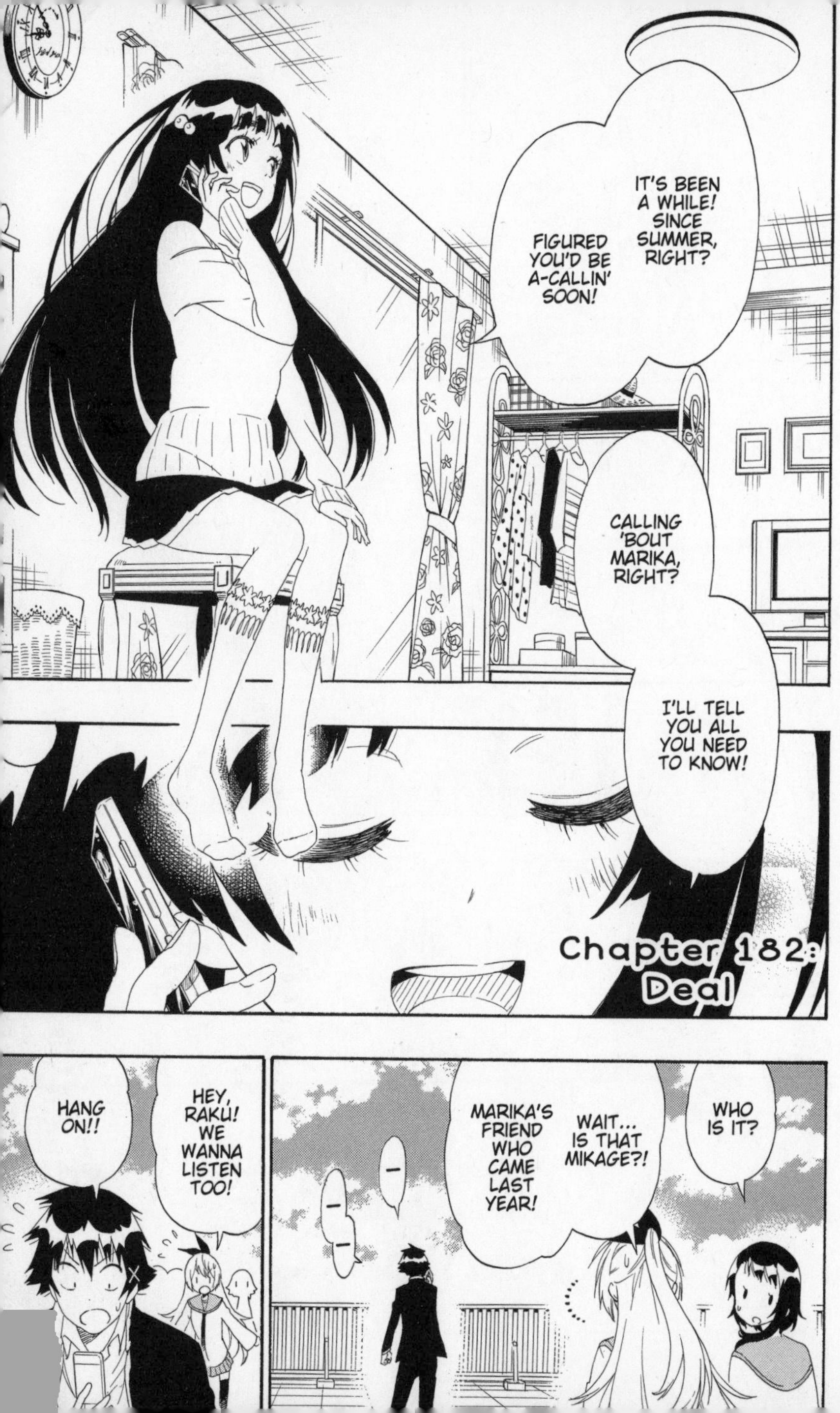
IT'S BEEN A WHILE! SINCE SUMMER, RIGHT?
FIGURED YOU'D BE A-CALLIN' SOON!
CALLING 'BOUT MARIKA, RIGHT?
I'LL TELL YOU ALL YOU NEED TO KNOW!
Chapter 182: Deal
WHO IS IT?
WAIT... IS THAT MIKAGE?!
MARIKA'S FRIEND WHO CAME LAST YEAR!
—
—
—
HEY, RAKU! WE WANNA LISTEN TOO!
HANG ON!!

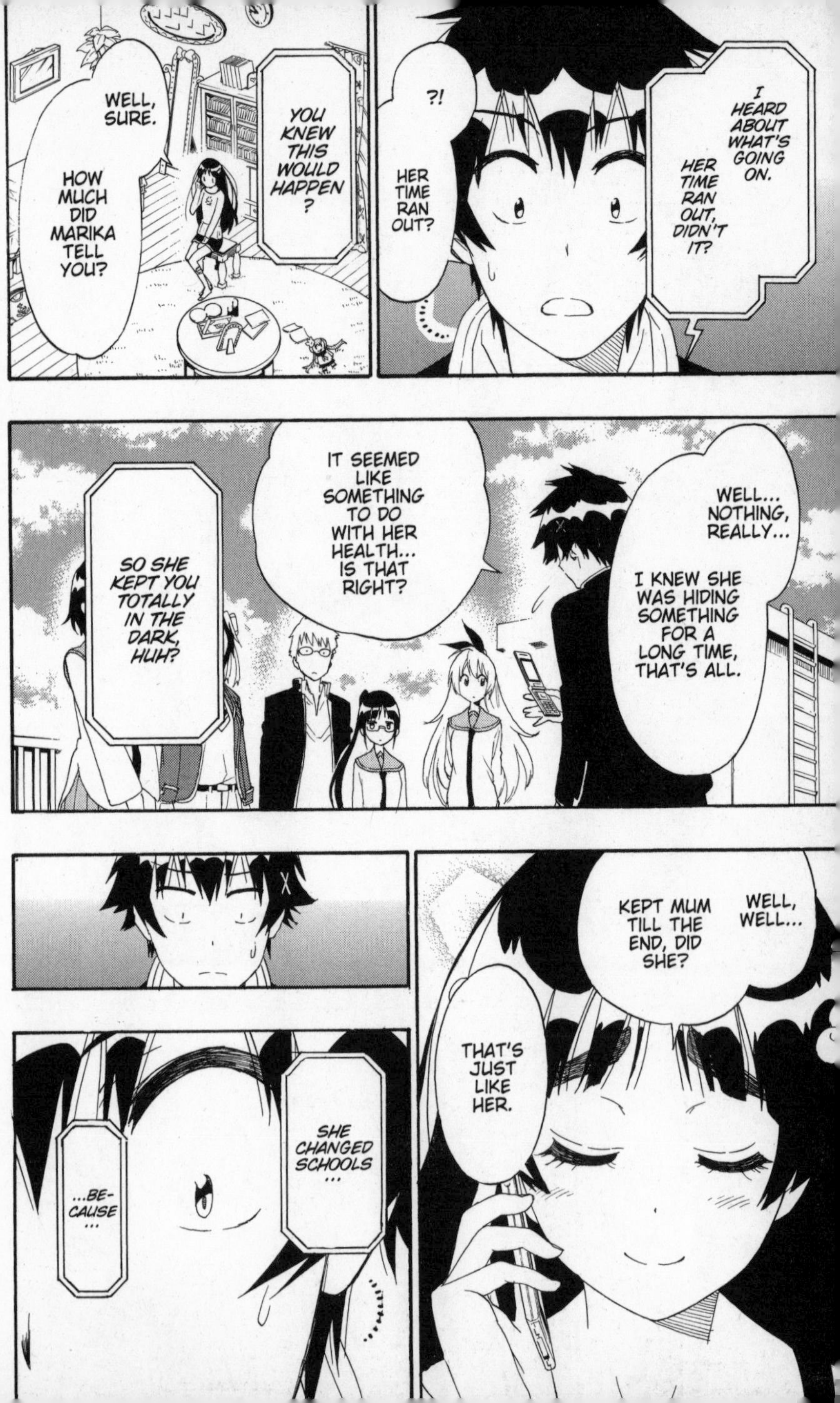
I HEARD ABOUT WHAT'S GOING ON.
HER TIME RAN OUT, DIDN'T IT?
?!
HER TIME RAN OUT?
YOU KNEW THIS WOULD HAPPEN?
WELL, SURE.
HOW MUCH DID MARIKA TELL YOU?
WELL... NOTHING, REALLY...
I KNEW SHE WAS HIDING SOMETHING FOR A LONG TIME, THAT'S ALL.
IT SEEMED LIKE SOMETHING TO DO WITH HER HEALTH... IS THAT RIGHT?
SO SHE KEPT YOU TOTALLY IN THE DARK, HUH?
WELL, WELL...
KEPT MUM TILL THE END, DID SHE?
THAT'S JUST LIKE HER.
SHE CHANGED SCHOOLS...
...BE-CAUSE...

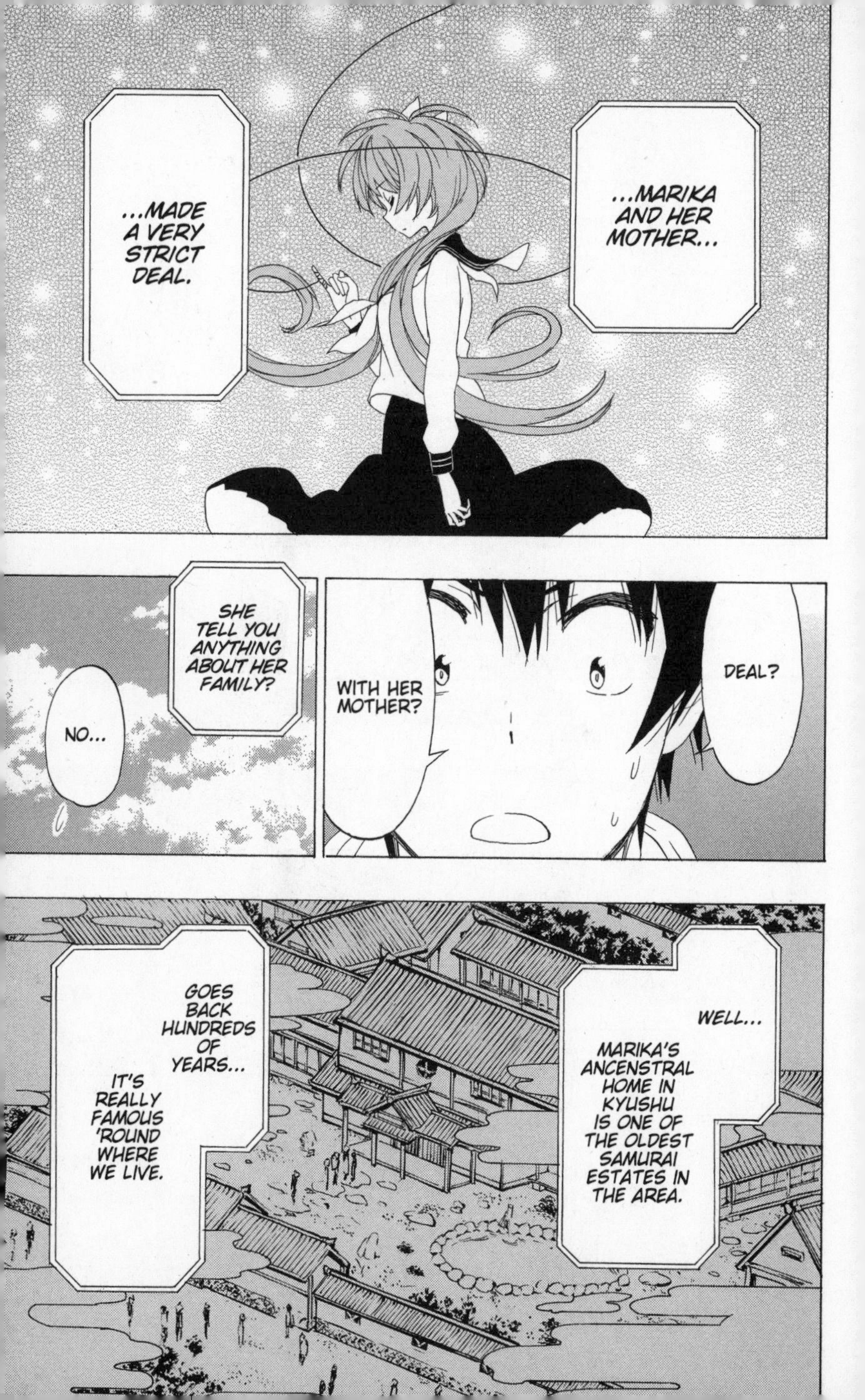

...MARIKA AND HER MOTHER...
...MADE A VERY STRICT DEAL.
DEAL?
WITH HER MOTHER?
SHE TELL YOU ANYTHING ABOUT HER FAMILY?
NO...
WELL...
MARIKA'S ANCENSTRAL HOME IN KYUSHU IS ONE OF THE OLDEST SAMURAI ESTATES IN THE AREA.
GOES BACK HUNDREDS OF YEARS...
IT'S REALLY FAMOUS 'ROUND WHERE WE LIVE.

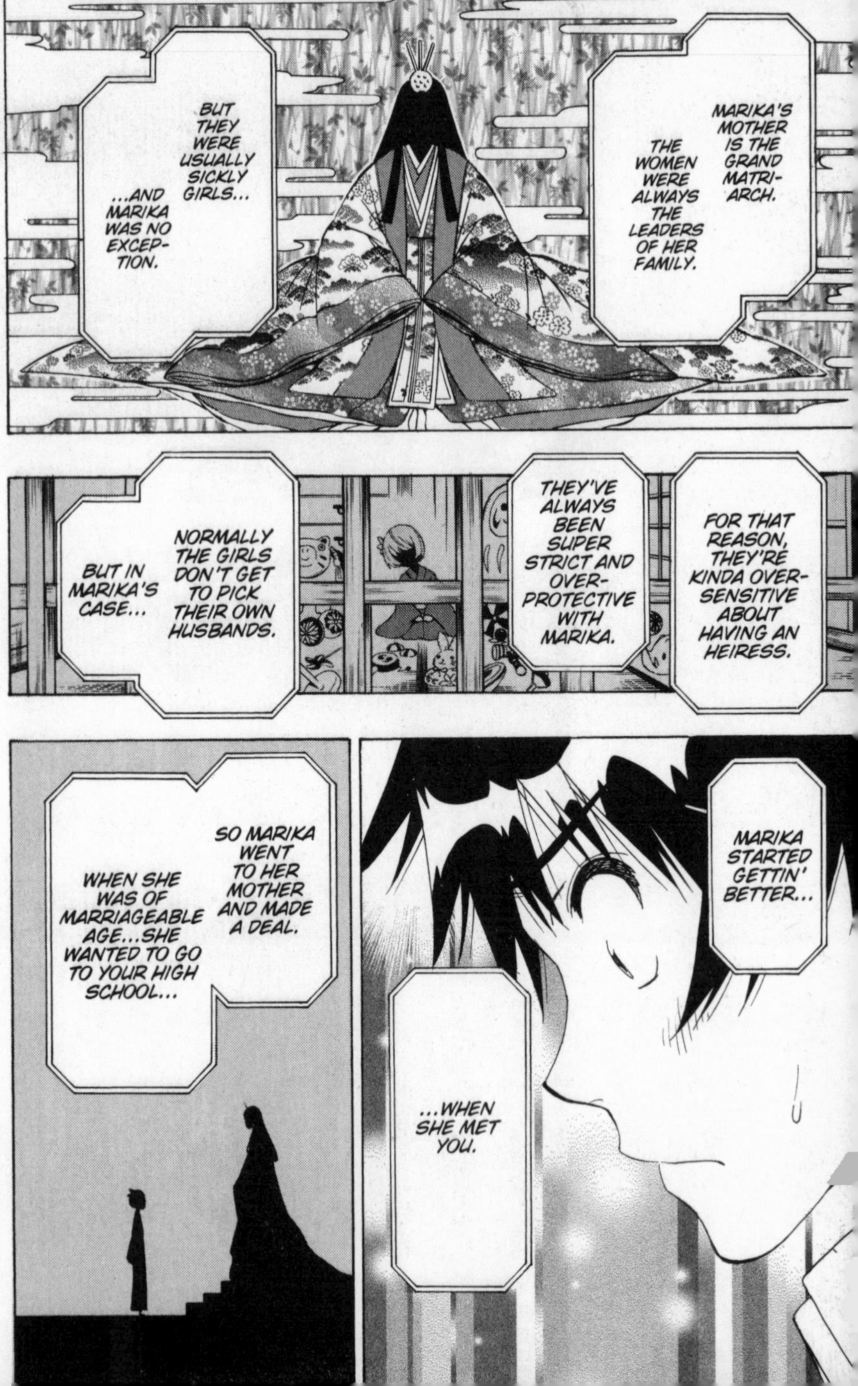
MARIKA'S MOTHER IS THE GRAND MATRI-ARCH.
THE WOMEN WERE ALWAYS THE LEADERS OF HER FAMILY.
BUT THEY WERE USUALLY SICKLY GIRLS...
...AND MARIKA WAS NO EXCEP-TION.
FOR THAT REASON, THEY'RE KINDA OVER-SENSITIVE ABOUT HAVING AN HEIRESS.
THEY'VE ALWAYS BEEN SUPER STRICT AND OVER-PROTECTIVE WITH MARIKA.
NORMALLY THE GIRLS DON'T GET TO PICK THEIR OWN HUSBANDS.
BUT IN MARIKA'S CASE...
MARIKA STARTED GETTIN' BETTER...
...WHEN SHE MET YOU.
SO MARIKA WENT TO HER MOTHER AND MADE A DEAL.
WHEN SHE WAS OF MARRIAGEABLE AGE...SHE WANTED TO GO TO YOUR HIGH SCHOOL...

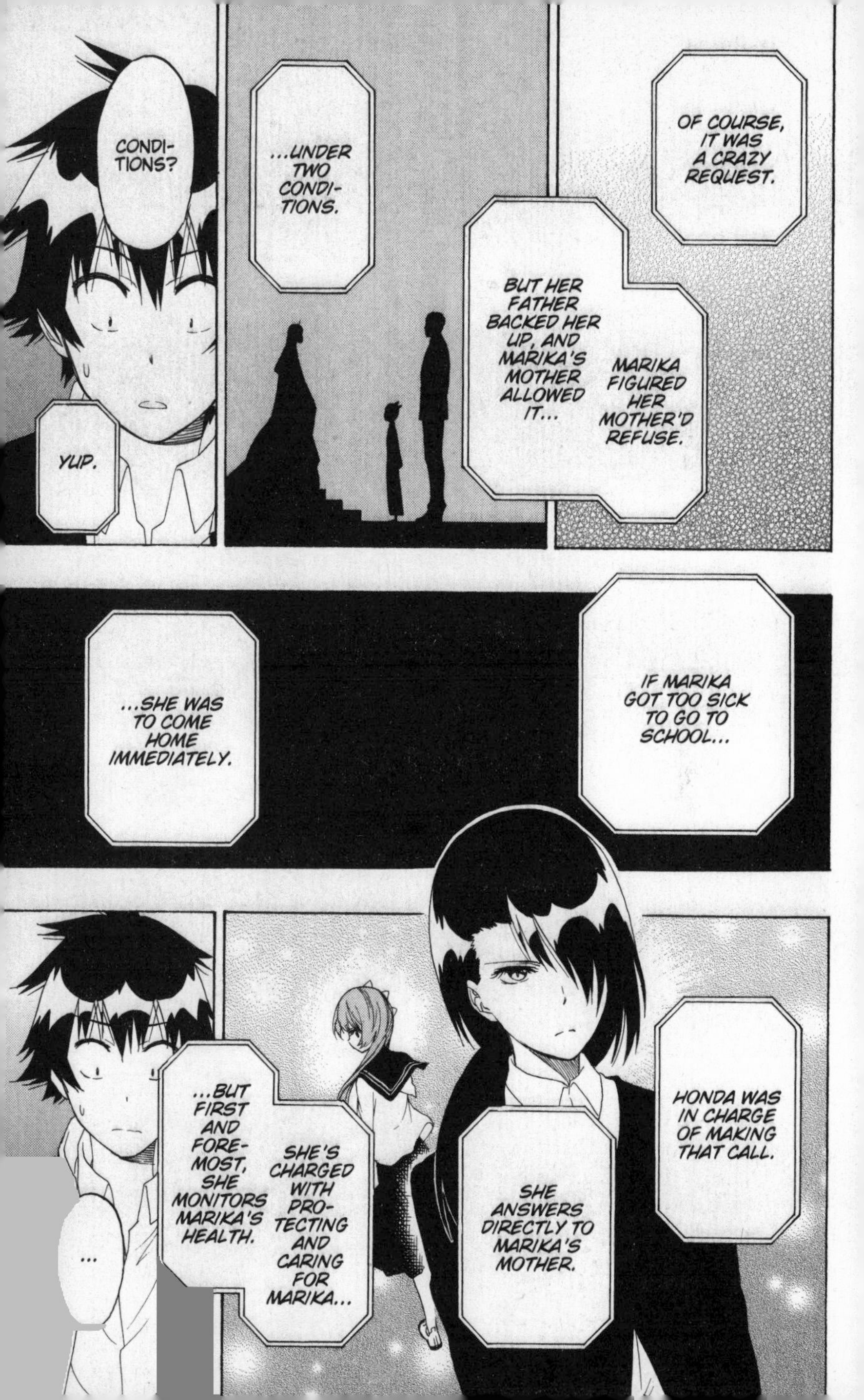
OF COURSE, IT WAS A CRAZY REQUEST.
MARIKA FIGURED HER MOTHER'D REFUSE.
BUT HER FATHER BACKED HER UP, AND MARIKA'S MOTHER ALLOWED IT...
...UNDER TWO CONDITIONS.
CONDITIONS?
YUP.
IF MARIKA GOT TOO SICK TO GO TO SCHOOL...
...SHE WAS TO COME HOME IMMEDIATELY.
HONDA WAS IN CHARGE OF MAKING THAT CALL.
SHE ANSWERS DIRECTLY TO MARIKA'S MOTHER.
SHE'S CHARGED WITH PROTECTING AND CARING FOR MARIKA...
...BUT FIRST AND FOREMOST, SHE MONITORS MARIKA'S HEALTH.
...

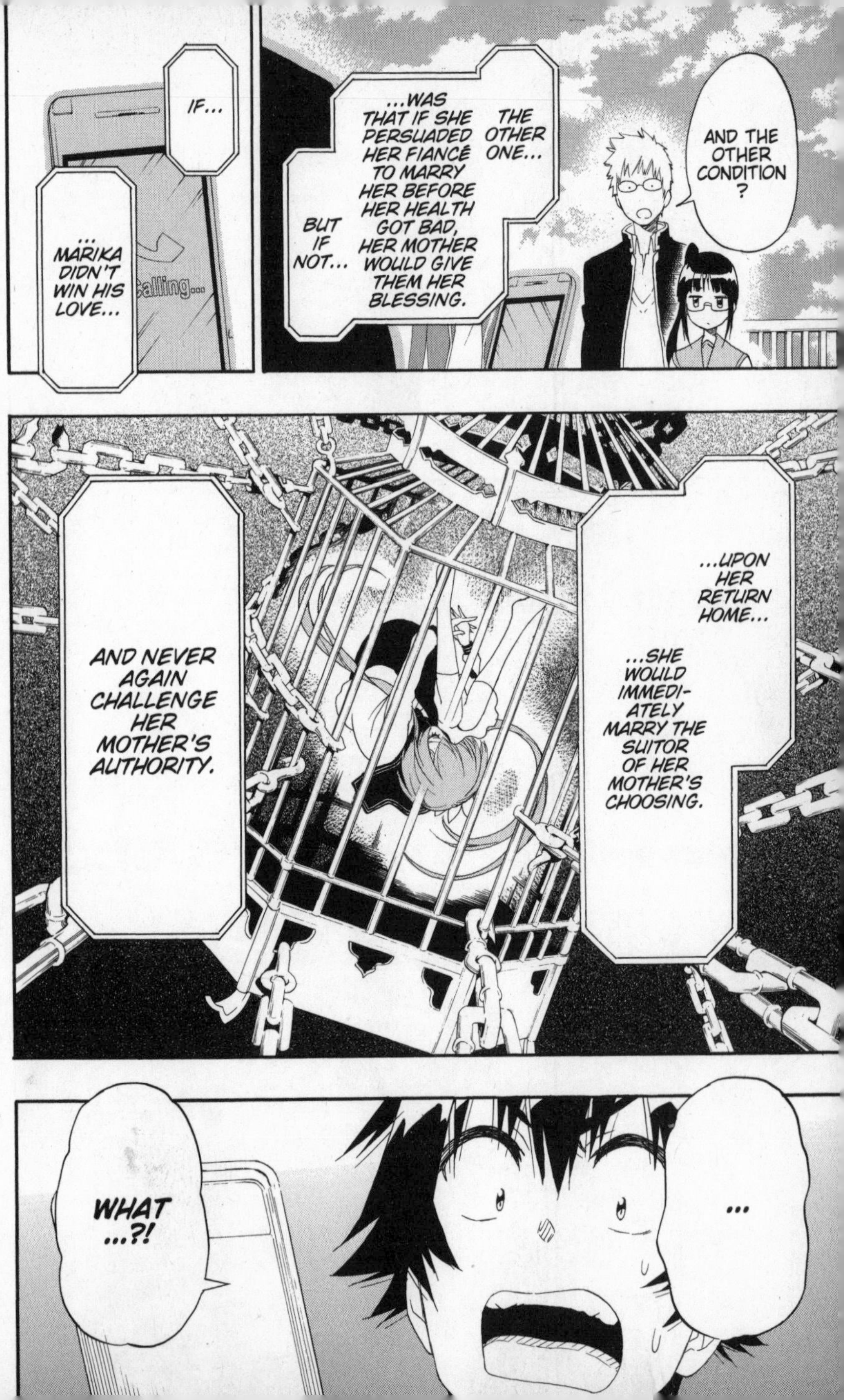
AND THE OTHER CONDITION?
THE OTHER ONE...
...WAS THAT IF SHE PERSUADED HER FIANCÉ TO MARRY HER BEFORE HER HEALTH GOT BAD, HER MOTHER WOULD GIVE THEM HER BLESSING.
BUT IF NOT...
IF...
...MÄRIKA DIDN'T WIN HIS LOVE...
Calling...
...UPON HER RETURN HOME...
...SHE WOULD IMMEDI-ATELY MARRY THE SUITOR OF HER MOTHER'S CHOOSING.
AND NEVER AGAIN CHALLENGE HER MOTHER'S AUTHORITY.
...
WHAT ...?!

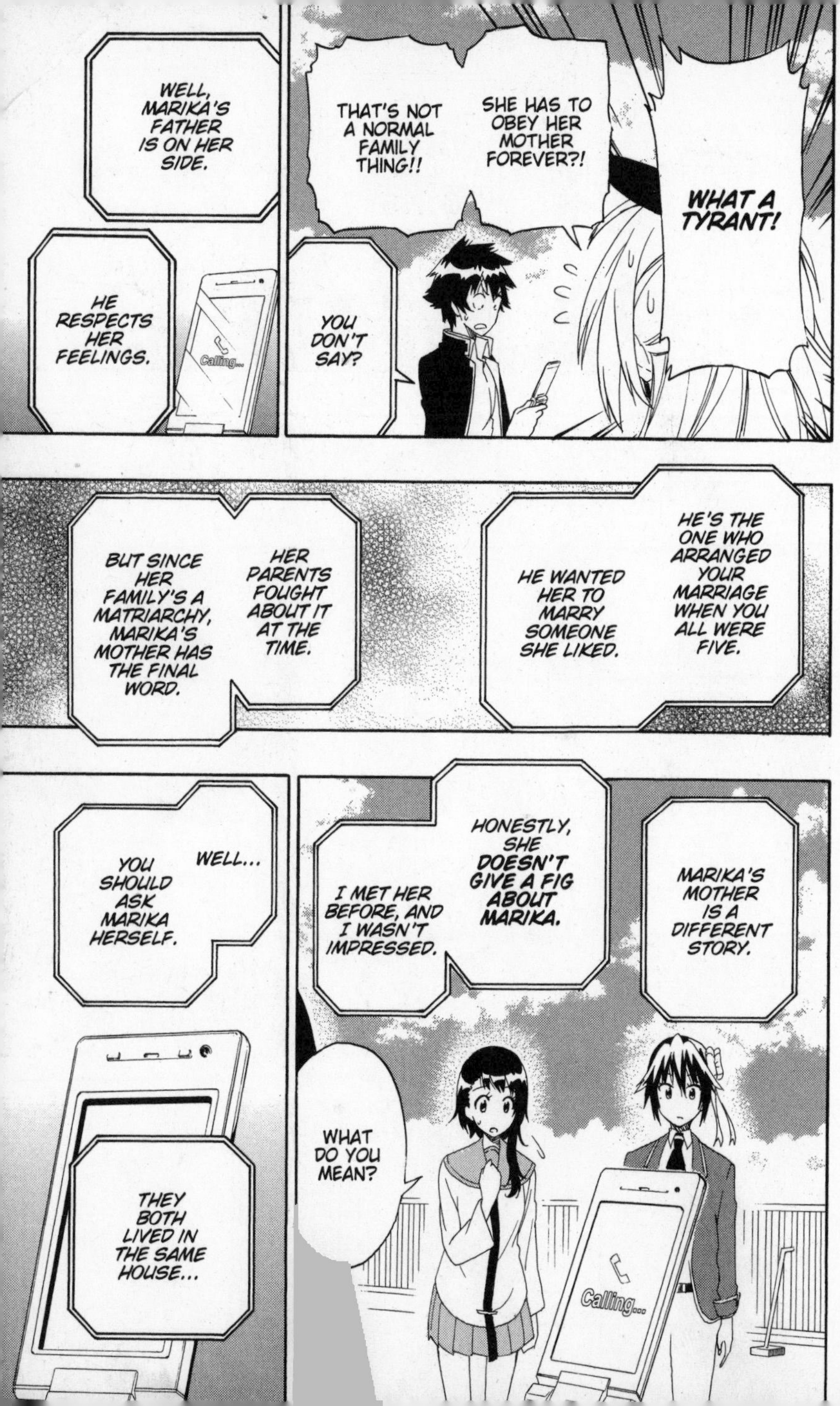
WHAT A TYRANT!
SHE HAS TO OBEY HER MOTHER FOREVER?!
THAT'S NOT A NORMAL FAMILY THING!!
YOU DON'T SAY?
WELL, MARIKA'S FATHER IS ON HER SIDE.
Calling...
HE RESPECTS HER FEELINGS.
HE'S THE ONE WHO ARRANGED YOUR MARRIAGE WHEN YOU ALL WERE FIVE.
HE WANTED HER TO MARRY SOMEONE SHE LIKED.
HER PARENTS FOUGHT ABOUT IT AT THE TIME.
BUT SINCE HER FAMILY'S A MATRIARCHY, MARIKA'S MOTHER HAS THE FINAL WORD.
MARIKA'S MOTHER IS A DIFFERENT STORY.
HONESTLY, SHE DOESN'T GIVE A FIG ABOUT MARIKA.
I MET HER BEFORE, AND I WASN'T IMPRESSED.
WHAT DO YOU MEAN?
Calling...
WELL...
YOU SHOULD ASK MARIKA HERSELF.
THEY BOTH LIVED IN THE SAME HOUSE...

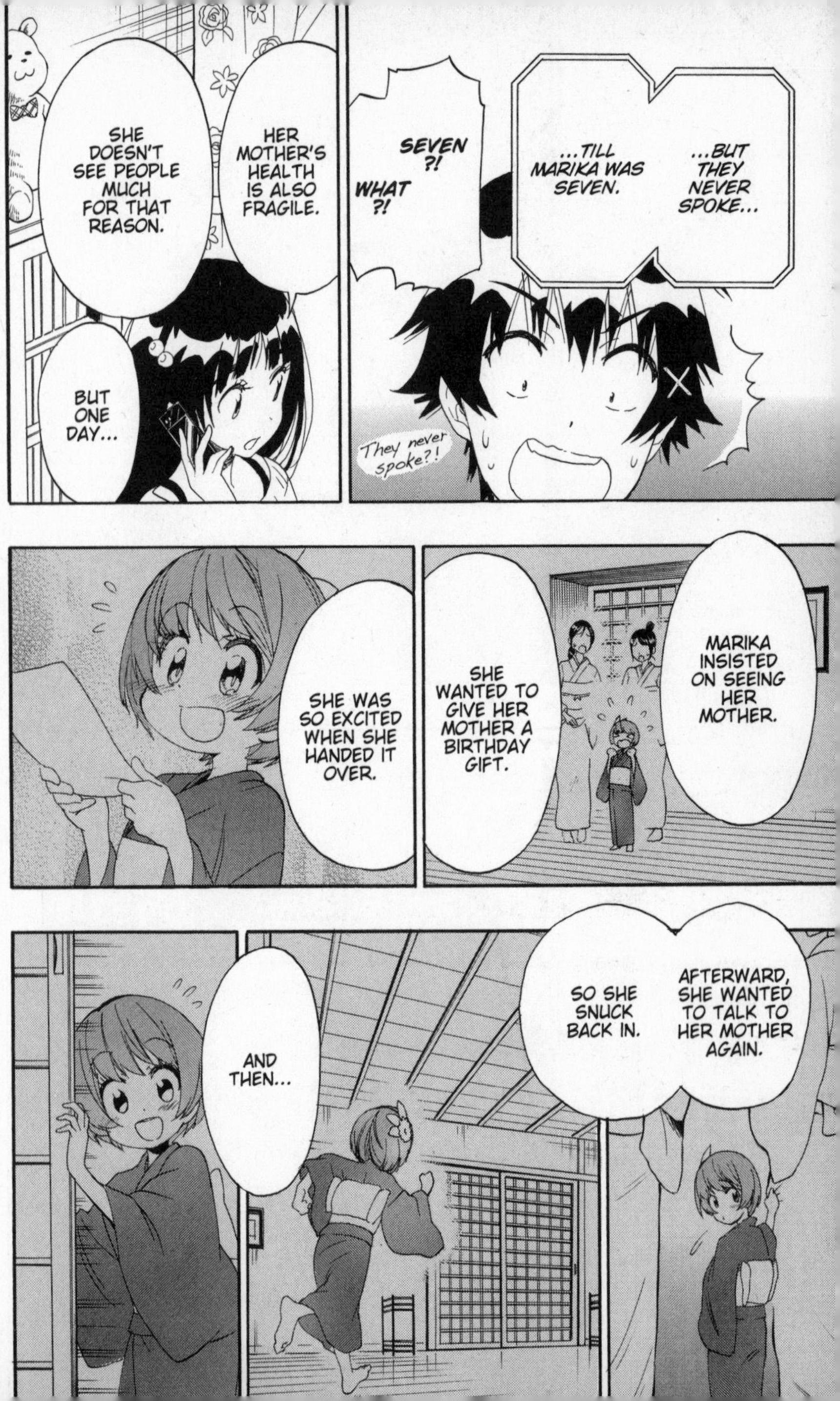
...BUT THEY NEVER SPOKE...
...TILL MARIKA WAS SEVEN.
SEVEN?!
WHAT?!
They never spoke?!
HER MOTHER'S HEALTH IS ALSO FRAGILE.
SHE DOESN'T SEE PEOPLE MUCH FOR THAT REASON.
BUT ONE DAY...
MARIKA INSISTED ON SEEING HER MOTHER.
SHE WANTED TO GIVE HER MOTHER A BIRTHDAY GIFT.
SHE WAS SO EXCITED WHEN SHE HANDED IT OVER.
AFTERWARD, SHE WANTED TO TALK TO HER MOTHER AGAIN.
SO SHE SNUCK BACK IN.
AND THEN...

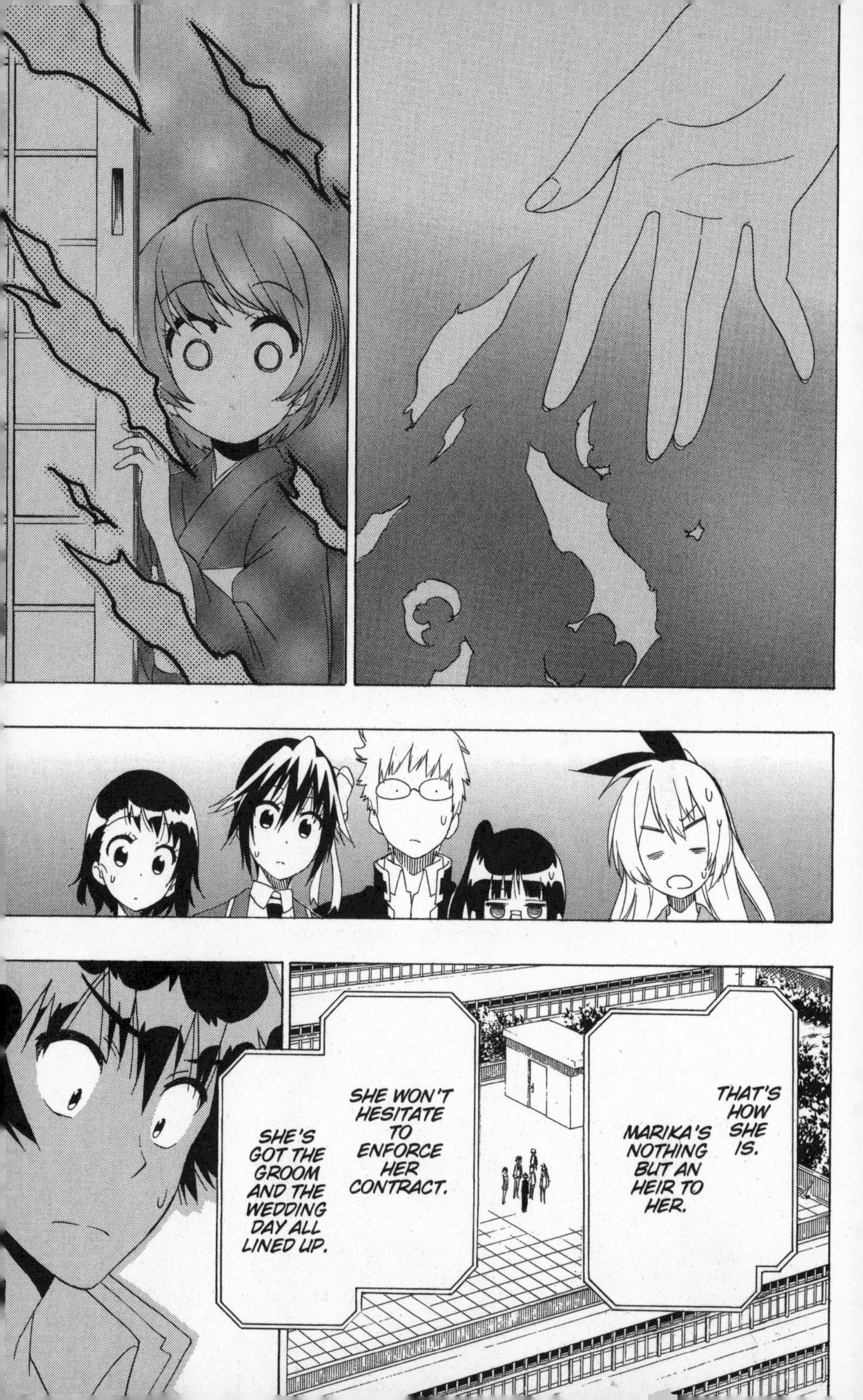
THAT'S HOW SHE IS.
MARIKA'S NOTHING BUT AN HEIR TO HER.
SHE WON'T HESITATE TO ENFORCE HER CONTRACT.
SHE'S GOT THE GROOM AND THE WEDDING DAY ALL LINED UP.

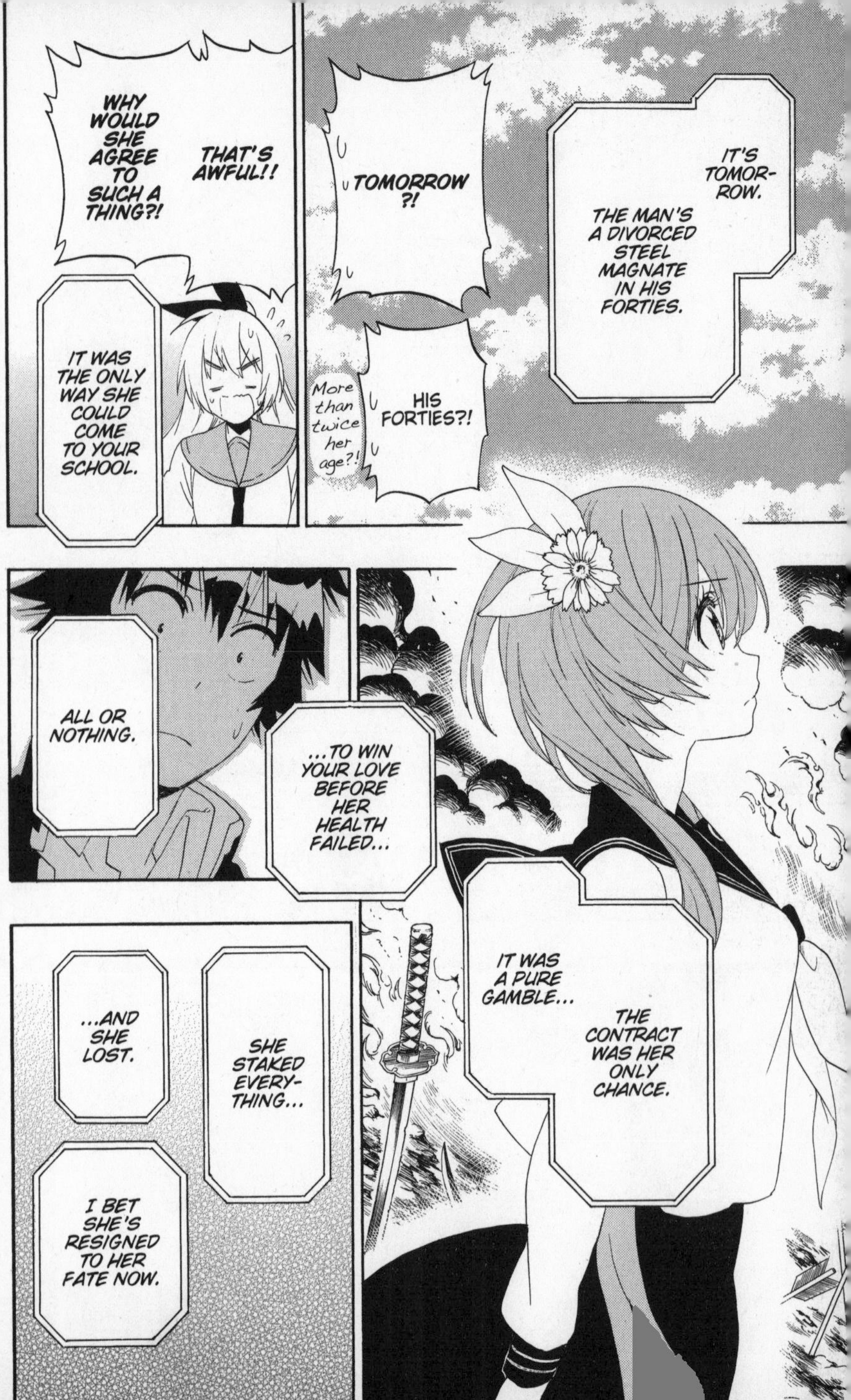
IT'S TOMORROW.
THE MAN'S A DIVORCED STEEL MAGNATE IN HIS FORTIES.
TOMORROW?!
HIS FORTIES?!
More than twice her age?!
THAT'S AWFUL!!
WHY WOULD SHE AGREE TO SUCH A THING?!
IT WAS THE ONLY WAY SHE COULD COME TO YOUR SCHOOL.
IT WAS A PURE GAMBLE...
THE CONTRACT WAS HER ONLY CHANCE.
...TO WIN YOUR LOVE BEFORE HER HEALTH FAILED...
ALL OR NOTHING.
SHE STAKED EVERYTHING...
...AND SHE LOST.
I BET SHE'S RESIGNED TO HER FATE NOW.

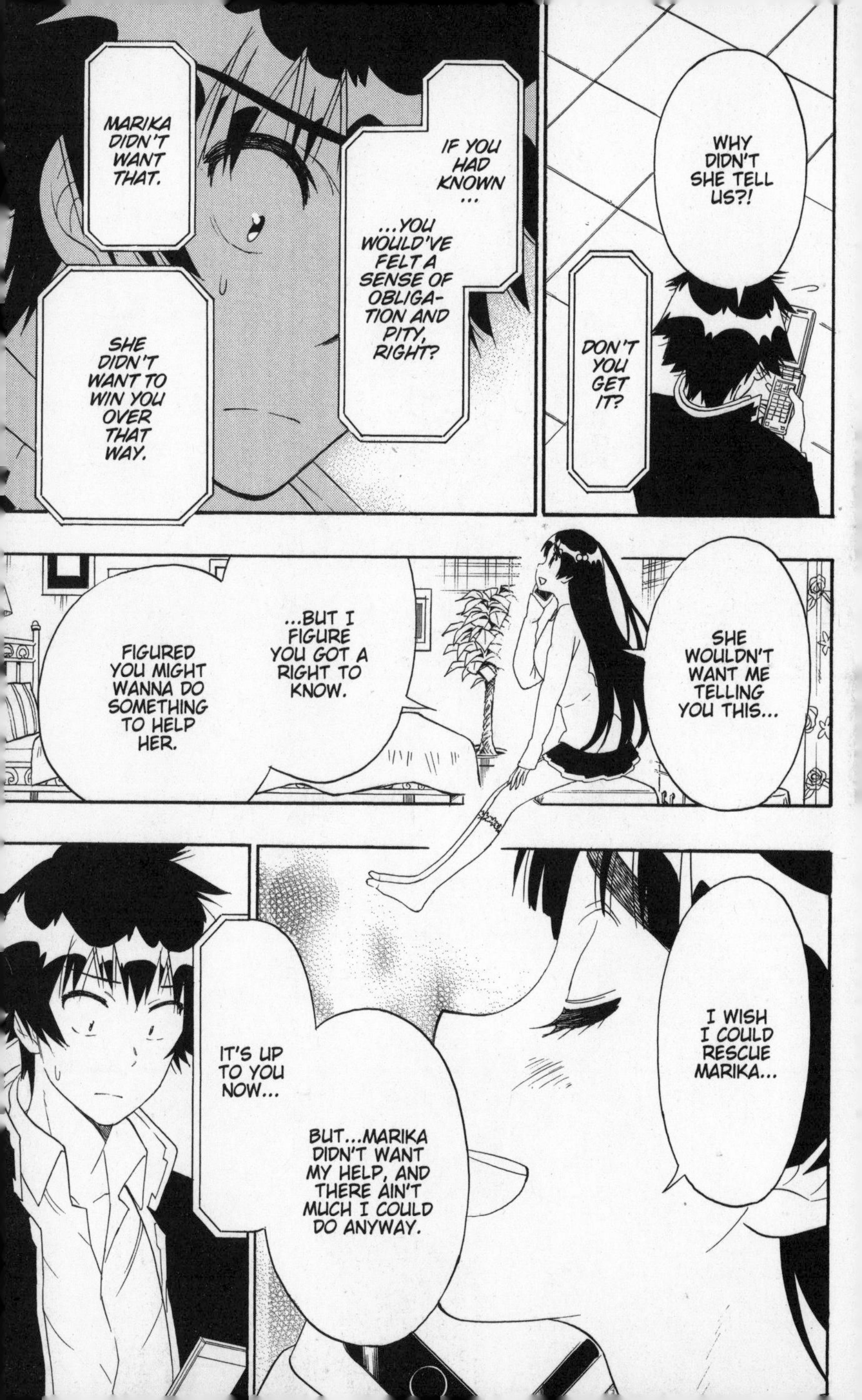
WHY DIDN'T SHE TELL US?!
DON'T YOU GET IT?
IF YOU HAD KNOWN...
...YOU WOULD'VE FELT A SENSE OF OBLIGATION AND PITY, RIGHT?
MARIKA DIDN'T WANT THAT.
SHE DIDN'T WANT TO WIN YOU OVER THAT WAY.
SHE WOULDN'T WANT ME TELLING YOU THIS...
...BUT I FIGURE YOU GOT A RIGHT TO KNOW.
FIGURED YOU MIGHT WANNA DO SOMETHING TO HELP HER.
I WISH I COULD RESCUE MARIKA...
BUT...MARIKA DIDN'T WANT MY HELP, AND THERE AIN'T MUCH I COULD DO ANYWAY.
IT'S UP TO YOU NOW...

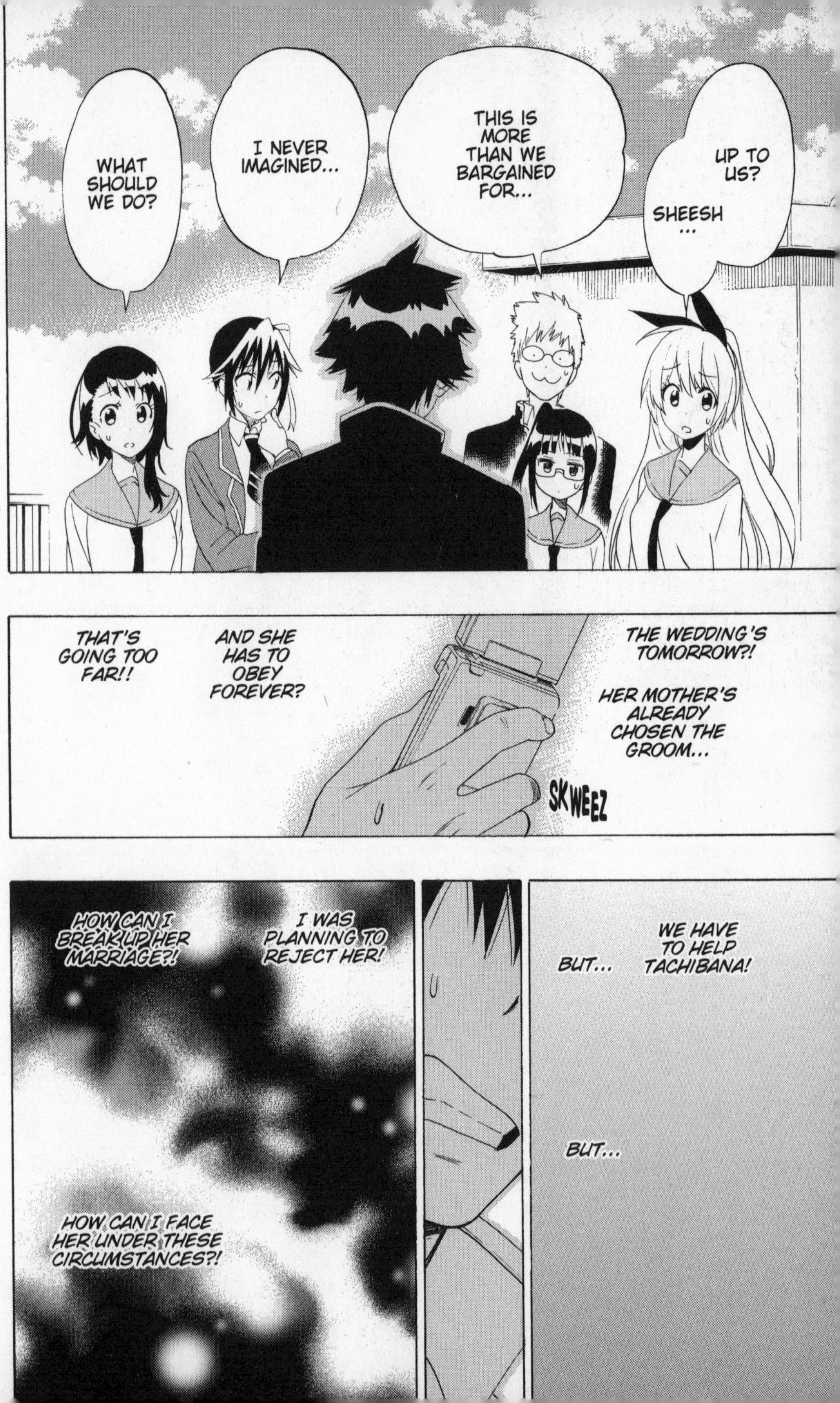
UP TO US?
SHEESH...
THIS IS MORE THAN WE BARGAINED FOR...
I NEVER IMAGINED...
WHAT SHOULD WE DO?
THE WEDDING'S TOMORROW?!
HER MOTHER'S ALREADY CHOSEN THE GROOM...
SKWEEZ
AND SHE HAS TO OBEY FOREVER?
THAT'S GOING TOO FAR!!
WE HAVE TO HELP TACHIBANA!
BUT...
BUT...
I WAS PLANNING TO REJECT HER!
HOW CAN I BREAK UP HER MARRIAGE?!
HOW CAN I FACE HER UNDER THESE CIRCUMSTANCES?!

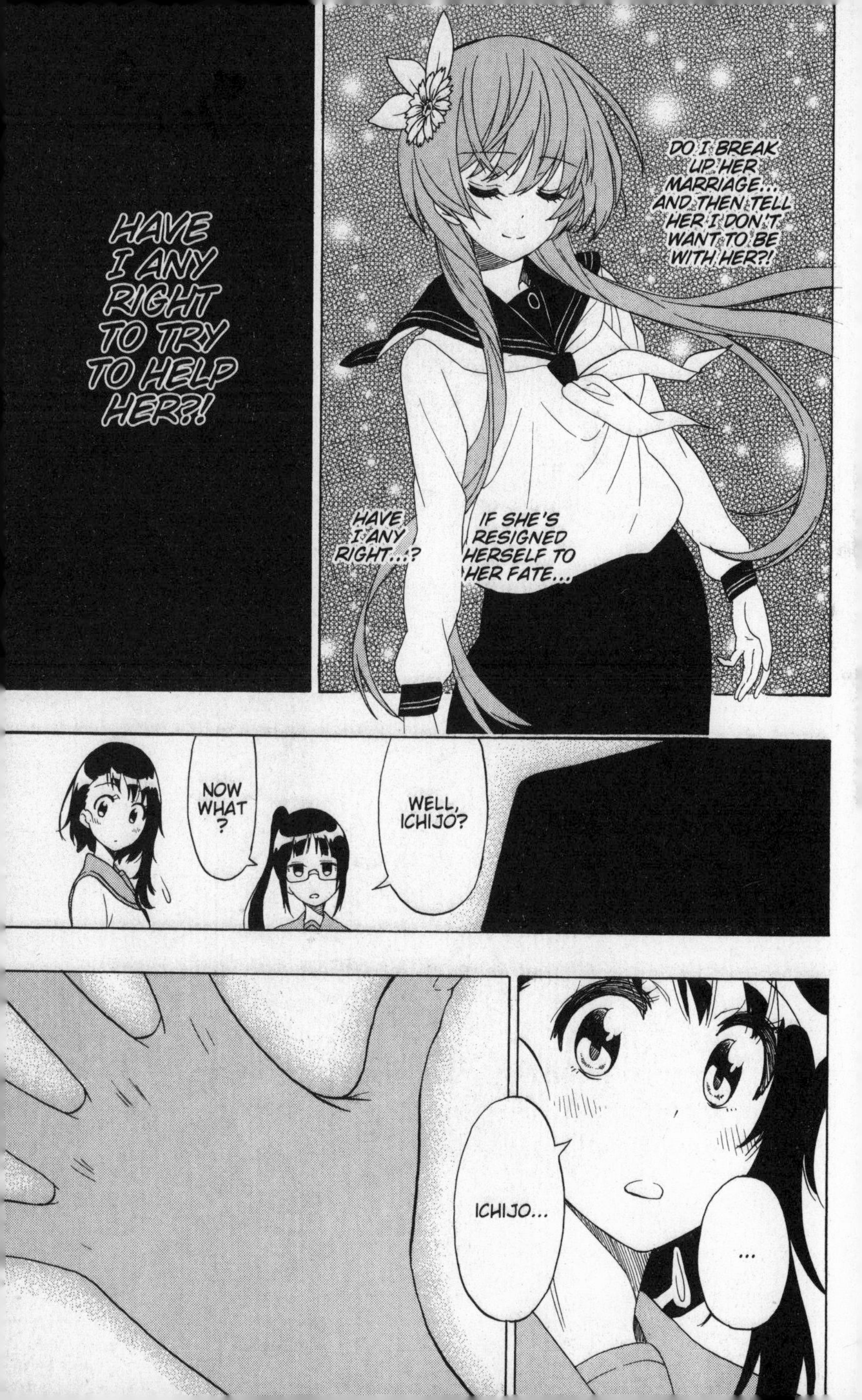
DO I BREAK UP HER MARRIAGE... AND THEN TELL HER I DON'T WANT TO BE WITH HER?!
IF SHE'S RESIGNED HERSELF TO HER FATE...
HAVE I ANY RIGHT...?
HAVE I ANY RIGHT TO TRY TO HELP HER?!
WELL, ICHIJO?
NOW WHAT?
ICHIJO...
...

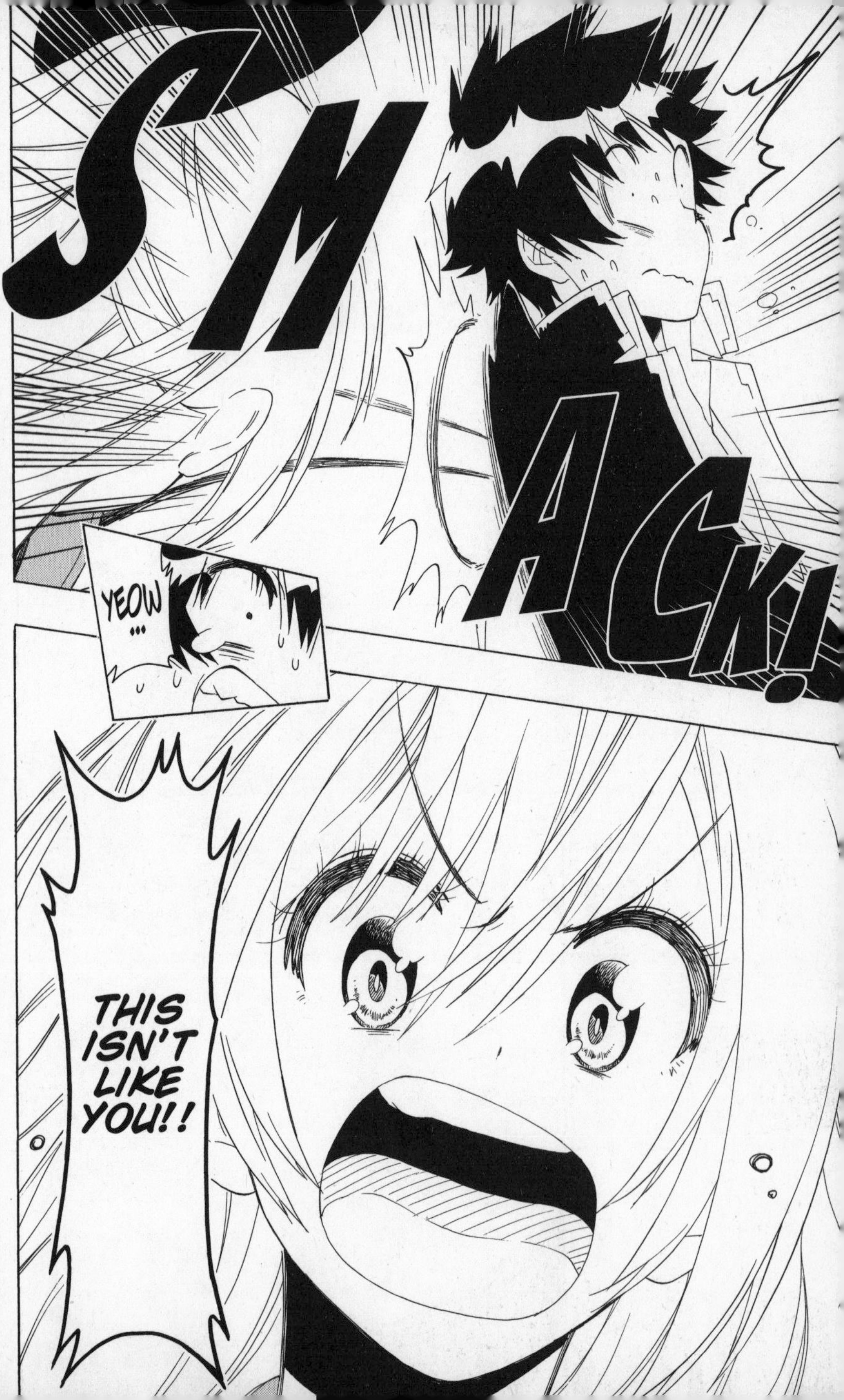
SMACK!
YEOW ...
THIS ISN'T LIKE YOU!!

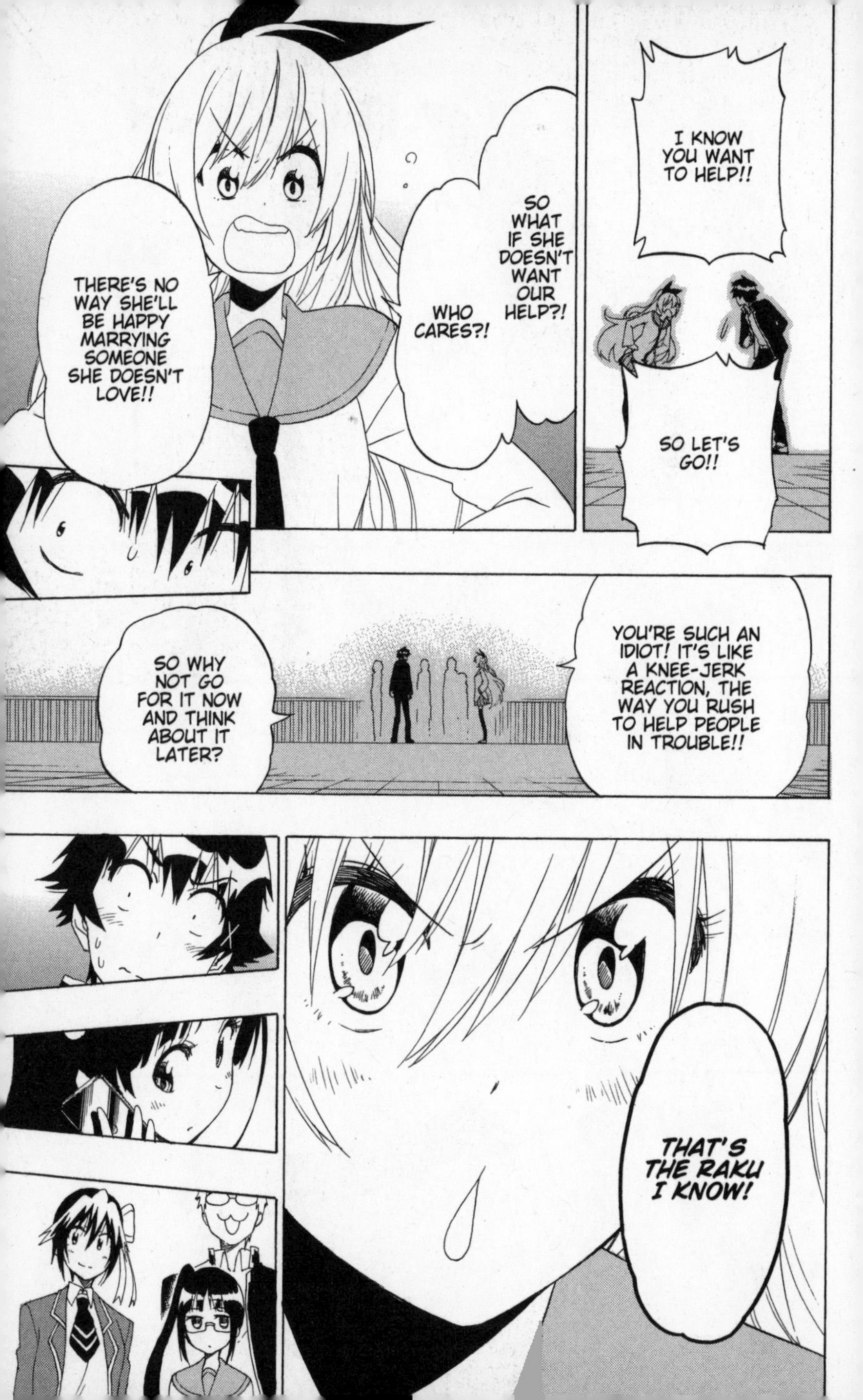
I KNOW YOU WANT TO HELP!!
SO LET'S GO!!
SO WHAT IF SHE DOESN'T WANT OUR HELP?!
WHO CARES?!
THERE'S NO WAY SHE'LL BE HAPPY MARRYING SOMEONE SHE DOESN'T LOVE!!
YOU'RE SUCH AN IDIOT! IT'S LIKE A KNEE-JERK REACTION, THE WAY YOU RUSH TO HELP PEOPLE IN TROUBLE!!
SO WHY NOT GO FOR IT NOW AND THINK ABOUT IT LATER?
THAT'S THE RAKU I KNOW!

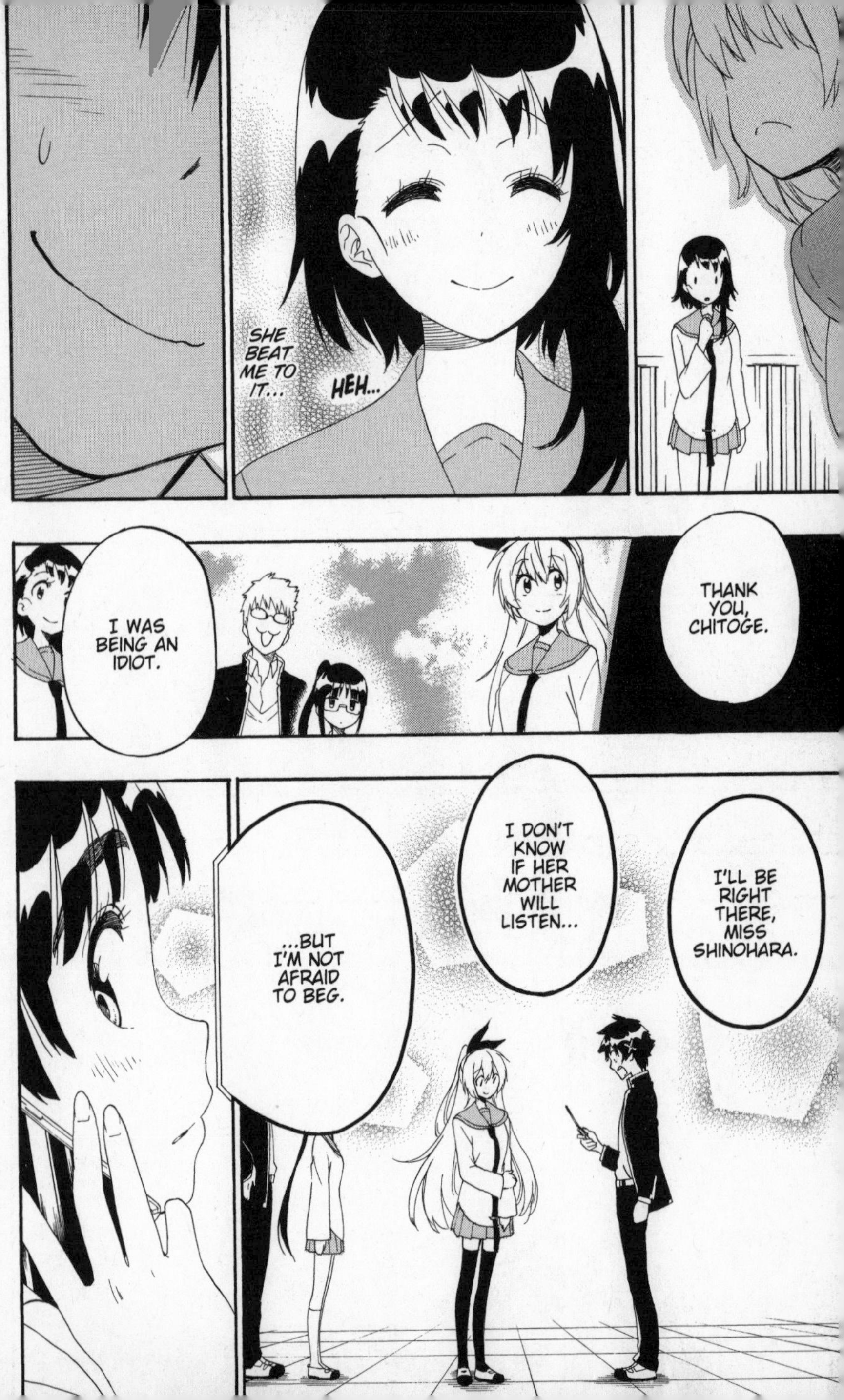
HEH...
SHE BEAT ME TO IT...
THANK YOU, CHITOGE.
I WAS BEING AN IDIOT.
I'LL BE RIGHT THERE, MISS SHINOHARA.
I DON'T KNOW IF HER MOTHER WILL LISTEN...
...BUT I'M NOT AFRAID TO BEG.

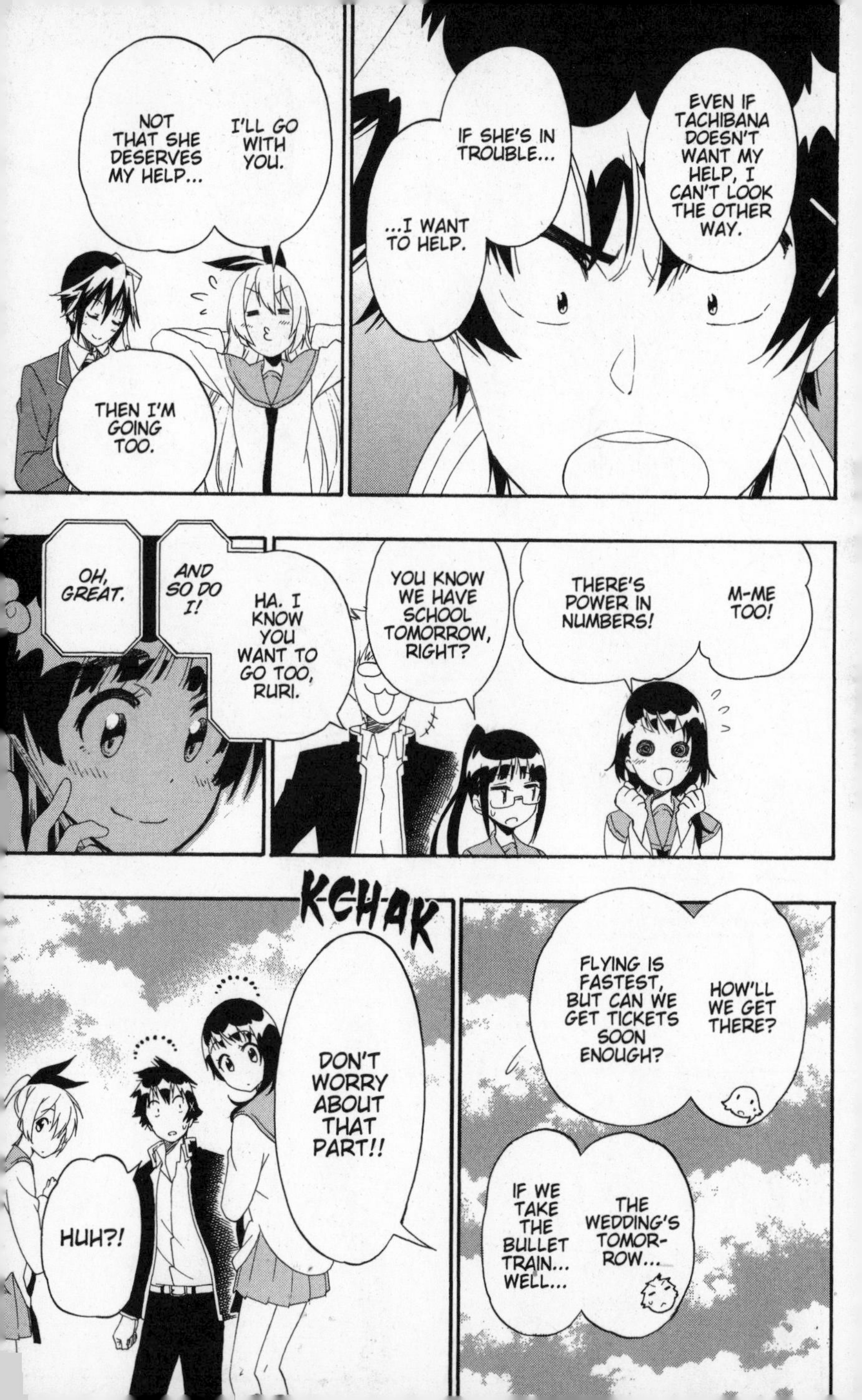
EVEN IF TACHIBANA DOESN'T WANT MY HELP, I CAN'T LOOK THE OTHER WAY.
IF SHE'S IN TROUBLE...
...I WANT TO HELP.
I'LL GO WITH YOU.
NOT THAT SHE DESERVES MY HELP...
THEN I'M GOING TOO.
M-ME TOO!
THERE'S POWER IN NUMBERS!
YOU KNOW WE HAVE SCHOOL TOMORROW, RIGHT?
HA. I KNOW YOU WANT TO GO TOO, RURI.
AND SO DO I!
OH, GREAT.
HOW'LL WE GET THERE?
FLYING IS FASTEST, BUT CAN WE GET TICKETS SOON ENOUGH?
THE WEDDING'S TOMORROW...
IF WE TAKE THE BULLET TRAIN... WELL...
KCHAK
DON'T WORRY ABOUT THAT PART!!
HUH?!

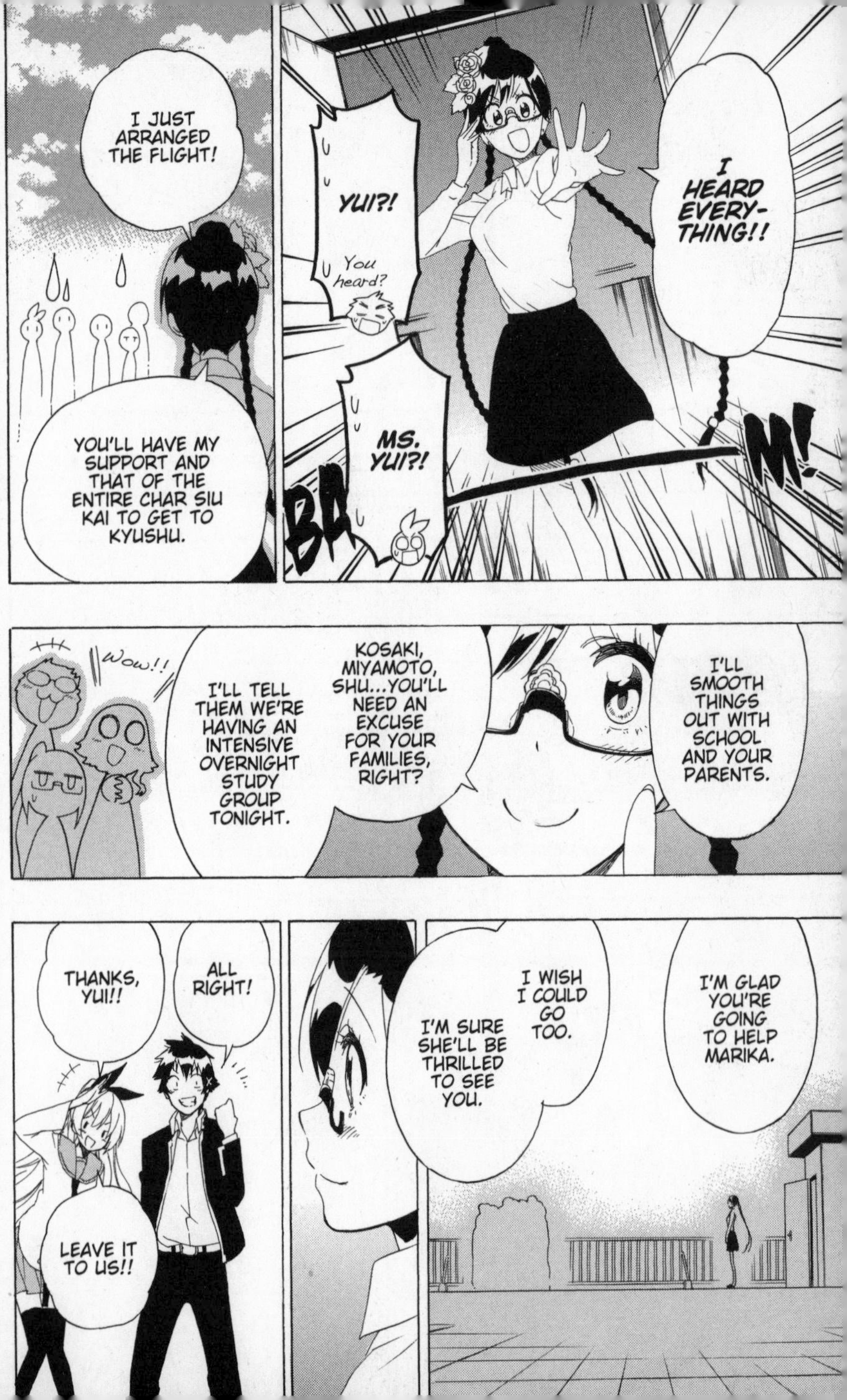
I HEARD EVERY-THING!!
BAM!
YUI?!
You heard?
MS. YUI?!
I JUST ARRANGED THE FLIGHT!
YOU'LL HAVE MY SUPPORT AND THAT OF THE ENTIRE CHAR SIU KAI TO GET TO KYUSHU.
I'LL SMOOTH THINGS OUT WITH SCHOOL AND YOUR PARENTS.
KOSAKI, MIYAMOTO, SHU...YOU'LL NEED AN EXCUSE FOR YOUR FAMILIES, RIGHT?
I'LL TELL THEM WE'RE HAVING AN INTENSIVE OVERNIGHT STUDY GROUP TONIGHT.
Wow!!
I'M GLAD YOU'RE GOING TO HELP MARIKA.
I WISH I COULD GO TOO.
I'M SURE SHE'LL BE THRILLED TO SEE YOU.
ALL RIGHT!
THANKS, YUI!!
LEAVE IT TO US!!

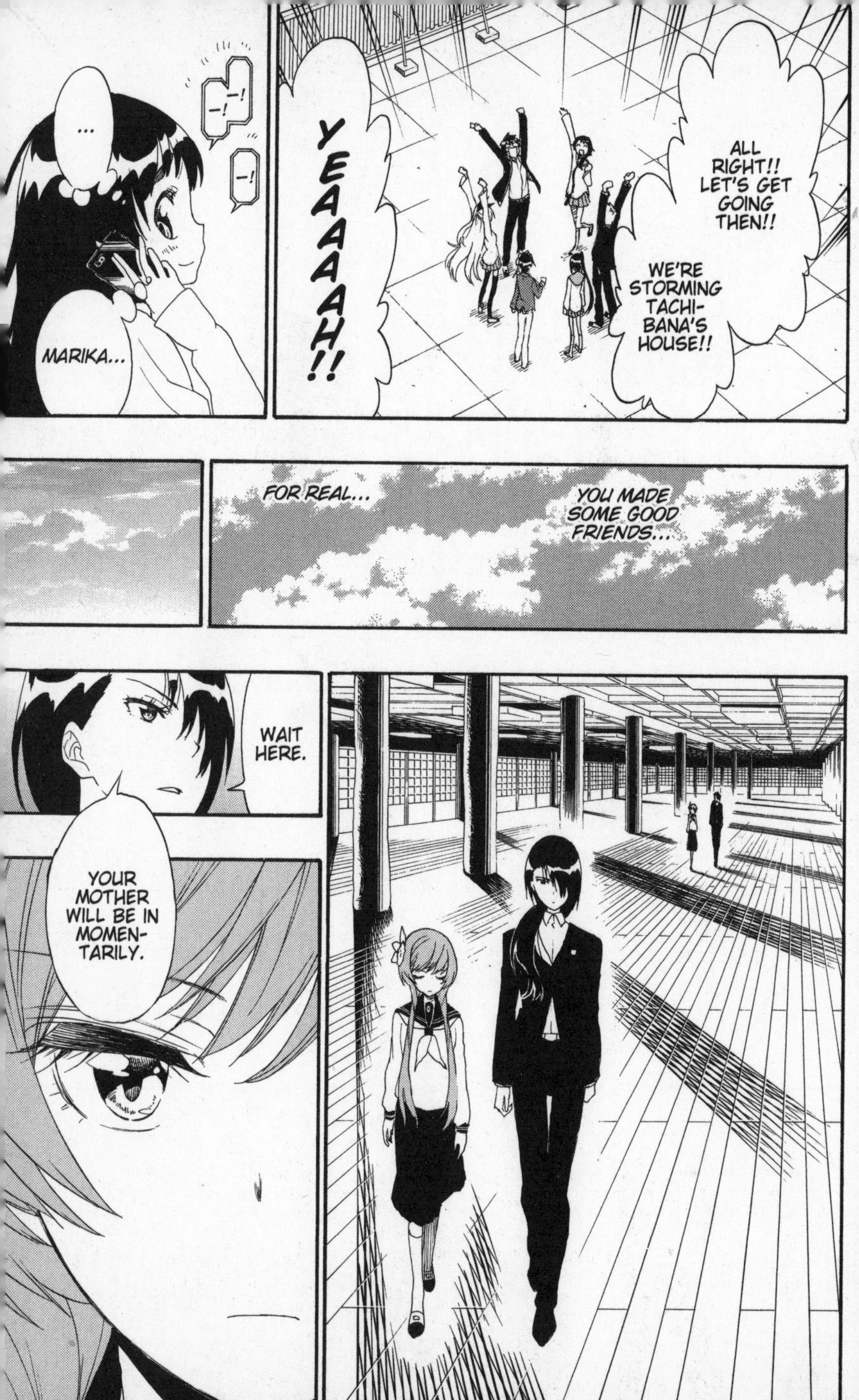

ALL RIGHT!! LET'S GET GOING THEN!!
WE'RE STORMING TACHI-BANA'S HOUSE!!
YEAAAAH!!
—! —!
—!
...
MARIKA...
FOR REAL...
YOU MADE SOME GOOD FRIENDS...
WAIT HERE.
YOUR MOTHER WILL BE IN MOMEN-TARILY.

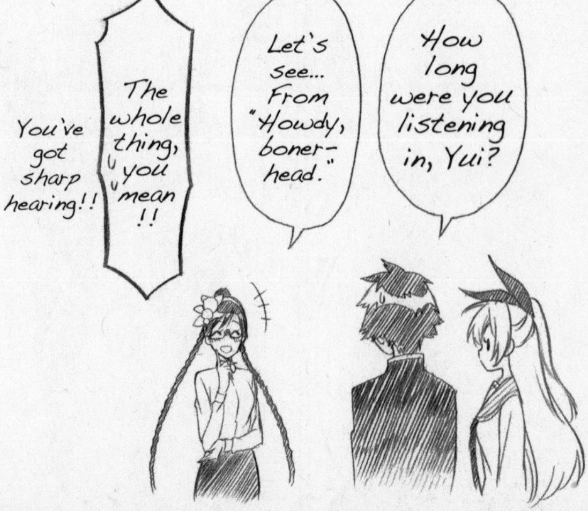
How long were you listening in, Yui?
Let's see... From "Howdy, boner-head."
The whole thing, you mean!!
You've got sharp hearing!!

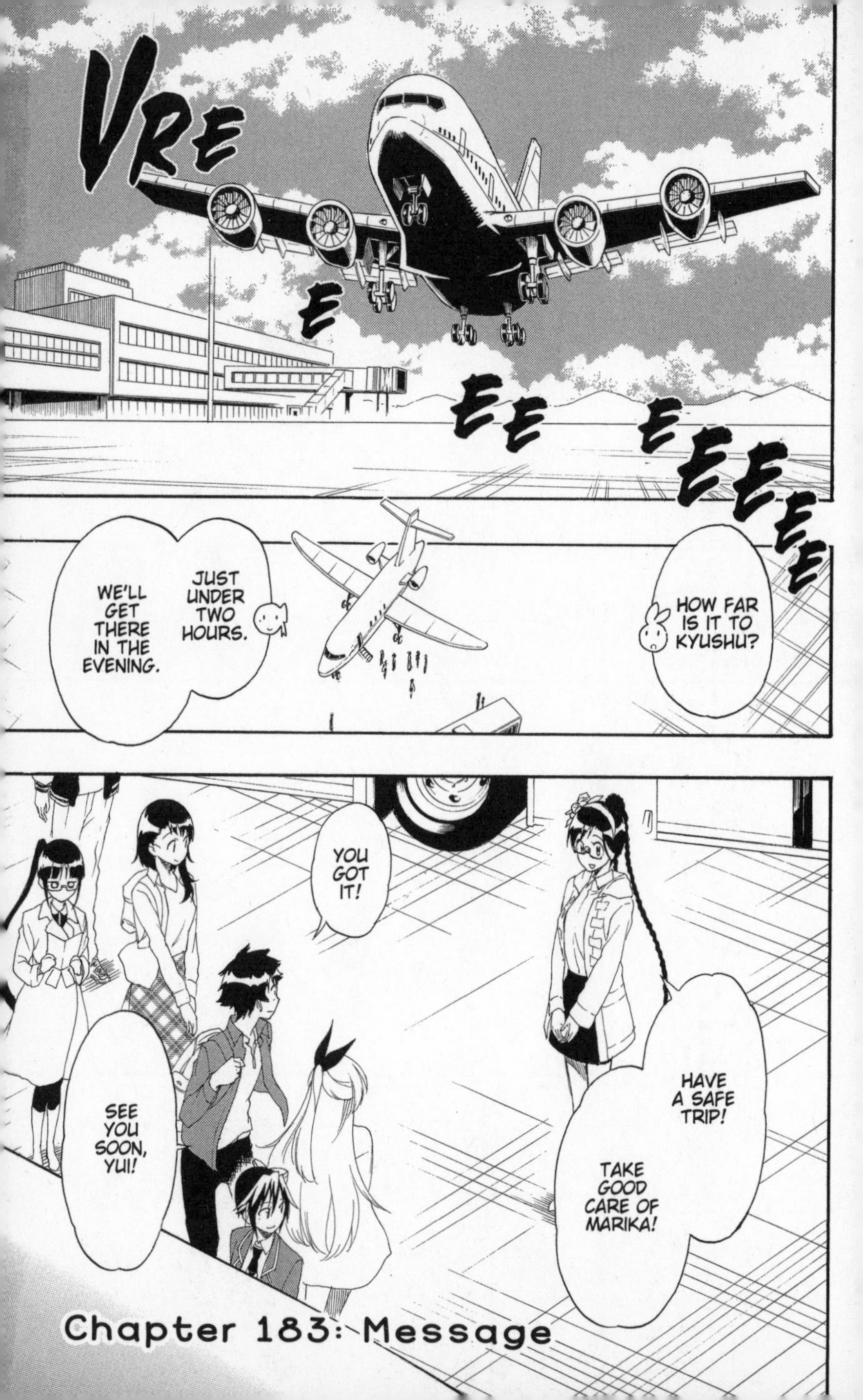
VREEEEEEEEEEE
HOW FAR IS IT TO KYUSHU?
JUST UNDER TWO HOURS.
WE'LL GET THERE IN THE EVENING.
HAVE A SAFE TRIP!
TAKE GOOD CARE OF MARIKA!
YOU GOT IT!
SEE YOU SOON, YUI!

Chapter 183: Message

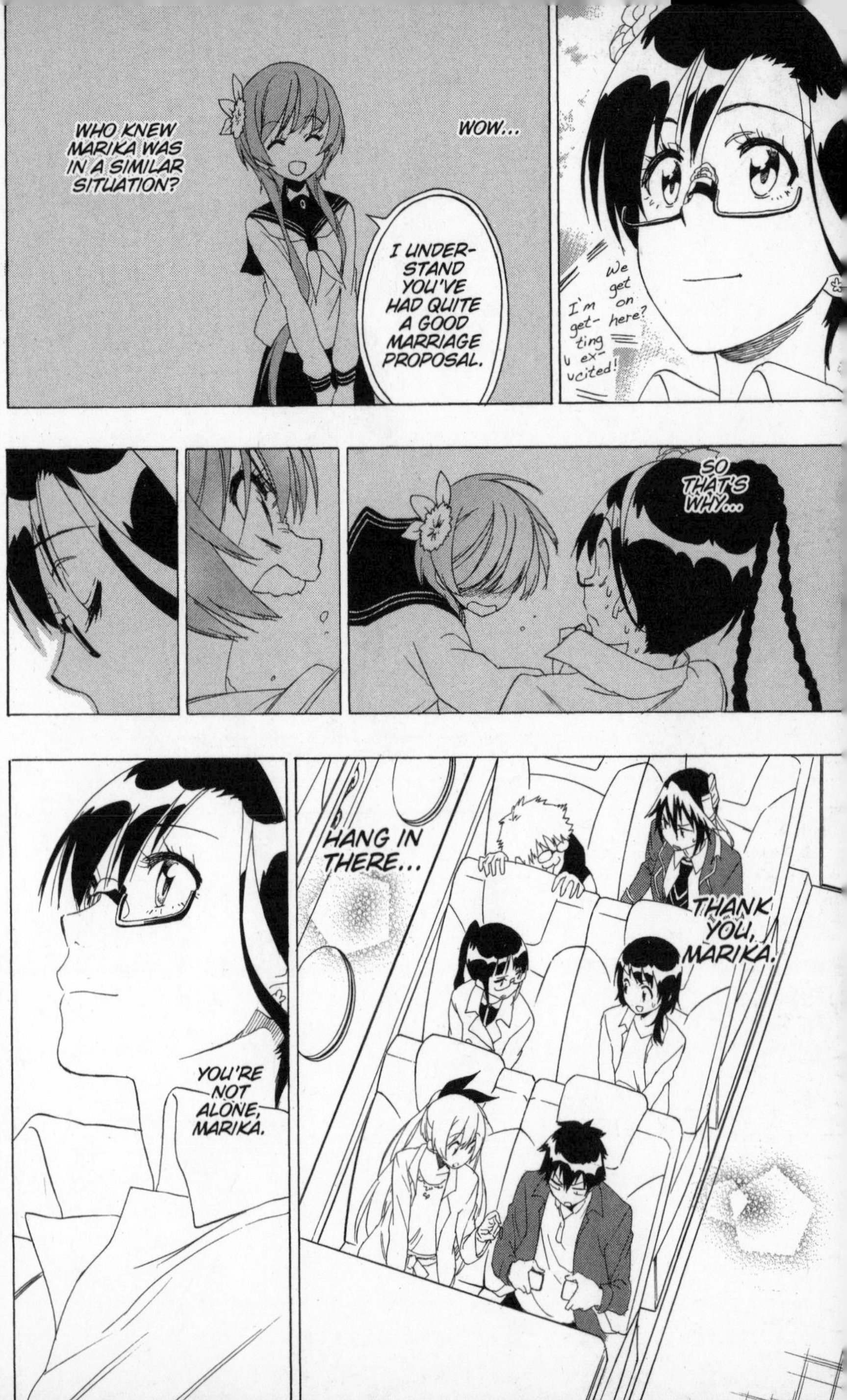
We get on here?
I'm get- ting ex- cited!
WOW...
I UNDER- STAND YOU'VE HAD QUITE A GOOD MARRIAGE PROPOSAL.
WHO KNEW MARIKA WAS IN A SIMILAR SITUATION?
SO THAT'S WHY...
HANG IN THERE...
THANK YOU, MARIKA.
YOU'RE NOT ALONE, MARIKA.

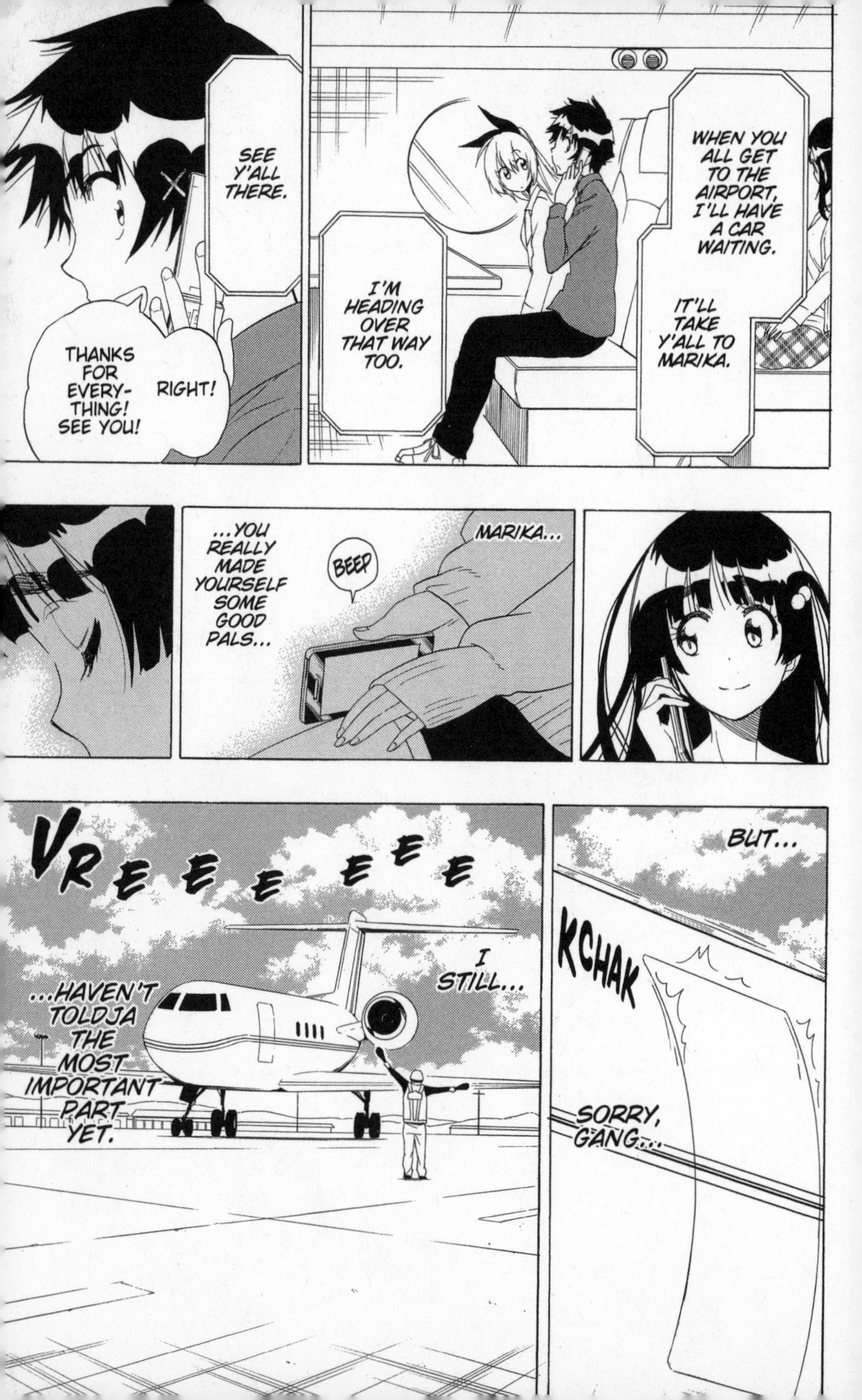
WHEN YOU ALL GET TO THE AIRPORT, I'LL HAVE A CAR WAITING.
IT'LL TAKE Y'ALL TO MARIKA.
I'M HEADING OVER THAT WAY TOO.
SEE Y'ALL THERE.
RIGHT!
THANKS FOR EVERY-THING! SEE YOU!
MARIKA...
BEEP
...YOU REALLY MADE YOURSELF SOME GOOD PALS...
BUT...
KCHAK
SORRY, GANG...
VREEEEEEE
I STILL...
...HAVEN'T TOLDJA THE MOST IMPORTANT PART YET.

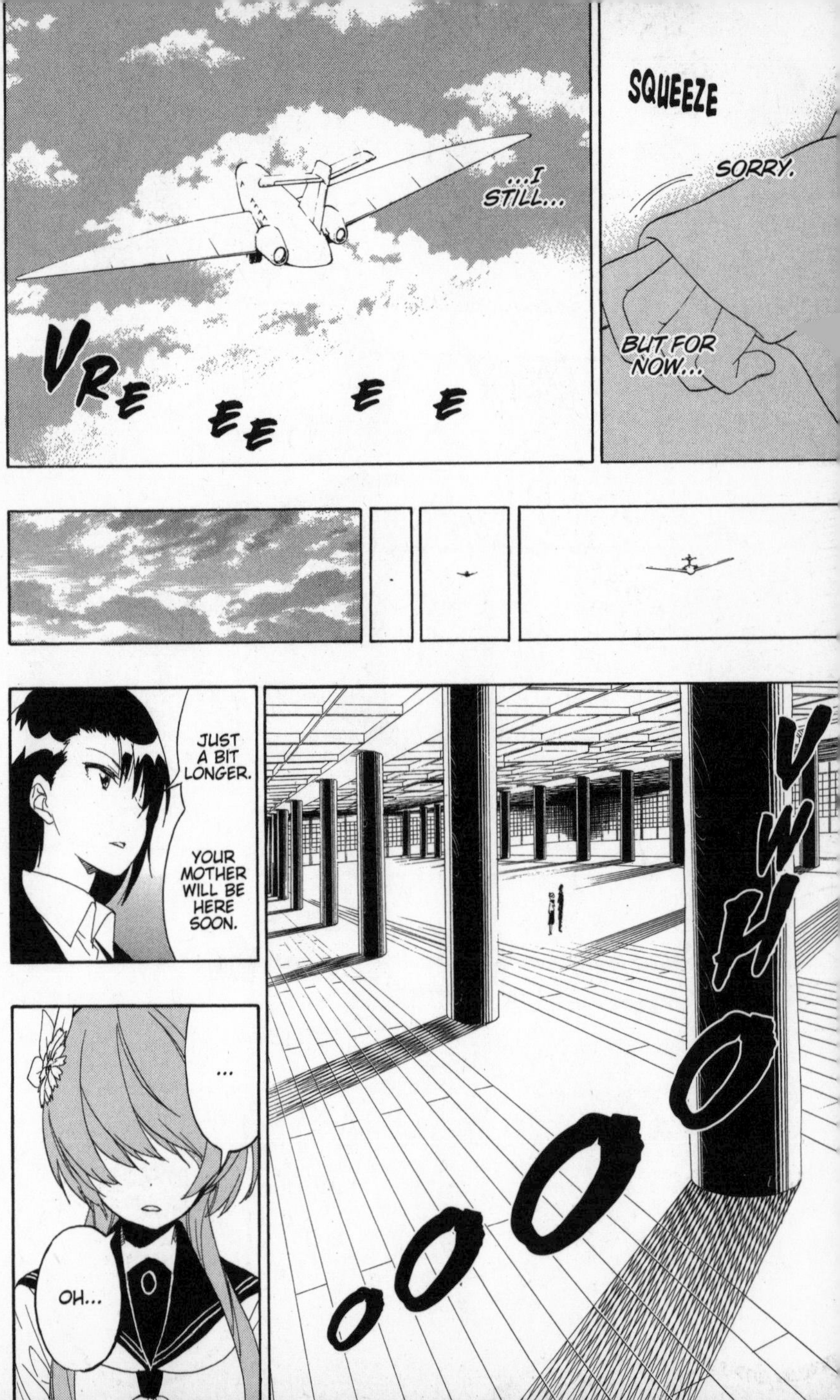
SQUEEZE
SORRY.
BUT FOR NOW...
...I STILL...
VREEEEEE
VWWHOOOOO
JUST A BIT LONGER.
YOUR MOTHER WILL BE HERE SOON.
...
OH...

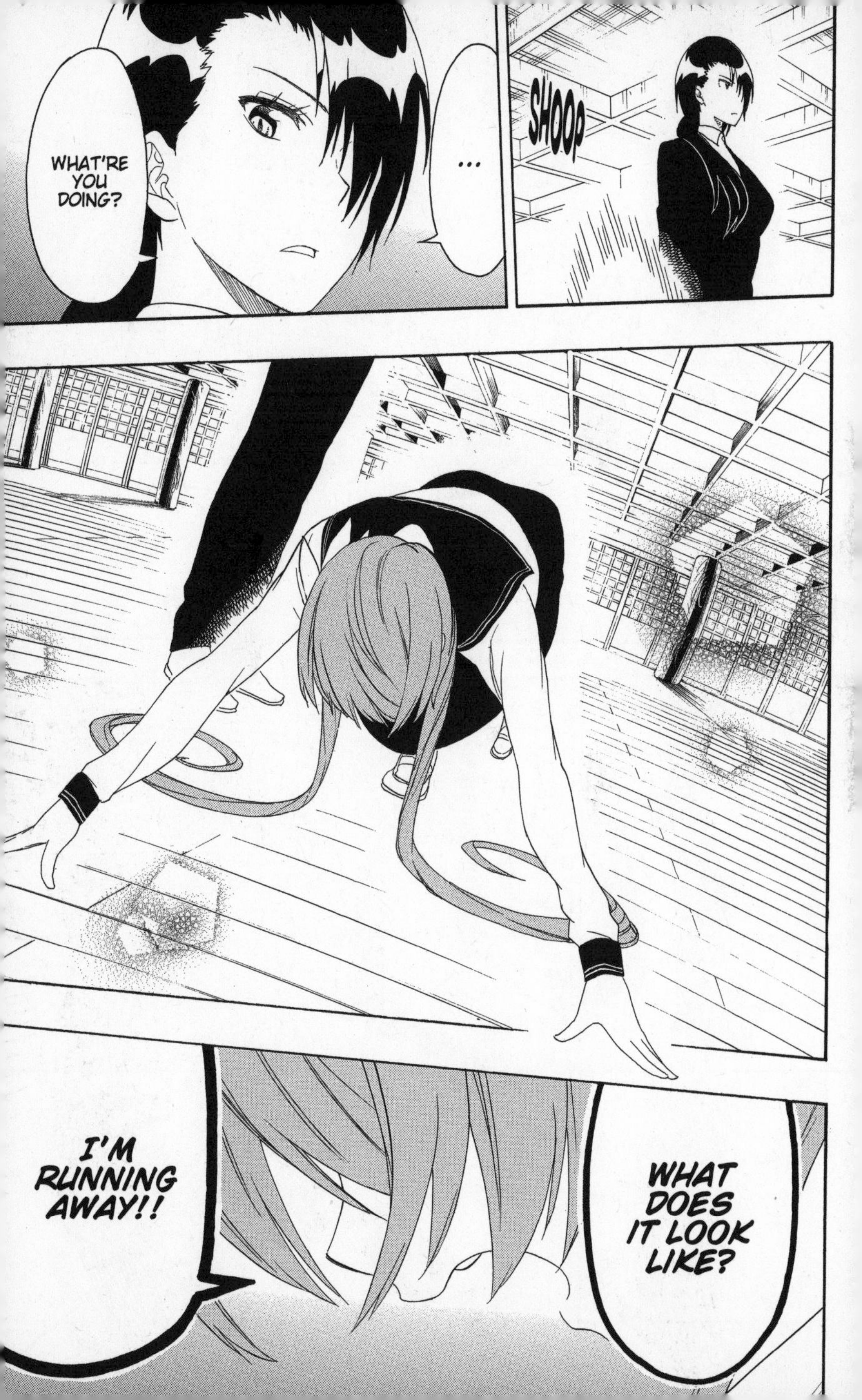
SHOOP
...
WHAT'RE YOU DOING?
WHAT DOES IT LOOK LIKE?
I'M RUNNING AWAY!!

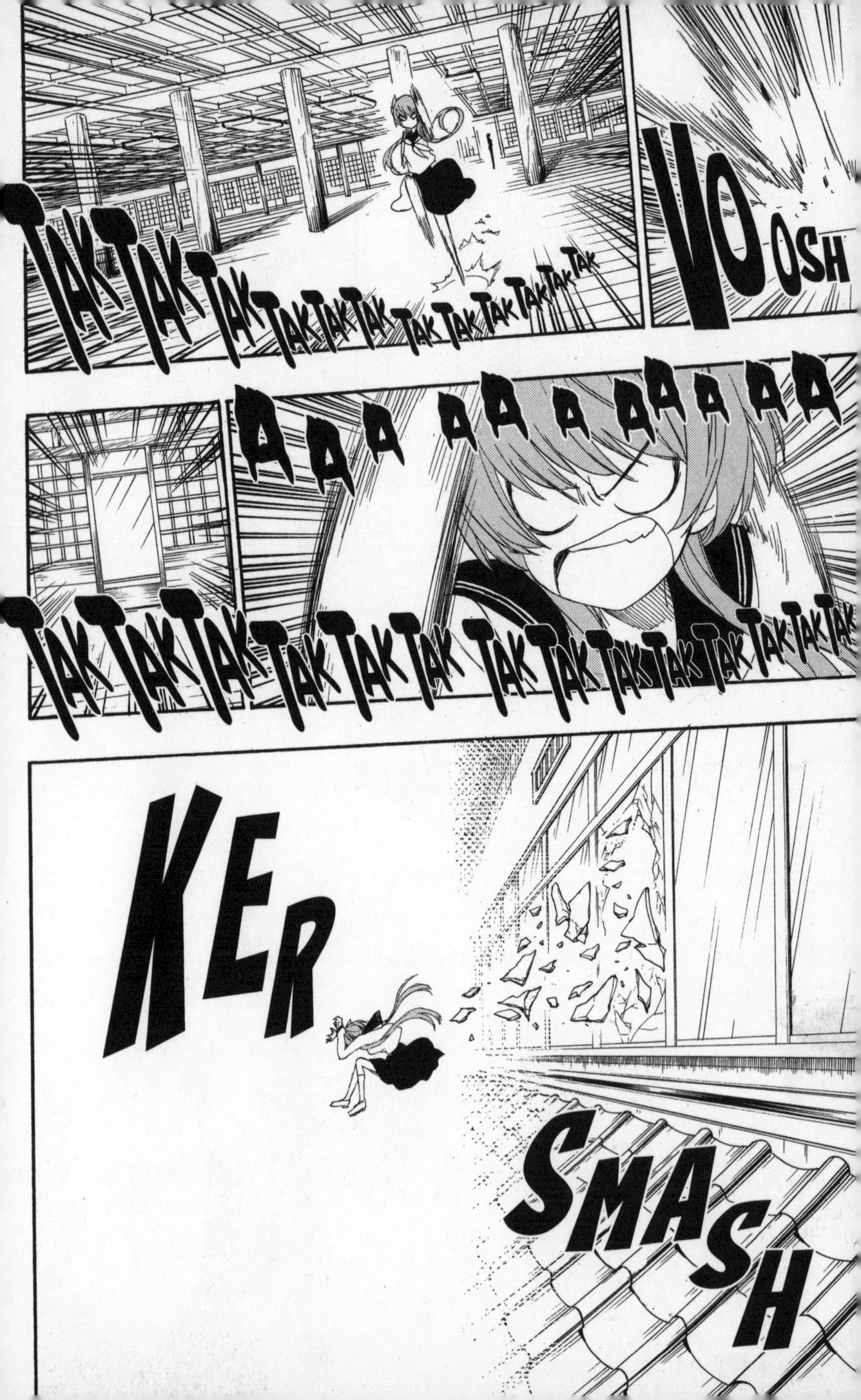
VOOSH
TAK TAK TAK TAKTAKTAK TAK TAK TAK TAK TAK TAK
AAAAAAAAAA
TAK TAK TAK TAK TAK TAK TAK TAK TAK TAK TAK TAK TAK TAK
KER
SMASH

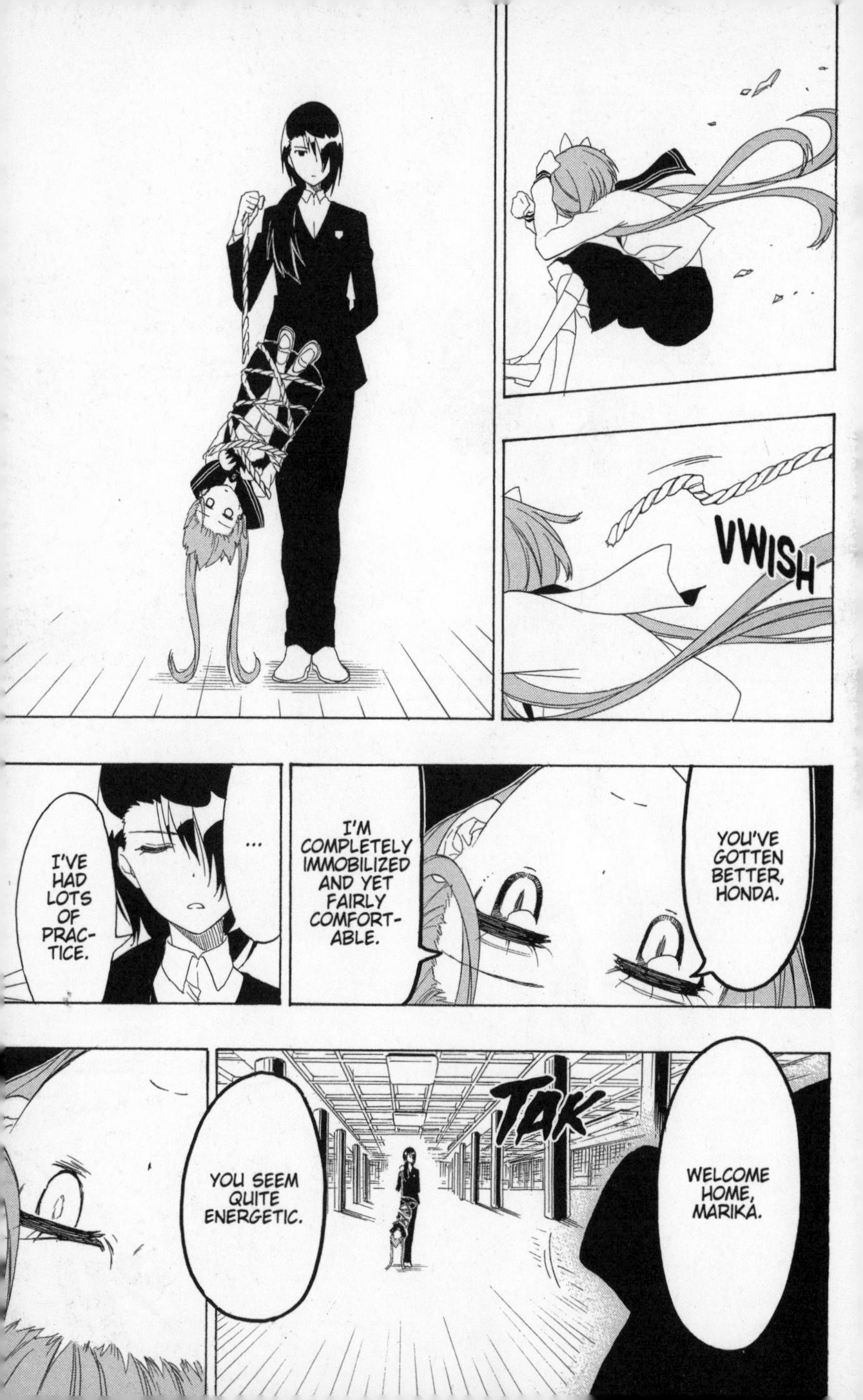
VWISH
YOU'VE GOTTEN BETTER, HONDA.
I'M COMPLETELY IMMOBILIZED AND YET FAIRLY COMFORT-ABLE.
...
I'VE HAD LOTS OF PRAC-TICE.
WELCOME HOME, MARIKA.
TAK
YOU SEEM QUITE ENERGETIC.

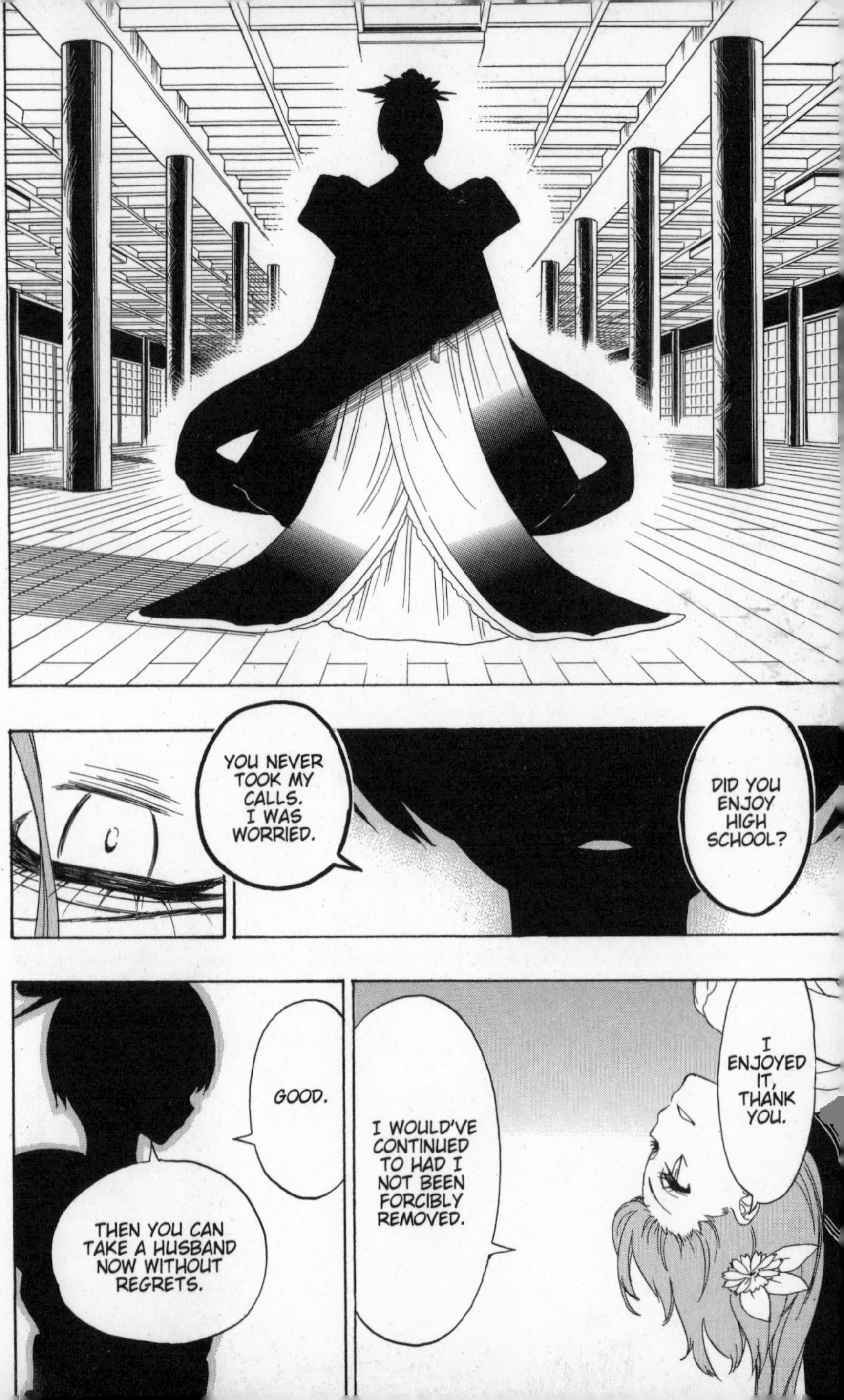
DID YOU ENJOY HIGH SCHOOL?
YOU NEVER TOOK MY CALLS. I WAS WORRIED.
I ENJOYED IT, THANK YOU.
I WOULD'VE CONTINUED TO HAD I NOT BEEN FORCIBLY REMOVED.
GOOD.
THEN YOU CAN TAKE A HUSBAND NOW WITHOUT REGRETS.

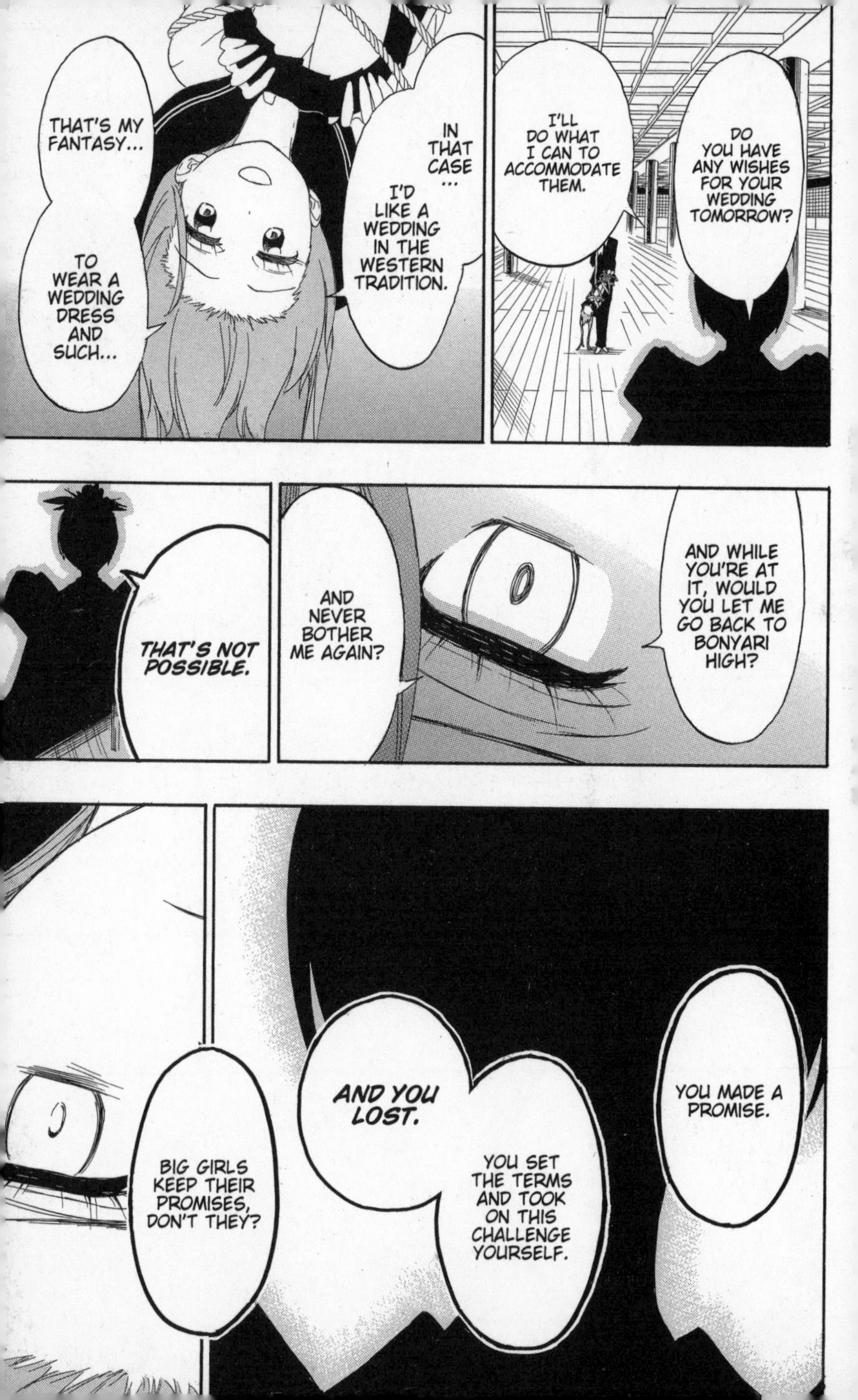
DO YOU HAVE ANY WISHES FOR YOUR WEDDING TOMORROW?
I'LL DO WHAT I CAN TO ACCOMMODATE THEM.
IN THAT CASE...
I'D LIKE A WEDDING IN THE WESTERN TRADITION.
THAT'S MY FANTASY...
TO WEAR A WEDDING DRESS AND SUCH...
AND WHILE YOU'RE AT IT, WOULD YOU LET ME GO BACK TO BONYARI HIGH?
AND NEVER BOTHER ME AGAIN?
THAT'S NOT POSSIBLE.
YOU MADE A PROMISE.
AND YOU LOST.
YOU SET THE TERMS AND TOOK ON THIS CHALLENGE YOURSELF.
BIG GIRLS KEEP THEIR PROMISES, DON'T THEY?

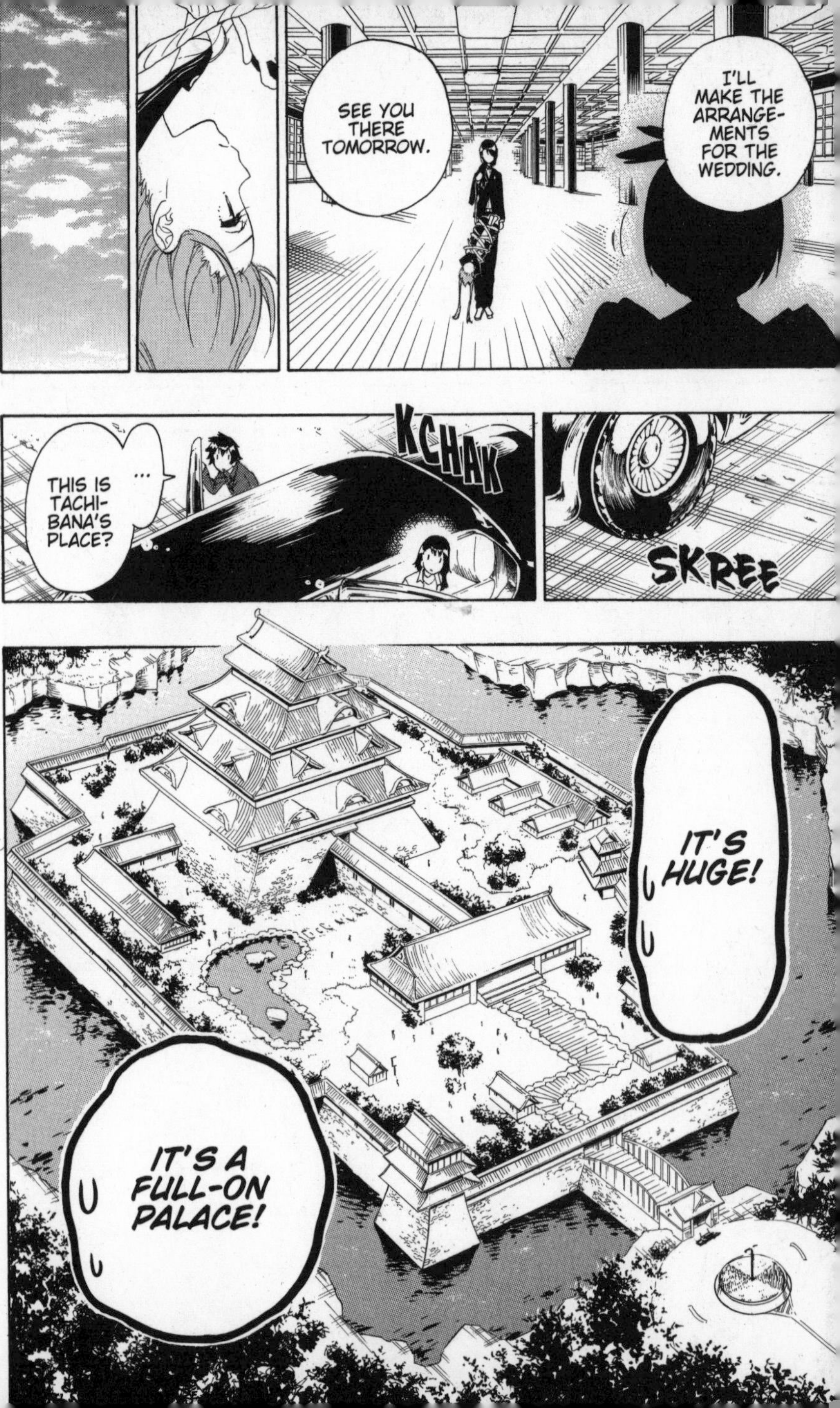
I'LL MAKE THE ARRANGE-MENTS FOR THE WEDDING.
SEE YOU THERE TOMORROW.
SKREE
KCHAK
...
THIS IS TACHI-BANA'S PLACE?
IT'S HUGE!
IT'S A FULL-ON PALACE!

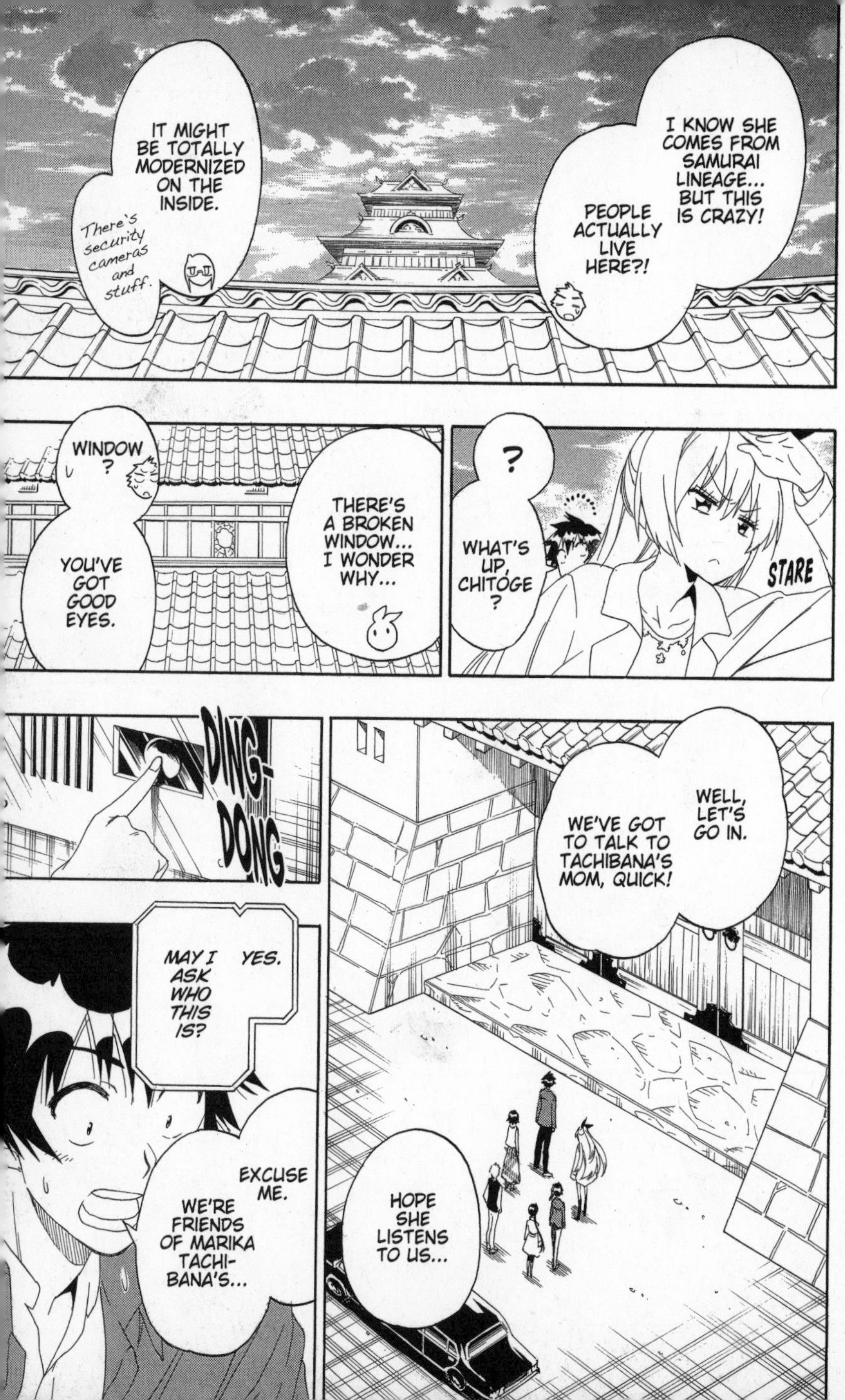

I KNOW SHE COMES FROM SAMURAI LINEAGE... BUT THIS IS CRAZY!
PEOPLE ACTUALLY LIVE HERE?!
IT MIGHT BE TOTALLY MODERNIZED ON THE INSIDE.
There's security cameras and stuff.
?
WHAT'S UP, CHITOGE?
STARE
THERE'S A BROKEN WINDOW... I WONDER WHY...
WINDOW?
YOU'VE GOT GOOD EYES.
WELL, LET'S GO IN.
WE'VE GOT TO TALK TO TACHIBANA'S MOM, QUICK!
HOPE SHE LISTENS TO US...
DING-DONG
YES.
MAY I ASK WHO THIS IS?
EXCUSE ME.
WE'RE FRIENDS OF MARIKA TACHIBANA'S...

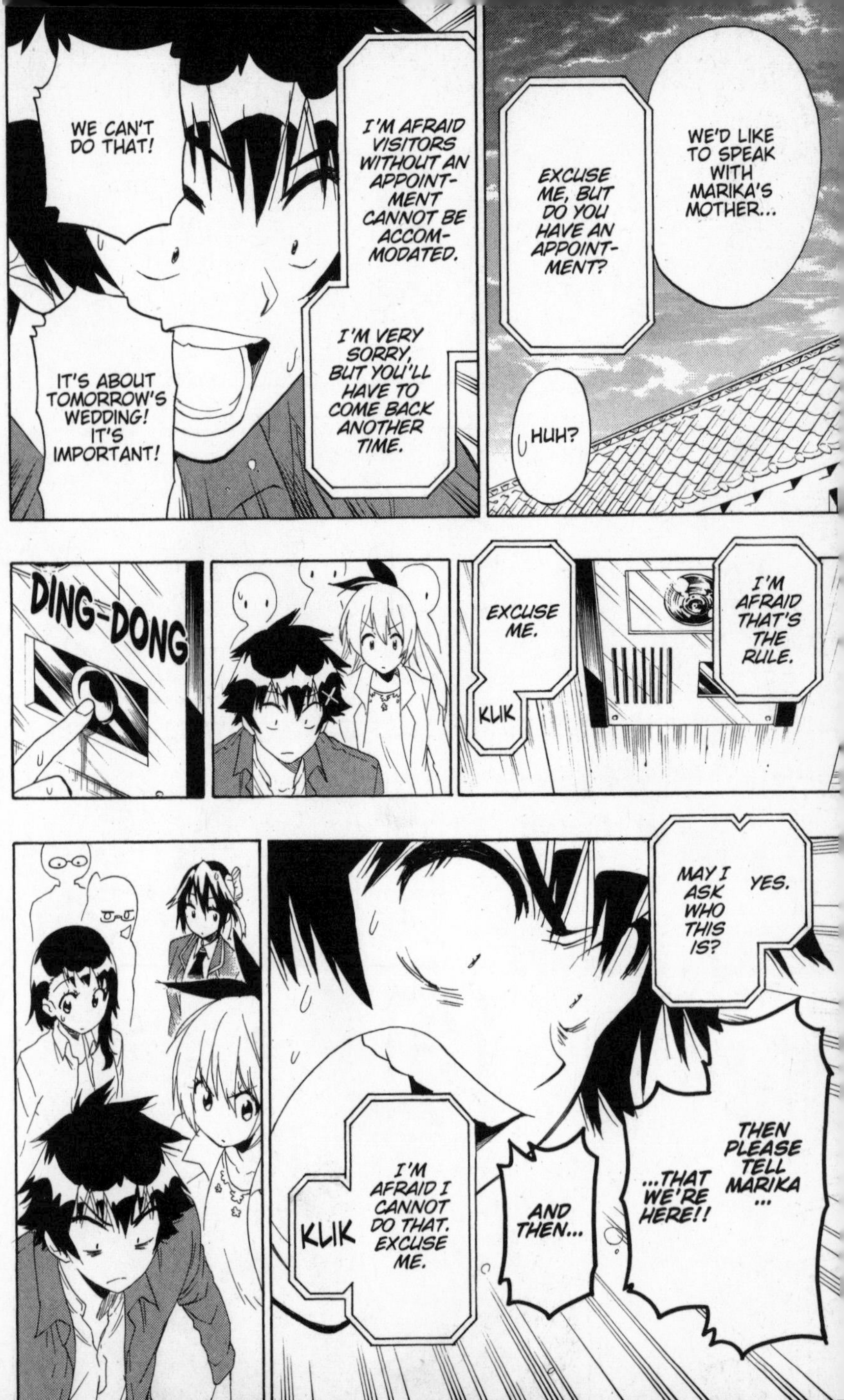
WE'D LIKE TO SPEAK WITH MARIKA'S MOTHER...
EXCUSE ME, BUT DO YOU HAVE AN APPOINT-MENT?
HUH?
I'M AFRAID VISITORS WITHOUT AN APPOINT-MENT CANNOT BE ACCOM-MODATED.
WE CAN'T DO THAT!
I'M VERY SORRY, BUT YOU'LL HAVE TO COME BACK ANOTHER TIME.
IT'S ABOUT TOMORROW'S WEDDING! IT'S IMPORTANT!
I'M AFRAID THAT'S THE RULE.
EXCUSE ME.
KLIK
DING-DONG
YES.
MAY I ASK WHO THIS IS?
THEN PLEASE TELL MARIKA...
...THAT WE'RE HERE!!
AND THEN...
I'M AFRAID I CANNOT DO THAT. EXCUSE ME.
KLIK

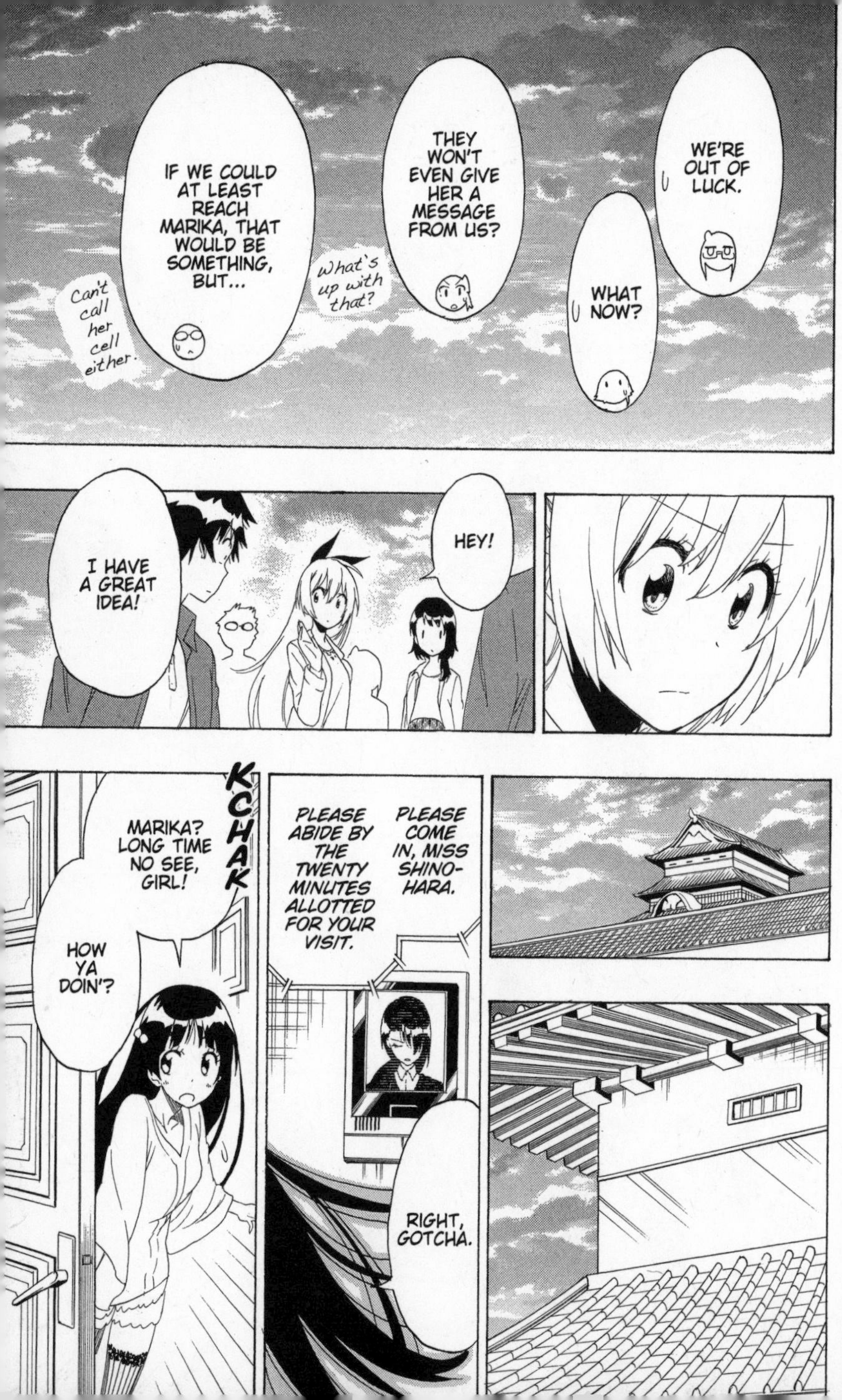
WE'RE OUT OF LUCK.
WHAT NOW?
THEY WON'T EVEN GIVE HER A MESSAGE FROM US?
What's up with that?
IF WE COULD AT LEAST REACH MARIKA, THAT WOULD BE SOMETHING, BUT...
Can't call her cell either.
HEY!
I HAVE A GREAT IDEA!
PLEASE COME IN, MISS SHINO-HARA.
PLEASE ABIDE BY THE TWENTY MINUTES ALLOTTED FOR YOUR VISIT.
RIGHT, GOTCHA.
KCHAK
MARIKA? LONG TIME NO SEE, GIRL!
HOW YA DOIN'?

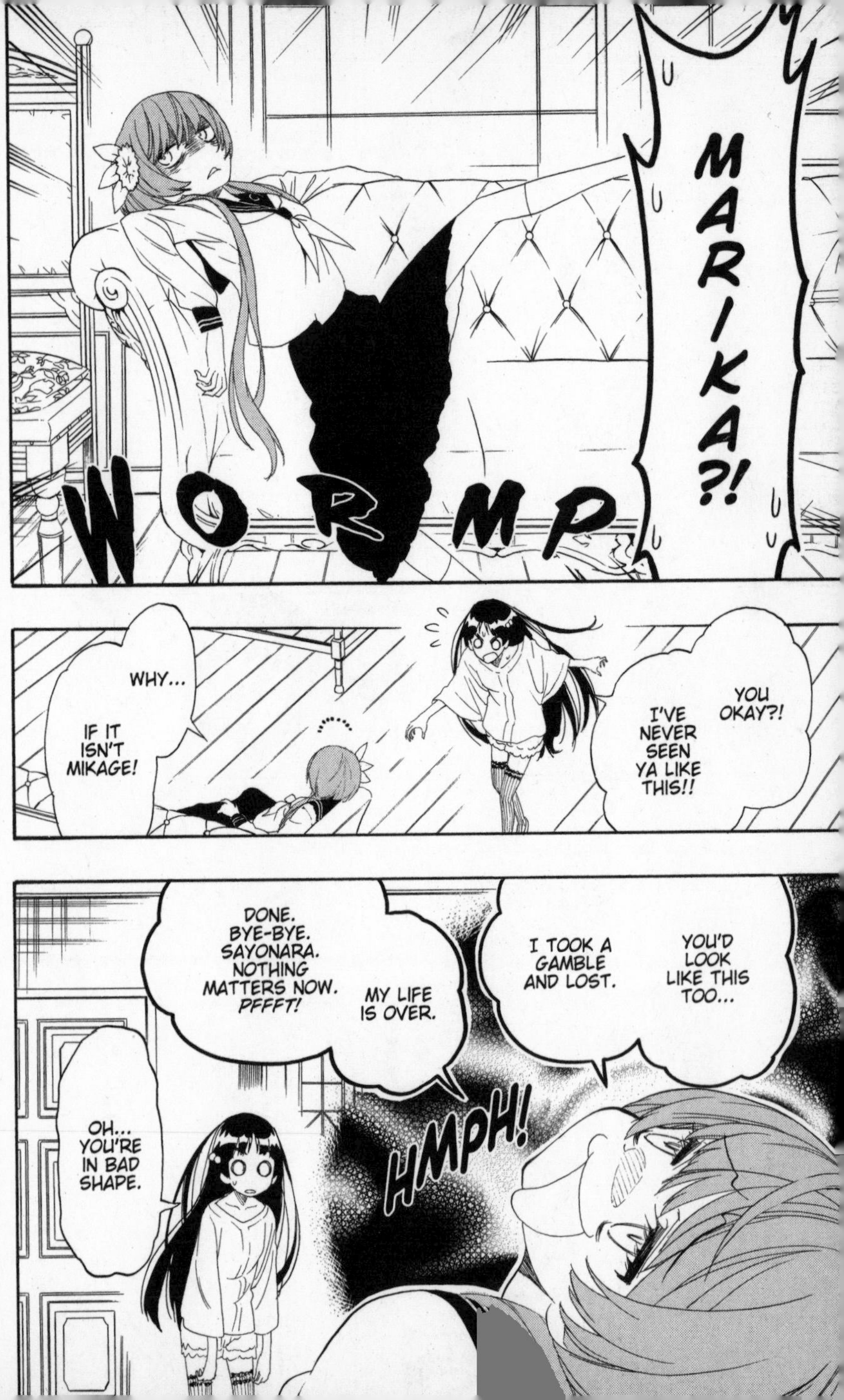
MARIKA?!
WORMP
YOU OKAY?!
I'VE NEVER SEEN YA LIKE THIS!!
WHY...
IF IT ISN'T MIKAGE!
YOU'D LOOK LIKE THIS TOO...
I TOOK A GAMBLE AND LOST.
MY LIFE IS OVER.
DONE. BYE-BYE. SAYONARA. NOTHING MATTERS NOW. PFFFT!
HMPH!
OH... YOU'RE IN BAD SHAPE.

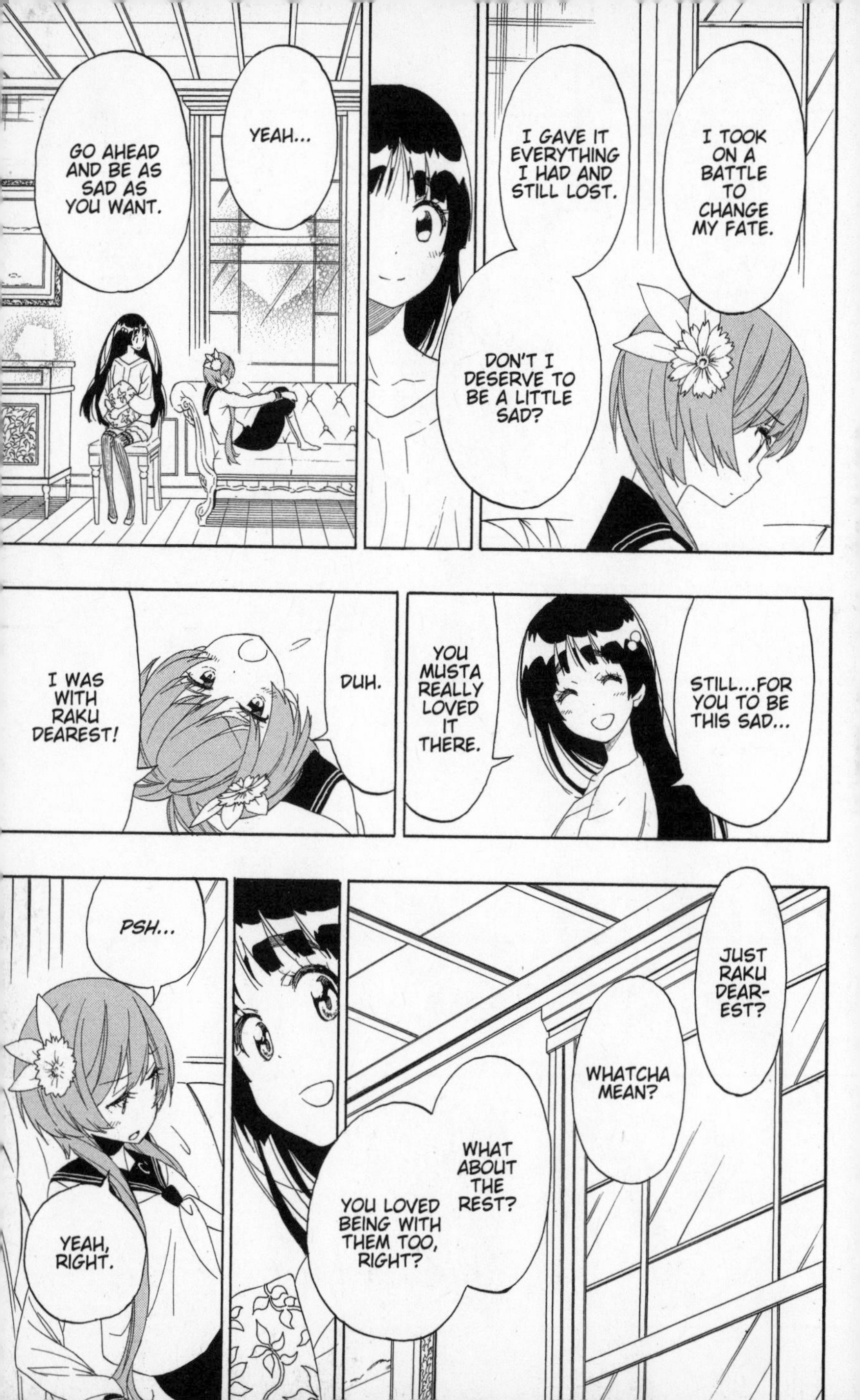
I TOOK ON A BATTLE TO CHANGE MY FATE.
I GAVE IT EVERYTHING I HAD AND STILL LOST.
DON'T I DESERVE TO BE A LITTLE SAD?
YEAH...
GO AHEAD AND BE AS SAD AS YOU WANT.
STILL...FOR YOU TO BE THIS SAD...
YOU MUSTA REALLY LOVED IT THERE.
DUH.
I WAS WITH RAKU DEAREST!
JUST RAKU DEAREST?
WHATCHA MEAN?
WHAT ABOUT THE REST?
YOU LOVED BEING WITH THEM TOO, RIGHT?
PSH...
YEAH, RIGHT.

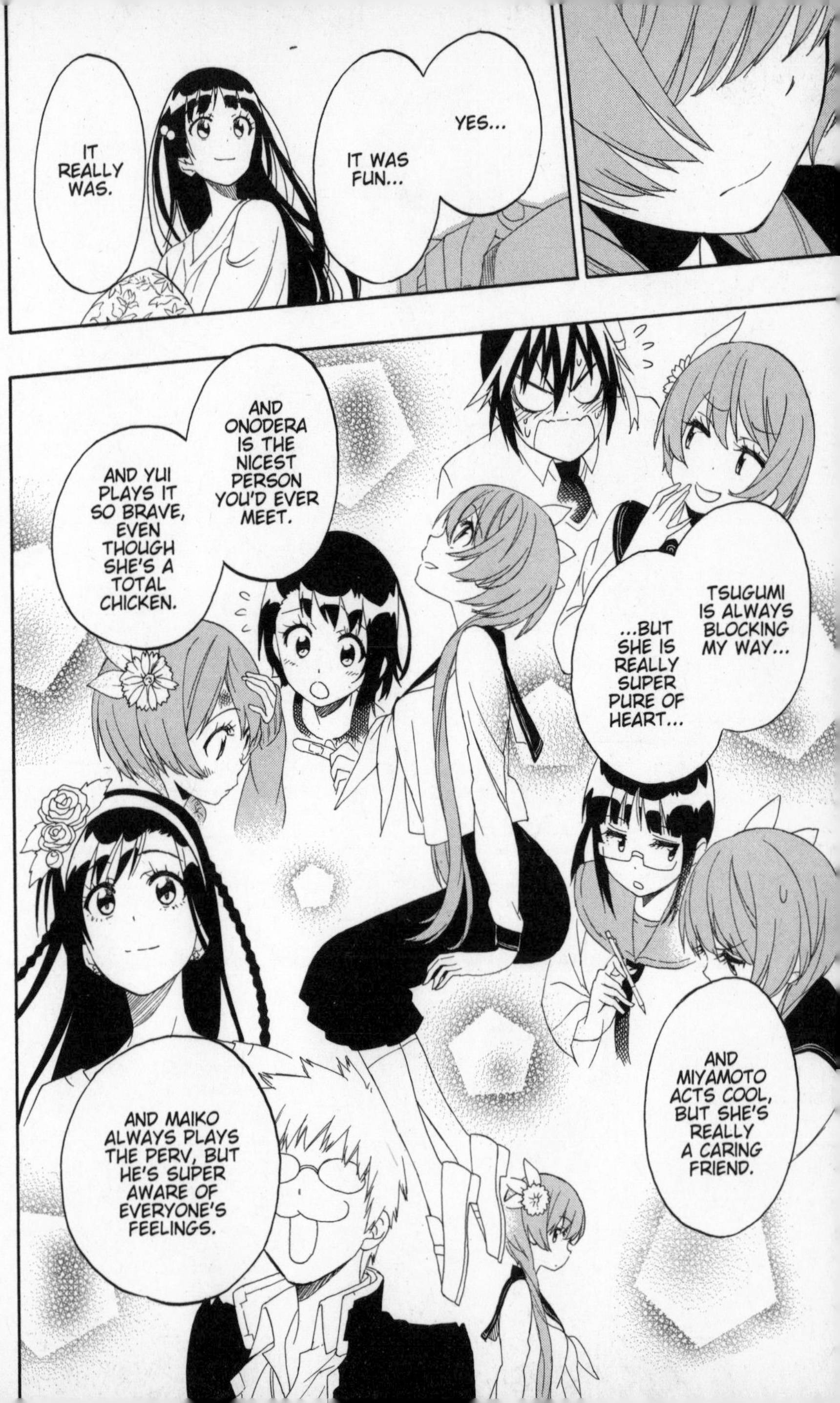
YES... IT WAS FUN...
IT REALLY WAS.
TSUGUMI IS ALWAYS BLOCKING MY WAY...
...BUT SHE IS REALLY SUPER PURE OF HEART...
AND ONODERA IS THE NICEST PERSON YOU'D EVER MEET.
AND YUI PLAYS IT SO BRAVE, EVEN THOUGH SHE'S A TOTAL CHICKEN.
AND MIYAMOTO ACTS COOL, BUT SHE'S REALLY A CARING FRIEND.
AND MAIKO ALWAYS PLAYS THE PERV, BUT HE'S SUPER AWARE OF EVERYONE'S FEELINGS.

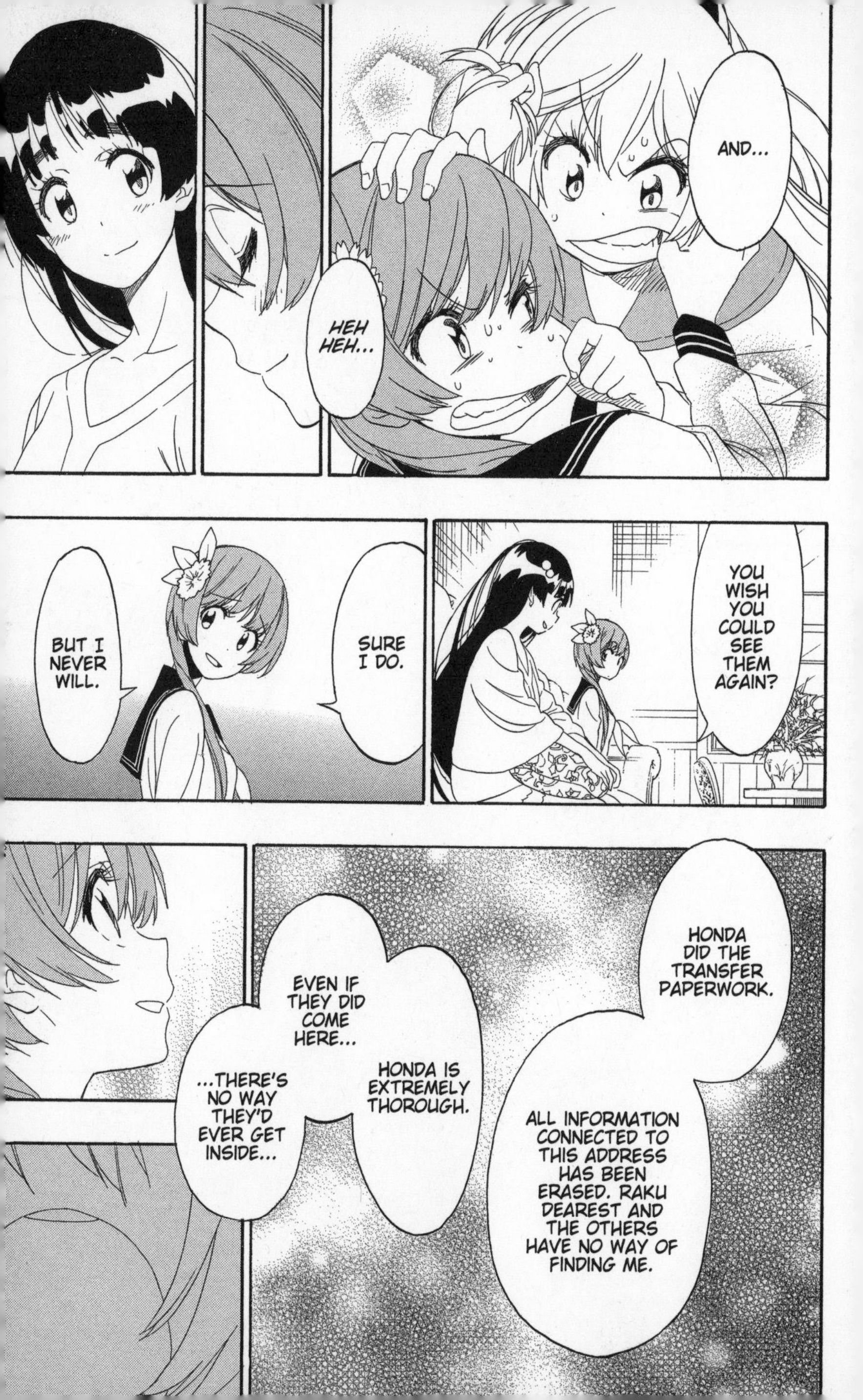
AND...
HEH HEH...
YOU WISH YOU COULD SEE THEM AGAIN?
SURE I DO.
BUT I NEVER WILL.
HONDA DID THE TRANSFER PAPERWORK.
ALL INFORMATION CONNECTED TO THIS ADDRESS HAS BEEN ERASED. RAKU DEAREST AND THE OTHERS HAVE NO WAY OF FINDING ME.
HONDA IS EXTREMELY THOROUGH.
EVEN IF THEY DID COME HERE...
...THERE'S NO WAY THEY'D EVER GET INSIDE...

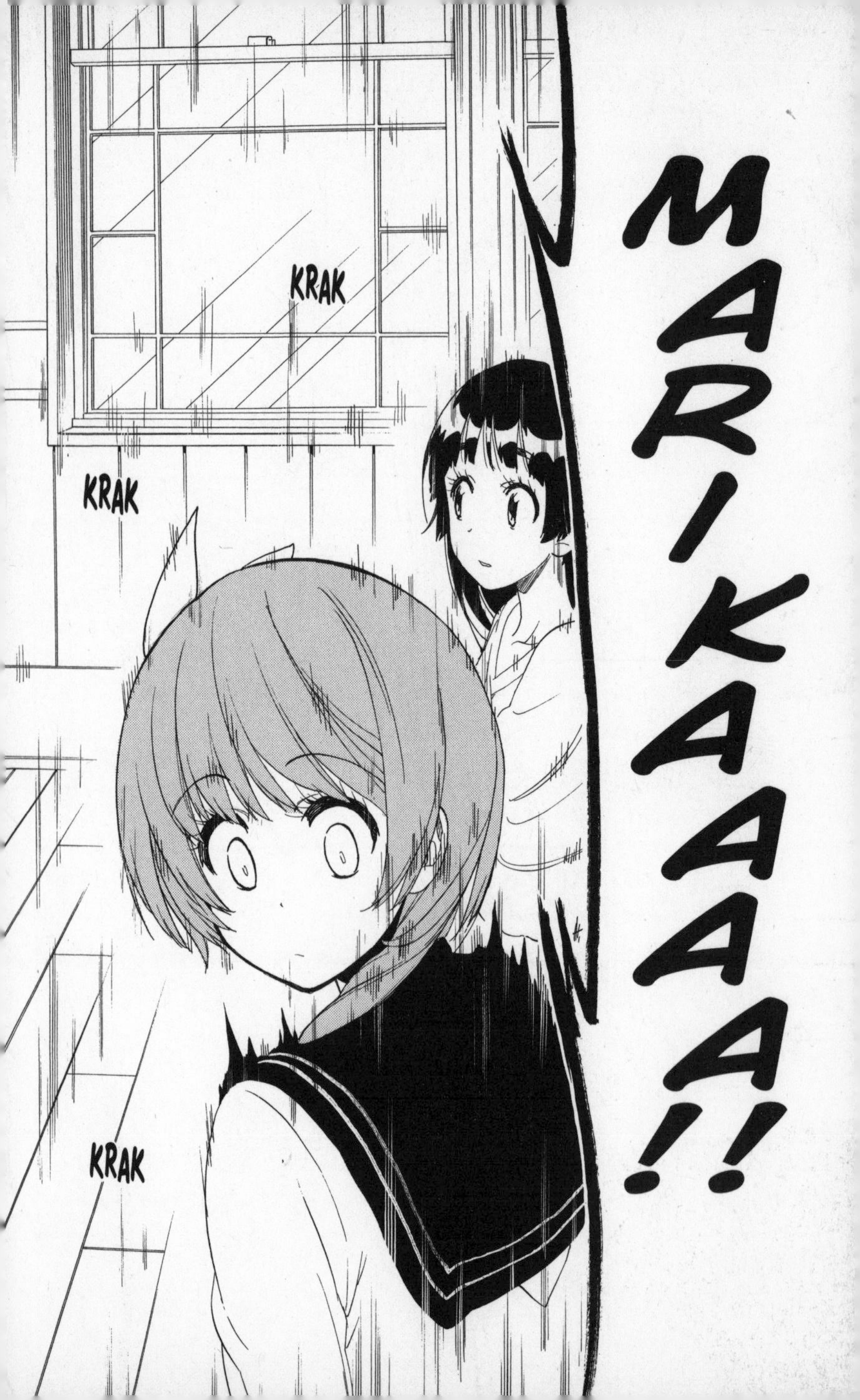
MARIKAAAA!!
KRAK
KRAK
KRAK

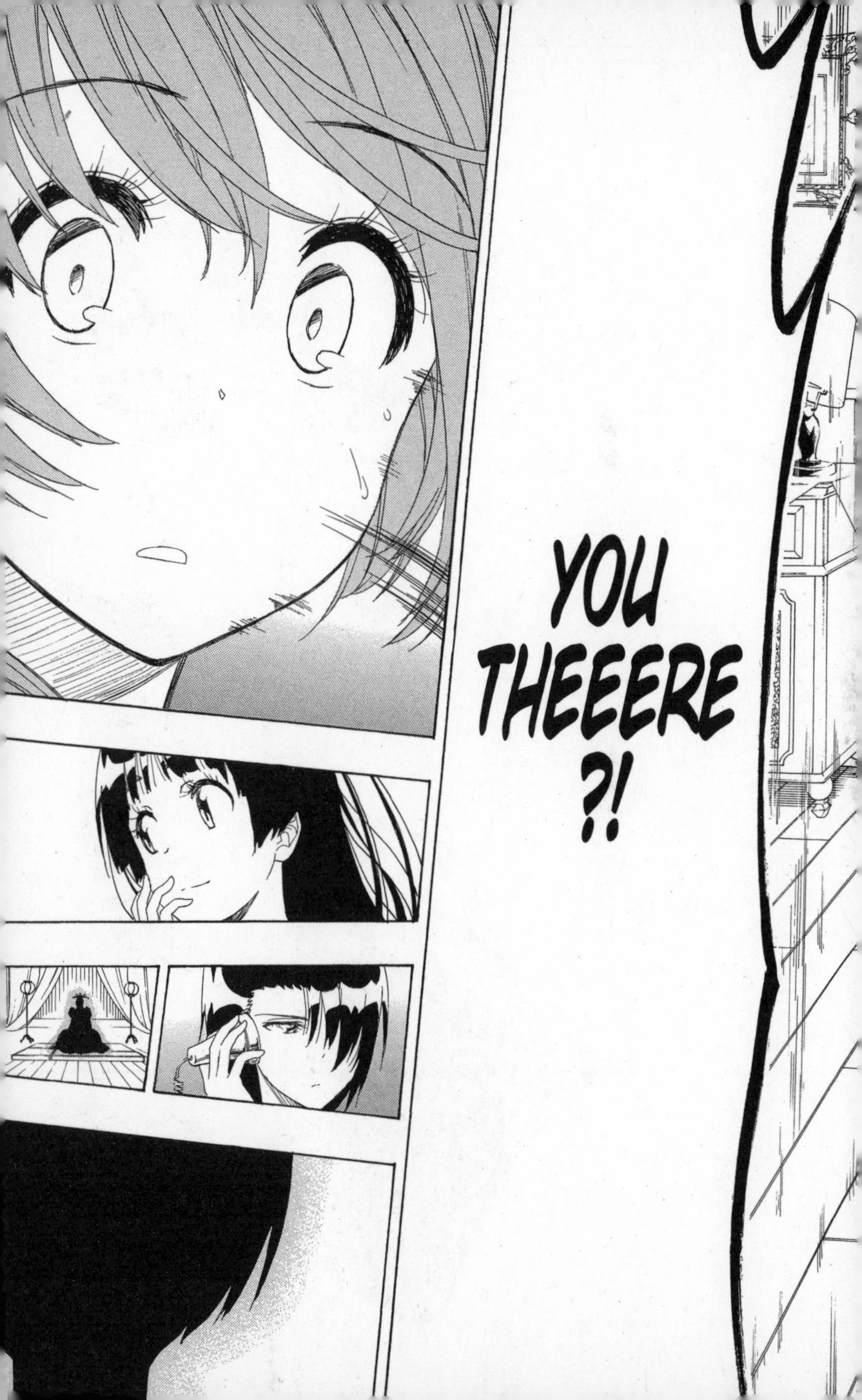
YOU THEEERE ?!

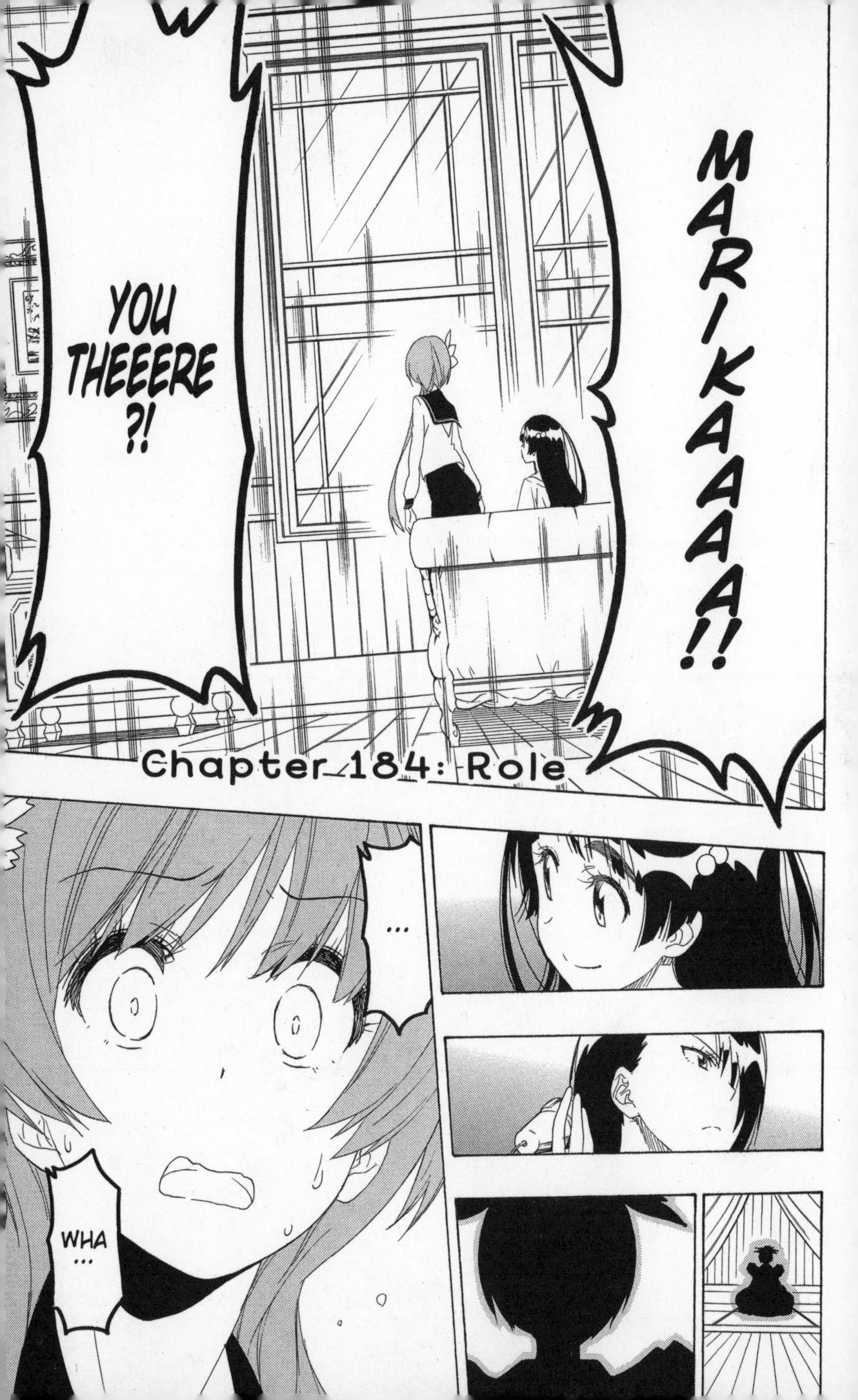
MARIKAAAAA!!
YOU THEEERE ?!
Chapter 184: Role
...
WHA ...

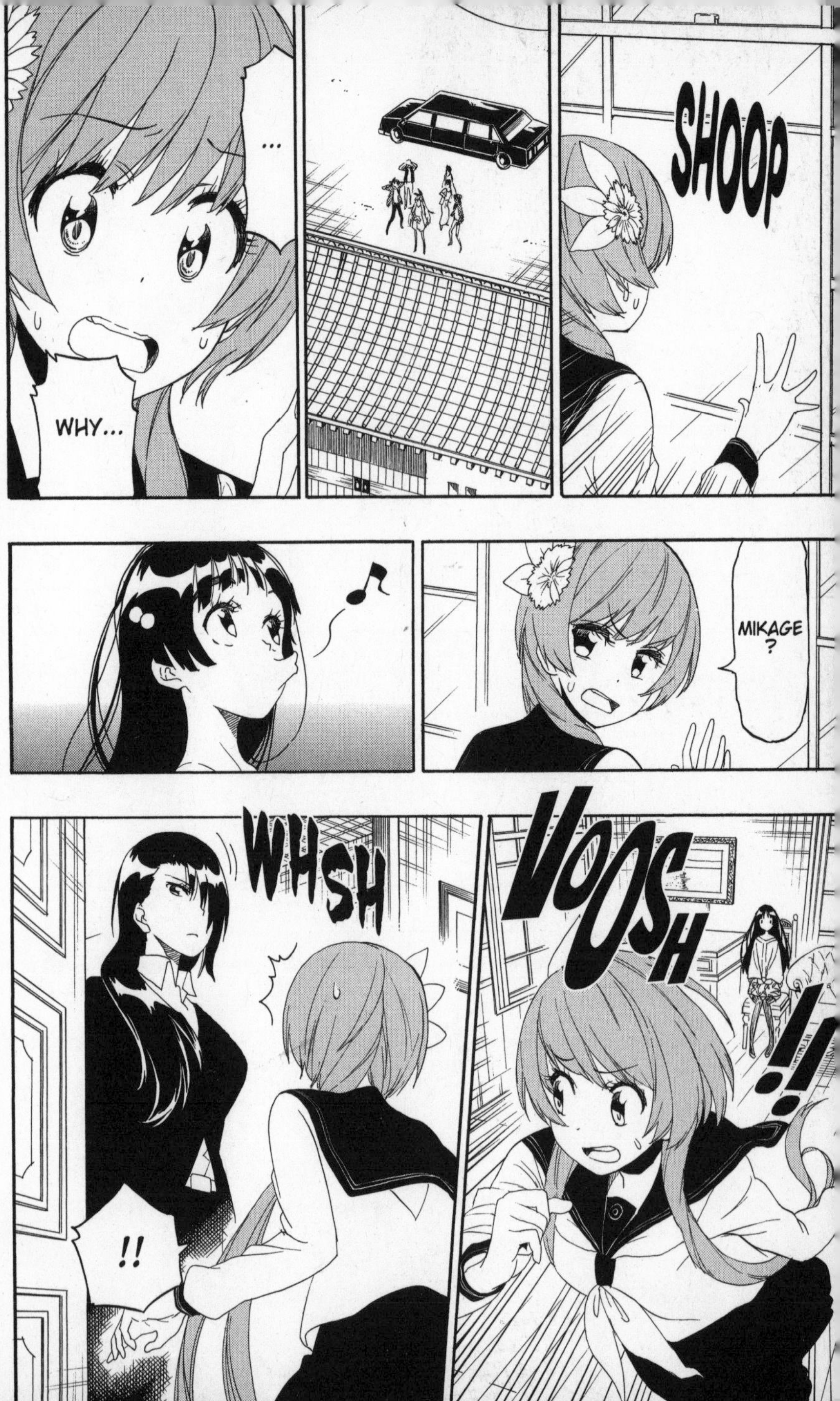
SHOOP
...
WHY...
MIKAGE?
♪
VOOSH
!!
WHSH
!!

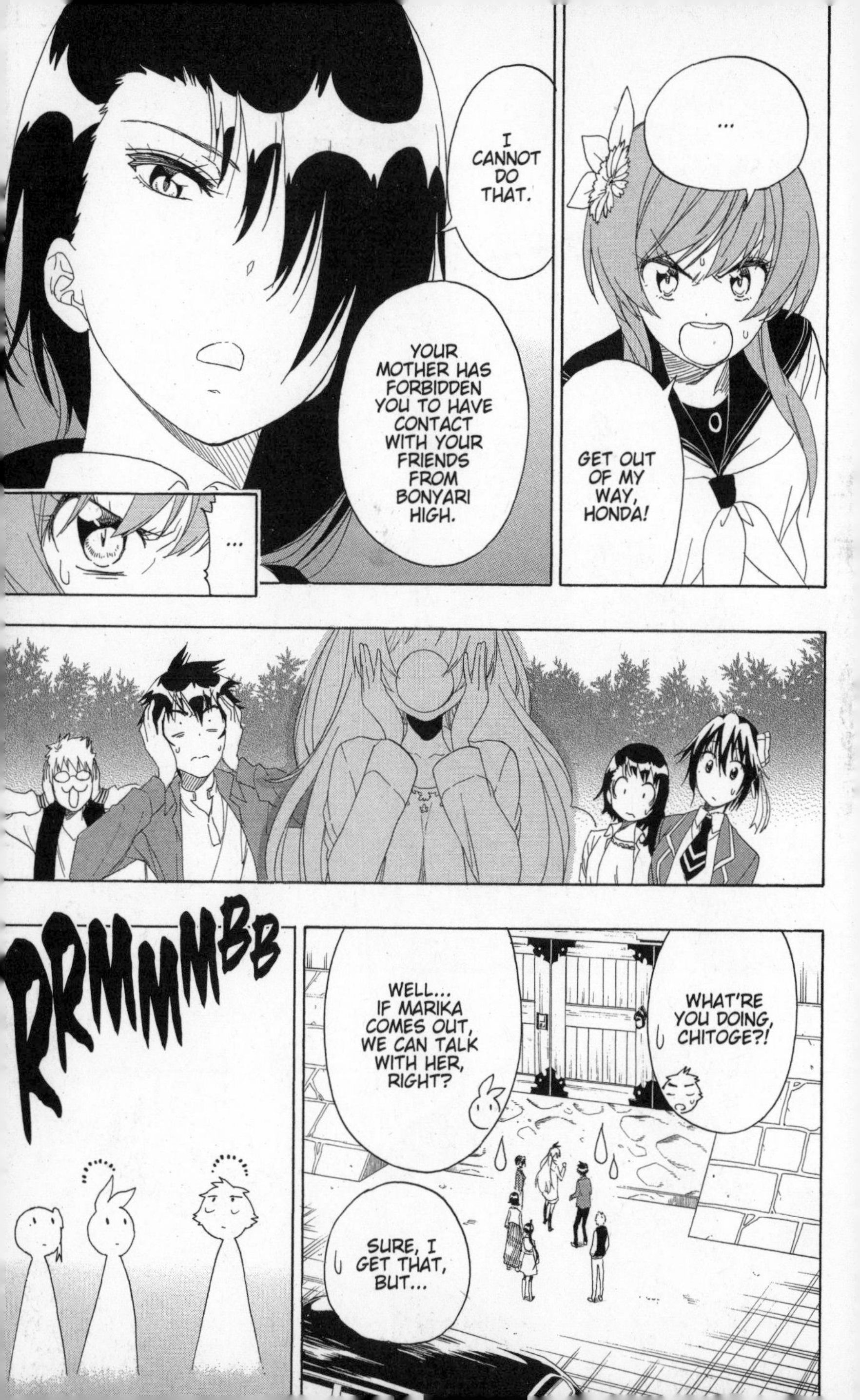
...
GET OUT OF MY WAY, HONDA!
I CANNOT DO THAT.
YOUR MOTHER HAS FORBIDDEN YOU TO HAVE CONTACT WITH YOUR FRIENDS FROM BONYARI HIGH.
...
WHAT'RE YOU DOING, CHITOGE?!
WELL... IF MARIKA COMES OUT, WE CAN TALK WITH HER, RIGHT?
SURE, I GET THAT, BUT...
RRMMMBB

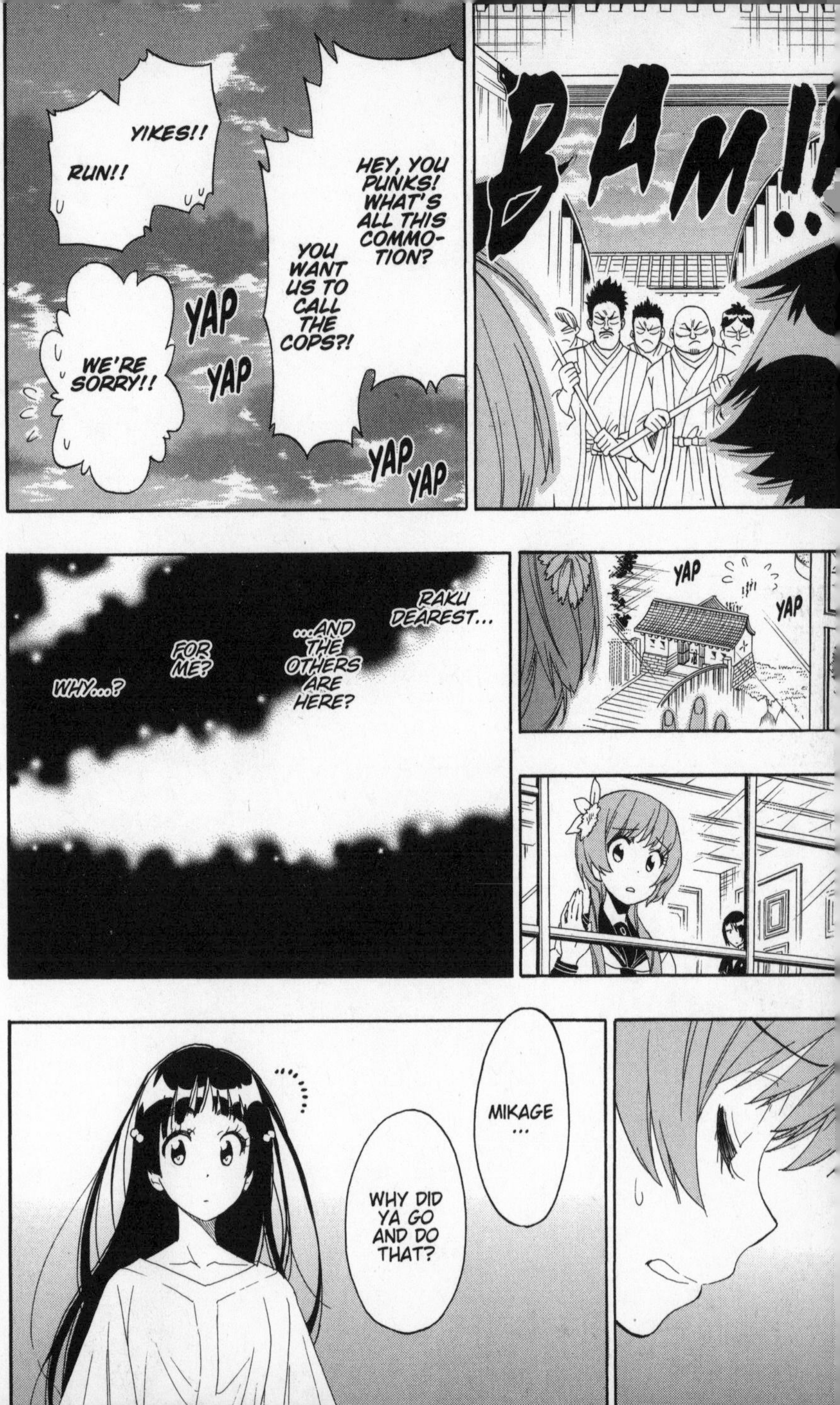
BAM!!
HEY, YOU PUNKS! WHAT'S ALL THIS COMMOTION?
YOU WANT US TO CALL THE COPS?!
YAP YAP
YIKES!!
RUN!!
YAP
YAP
WE'RE SORRY!!
YAP
YAP
RAKU DEAREST...
...AND THE OTHERS ARE HERE?
FOR ME?
WHY...?
MIKAGE...
WHY DID YA GO AND DO THAT?

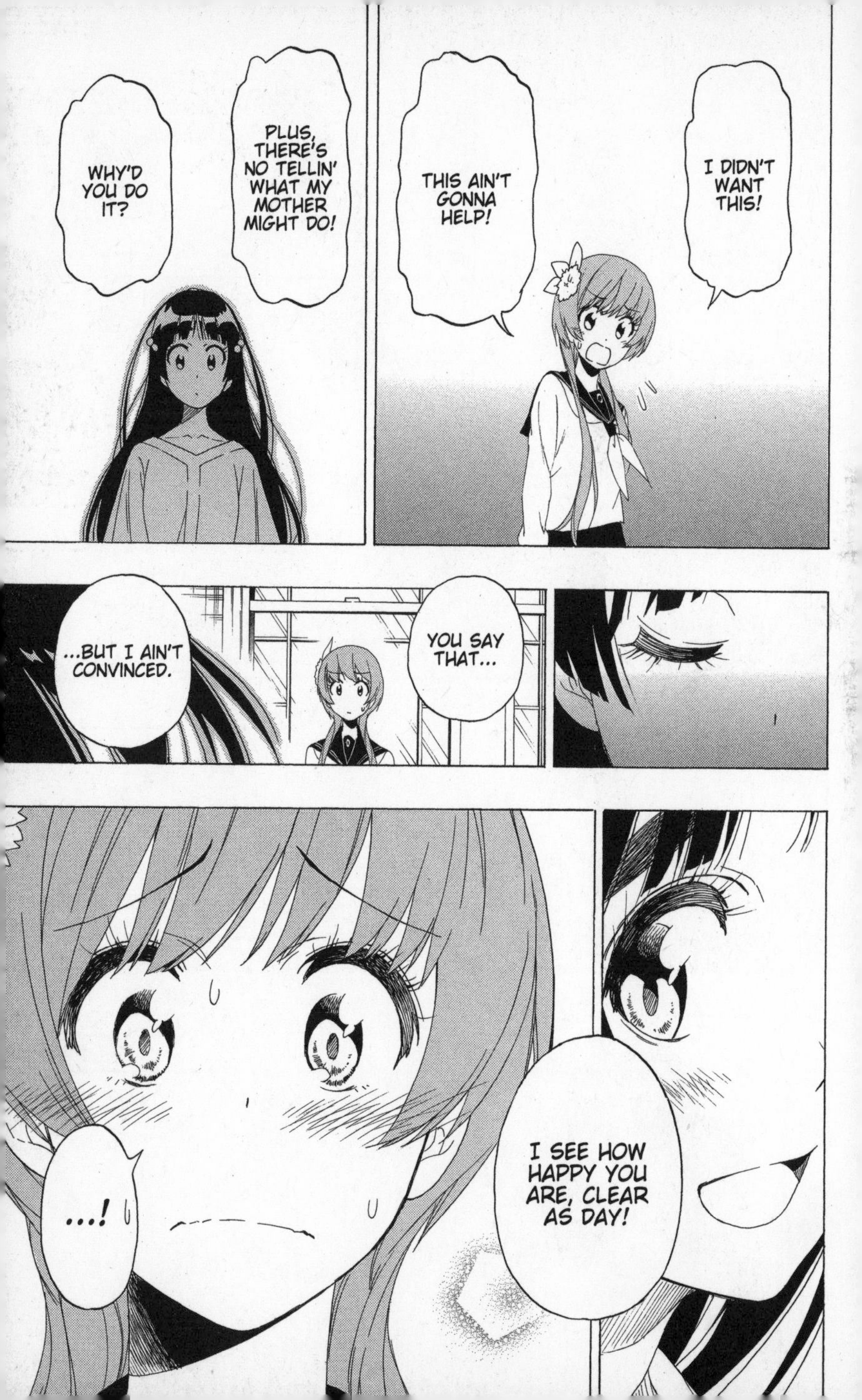
I DIDN'T WANT THIS!
THIS AIN'T GONNA HELP!
PLUS, THERE'S NO TELLIN' WHAT MY MOTHER MIGHT DO!
WHY'D YOU DO IT?
YOU SAY THAT...
...BUT I AIN'T CONVINCED.
I SEE HOW HAPPY YOU ARE, CLEAR AS DAY!
...!

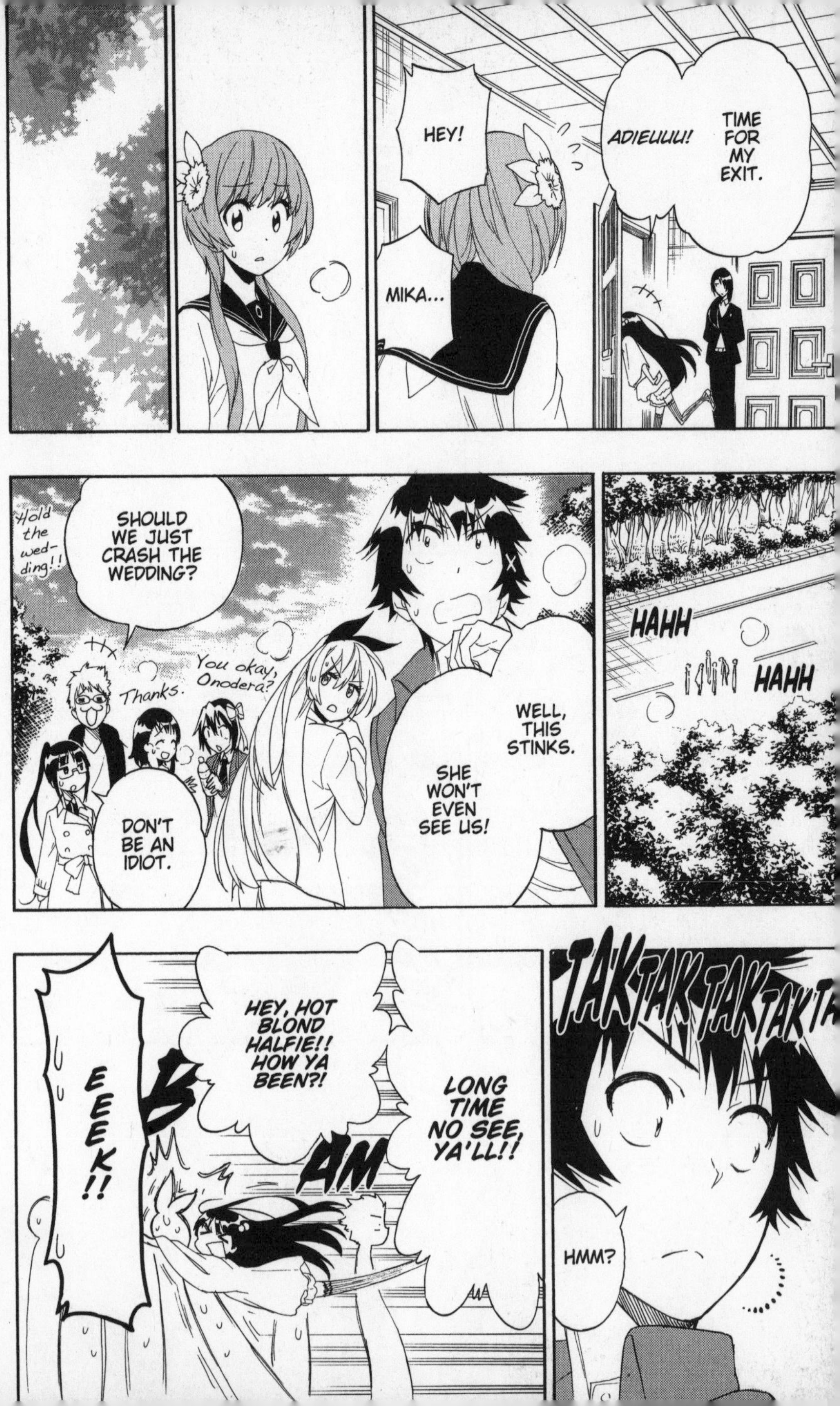
TIME FOR MY EXIT.
ADIEUUU!
HEY!
MIKA...
HAHH
HAHH
WELL, THIS STINKS.
SHE WON'T EVEN SEE US!
You okay, Onodera?
Thanks.
SHOULD WE JUST CRASH THE WEDDING?
Hold the wed-ding!!
DON'T BE AN IDIOT.
TAK TAK TAK TAK
HMM?
LONG TIME NO SEE, YA'LL!!
HEY, HOT BLOND HALFIE!! HOW YA BEEN?!
EEEK!!

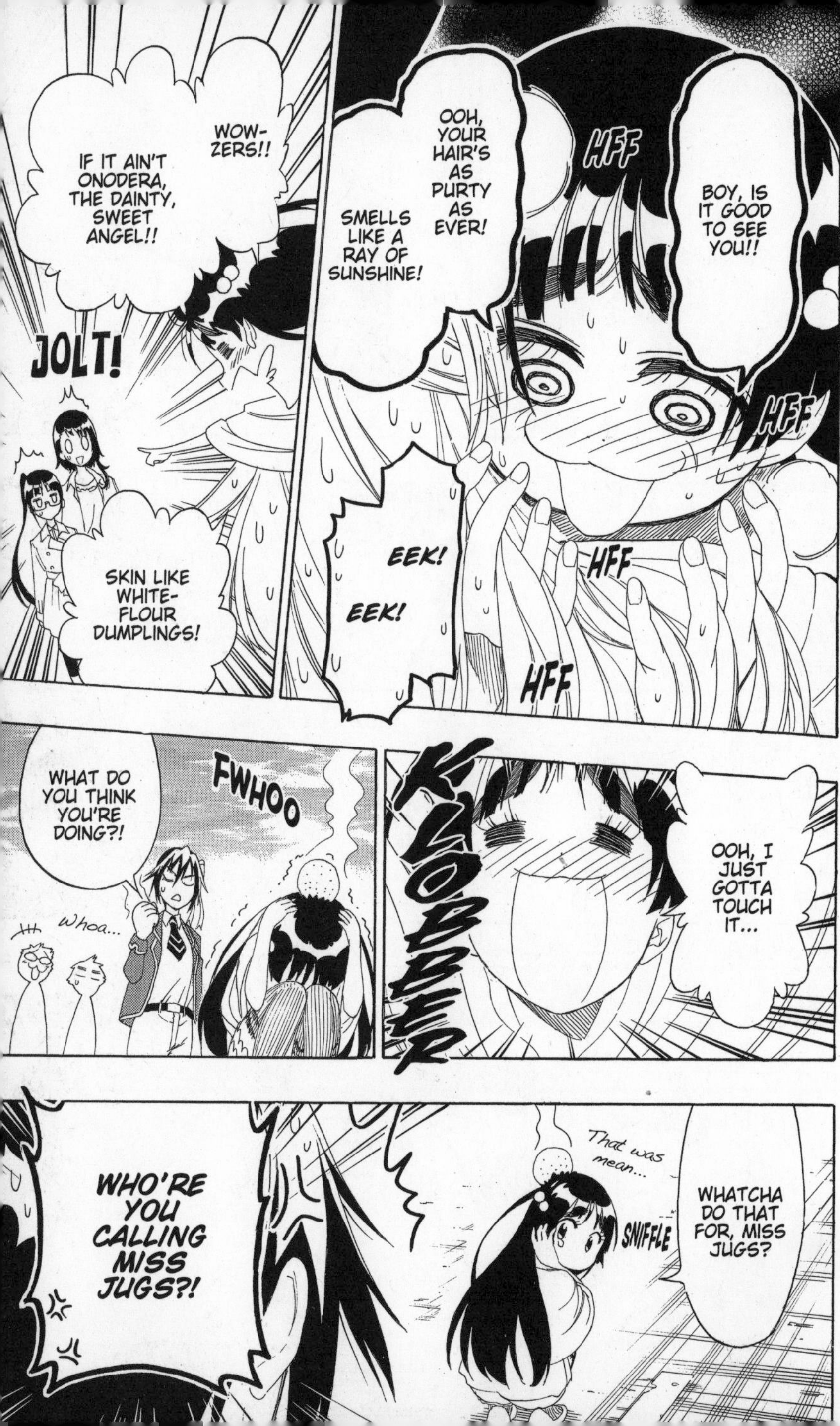
BOY, IS IT GOOD TO SEE YOU!!
HFF
OOH, YOUR HAIR'S AS PURTY AS EVER!
SMELLS LIKE A RAY OF SUNSHINE!
HFF
HFF
EEK!
EEK!
HFF
WOW-ZERS!!
IF IT AIN'T ONODERA, THE DAINTY, SWEET ANGEL!!
JOLT!
SKIN LIKE WHITE-FLOUR DUMPLINGS!
OOH, I JUST GOTTA TOUCH IT...
KLOBBER
FWHOO
WHAT DO YOU THINK YOU'RE DOING?!
Whoa...
WHATCHA DO THAT FOR, MISS JUGS?
SNIFFLE
That was mean...
WHO'RE YOU CALLING MISS JUGS?!

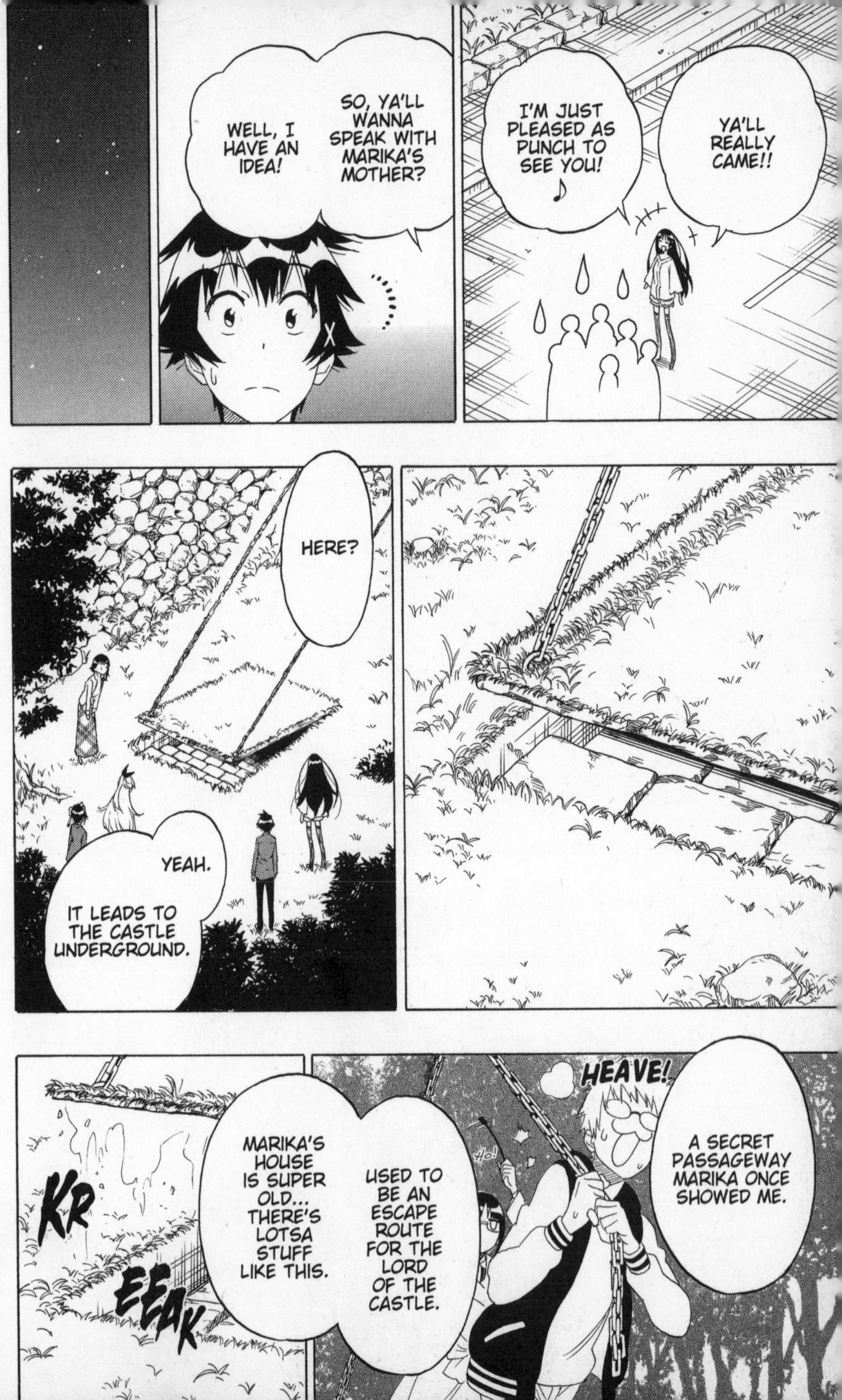
YA'LL REALLY CAME!!
I'M JUST PLEASED AS PUNCH TO SEE YOU! ♪
SO, YA'LL WANNA SPEAK WITH MARIKA'S MOTHER?
WELL, I HAVE AN IDEA!
HERE?
YEAH.
IT LEADS TO THE CASTLE UNDERGROUND.
HEAVE!
A SECRET PASSAGEWAY MARIKA ONCE SHOWED ME.
USED TO BE AN ESCAPE ROUTE FOR THE LORD OF THE CASTLE.
MARIKA'S HOUSE IS SUPER OLD... THERE'S LOTSA STUFF LIKE THIS.
KR
EEEAK

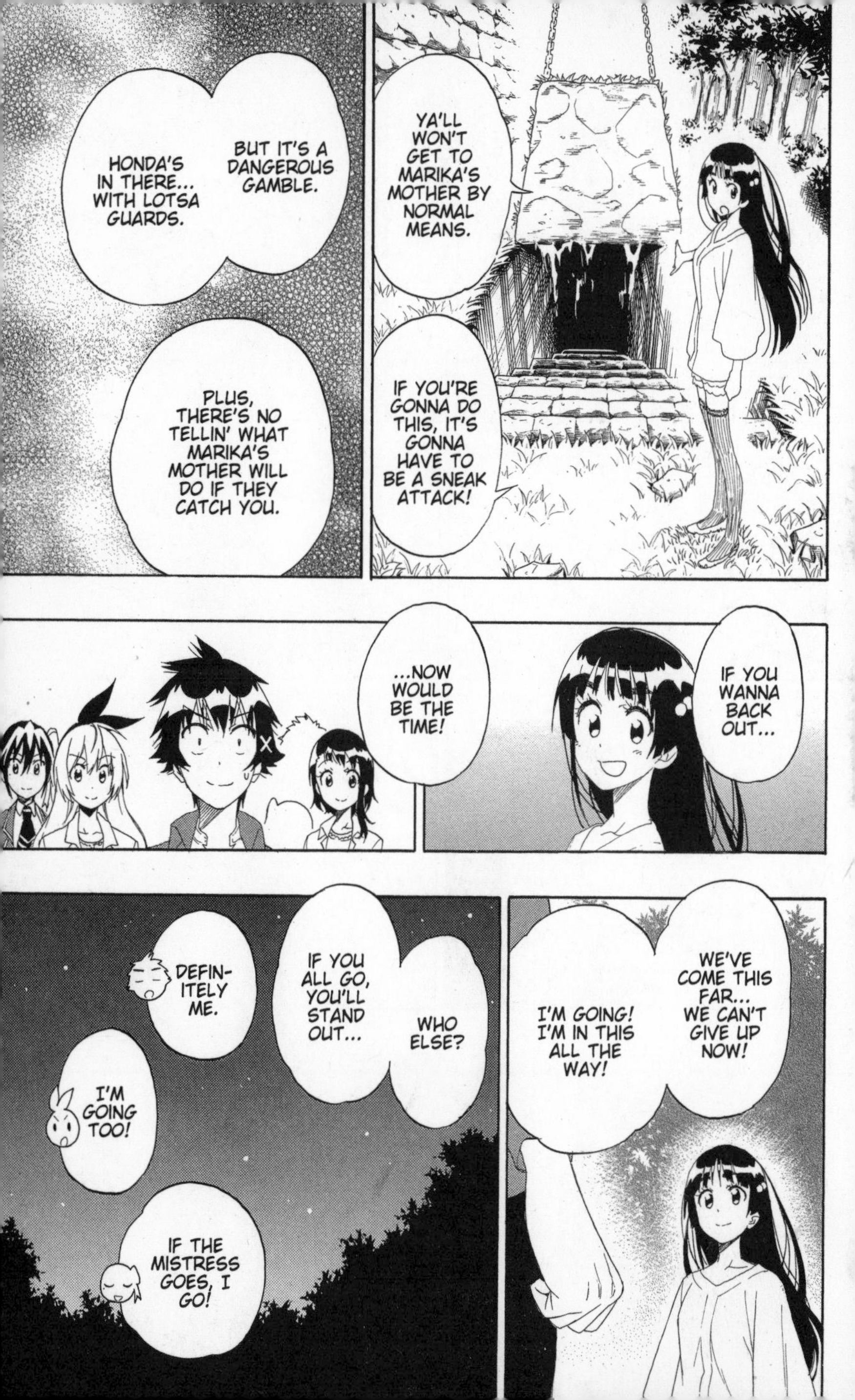
YA'LL WON'T GET TO MARIKA'S MOTHER BY NORMAL MEANS.
IF YOU'RE GONNA DO THIS, IT'S GONNA HAVE TO BE A SNEAK ATTACK!
BUT IT'S A DANGEROUS GAMBLE.
HONDA'S IN THERE... WITH LOTSA GUARDS.
PLUS, THERE'S NO TELLIN' WHAT MARIKA'S MOTHER WILL DO IF THEY CATCH YOU.
IF YOU WANNA BACK OUT...
...NOW WOULD BE THE TIME!
WE'VE COME THIS FAR... WE CAN'T GIVE UP NOW!
I'M GOING! I'M IN THIS ALL THE WAY!
WHO ELSE?
IF YOU ALL GO, YOU'LL STAND OUT...
DEFIN-ITELY ME.
I'M GOING TOO!
IF THE MISTRESS GOES, I GO!

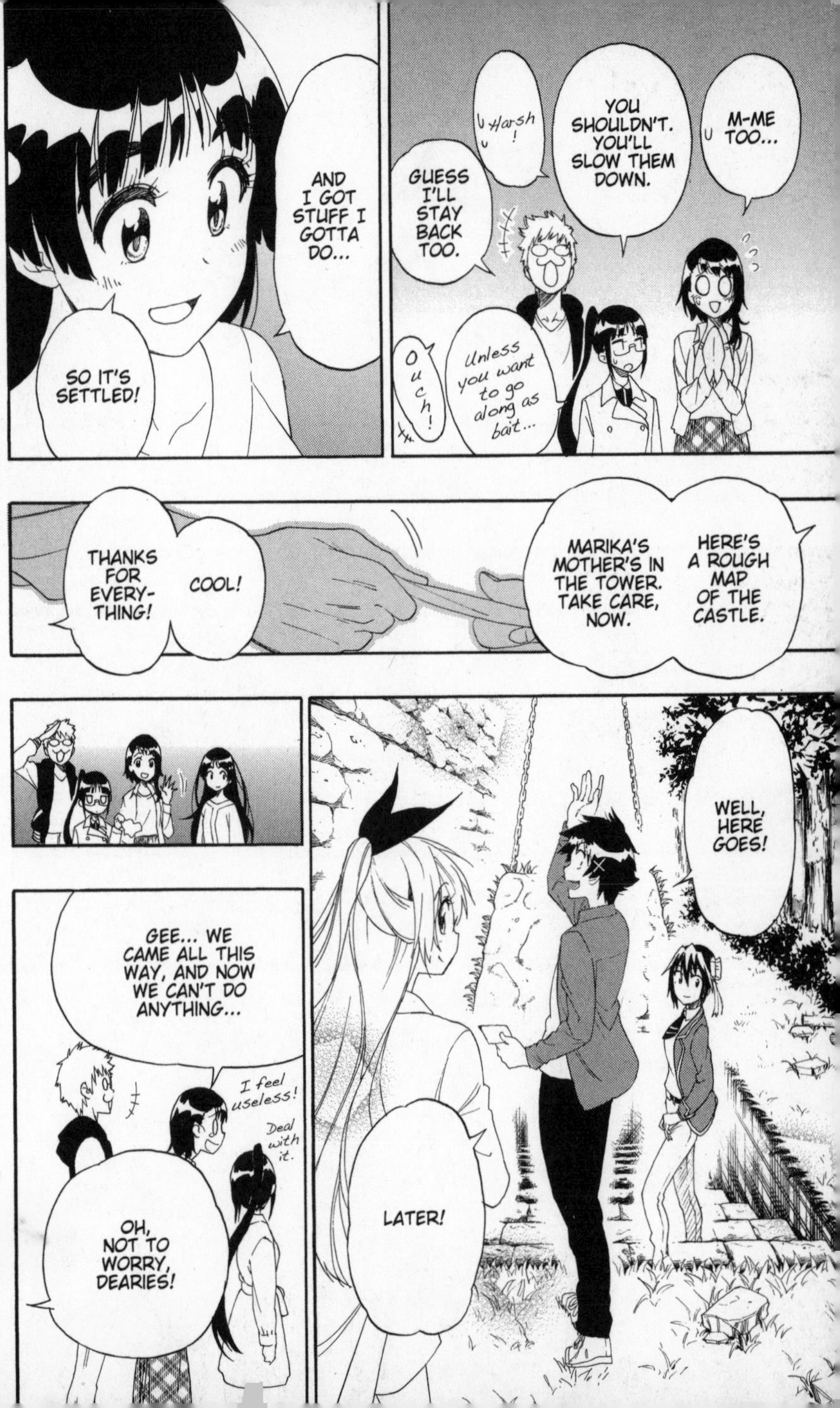
M-ME TOO...
YOU SHOULDN'T. YOU'LL SLOW THEM DOWN.
Harsh!
GUESS I'LL STAY BACK TOO.
Unless you want to go along as bait...
Ouch!
AND I GOT STUFF I GOTTA DO...
SO IT'S SETTLED!
HERE'S A ROUGH MAP OF THE CASTLE.
MARIKA'S MOTHER'S IN THE TOWER. TAKE CARE, NOW.
COOL!
THANKS FOR EVERYTHING!
WELL, HERE GOES!
LATER!
GEE... WE CAME ALL THIS WAY, AND NOW WE CAN'T DO ANYTHING...
I feel useless!
Deal with it.
OH, NOT TO WORRY, DEARIES!

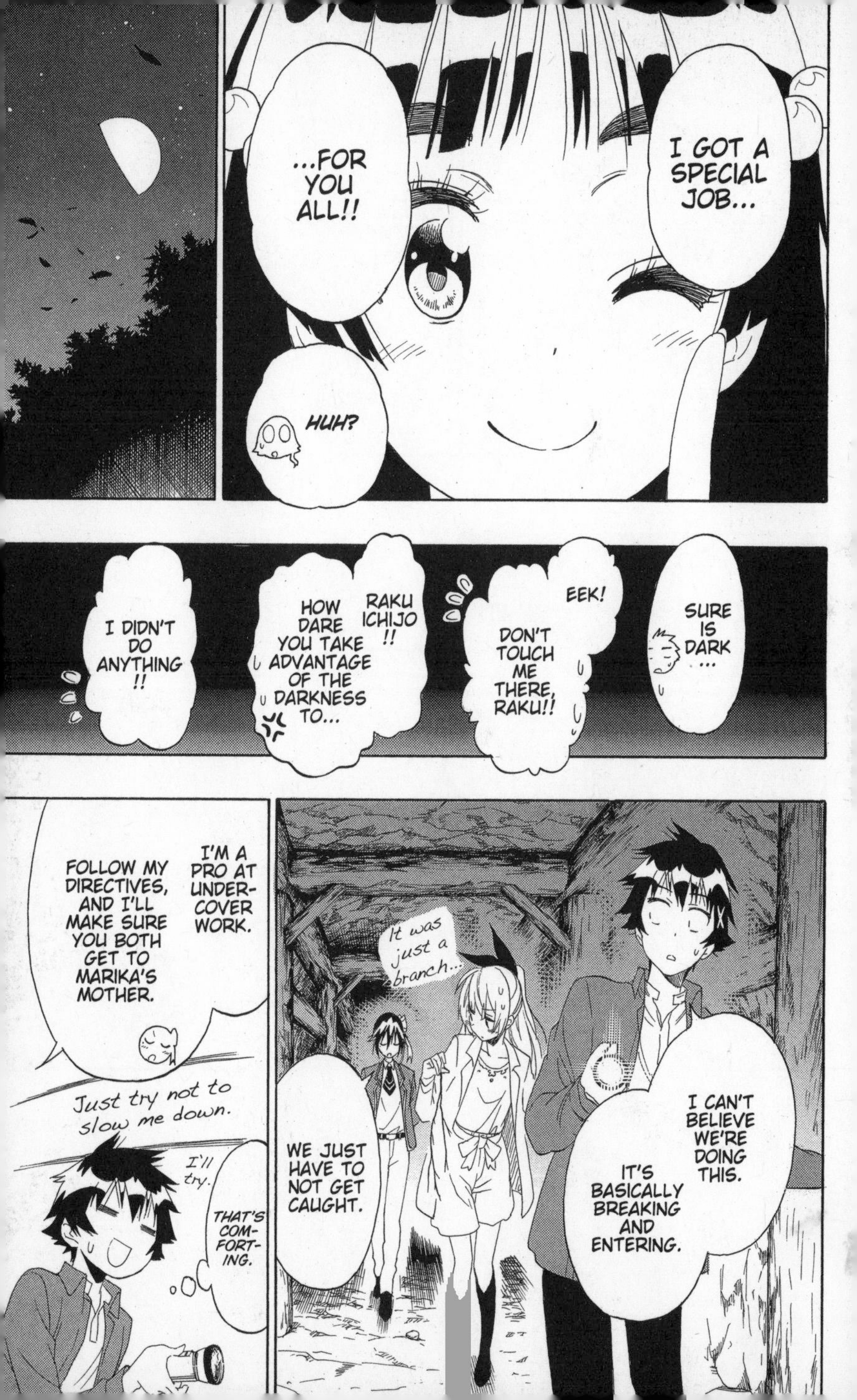
I GOT A SPECIAL JOB...
...FOR YOU ALL!!
HUH?
SURE IS DARK...
EEK!
DON'T TOUCH ME THERE, RAKU!!
RAKU ICHIJO!!
HOW DARE YOU TAKE ADVANTAGE OF THE DARKNESS TO...
I DIDN'T DO ANYTHING!!
I CAN'T BELIEVE WE'RE DOING THIS.
IT'S BASICALLY BREAKING AND ENTERING.
It was just a branch...
WE JUST HAVE TO NOT GET CAUGHT.
I'M A PRO AT UNDER-COVER WORK.
FOLLOW MY DIRECTIVES, AND I'LL MAKE SURE YOU BOTH GET TO MARIKA'S MOTHER.
Just try not to slow me down.
I'll try.
THAT'S COM-FORT-ING.

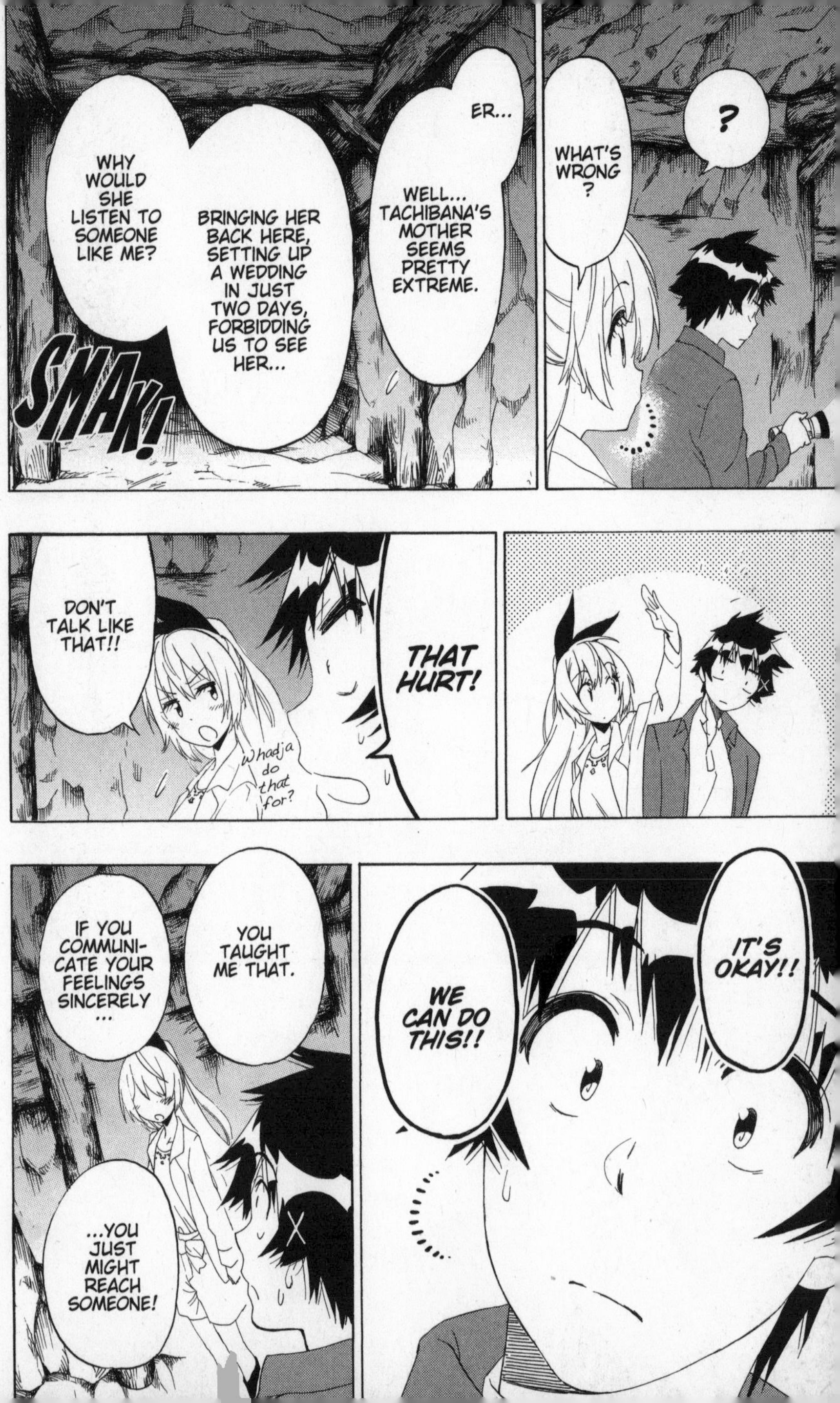
?
WHAT'S WRONG?
ER...
WELL... TACHIBANA'S MOTHER SEEMS PRETTY EXTREME.
BRINGING HER BACK HERE, SETTING UP A WEDDING IN JUST TWO DAYS, FORBIDDING US TO SEE HER...
WHY WOULD SHE LISTEN TO SOMEONE LIKE ME?
SMAK!
THAT HURT!
Whadja do that for?
DON'T TALK LIKE THAT!!
IT'S OKAY!!
WE CAN DO THIS!!
YOU TAUGHT ME THAT.
IF YOU COMMUNI-CATE YOUR FEELINGS SINCERELY...
...YOU JUST MIGHT REACH SOMEONE!

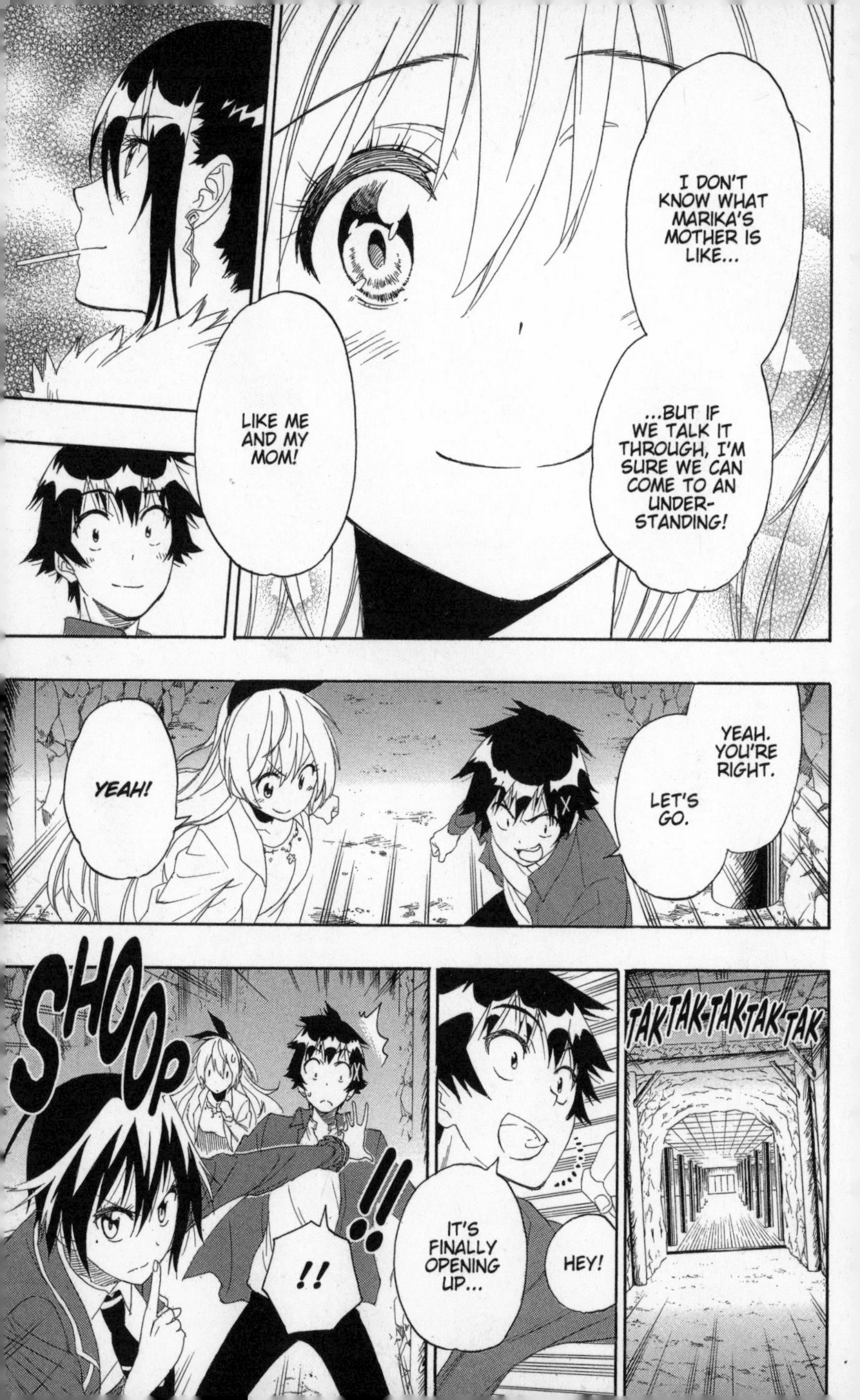
I DON'T KNOW WHAT MARIKA'S MOTHER IS LIKE...
...BUT IF WE TALK IT THROUGH, I'M SURE WE CAN COME TO AN UNDER-STANDING!
LIKE ME AND MY MOM!
YEAH. YOU'RE RIGHT.
LET'S GO.
YEAH!
TAK TAK TAK TAK TAK
HEY!
IT'S FINALLY OPENING UP...
!!
SHOOP
!!

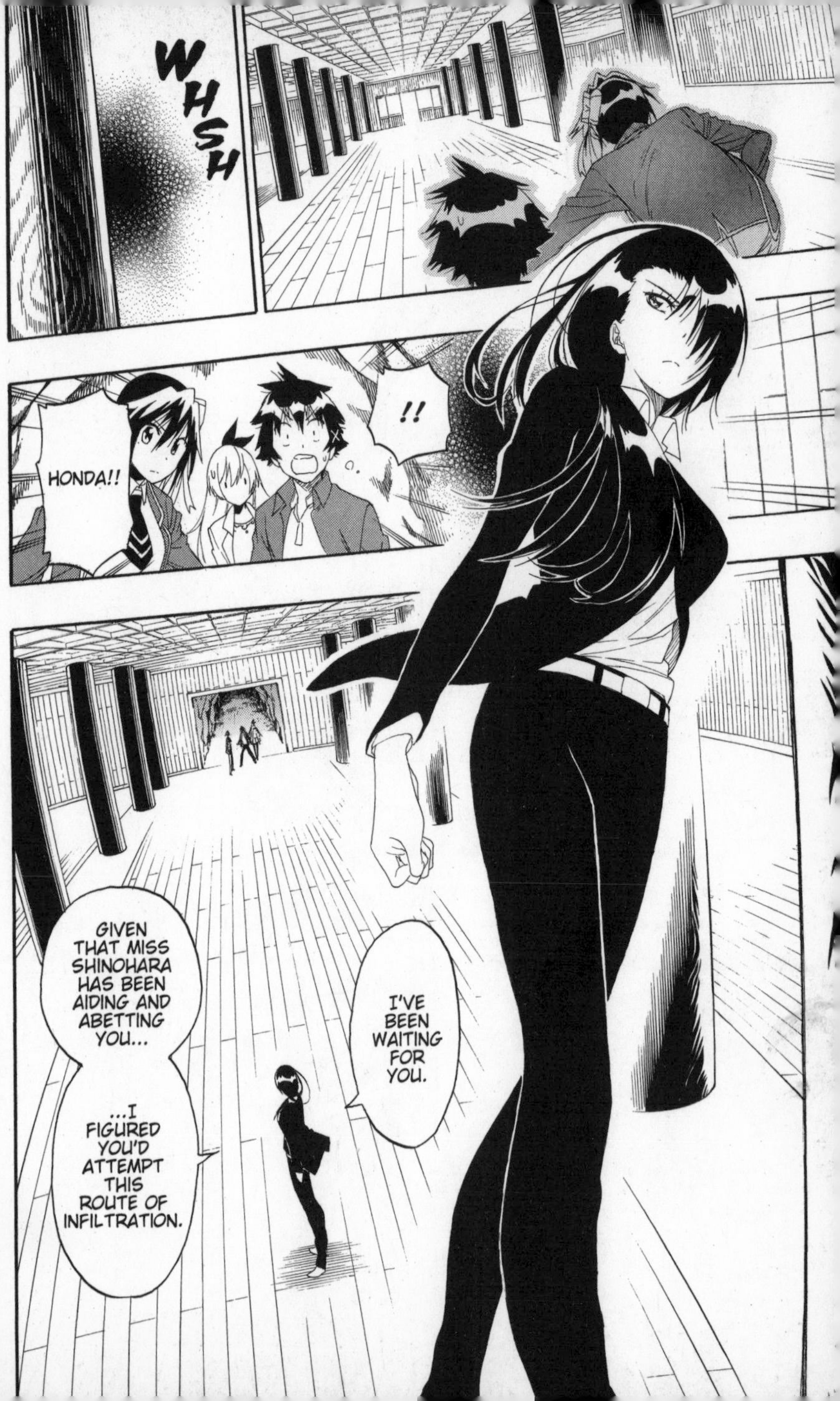
WHSH
!!
HONDA!!
I'VE BEEN WAITING FOR YOU.
GIVEN THAT MISS SHINOHARA HAS BEEN AIDING AND ABETTING YOU...
...I FIGURED YOU'D ATTEMPT THIS ROUTE OF INFILTRATION.

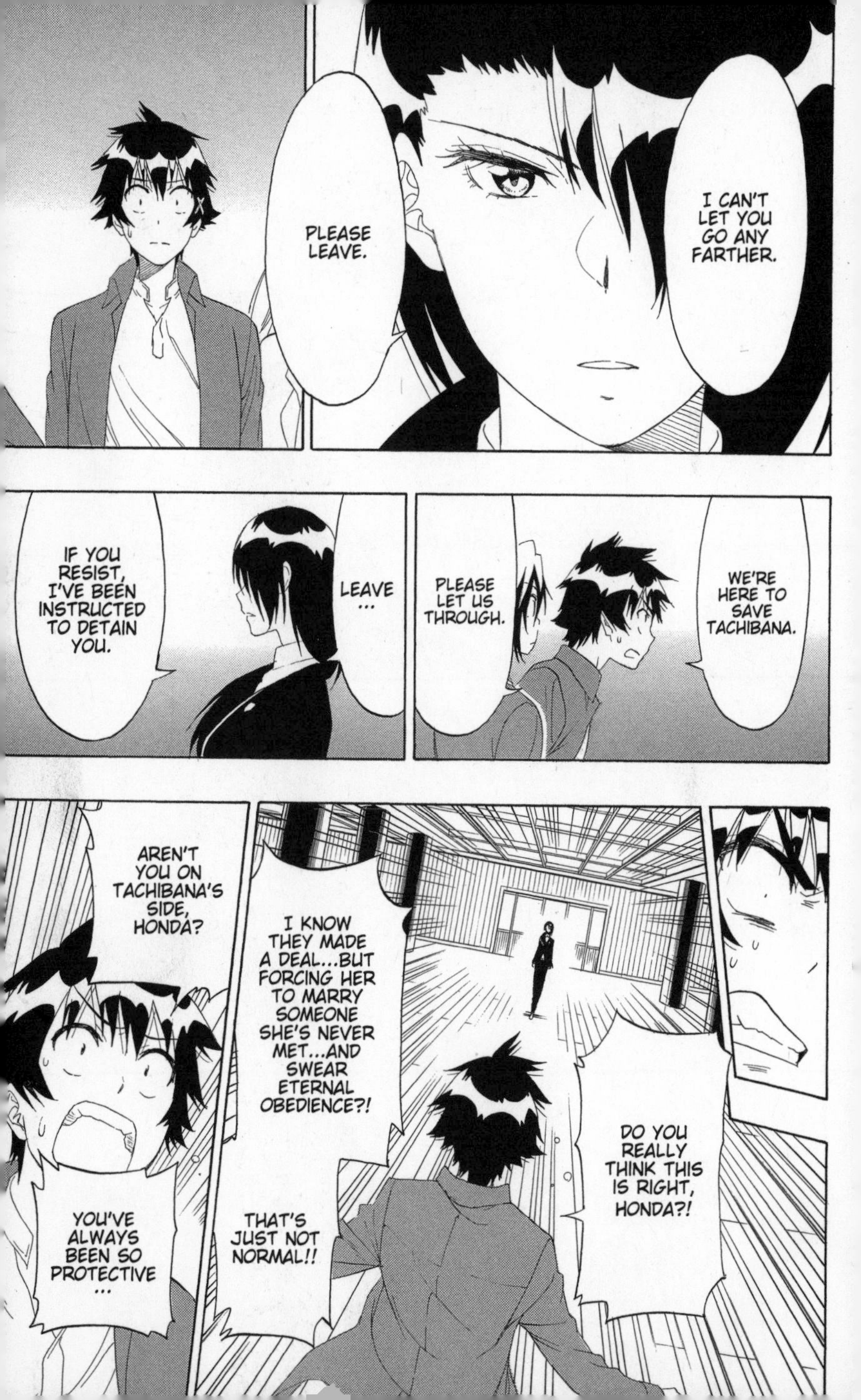
I CAN'T LET YOU GO ANY FARTHER.
PLEASE LEAVE.
WE'RE HERE TO SAVE TACHIBANA.
PLEASE LET US THROUGH.
LEAVE ...
IF YOU RESIST, I'VE BEEN INSTRUCTED TO DETAIN YOU.
I KNOW THEY MADE A DEAL...BUT FORCING HER TO MARRY SOMEONE SHE'S NEVER MET...AND SWEAR ETERNAL OBEDIENCE?!
THAT'S JUST NOT NORMAL!!
DO YOU REALLY THINK THIS IS RIGHT, HONDA?!
AREN'T YOU ON TACHIBANA'S SIDE, HONDA?
YOU'VE ALWAYS BEEN SO PROTECTIVE ...

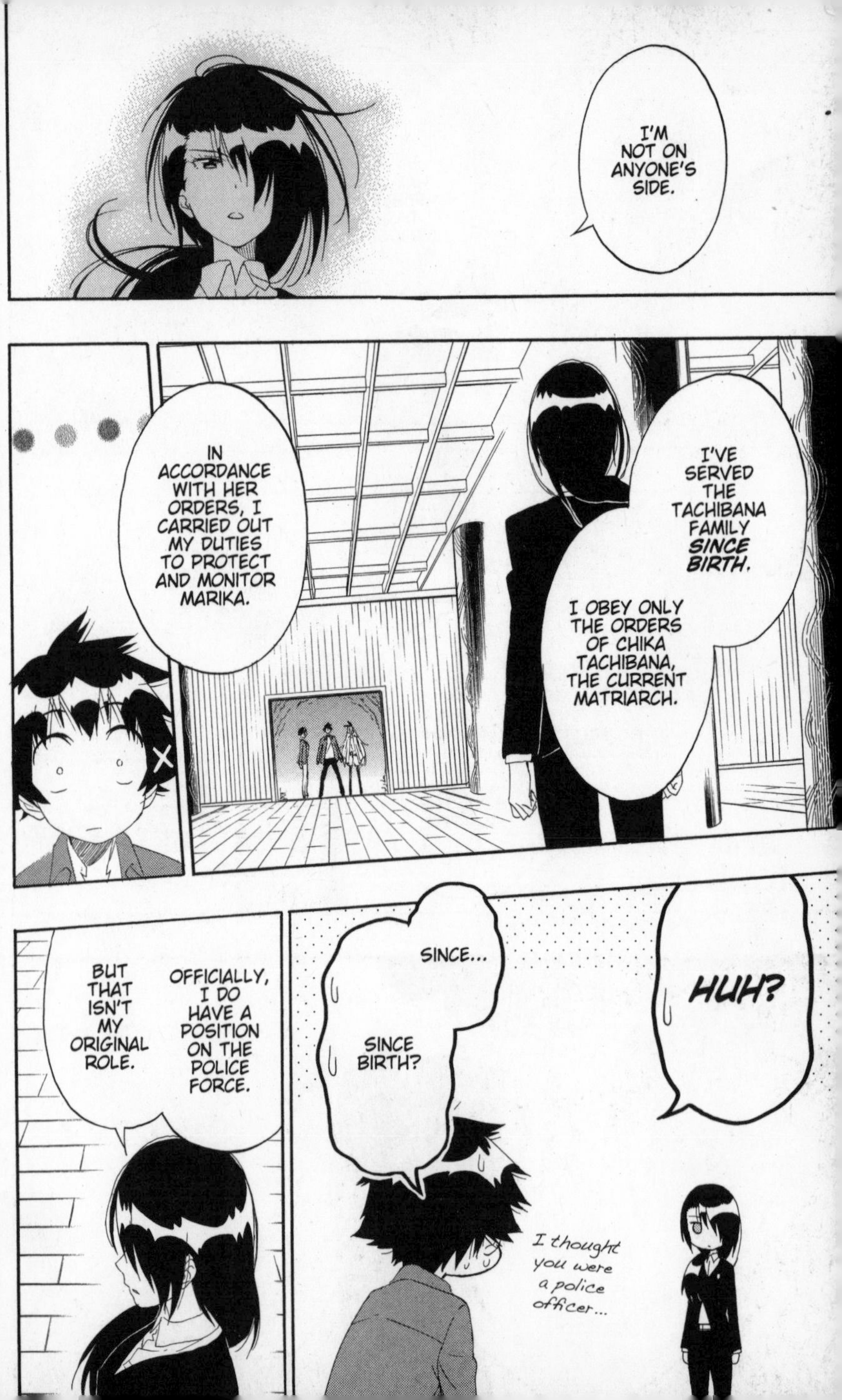
I'M NOT ON ANYONE'S SIDE.
I'VE SERVED THE TACHIBANA FAMILY *SINCE BIRTH*.
I OBEY ONLY THE ORDERS OF CHIKA TACHIBANA, THE CURRENT MATRIARCH.
IN ACCORDANCE WITH HER ORDERS, I CARRIED OUT MY DUTIES TO PROTECT AND MONITOR MARIKA.
...
HUH?
SINCE...
SINCE BIRTH?
I thought you were a police officer...
OFFICIALLY, I DO HAVE A POSITION ON THE POLICE FORCE.
BUT THAT ISN'T MY ORIGINAL ROLE.

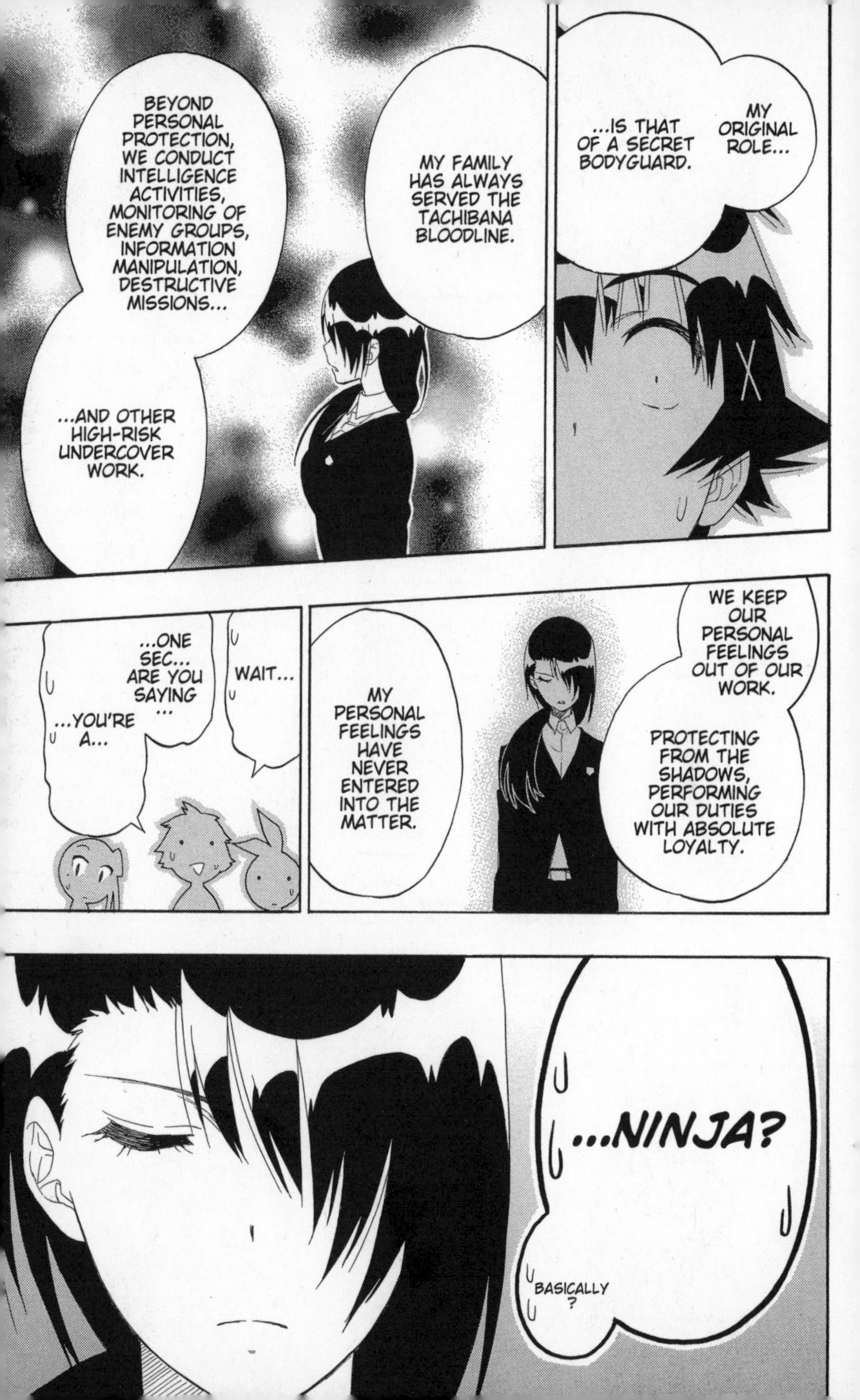
MY ORIGINAL ROLE...
...IS THAT OF A SECRET BODYGUARD.
MY FAMILY HAS ALWAYS SERVED THE TACHIBANA BLOODLINE.
BEYOND PERSONAL PROTECTION, WE CONDUCT INTELLIGENCE ACTIVITIES, MONITORING OF ENEMY GROUPS, INFORMATION MANIPULATION, DESTRUCTIVE MISSIONS...
...AND OTHER HIGH-RISK UNDERCOVER WORK.
WE KEEP OUR PERSONAL FEELINGS OUT OF OUR WORK.
PROTECTING FROM THE SHADOWS, PERFORMING OUR DUTIES WITH ABSOLUTE LOYALTY.
MY PERSONAL FEELINGS HAVE NEVER ENTERED INTO THE MATTER.
WAIT...
...ONE SEC... ARE YOU SAYING ...
...YOU'RE A...
...NINJA?
BASICALLY?

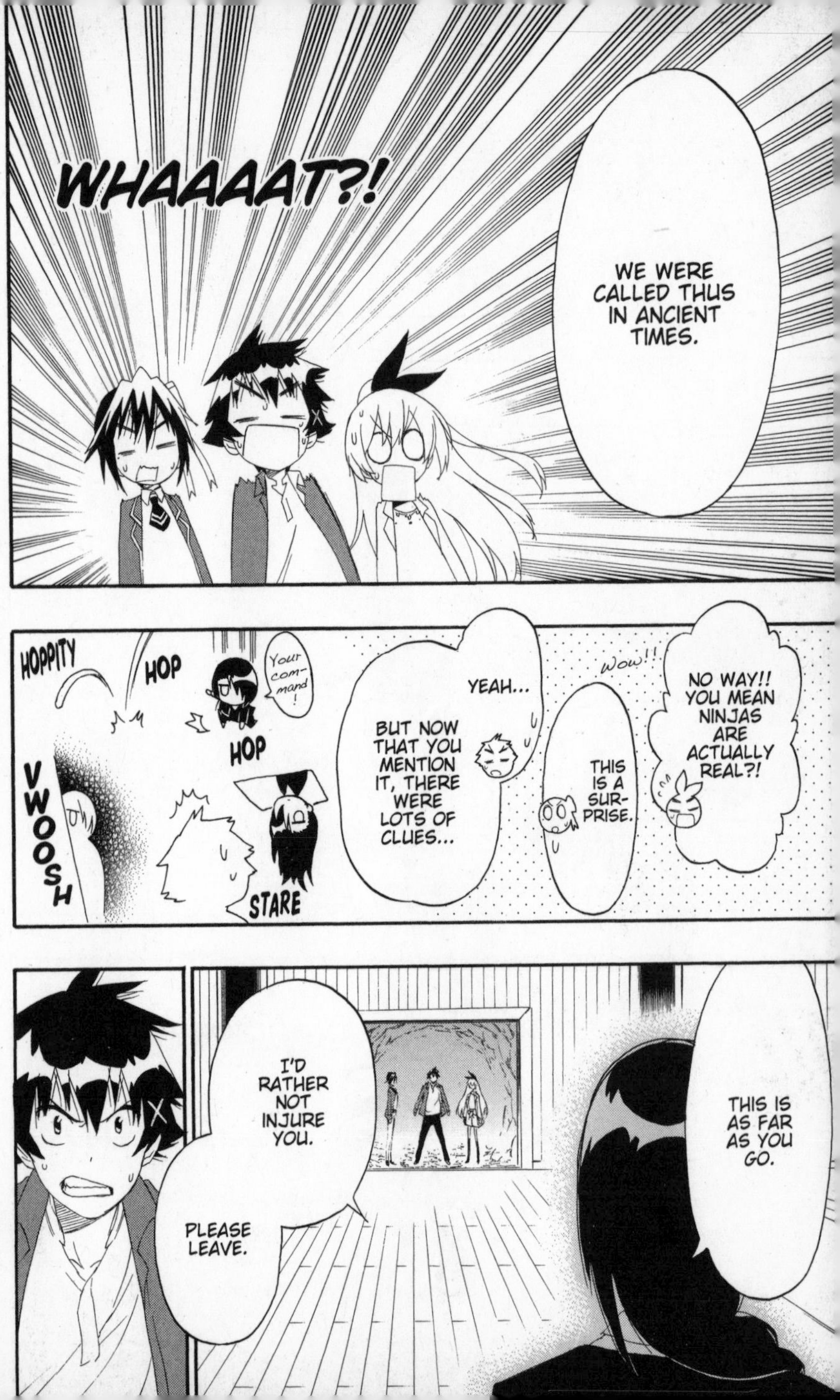
WE WERE CALLED THUS IN ANCIENT TIMES.
WHAAAAT?!
NO WAY!! YOU MEAN NINJAS ARE ACTUALLY REAL?!
Wow!!
THIS IS A SUR-PRISE.
YEAH...
BUT NOW THAT YOU MENTION IT, THERE WERE LOTS OF CLUES...
Your com-mand!
HOP
HOP
HOPPITY
STARE
VWOOSH
THIS IS AS FAR AS YOU GO.
I'D RATHER NOT INJURE YOU.
PLEASE LEAVE.

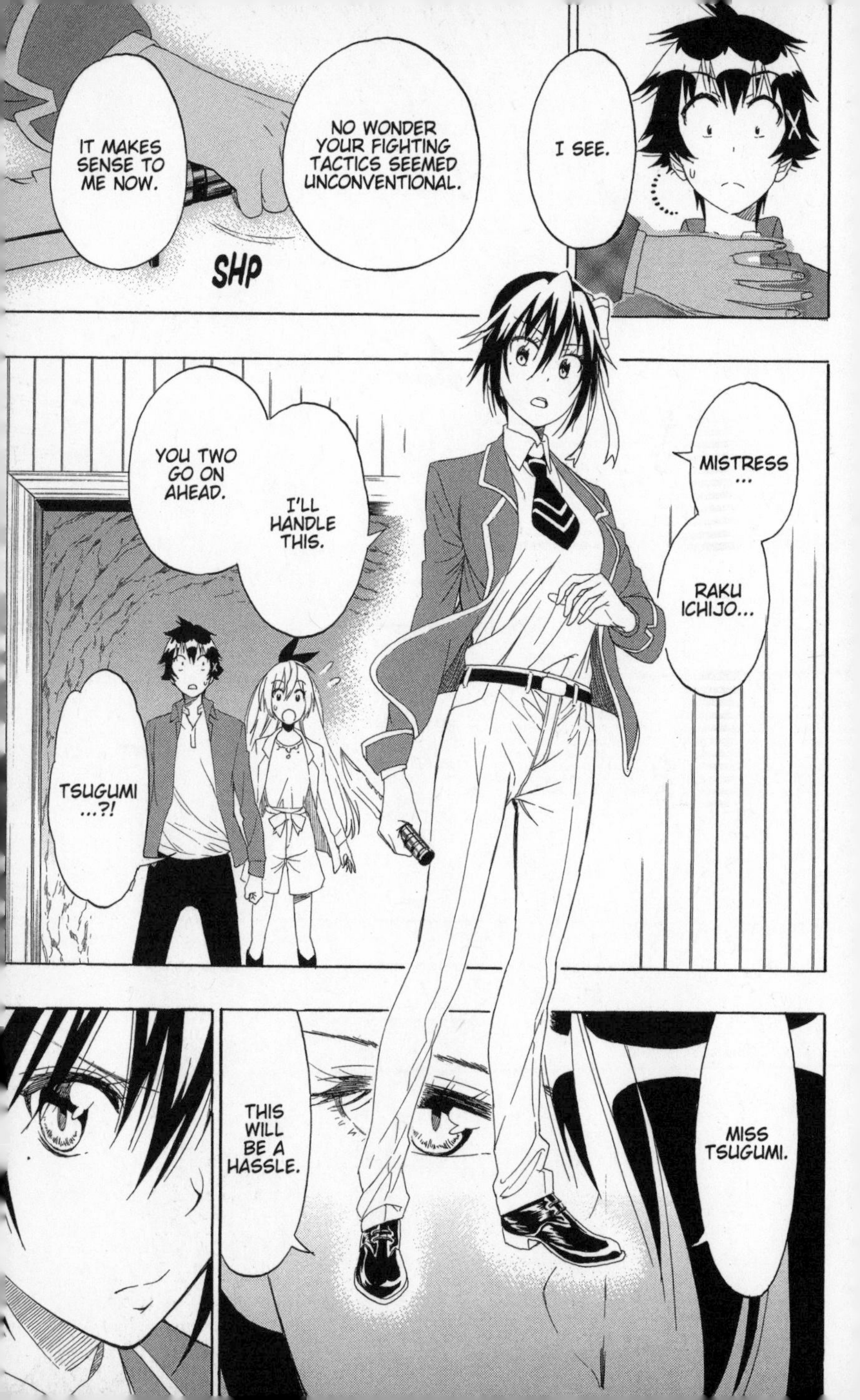
I SEE.
NO WONDER YOUR FIGHTING TACTICS SEEMED UNCONVENTIONAL.
IT MAKES SENSE TO ME NOW.
SHP
MISTRESS...
RAKU ICHIJO...
YOU TWO GO ON AHEAD.
I'LL HANDLE THIS.
TSUGUMI...?!
MISS TSUGUMI.
THIS WILL BE A HASSLE.

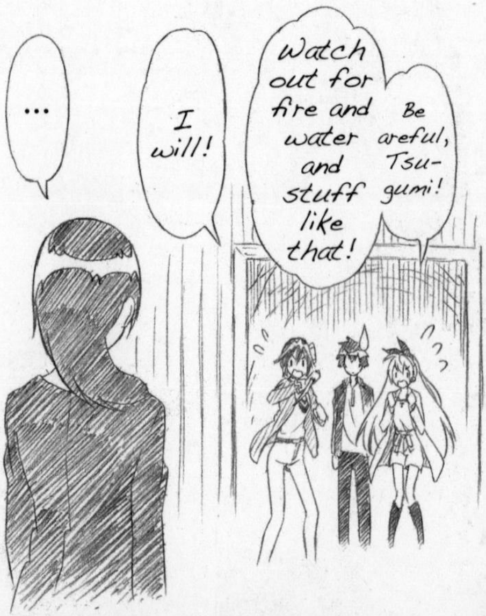
Be areful, Tsu-gumi!
Watch out for fire and water and stuff like that!
I will!
...

Chapter 185: Battle

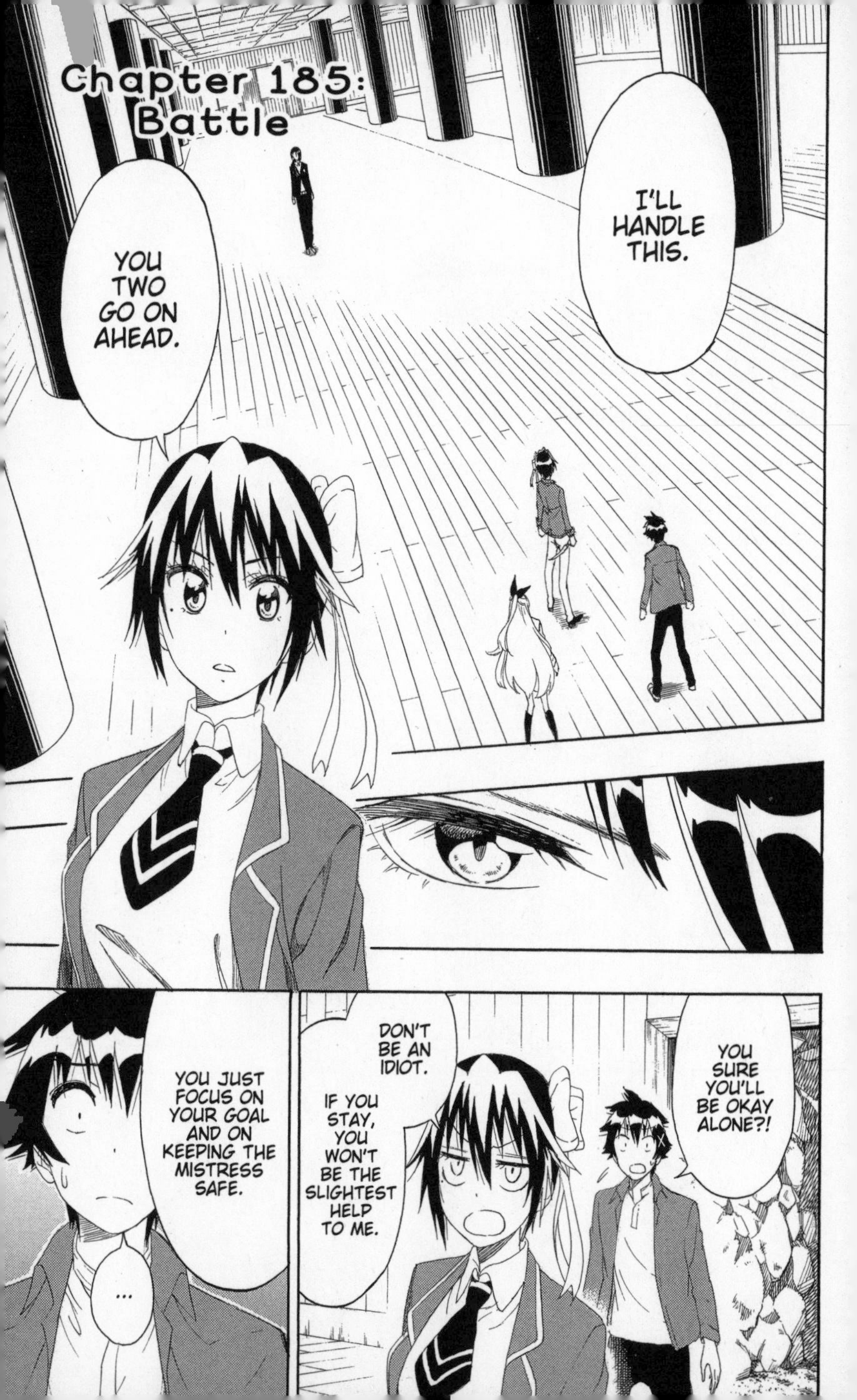
I'LL HANDLE THIS.
YOU TWO GO ON AHEAD.
YOU SURE YOU'LL BE OKAY ALONE?!
DON'T BE AN IDIOT.
IF YOU STAY, YOU WON'T BE THE SLIGHTEST HELP TO ME.
YOU JUST FOCUS ON YOUR GOAL AND ON KEEPING THE MISTRESS SAFE.
...

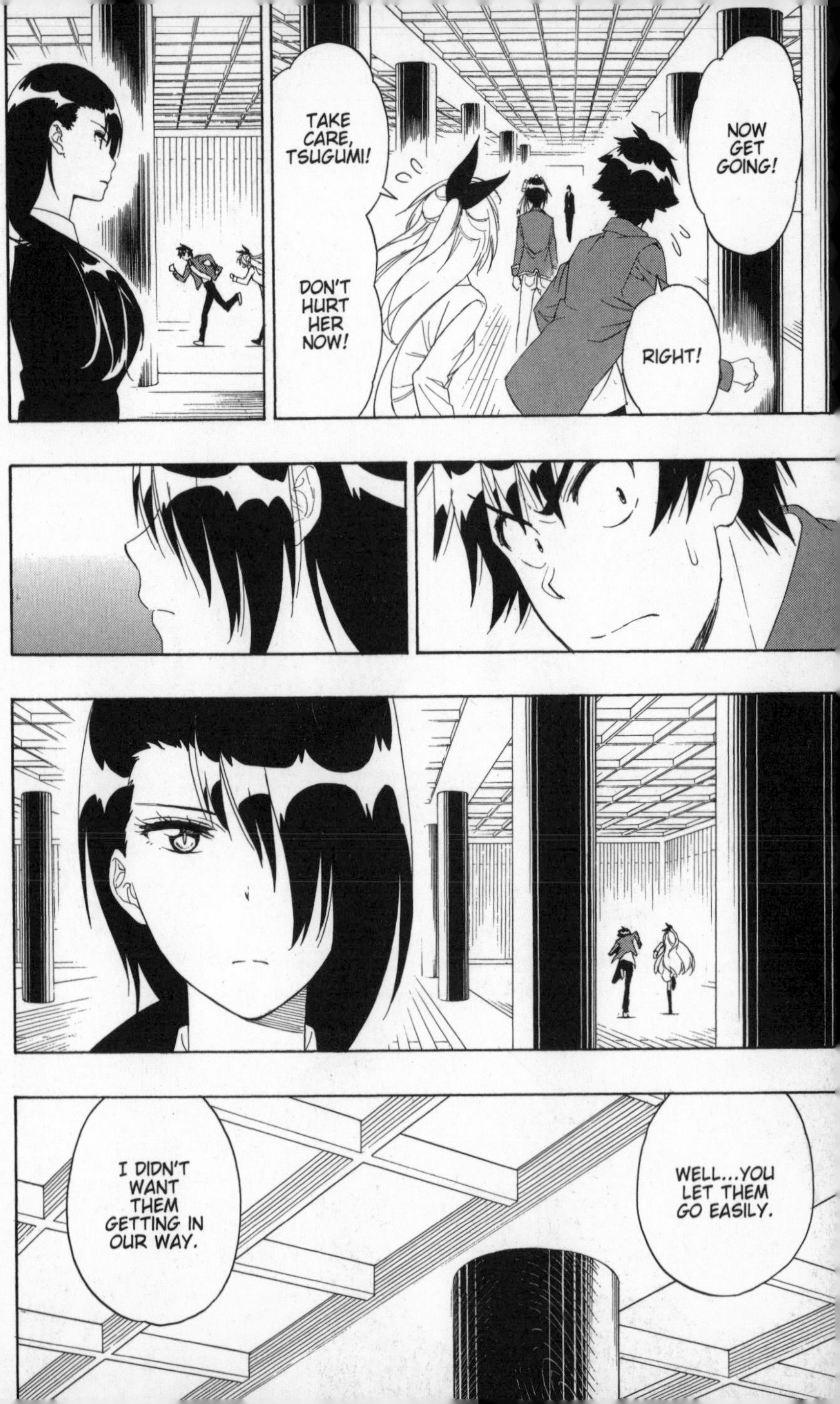
NOW GET GOING!
RIGHT!
TAKE CARE, TSUGUMI!
DON'T HURT HER NOW!
WELL...YOU LET THEM GO EASILY.
I DIDN'T WANT THEM GETTING IN OUR WAY.

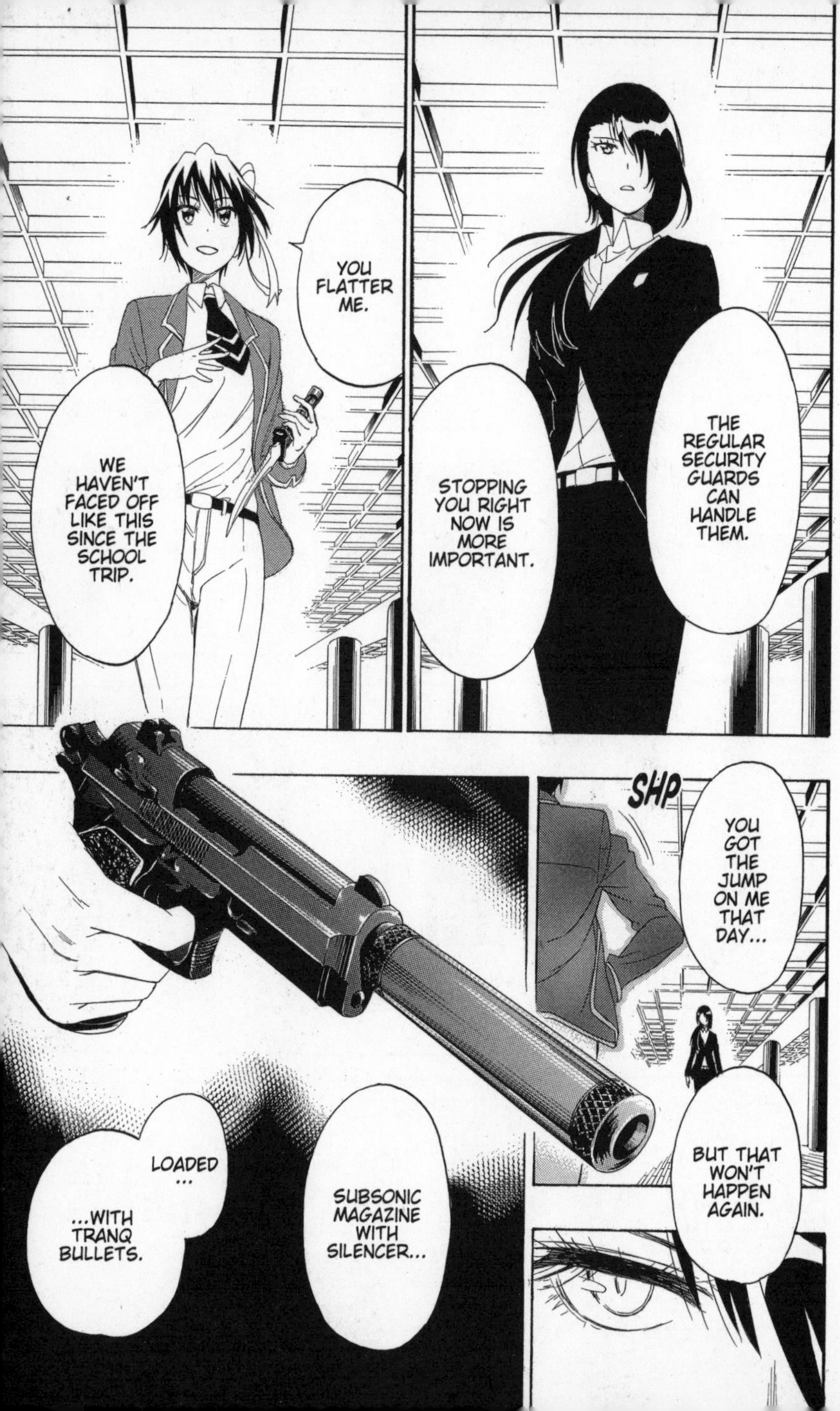
THE REGULAR SECURITY GUARDS CAN HANDLE THEM.
STOPPING YOU RIGHT NOW IS MORE IMPORTANT.
YOU FLATTER ME.
WE HAVEN'T FACED OFF LIKE THIS SINCE THE SCHOOL TRIP.
SHP
YOU GOT THE JUMP ON ME THAT DAY...
BUT THAT WON'T HAPPEN AGAIN.
SUBSONIC MAGAZINE WITH SILENCER...
LOADED ...
...WITH TRANQ BULLETS.

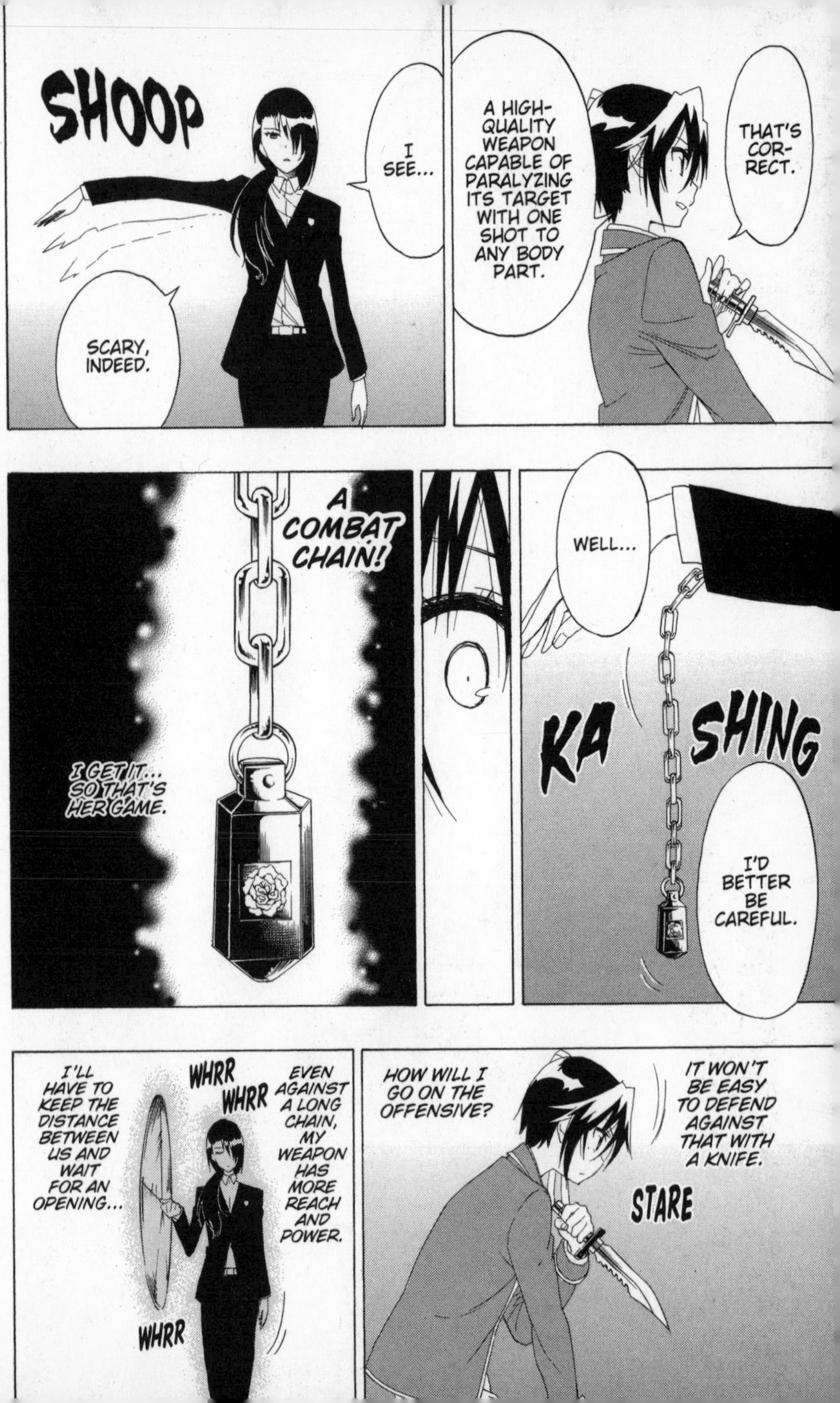
THAT'S COR-RECT.
A HIGH-QUALITY WEAPON CAPABLE OF PARALYZING ITS TARGET WITH ONE SHOT TO ANY BODY PART.
I SEE...
SHOOP
SCARY, INDEED.
WELL...
KA SHING
I'D BETTER BE CAREFUL.
A COMBAT CHAIN!
I GET IT... SO THAT'S HER GAME.
IT WON'T BE EASY TO DEFEND AGAINST THAT WITH A KNIFE.
HOW WILL I GO ON THE OFFENSIVE?
STARE
EVEN AGAINST A LONG CHAIN, MY WEAPON HAS MORE REACH AND POWER.
WHRR
WHRR
I'LL HAVE TO KEEP THE DISTANCE BETWEEN US AND WAIT FOR AN OPENING...
WHRR

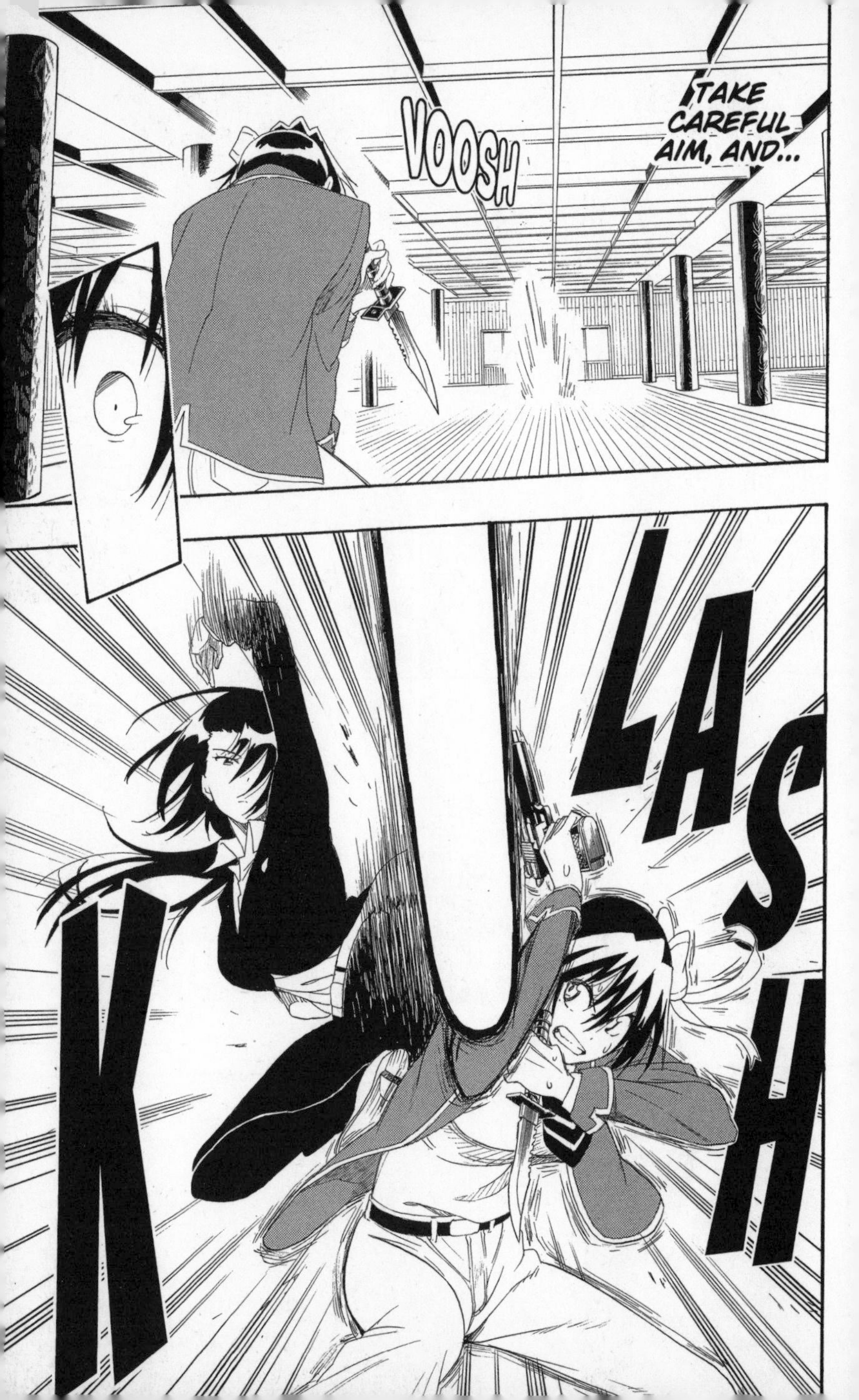
TAKE CAREFUL AIM, AND...
VOOSH
KLASH

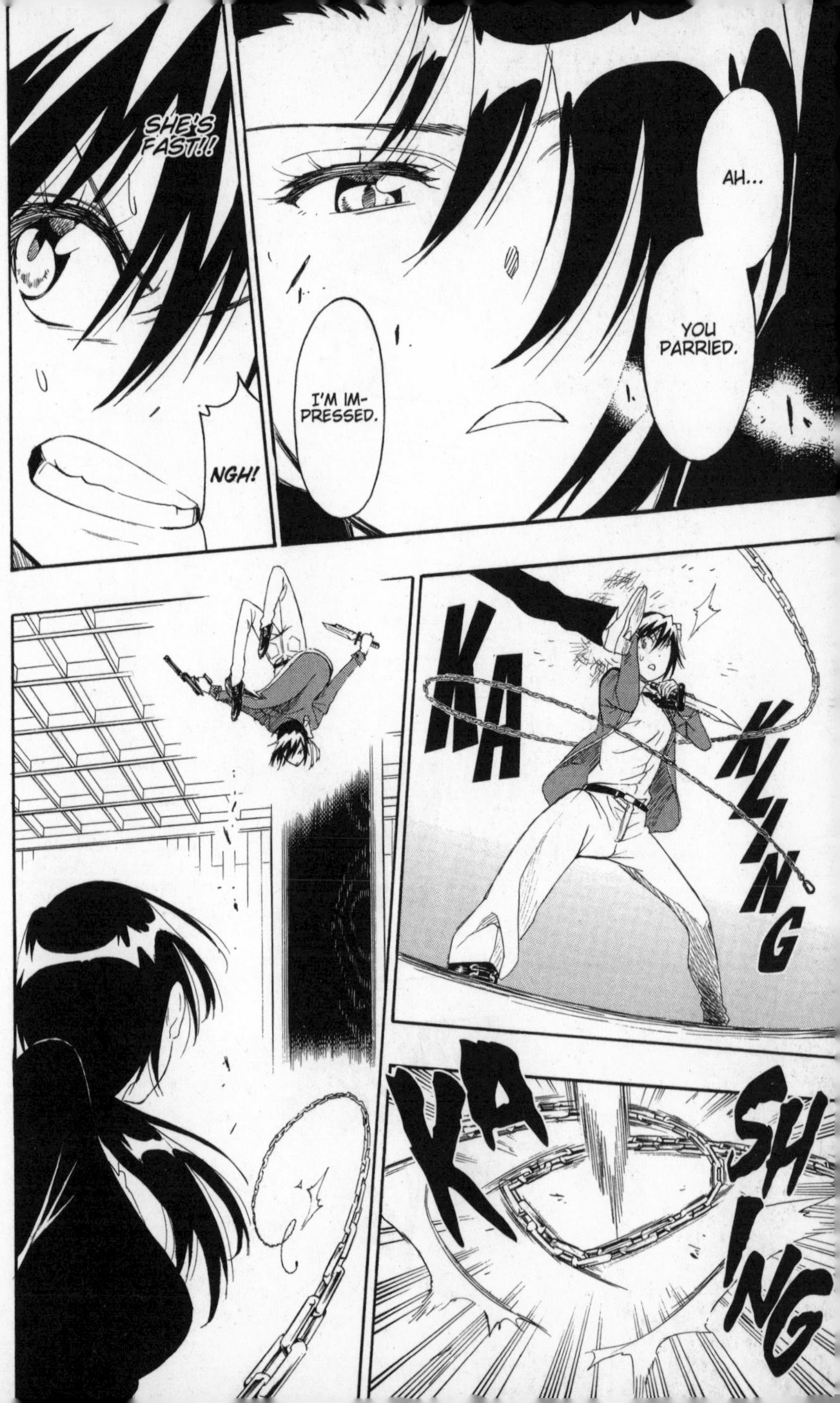
AH...
YOU PARRIED.
I'M IM-PRESSED.
SHE'S FAST!!
NGH!
KA
KLING
KA
SHING

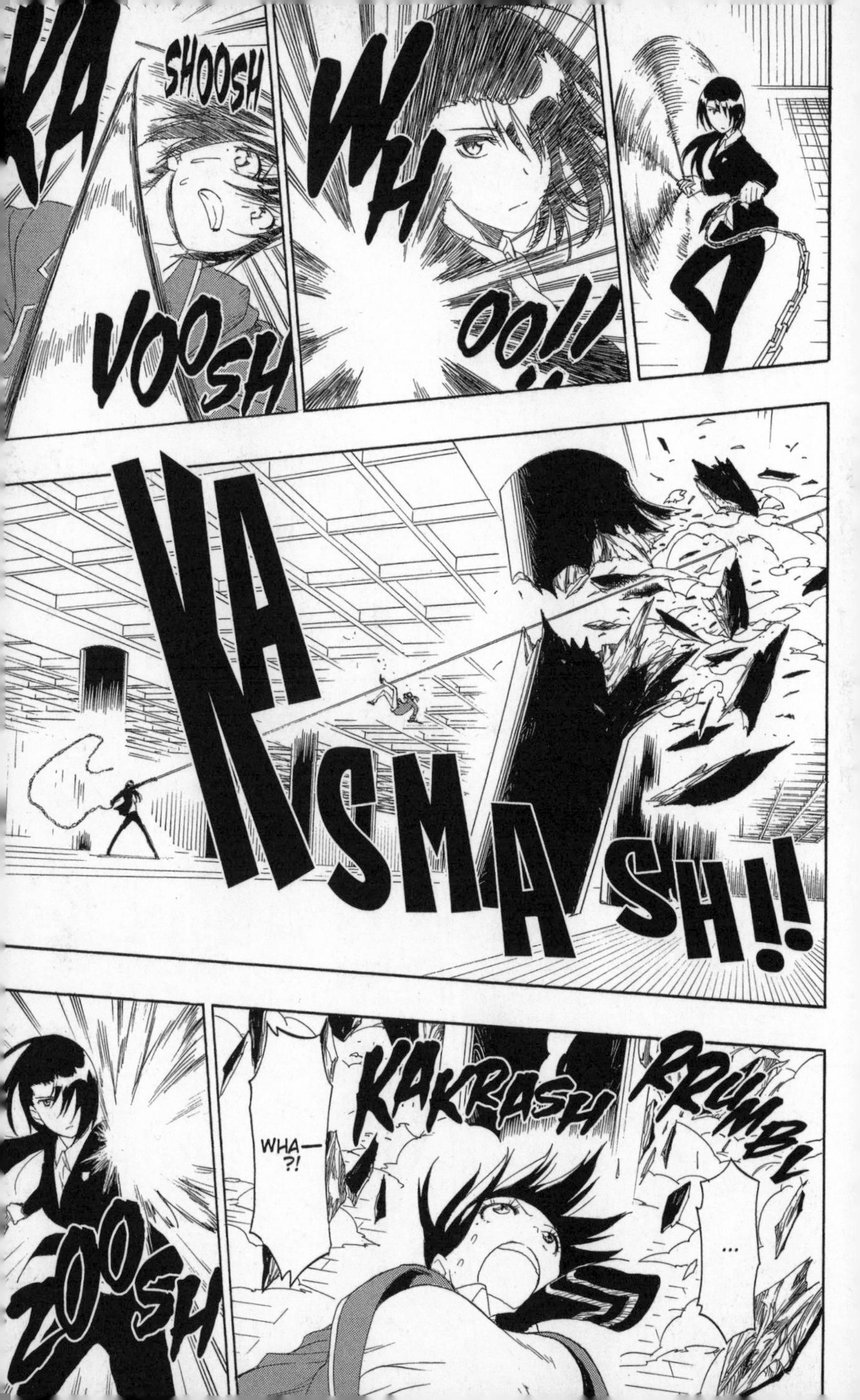
WH
OO!!
SHOOSH
KA
VOOSH
KA
SMASH!!
RRUMBL
KAKRASH
WHA— ?!
...
ZOOSH

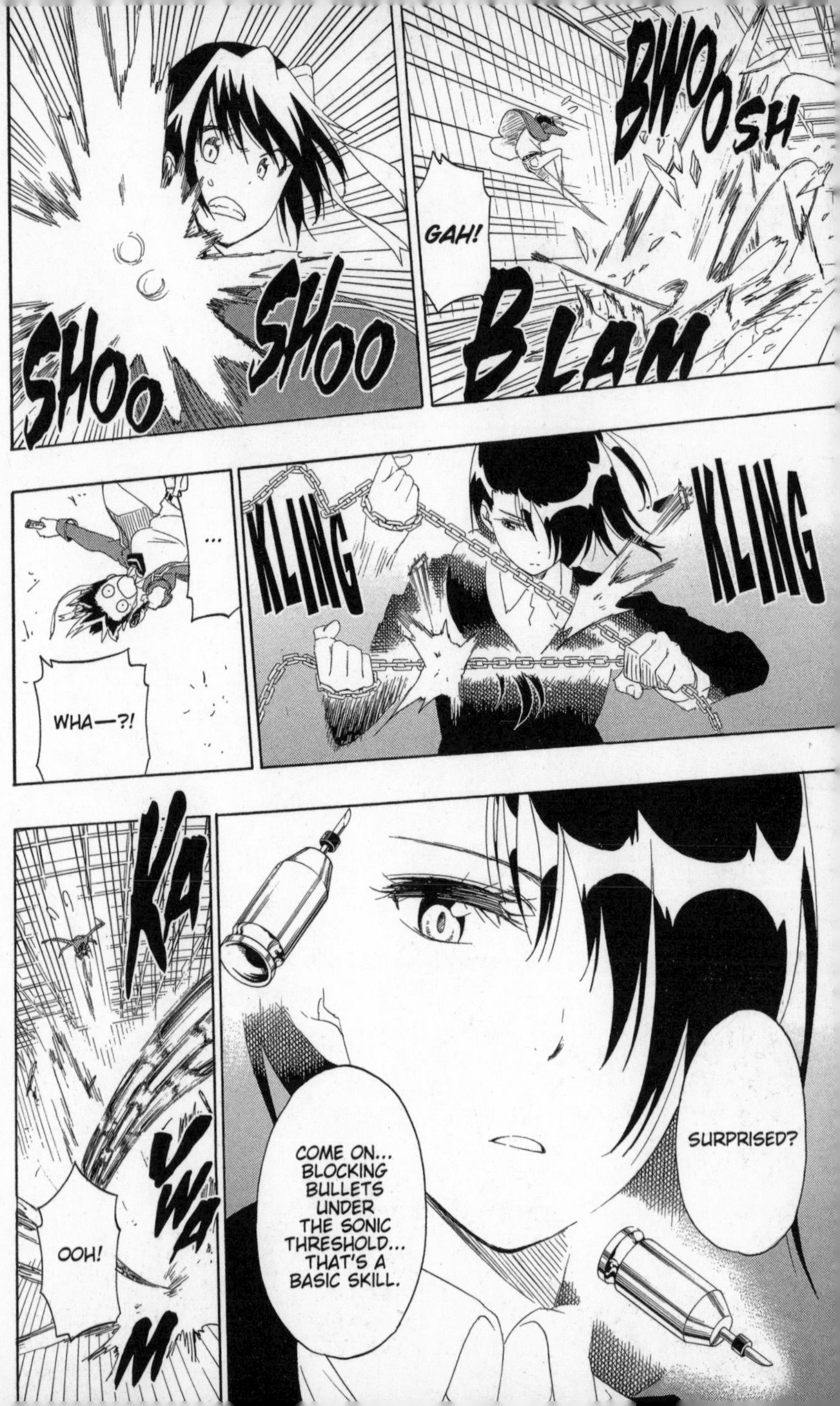
BWOOSH
GAH!
BLAM
SHOO
SHOO
KLING
KLING
...
WHA—?!
SURPRISED?
COME ON... BLOCKING BULLETS UNDER THE SONIC THRESHOLD... THAT'S A BASIC SKILL.
KA
JWAM
OOH!

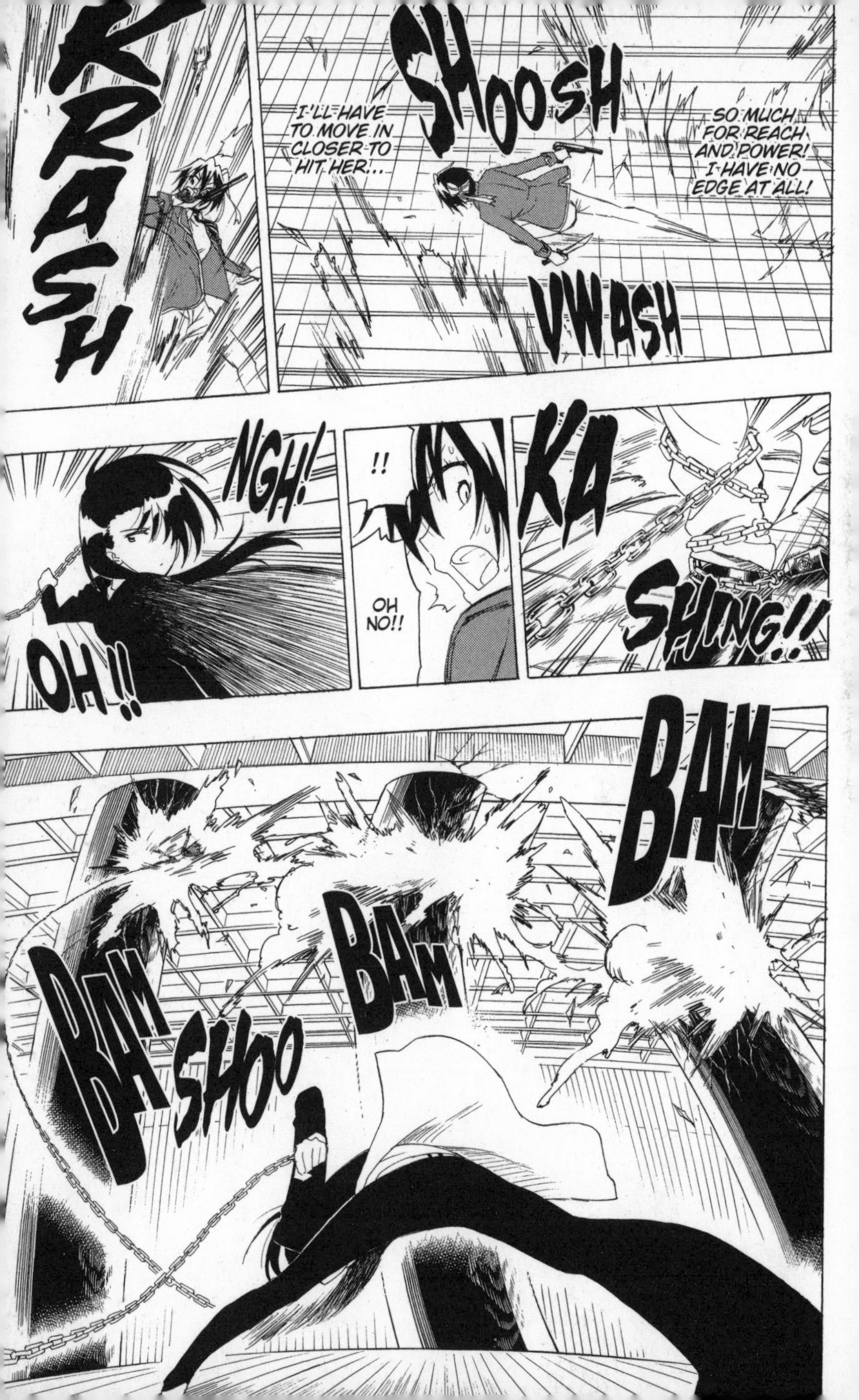
SO MUCH FOR REACH AND POWER! I HAVE NO EDGE AT ALL!
SHOOSH
I'LL HAVE TO MOVE IN CLOSER TO HIT HER...
UWASH
KRASH
KA
SHING!!
!!
OH NO!!
NGH!
OH!!
BAM
BAM
BAM
BASHOO

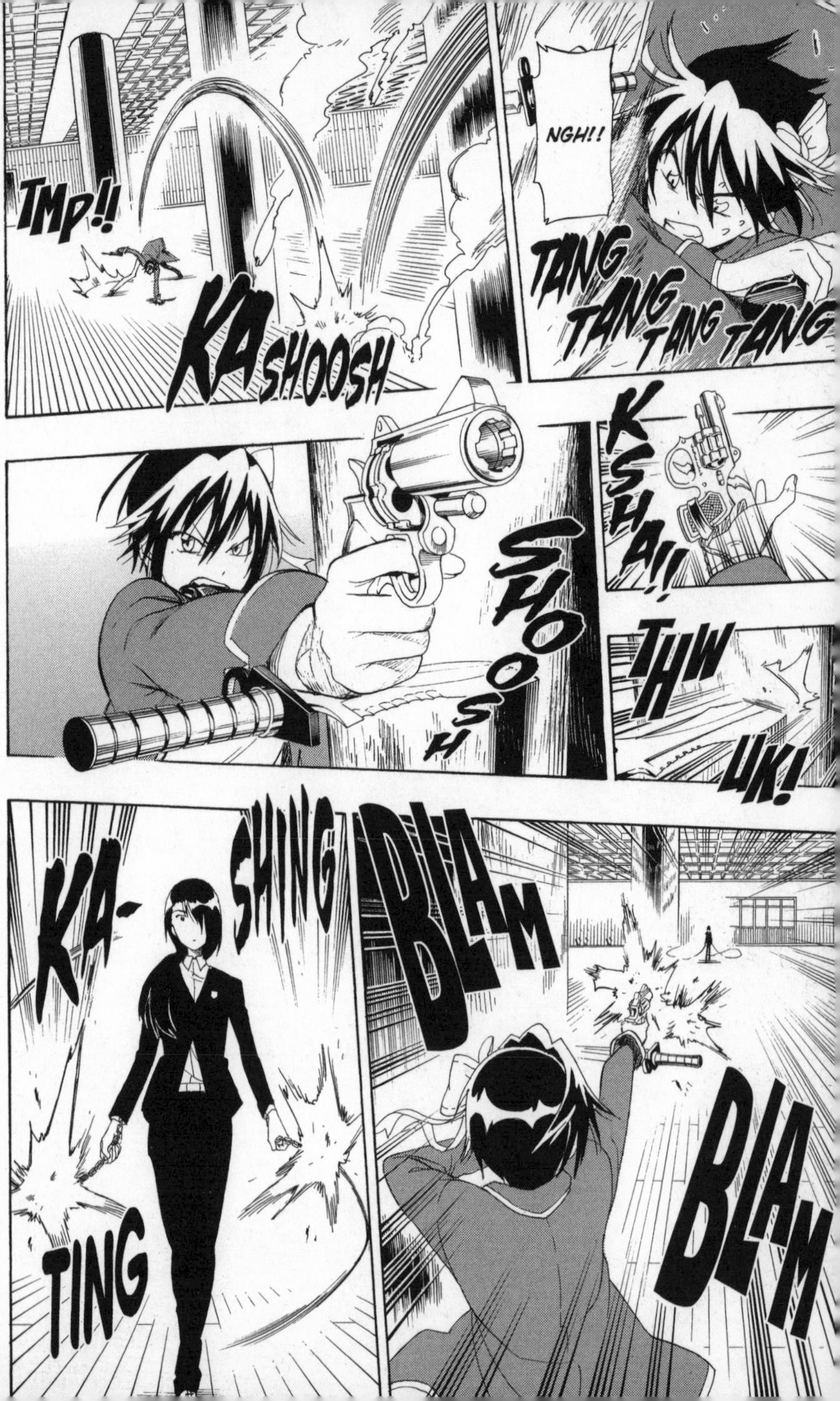
NGH!!
TANG TANG TANG TANG
TMP!!
KASHOOSH
KSHA!!
THWUK!
SHOOOSH
BLAM
BLAM
KA-SHING
TING

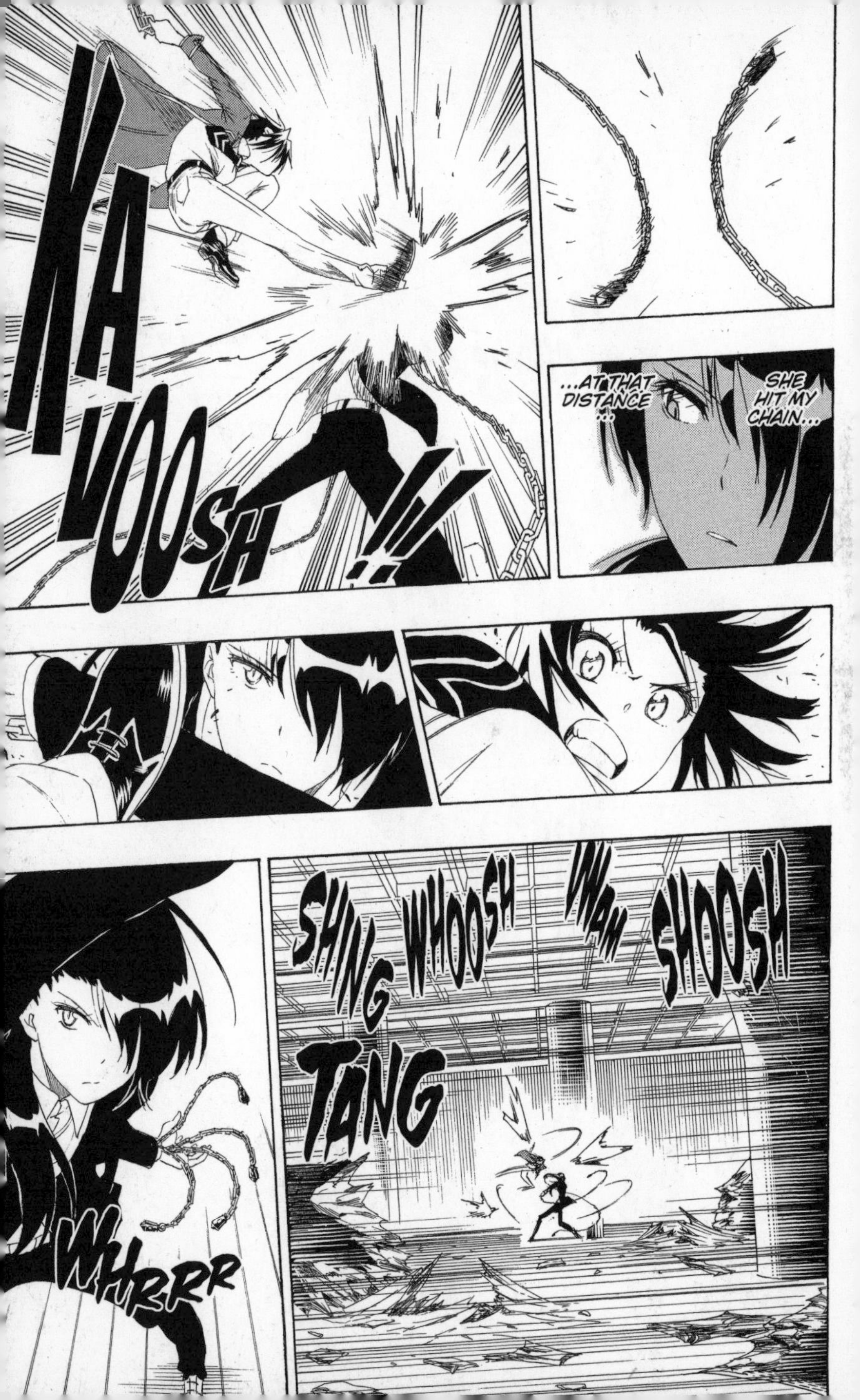
SHE HIT MY CHAIN...
...AT THAT DISTANCE...
VA VOOSH!!
SHOOSH
WHAM
WHOOSH
SHING
TANG
WHRRR

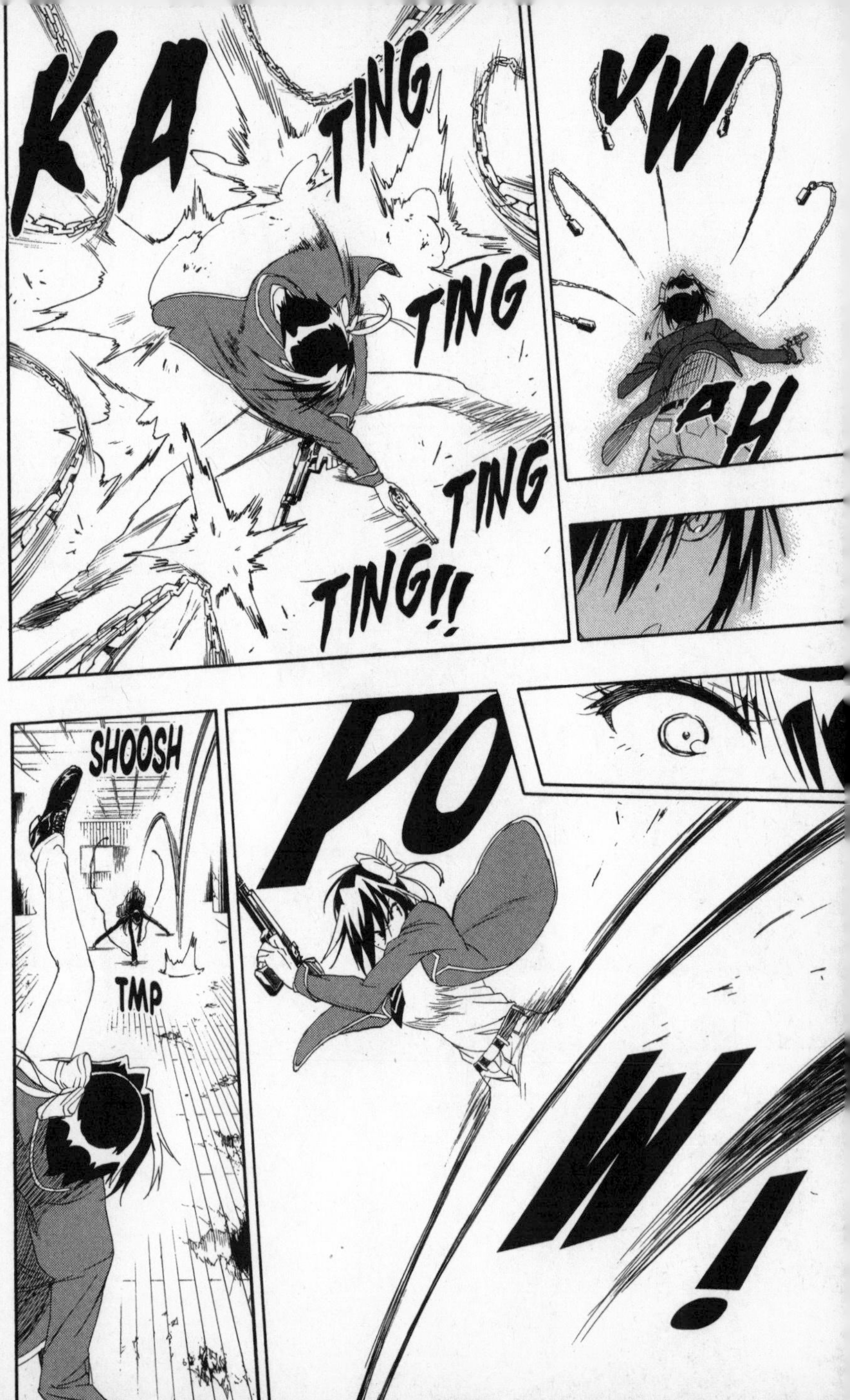
VW
AH
KA
TING
TING
TING
TING!!
PO
W!
SHOOSH
TMP

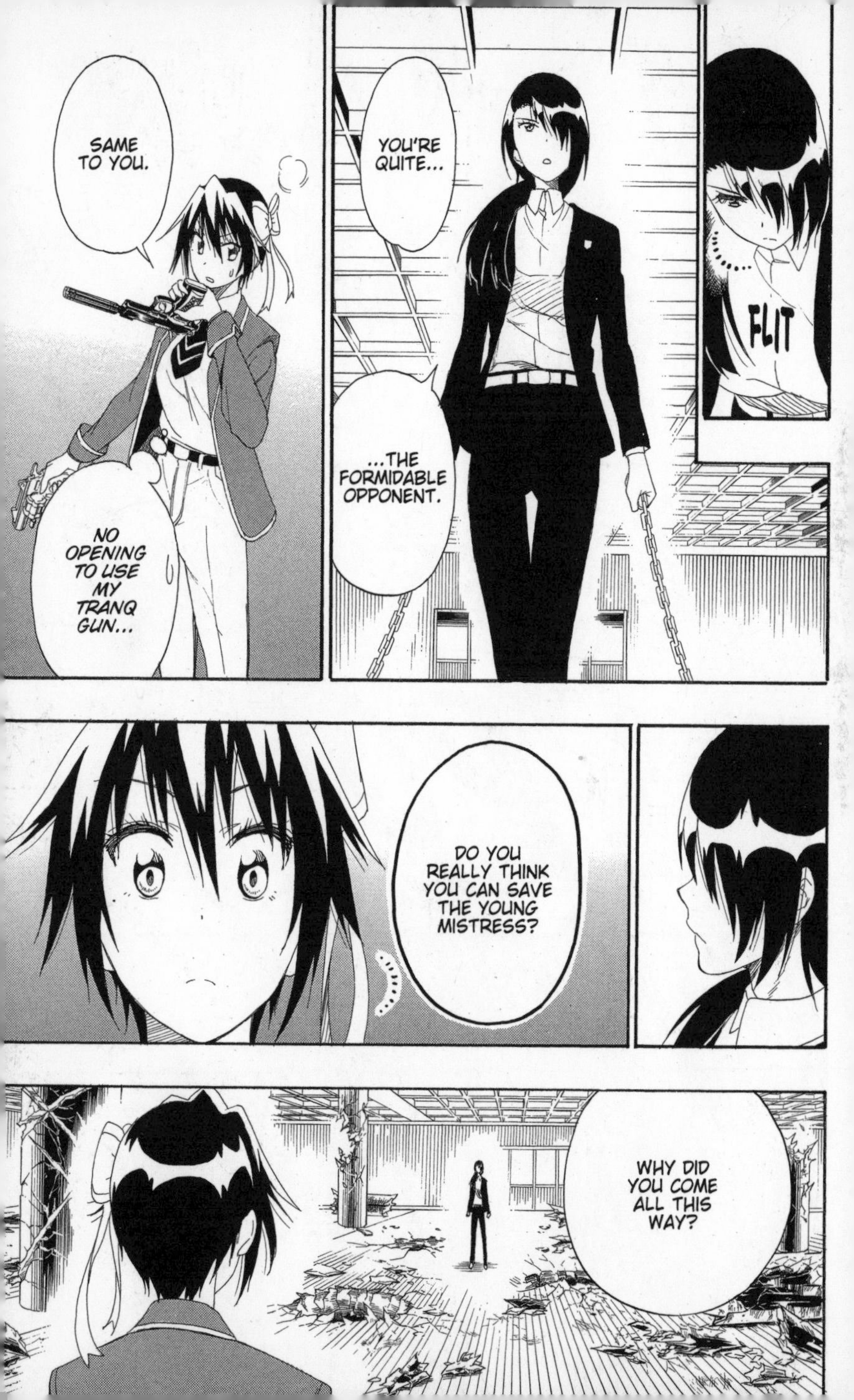
......
FLIT
YOU'RE QUITE...
...THE FORMIDABLE OPPONENT.
SAME TO YOU.
NO OPENING TO USE MY TRANQ GUN...
DO YOU REALLY THINK YOU CAN SAVE THE YOUNG MISTRESS?
......
WHY DID YOU COME ALL THIS WAY?

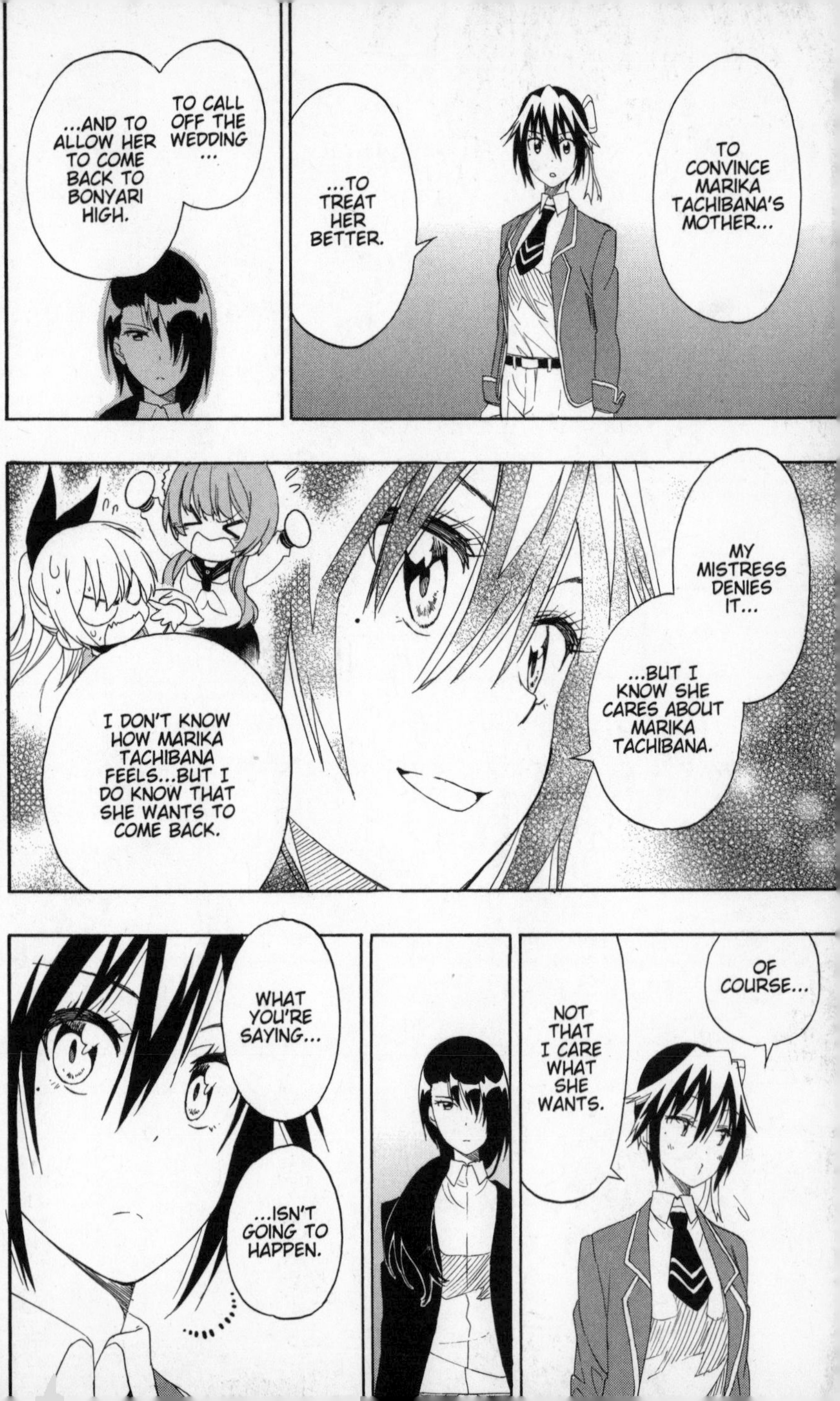
TO CONVINCE MARIKA TACHIBANA'S MOTHER...
...TO TREAT HER BETTER.
TO CALL OFF THE WEDDING...
...AND TO ALLOW HER TO COME BACK TO BONYARI HIGH.
MY MISTRESS DENIES IT...
...BUT I KNOW SHE CARES ABOUT MARIKA TACHIBANA.
I DON'T KNOW HOW MARIKA TACHIBANA FEELS...BUT I DO KNOW THAT SHE WANTS TO COME BACK.
OF COURSE...
NOT THAT I CARE WHAT SHE WANTS.
WHAT YOU'RE SAYING...
...ISN'T GOING TO HAPPEN.
......

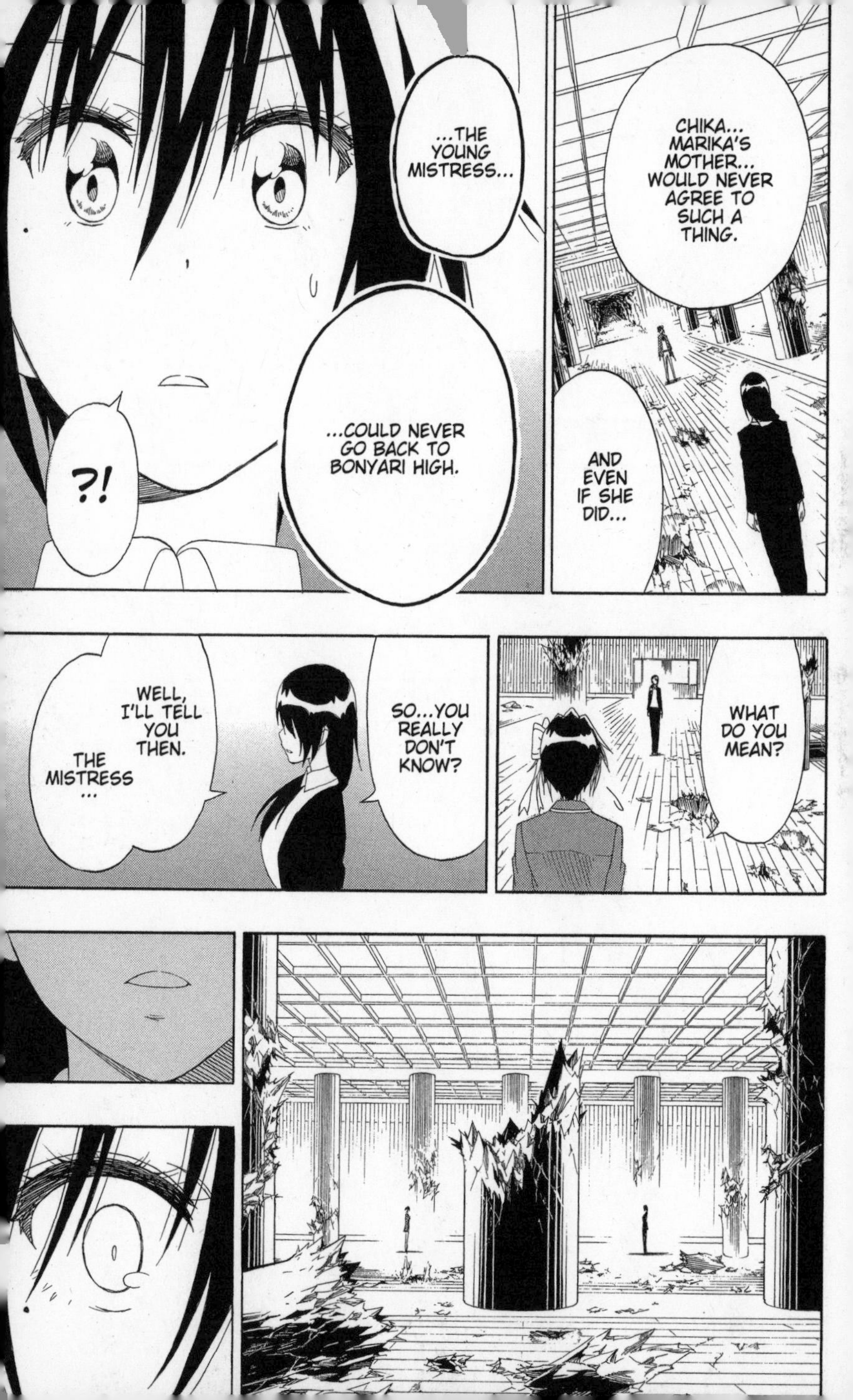
CHIKA... MARIKA'S MOTHER... WOULD NEVER AGREE TO SUCH A THING.
AND EVEN IF SHE DID...
...THE YOUNG MISTRESS...
...COULD NEVER GO BACK TO BONYARI HIGH.
?!
WHAT DO YOU MEAN?
SO...YOU REALLY DON'T KNOW?
WELL, I'LL TELL YOU THEN.
THE MISTRESS...

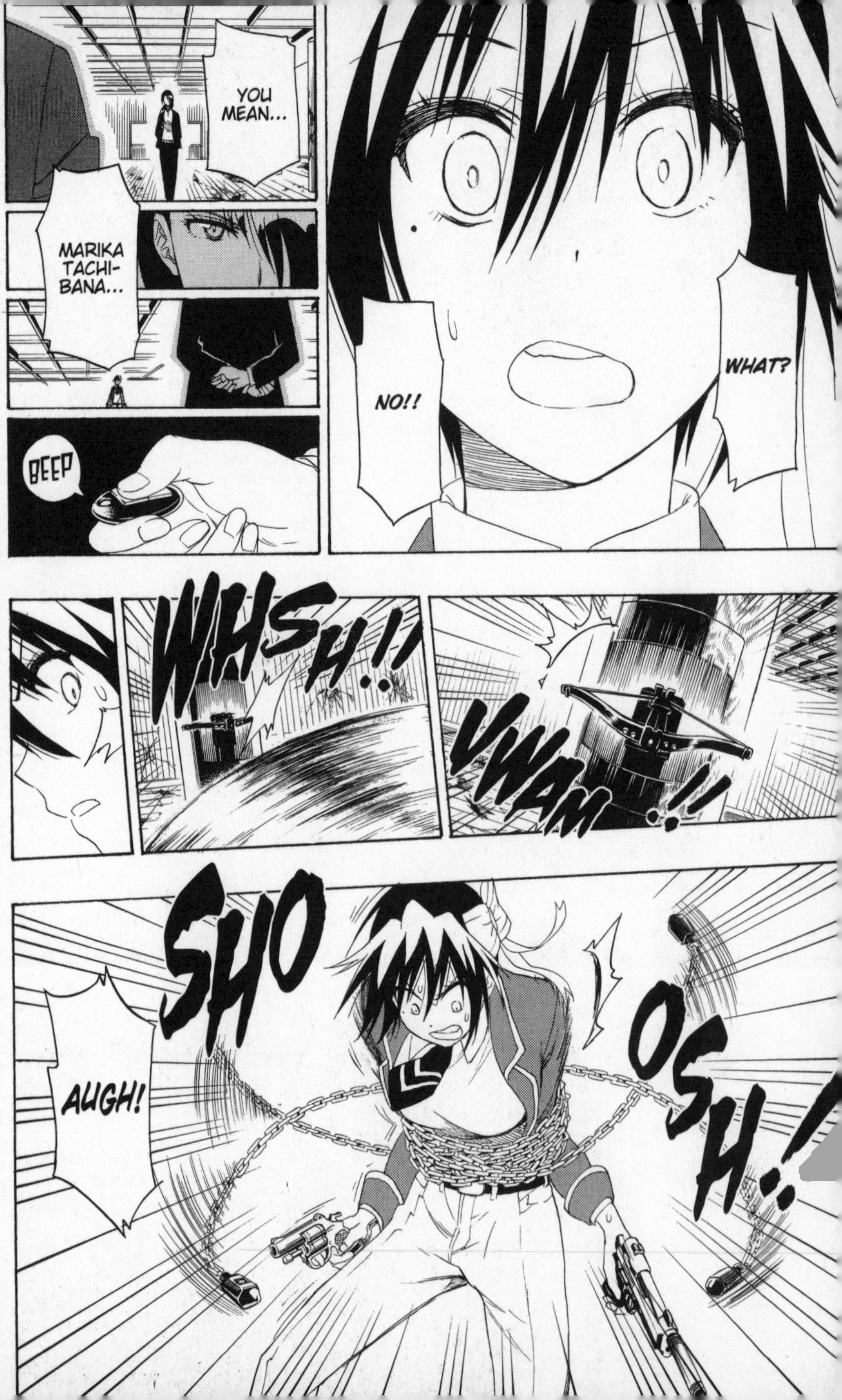
WHAT?
NO!!
YOU MEAN...
MARIKA TACHIBANA...
BEEP
VWAM!!
WHSH!!
SHO OSH!!
AUGH!

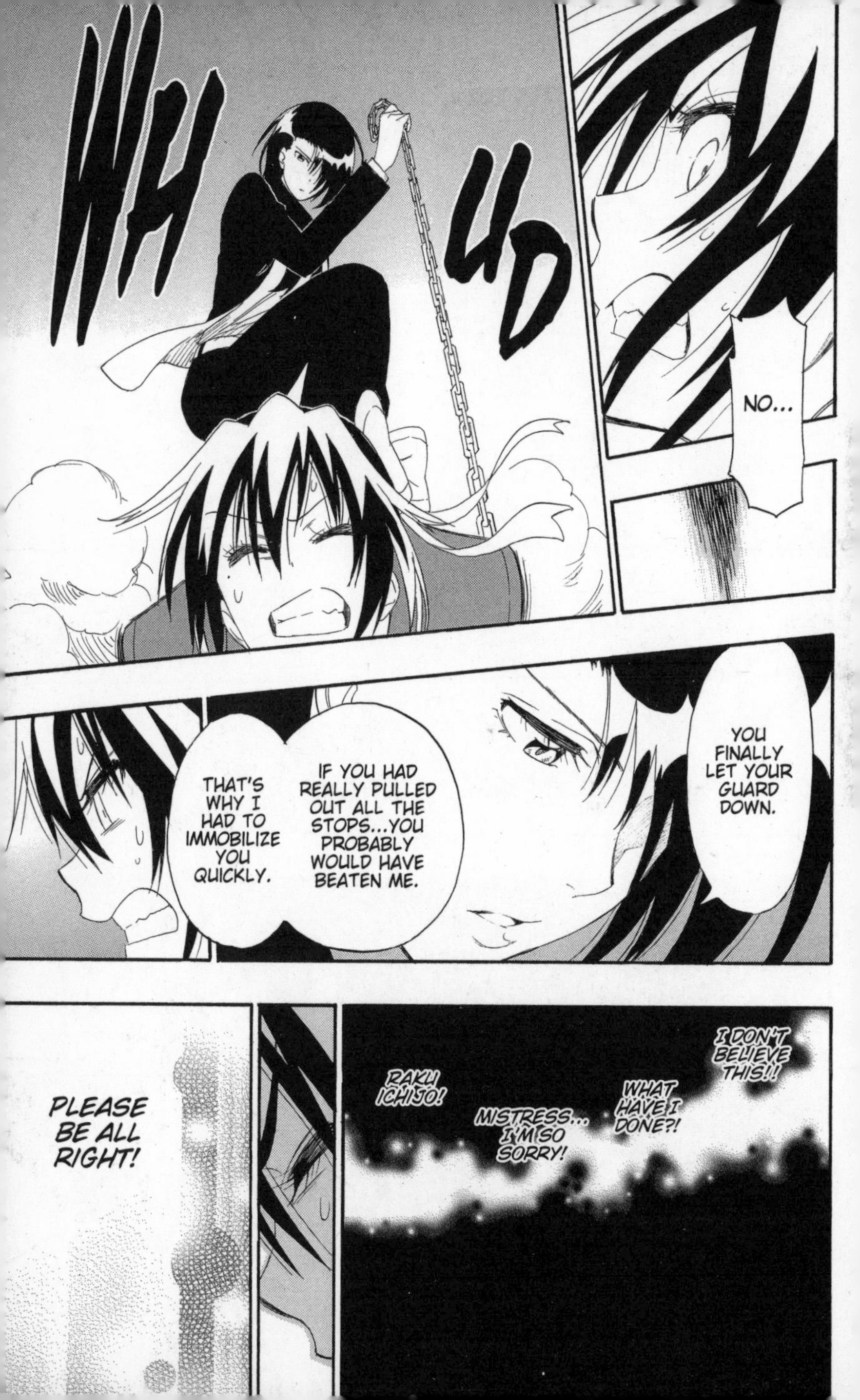
NO...
WHUD
YOU FINALLY LET YOUR GUARD DOWN.
IF YOU HAD REALLY PULLED OUT ALL THE STOPS...YOU PROBABLY WOULD HAVE BEATEN ME.
THAT'S WHY I HAD TO IMMOBILIZE YOU QUICKLY.
I DON'T BELIEVE THIS!!
WHAT HAVE I DONE?!
MISTRESS... I'M SO SORRY!
RAKU ICHIJO!
PLEASE BE ALL RIGHT!

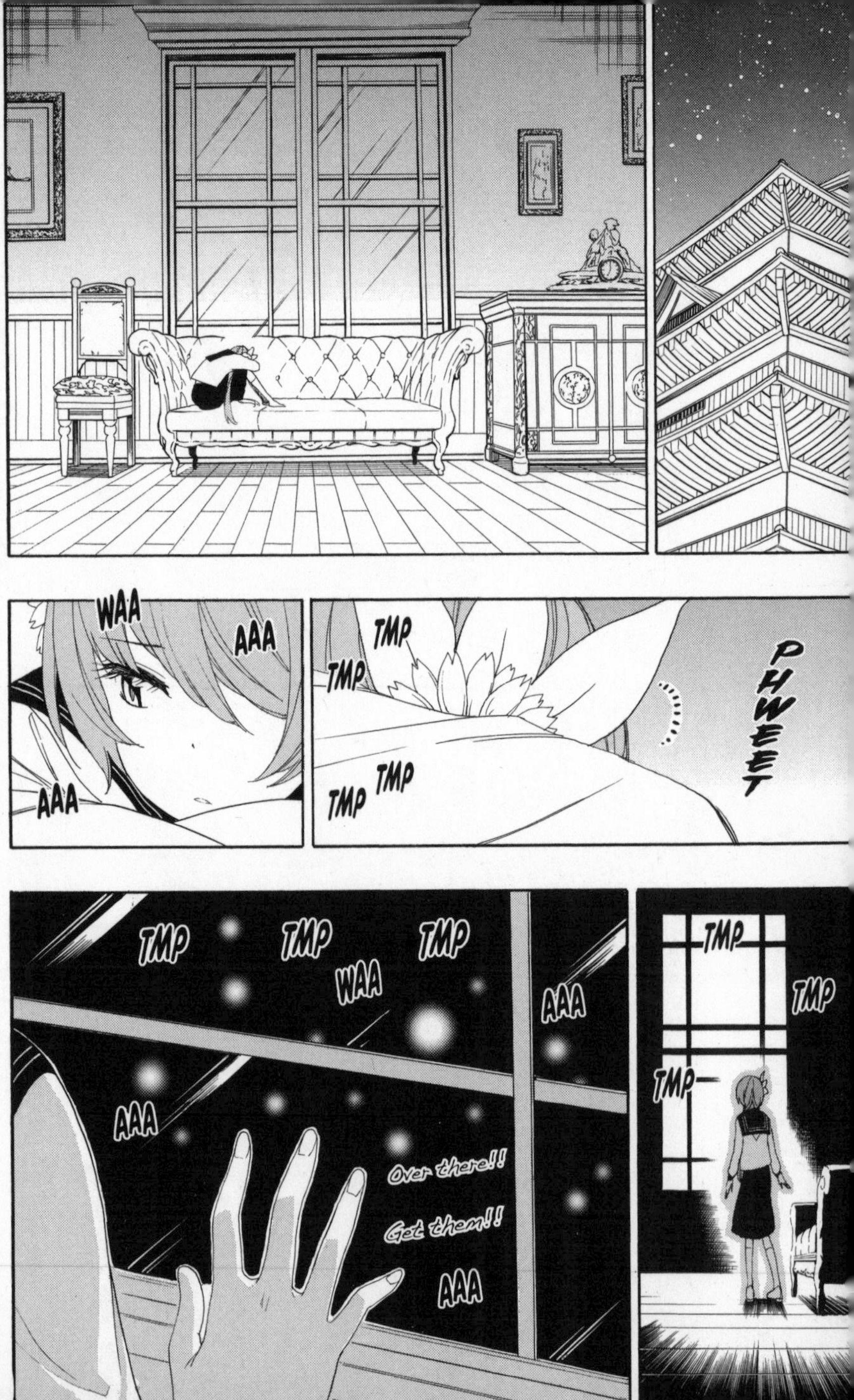
PHWEET
TMP
TMP
TMP
TMP
AAA
WAA
AAA
TMP
TMP
TMP
TMP
TMP
AAA
TMP
WAA
AAA
Over there!!
Get them!!
AAA

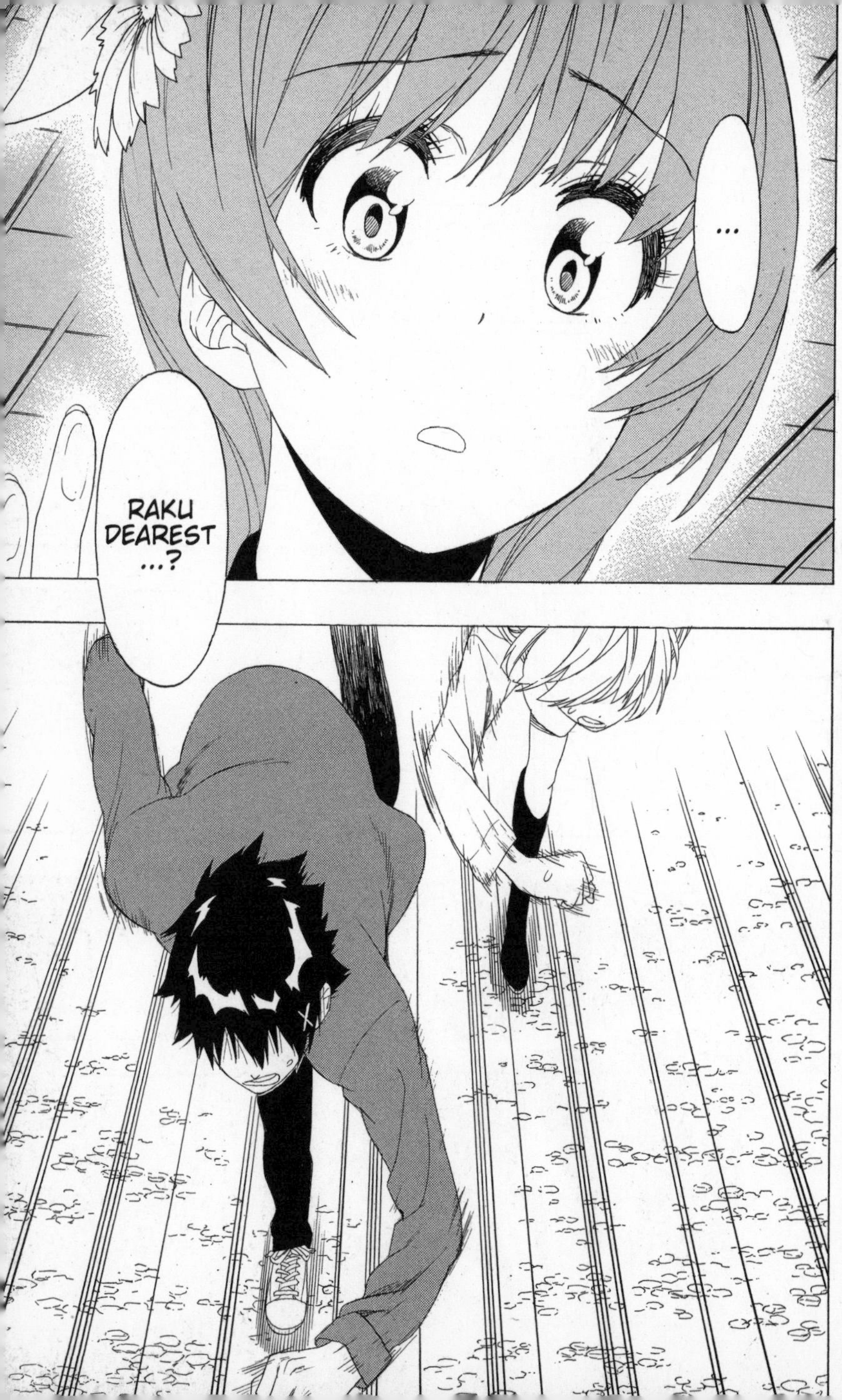
...
RAKU DEAREST ...?

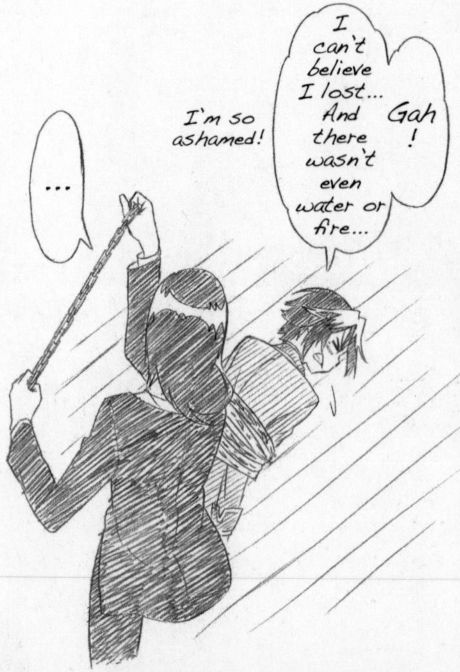
I can't believe I lost... And there wasn't even water or fire...
Gah!
I'm so ashamed!
...

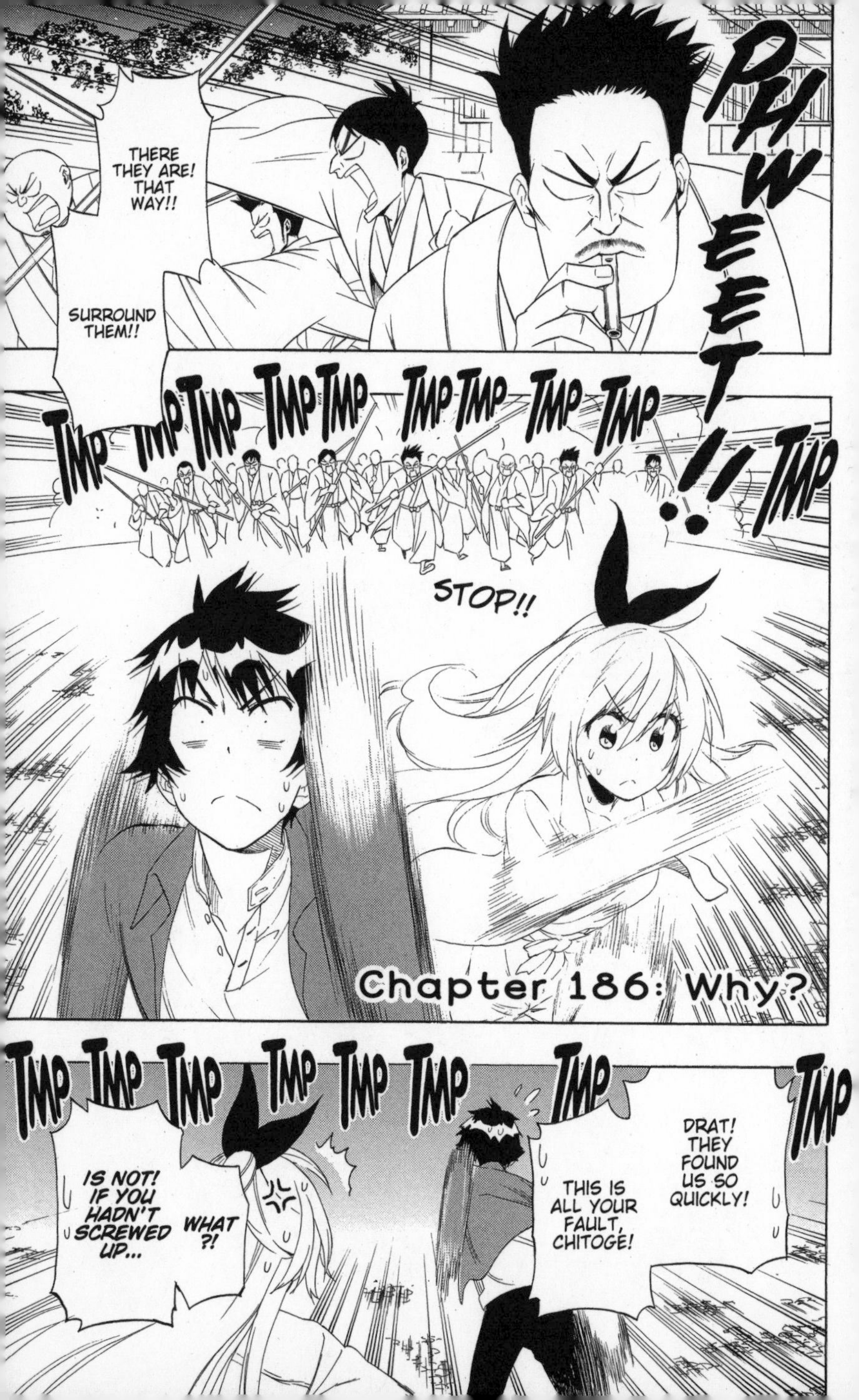
PHWEEET!!
THERE THEY ARE! THAT WAY!!
SURROUND THEM!!
TMP TMP TMP TMP TMP TMP TMP TMP TMP TMP
STOP!!
Chapter 186: Why?
TMP TMP TMP TMP TMP TMP TMP TMP
DRAT! THEY FOUND US SO QUICKLY!
THIS IS ALL YOUR FAULT, CHITOGE!
WHAT?!
IS NOT! IF YOU HADN'T SCREWED UP...

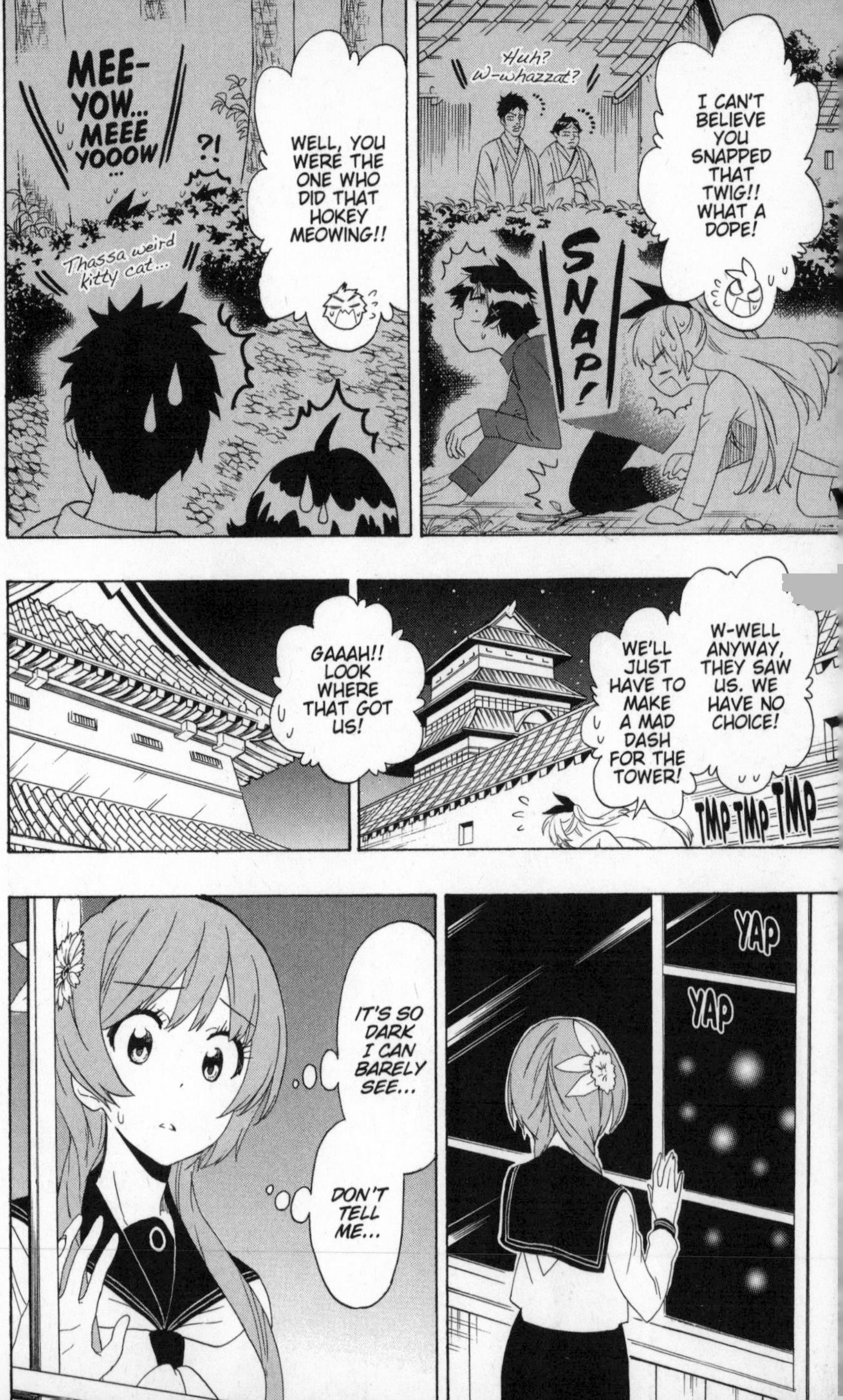
I CAN'T BELIEVE YOU SNAPPED THAT TWIG!! WHAT A DOPE!
Huh? W-whazzat?
SNAP!
WELL, YOU WERE THE ONE WHO DID THAT HOKEY MEOWING!!
MEE-YOW... MEEE YOOOW...
?!
Thassa weird kitty cat...
W-WELL ANYWAY, THEY SAW US. WE HAVE NO CHOICE!
WE'LL JUST HAVE TO MAKE A MAD DASH FOR THE TOWER!
TMP TMP TMP
GAAAH!! LOOK WHERE THAT GOT US!
YAP
YAP
IT'S SO DARK I CAN BARELY SEE...
DON'T TELL ME...

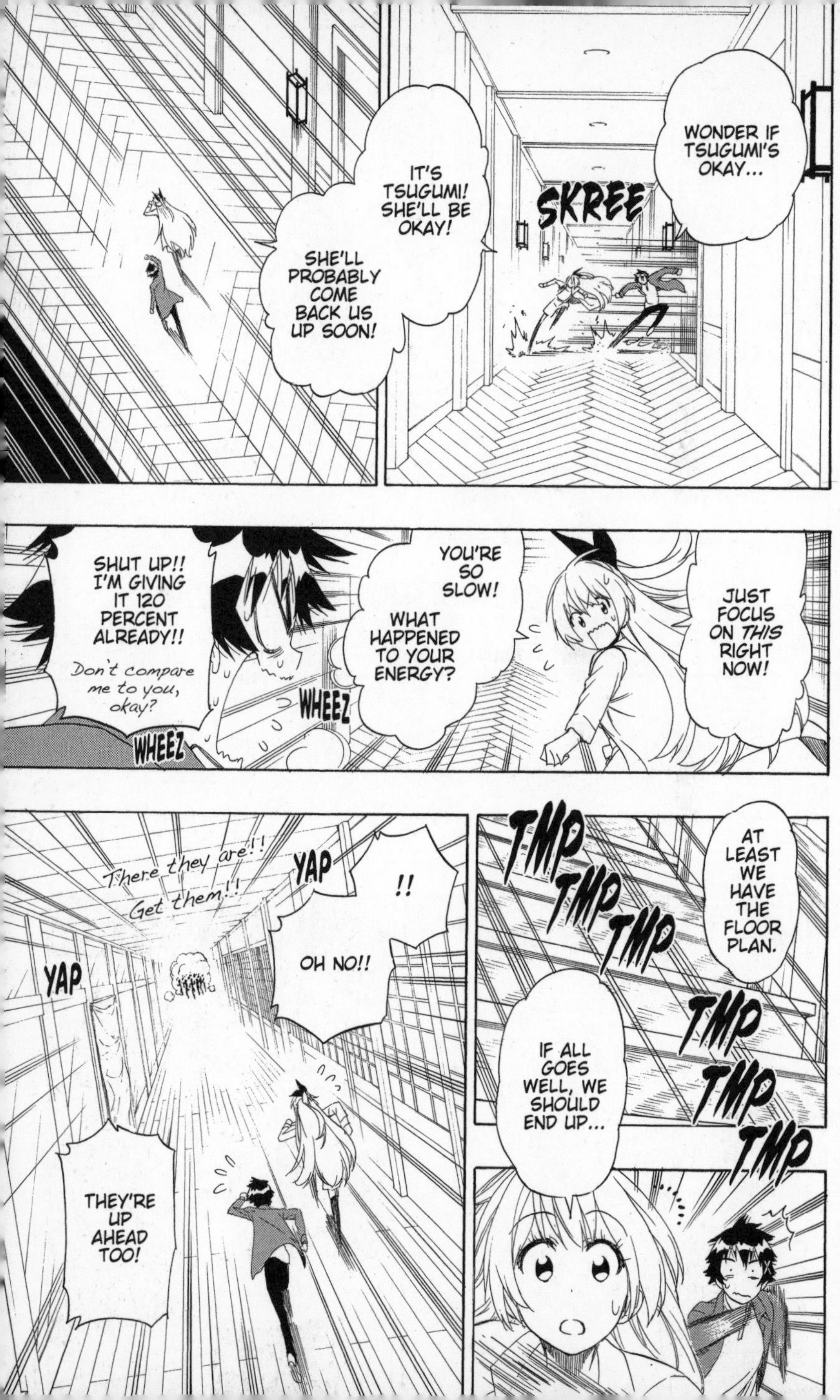
WONDER IF TSUGUMI'S OKAY...
SKREE
IT'S TSUGUMI! SHE'LL BE OKAY!
SHE'LL PROBABLY COME BACK US UP SOON!
JUST FOCUS ON *THIS* RIGHT NOW!
YOU'RE SO SLOW!
WHAT HAPPENED TO YOUR ENERGY?
SHUT UP!! I'M GIVING IT 120 PERCENT ALREADY!!
Don't compare me to you, okay?
WHEEZ
WHEEZ
AT LEAST WE HAVE THE FLOOR PLAN.
TMP TMP TMP
IF ALL GOES WELL, WE SHOULD END UP...
TMP TMP TMP
!!
OH NO!!
YAP
There they are!!
Get them!!
YAP
THEY'RE UP AHEAD TOO!

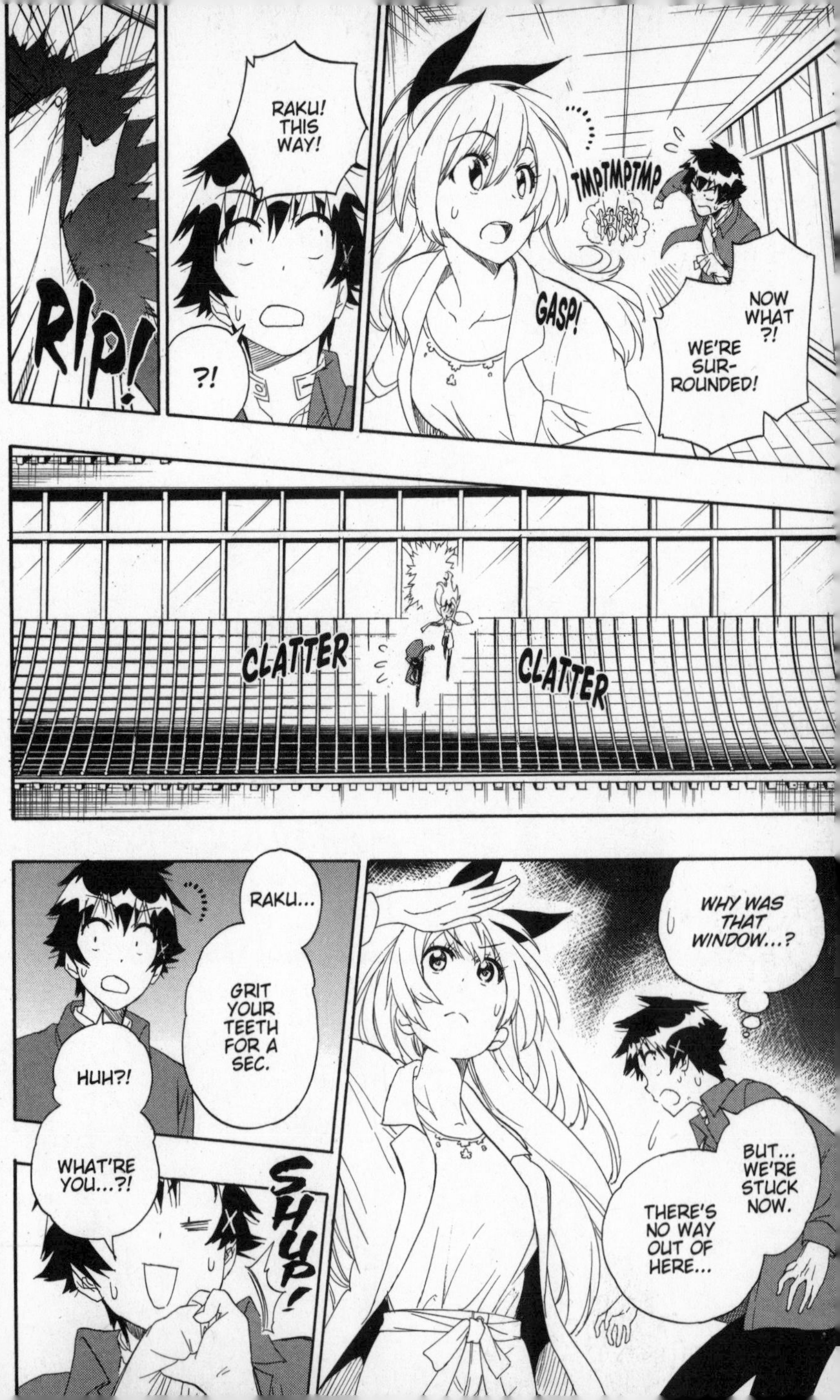
TMPTMPTMP
NOW WHAT?!
WE'RE SUR-ROUNDED!
GASP!
RAKU! THIS WAY!
?!
RIP!
CLATTER
CLATTER
WHY WAS THAT WINDOW...?
BUT... WE'RE STUCK NOW.
THERE'S NO WAY OUT OF HERE...
RAKU...
GRIT YOUR TEETH FOR A SEC.
HUH?!
SHUP!
WHAT'RE YOU...?!

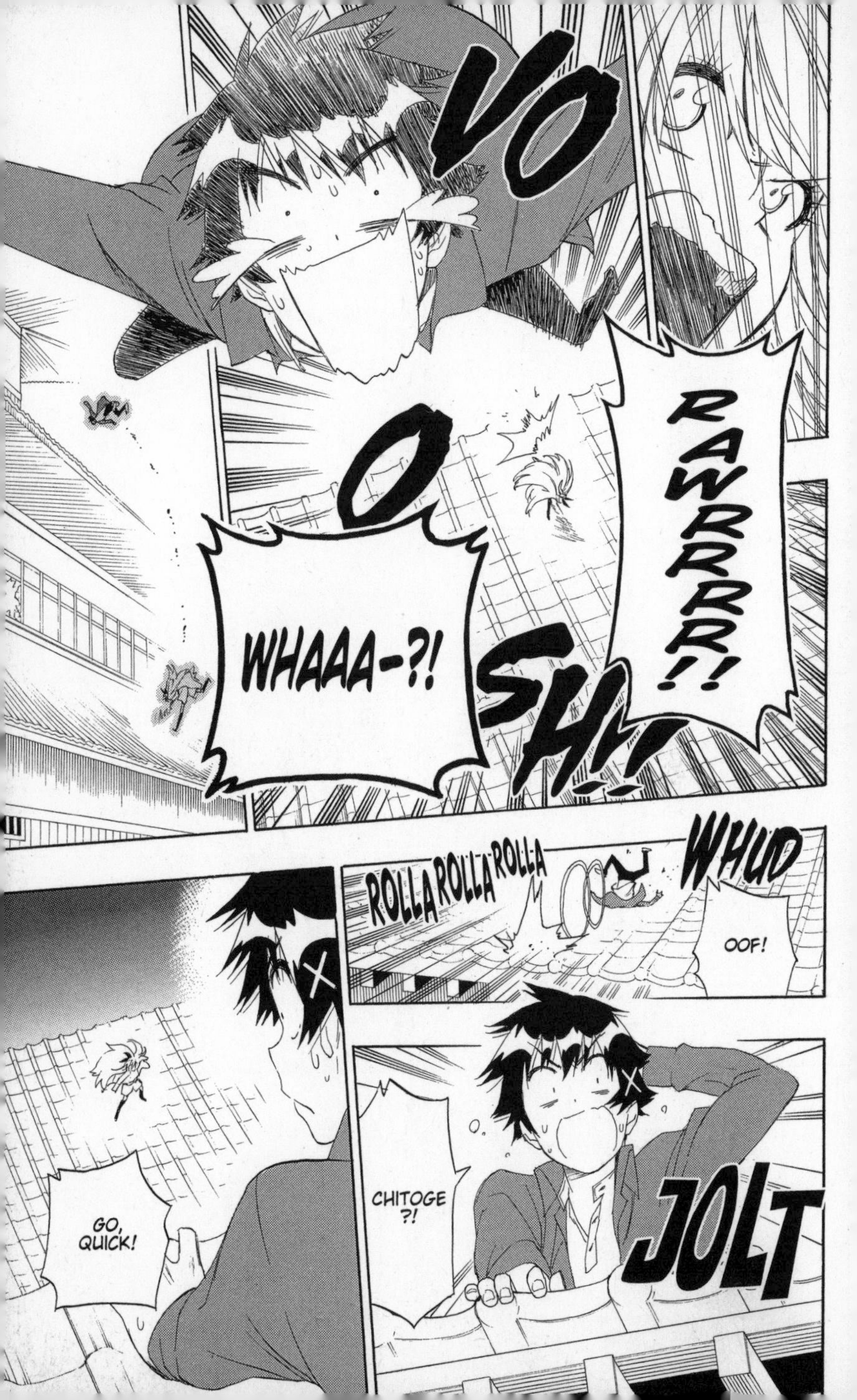
RAWRRRR!!
VO
O
SH!!
WHAAA-?!
WHUD
ROLLA ROLLA ROLLA
OOF!
JOLT
CHITOGE ?!
GO, QUICK!

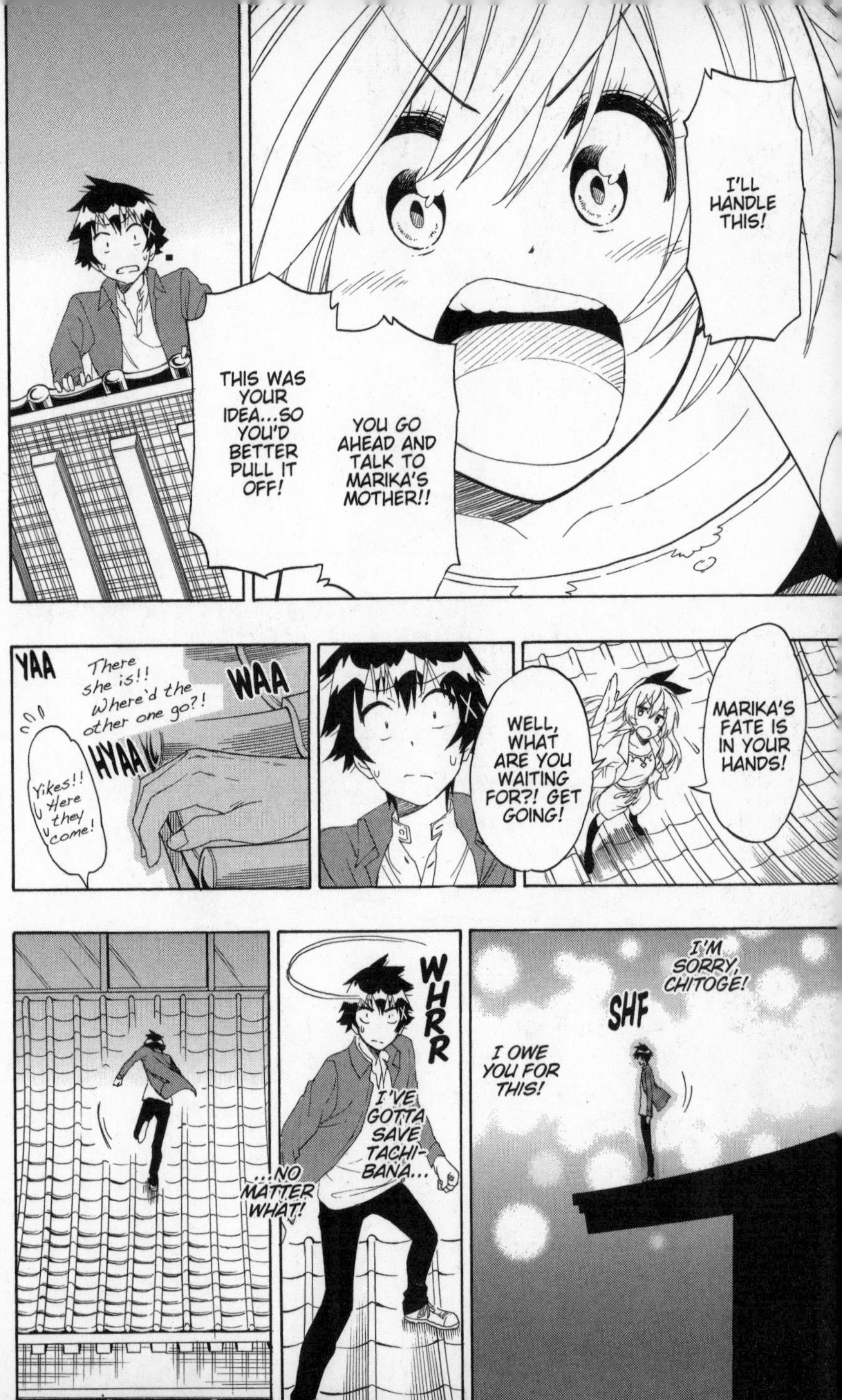
I'LL HANDLE THIS!
YOU GO AHEAD AND TALK TO MARIKA'S MOTHER!!
THIS WAS YOUR IDEA...SO YOU'D BETTER PULL IT OFF!
MARIKA'S FATE IS IN YOUR HANDS!
WELL, WHAT ARE YOU WAITING FOR?! GET GOING!
WAA
There she is!! Where'd the other one go?!
YAA
HYAA
Yikes!! Here they come!
I'M SORRY, CHITOGE!
SHF
I OWE YOU FOR THIS!
WHRR
I'VE GOTTA SAVE TACHIBANA...
...NO MATTER WHAT!

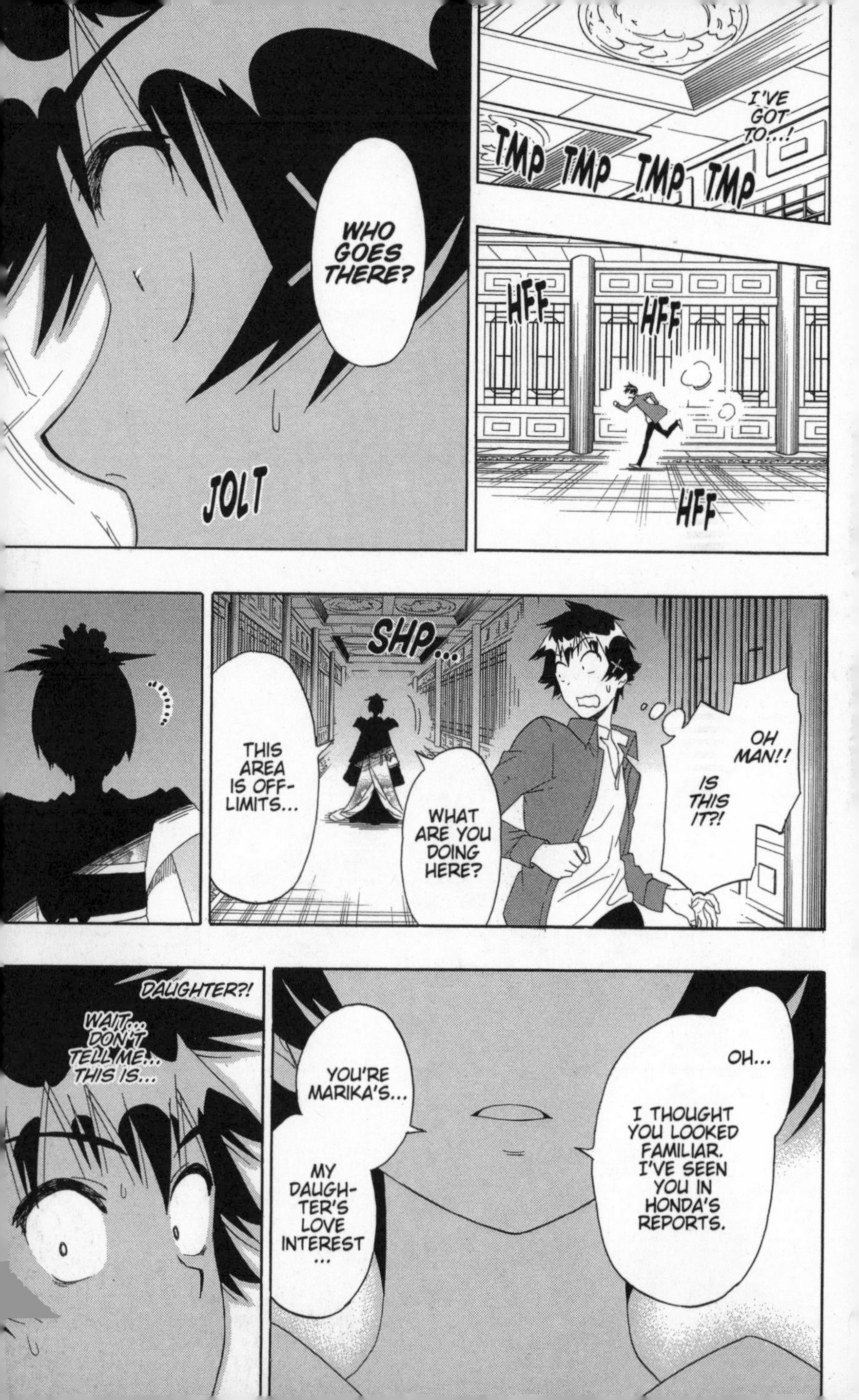
I'VE GOT TO...!
TMP TMP TMP TMP
HFF HFF
HFF
WHO GOES THERE?
JOLT
SHP...
OH MAN!!
IS THIS IT?!
WHAT ARE YOU DOING HERE?
THIS AREA IS OFF-LIMITS...
......
OH...
I THOUGHT YOU LOOKED FAMILIAR. I'VE SEEN YOU IN HONDA'S REPORTS.
YOU'RE MARIKA'S...
MY DAUGHTER'S LOVE INTEREST...
DAUGHTER?!
WAIT... DON'T TELL ME... THIS IS...

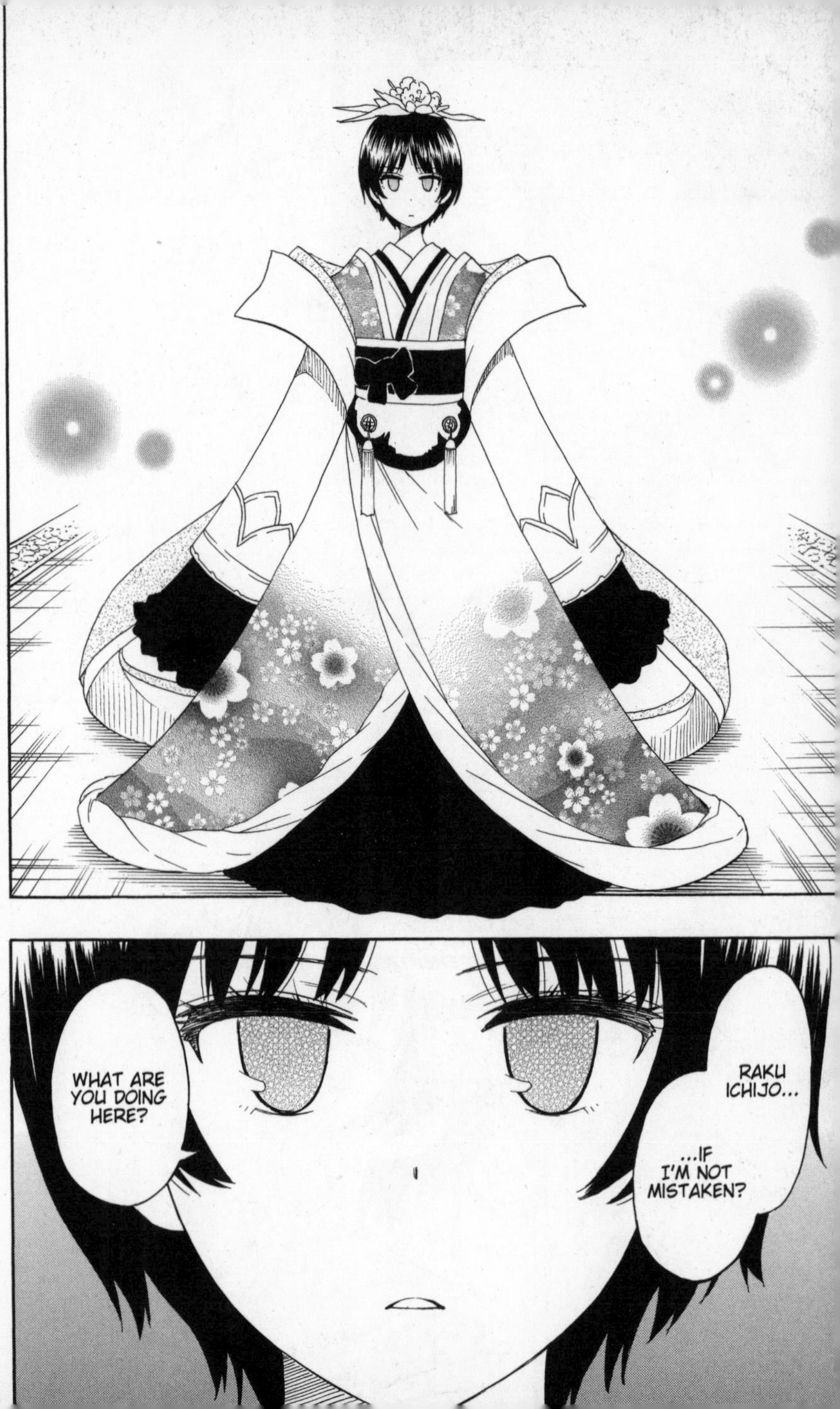
RAKU ICHIJO...
...IF I'M NOT MISTAKEN?
WHAT ARE YOU DOING HERE?

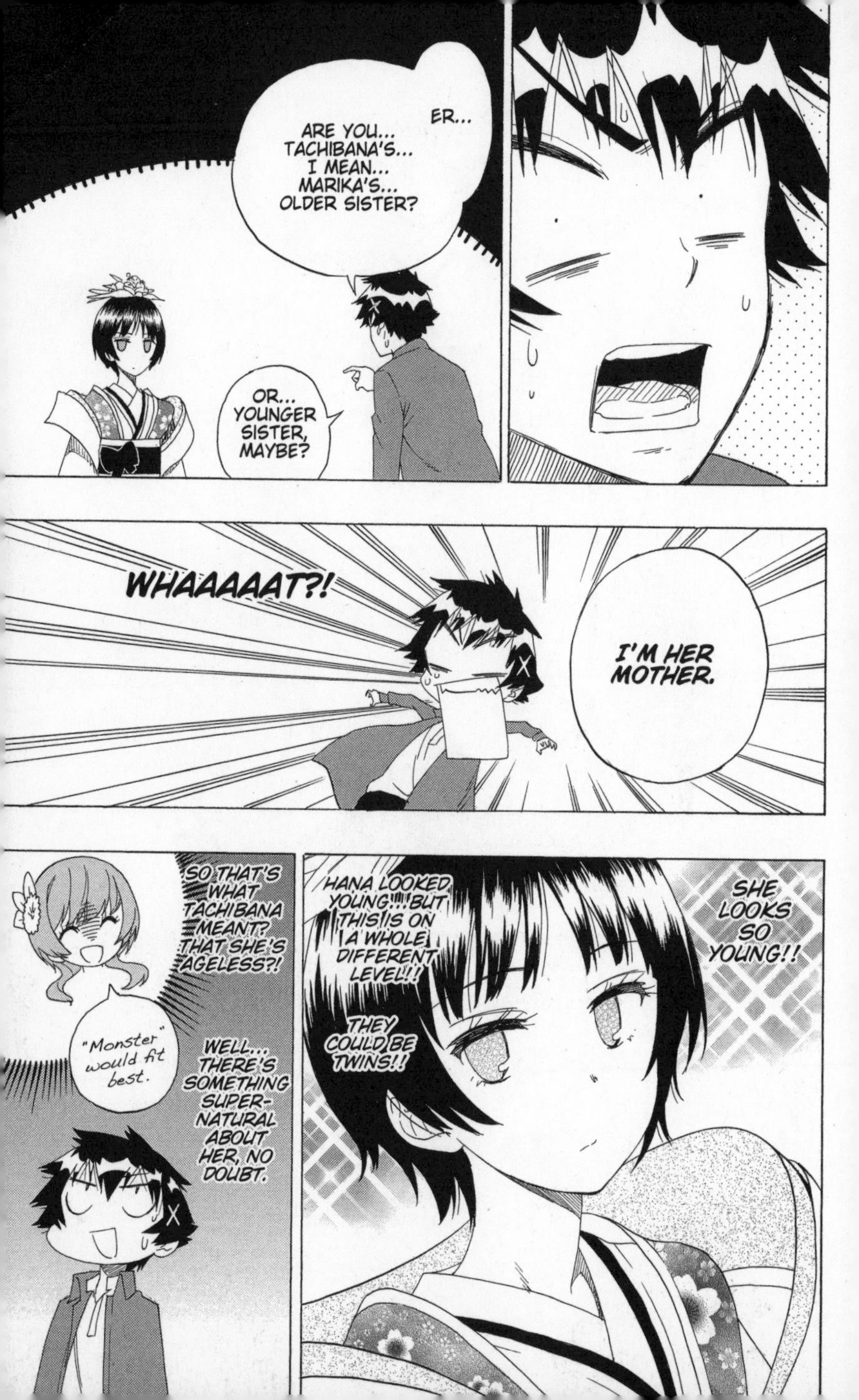
ER...
ARE YOU... TACHIBANA'S... I MEAN... MARIKA'S... OLDER SISTER?
OR... YOUNGER SISTER, MAYBE?
I'M HER MOTHER.
WHAAAAAT?!
SHE LOOKS SO YOUNG!!
HANA LOOKED YOUNG!!! BUT THIS IS ON A WHOLE DIFFERENT LEVEL!!
THEY COULD BE TWINS!!
SO THAT'S WHAT TACHIBANA MEANT? THAT SHE'S AGELESS?!
WELL... THERE'S SOMETHING SUPER-NATURAL ABOUT HER, NO DOUBT.
"Monster" would fit best.

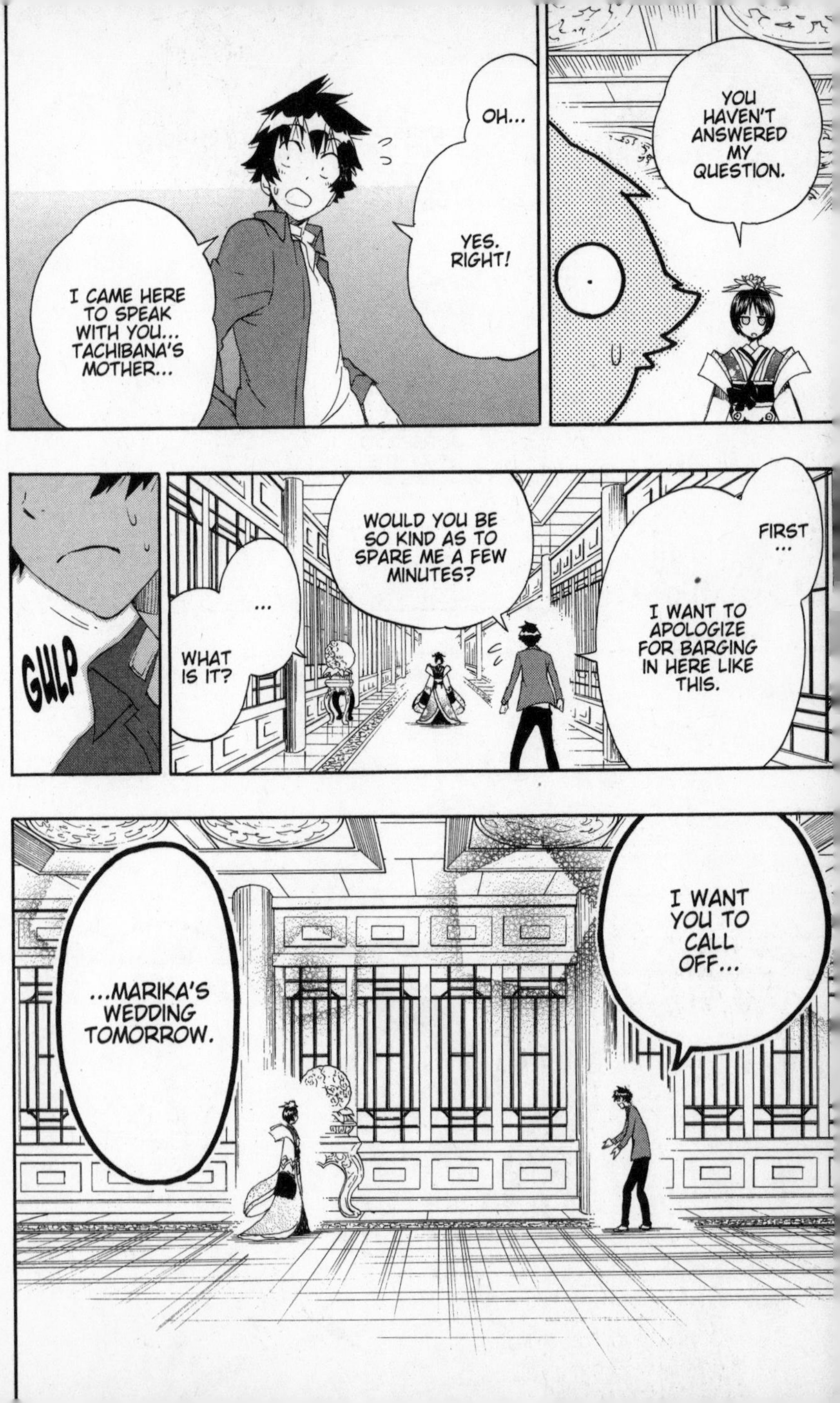
YOU HAVEN'T ANSWERED MY QUESTION.
OH...
YES. RIGHT!
I CAME HERE TO SPEAK WITH YOU... TACHIBANA'S MOTHER...
FIRST...
I WANT TO APOLOGIZE FOR BARGING IN HERE LIKE THIS.
WOULD YOU BE SO KIND AS TO SPARE ME A FEW MINUTES?
...
WHAT IS IT?
GULP
I WANT YOU TO CALL OFF...
...MARIKA'S WEDDING TOMORROW.

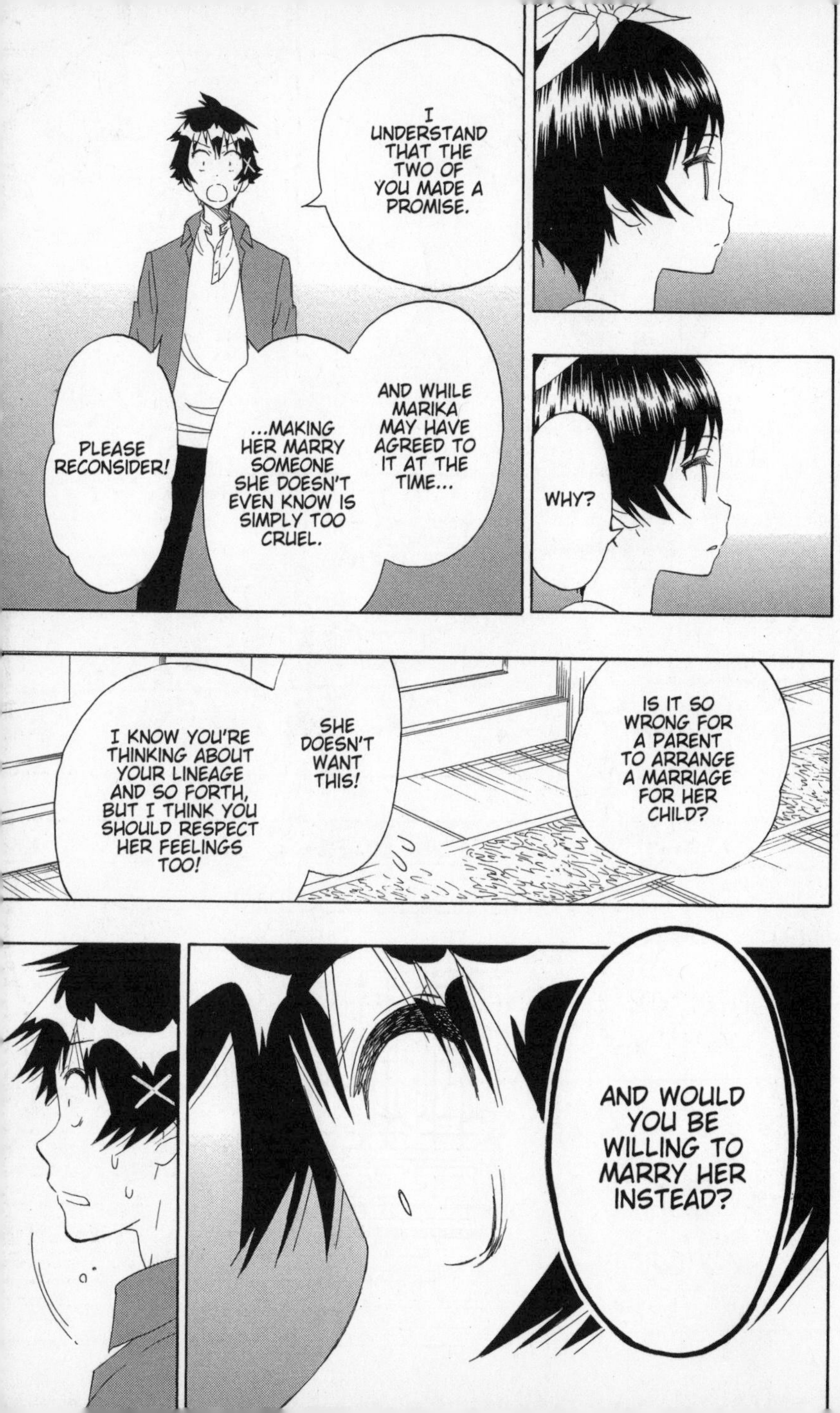
WHY?
I UNDERSTAND THAT THE TWO OF YOU MADE A PROMISE.
AND WHILE MARIKA MAY HAVE AGREED TO IT AT THE TIME...
...MAKING HER MARRY SOMEONE SHE DOESN'T EVEN KNOW IS SIMPLY TOO CRUEL.
PLEASE RECONSIDER!
IS IT SO WRONG FOR A PARENT TO ARRANGE A MARRIAGE FOR HER CHILD?
SHE DOESN'T WANT THIS!
I KNOW YOU'RE THINKING ABOUT YOUR LINEAGE AND SO FORTH, BUT I THINK YOU SHOULD RESPECT HER FEELINGS TOO!
AND WOULD YOU BE WILLING TO MARRY HER INSTEAD?

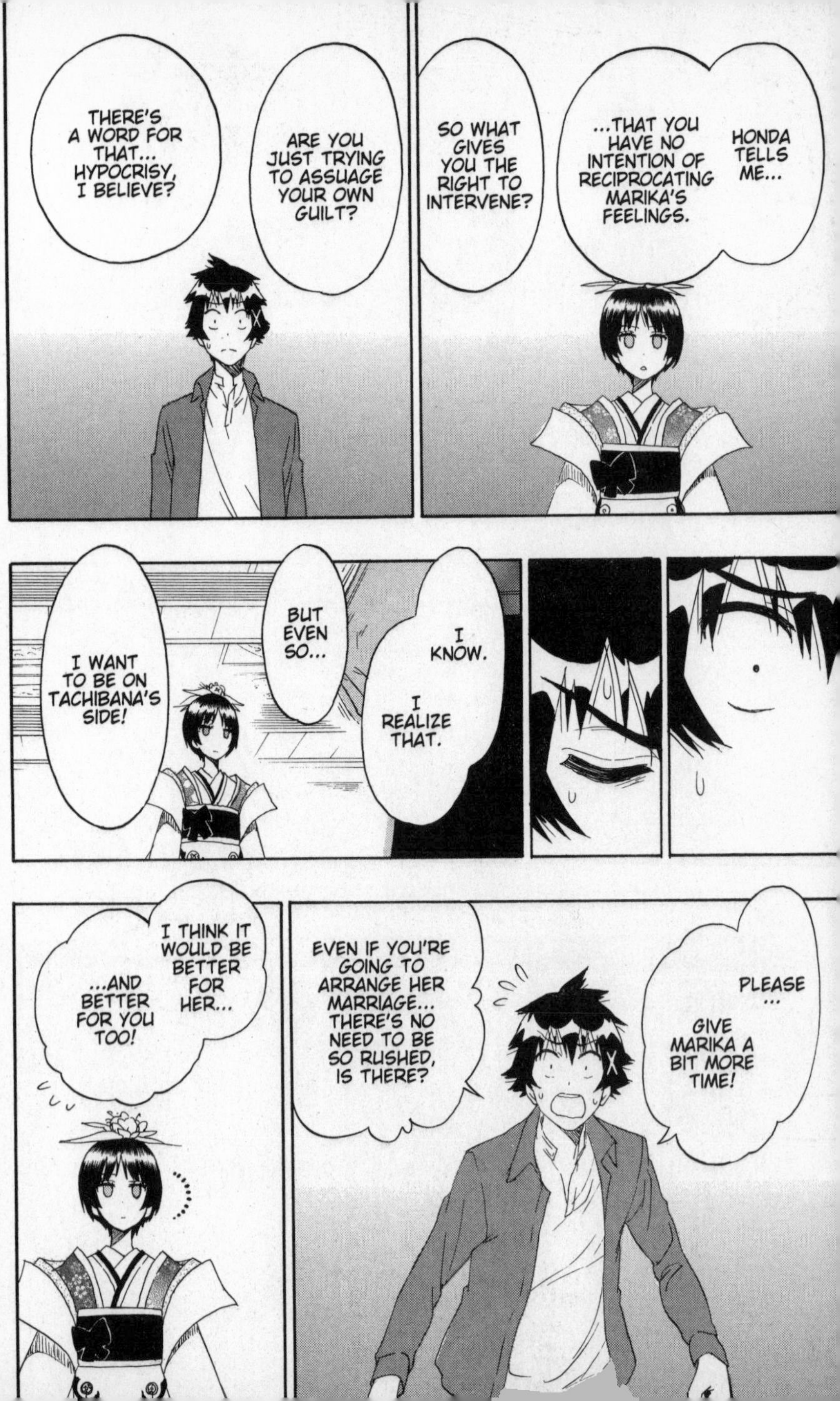
HONDA TELLS ME...
...THAT YOU HAVE NO INTENTION OF RECIPROCATING MARIKA'S FEELINGS.
SO WHAT GIVES YOU THE RIGHT TO INTERVENE?
ARE YOU JUST TRYING TO ASSUAGE YOUR OWN GUILT?
THERE'S A WORD FOR THAT... HYPOCRISY, I BELIEVE?
I KNOW.
I REALIZE THAT.
BUT EVEN SO...
I WANT TO BE ON TACHIBANA'S SIDE!
PLEASE...
GIVE MARIKA A BIT MORE TIME!
EVEN IF YOU'RE GOING TO ARRANGE HER MARRIAGE... THERE'S NO NEED TO BE SO RUSHED, IS THERE?
I THINK IT WOULD BE BETTER FOR HER...
...AND BETTER FOR YOU TOO!

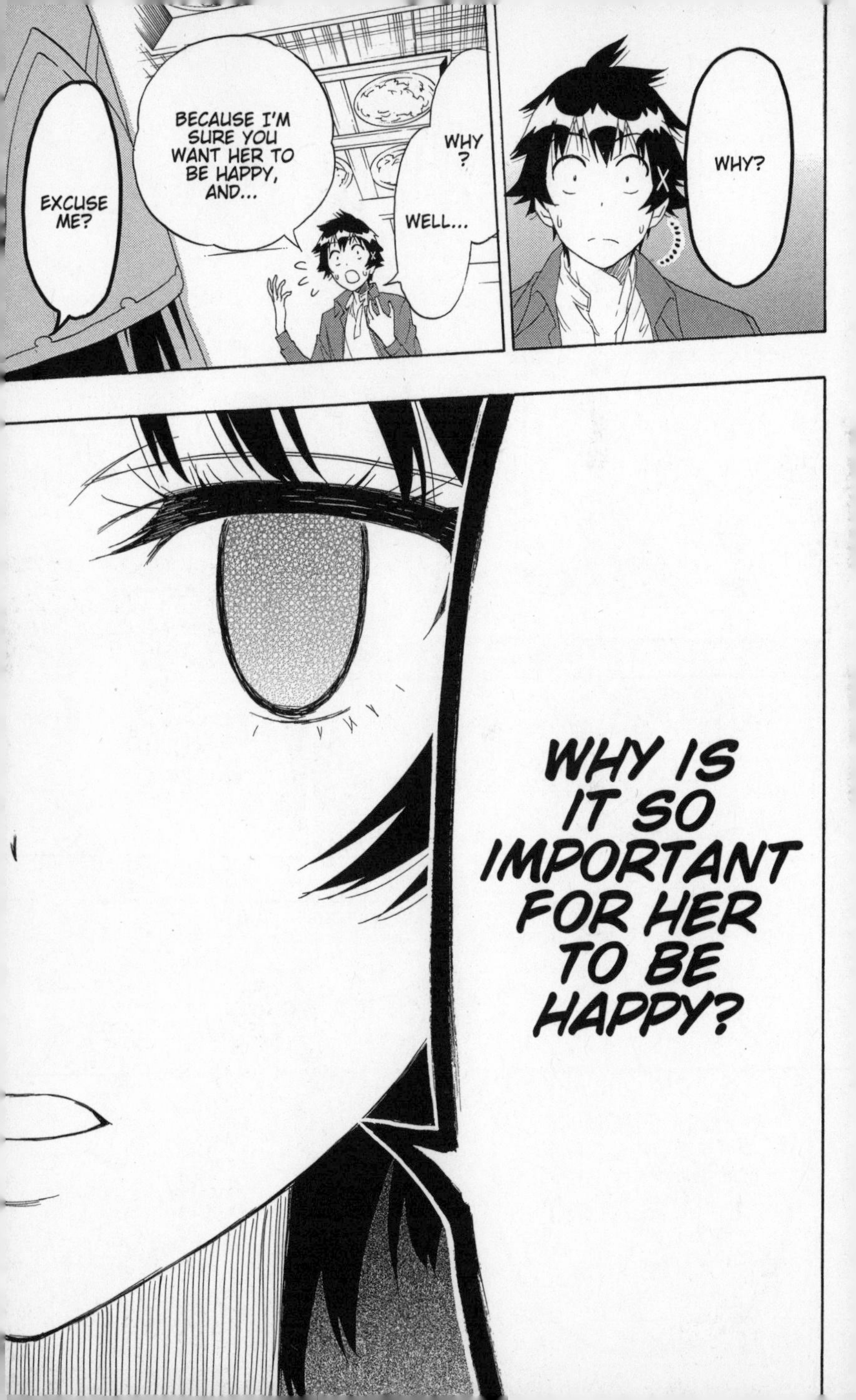
WHY?
WHY?
WELL...
BECAUSE I'M SURE YOU WANT HER TO BE HAPPY, AND...
EXCUSE ME?
WHY IS IT SO IMPORTANT FOR HER TO BE HAPPY?

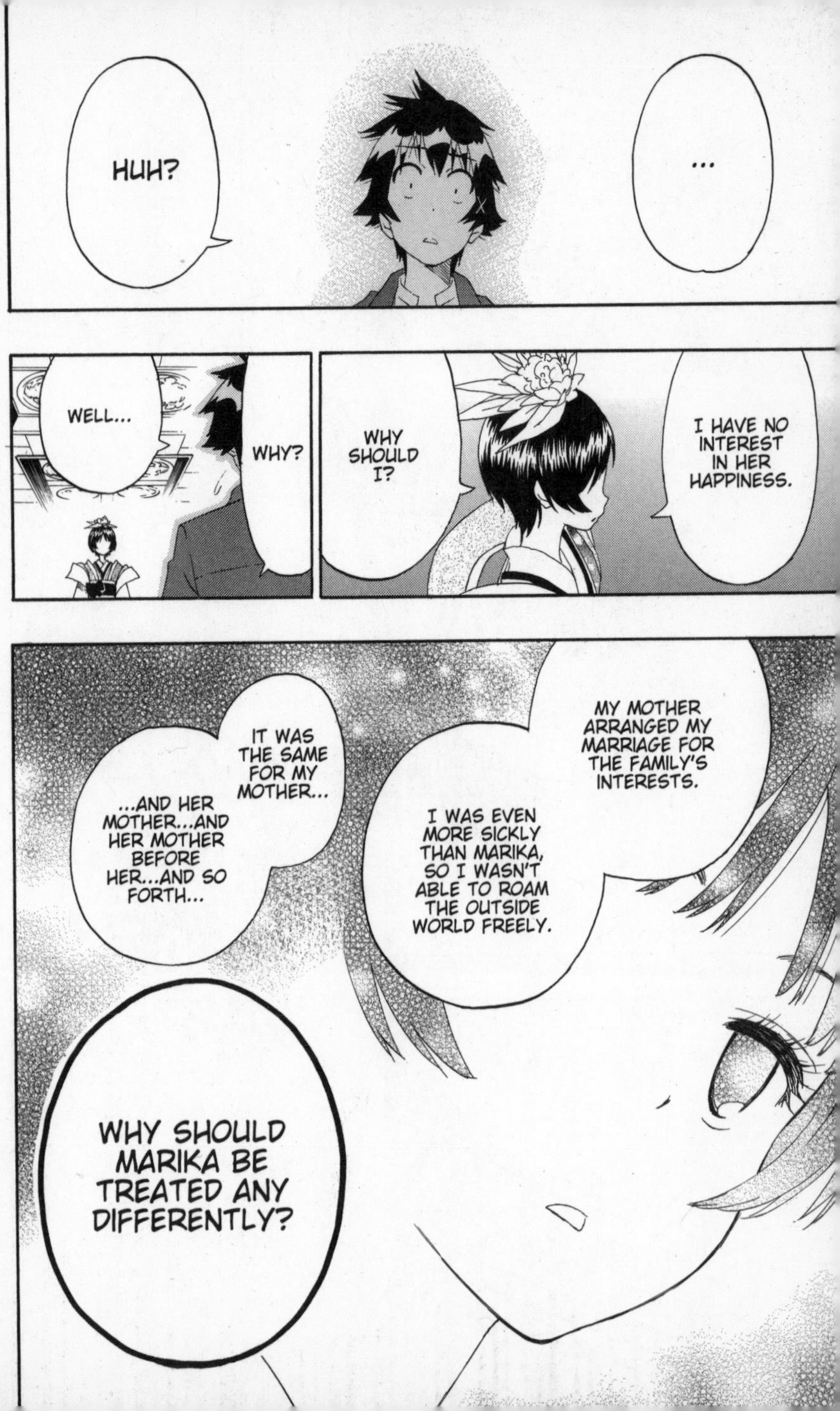
...
HUH?
I HAVE NO INTEREST IN HER HAPPINESS.
WHY SHOULD I?
WHY?
WELL...
MY MOTHER ARRANGED MY MARRIAGE FOR THE FAMILY'S INTERESTS.
I WAS EVEN MORE SICKLY THAN MARIKA, SO I WASN'T ABLE TO ROAM THE OUTSIDE WORLD FREELY.
IT WAS THE SAME FOR MY MOTHER...
...AND HER MOTHER...AND HER MOTHER BEFORE HER...AND SO FORTH...
WHY SHOULD MARIKA BE TREATED ANY DIFFERENTLY?

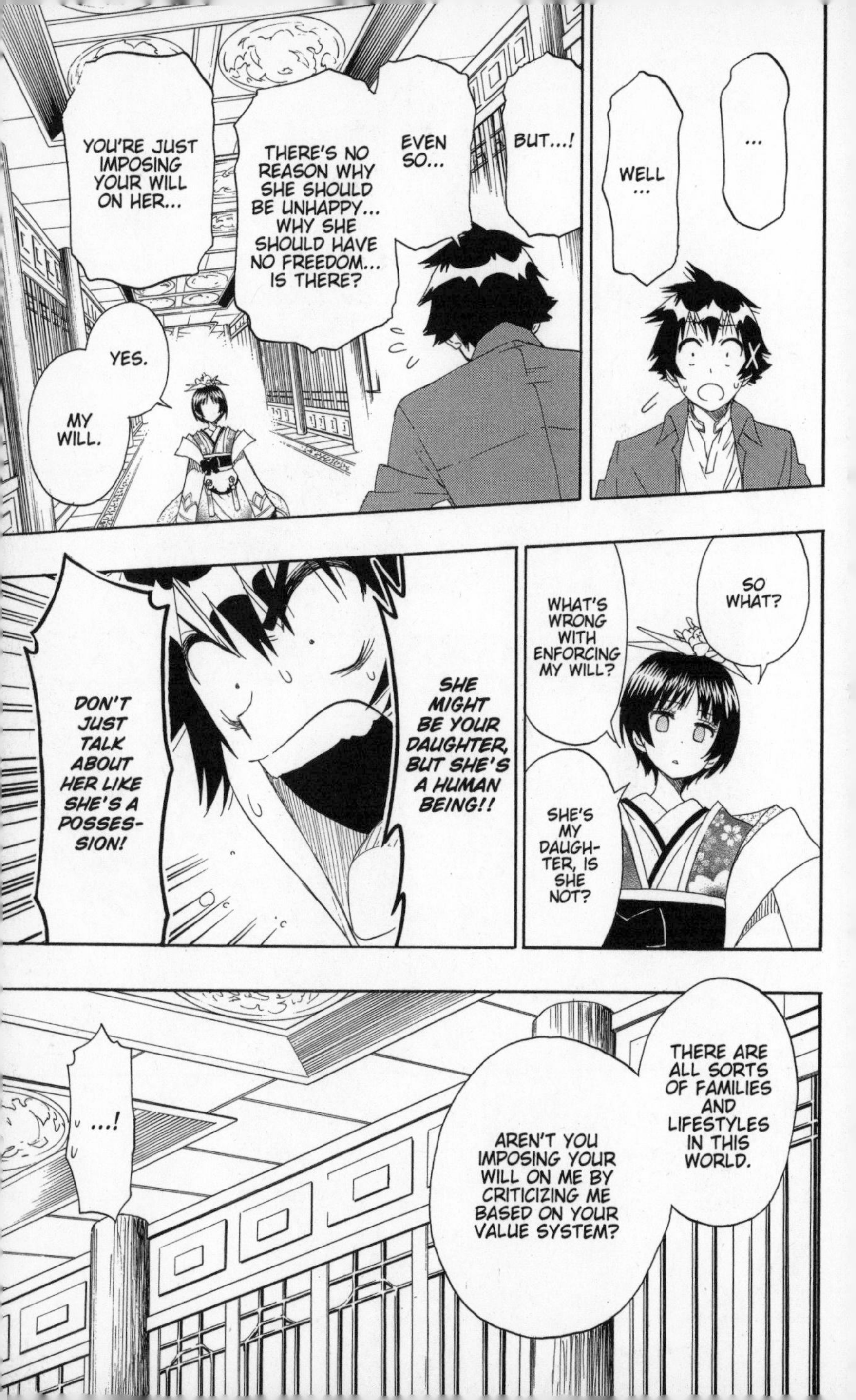
...
WELL...
BUT...!
EVEN SO...
THERE'S NO REASON WHY SHE SHOULD BE UNHAPPY... WHY SHE SHOULD HAVE NO FREEDOM... IS THERE?
YOU'RE JUST IMPOSING YOUR WILL ON HER...
YES.
MY WILL.
SO WHAT?
WHAT'S WRONG WITH ENFORCING MY WILL?
SHE'S MY DAUGHTER, IS SHE NOT?
SHE MIGHT BE YOUR DAUGHTER, BUT SHE'S A HUMAN BEING!!
DON'T JUST TALK ABOUT HER LIKE SHE'S A POSSESSION!
THERE ARE ALL SORTS OF FAMILIES AND LIFESTYLES IN THIS WORLD.
AREN'T YOU IMPOSING YOUR WILL ON ME BY CRITICIZING ME BASED ON YOUR VALUE SYSTEM?
...!

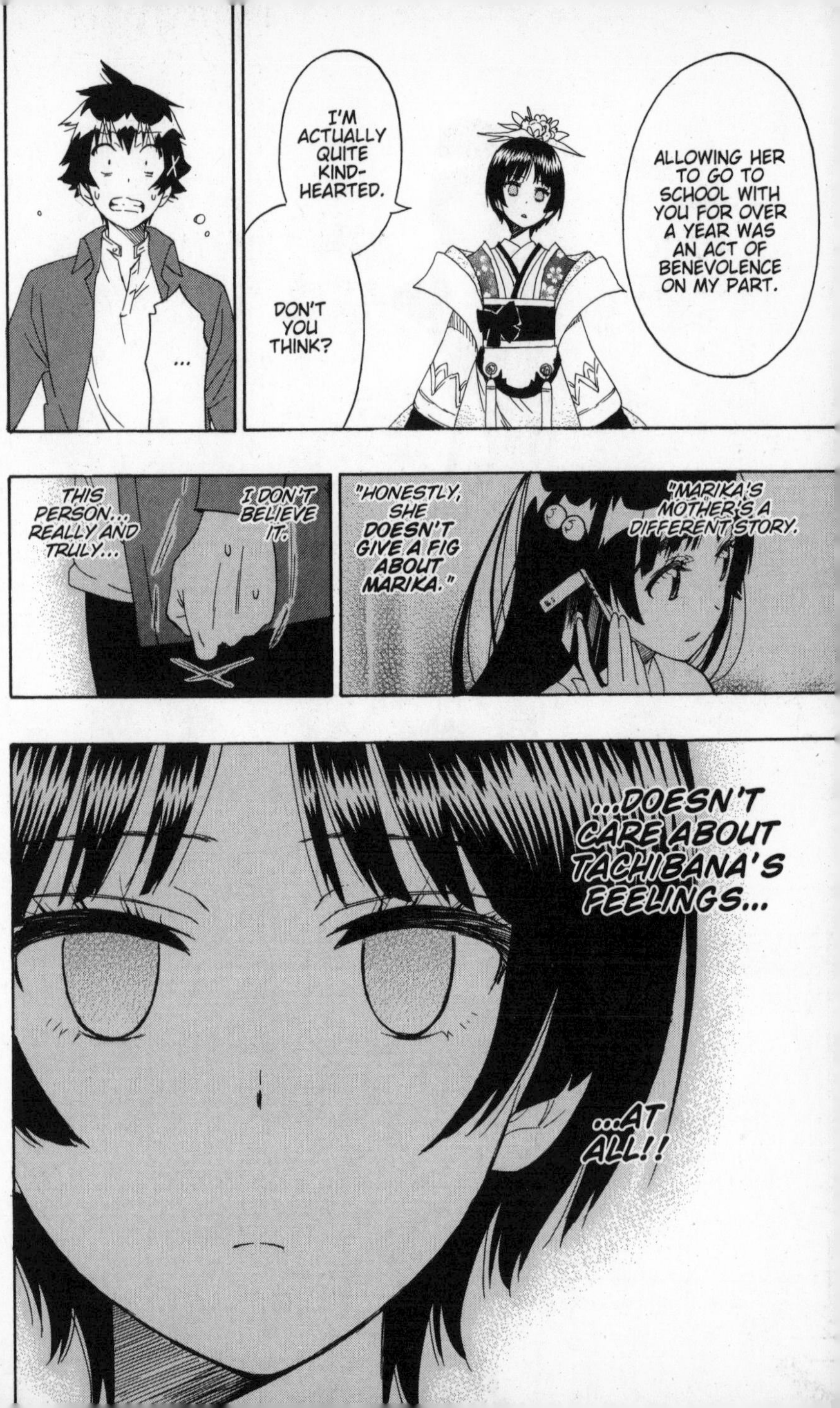
ALLOWING HER TO GO TO SCHOOL WITH YOU FOR OVER A YEAR WAS AN ACT OF BENEVOLENCE ON MY PART.
I'M ACTUALLY QUITE KIND-HEARTED.
DON'T YOU THINK?
...
"MARIKA'S MOTHER'S A DIFFERENT STORY.
"HONESTLY, SHE DOESN'T GIVE A FIG ABOUT MARIKA."
I DON'T BELIEVE IT.
THIS PERSON... REALLY AND TRULY...
...DOESN'T CARE ABOUT TACHIBANA'S FEELINGS...
...AT ALL!!

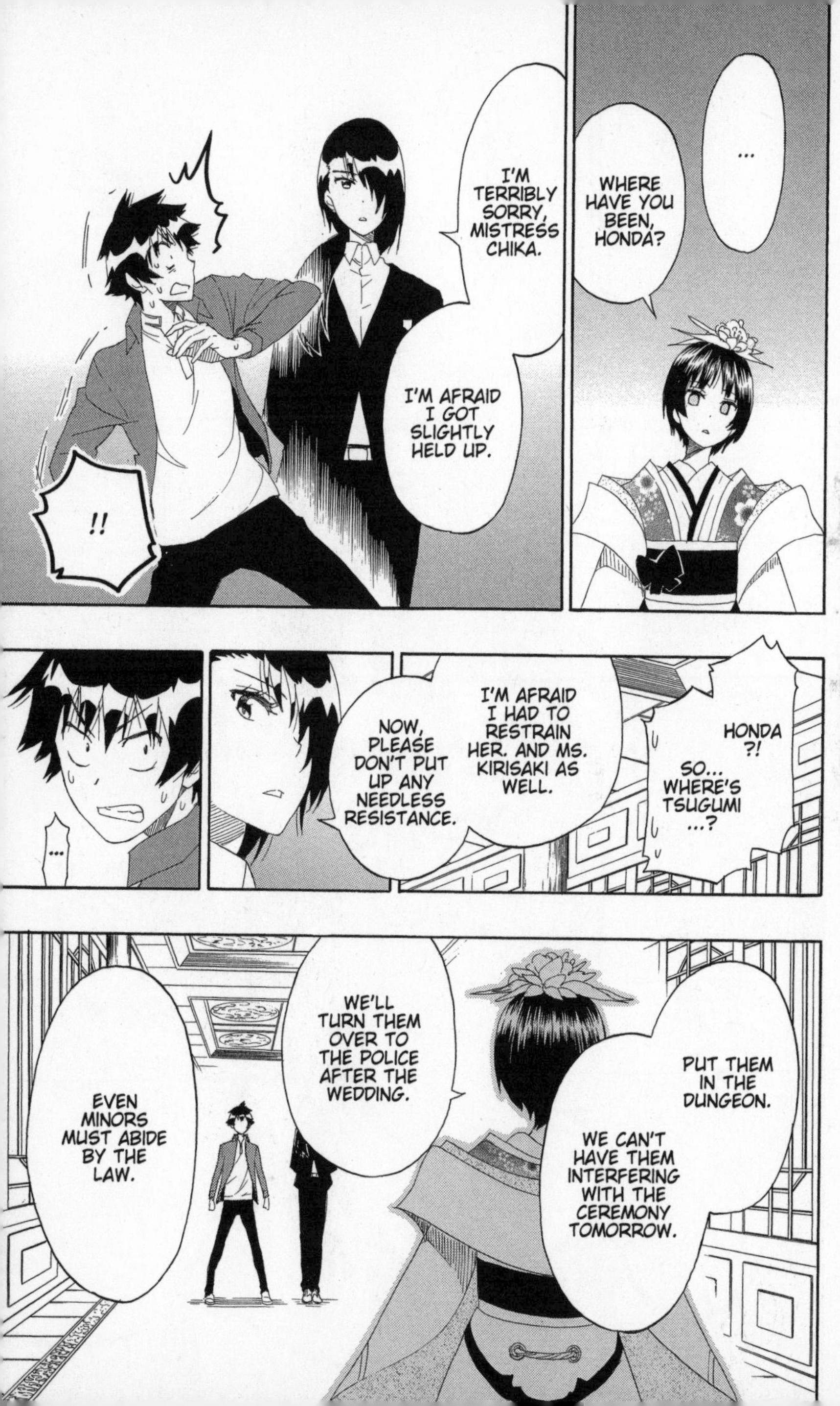
...
WHERE HAVE YOU BEEN, HONDA?
I'M TERRIBLY SORRY, MISTRESS CHIKA.
I'M AFRAID I GOT SLIGHTLY HELD UP.
!!
HONDA ?!
SO... WHERE'S TSUGUMI ...?
I'M AFRAID I HAD TO RESTRAIN HER. AND MS. KIRISAKI AS WELL.
NOW, PLEASE DON'T PUT UP ANY NEEDLESS RESISTANCE.
...
PUT THEM IN THE DUNGEON.
WE CAN'T HAVE THEM INTERFERING WITH THE CEREMONY TOMORROW.
WE'LL TURN THEM OVER TO THE POLICE AFTER THE WEDDING.
EVEN MINORS MUST ABIDE BY THE LAW.

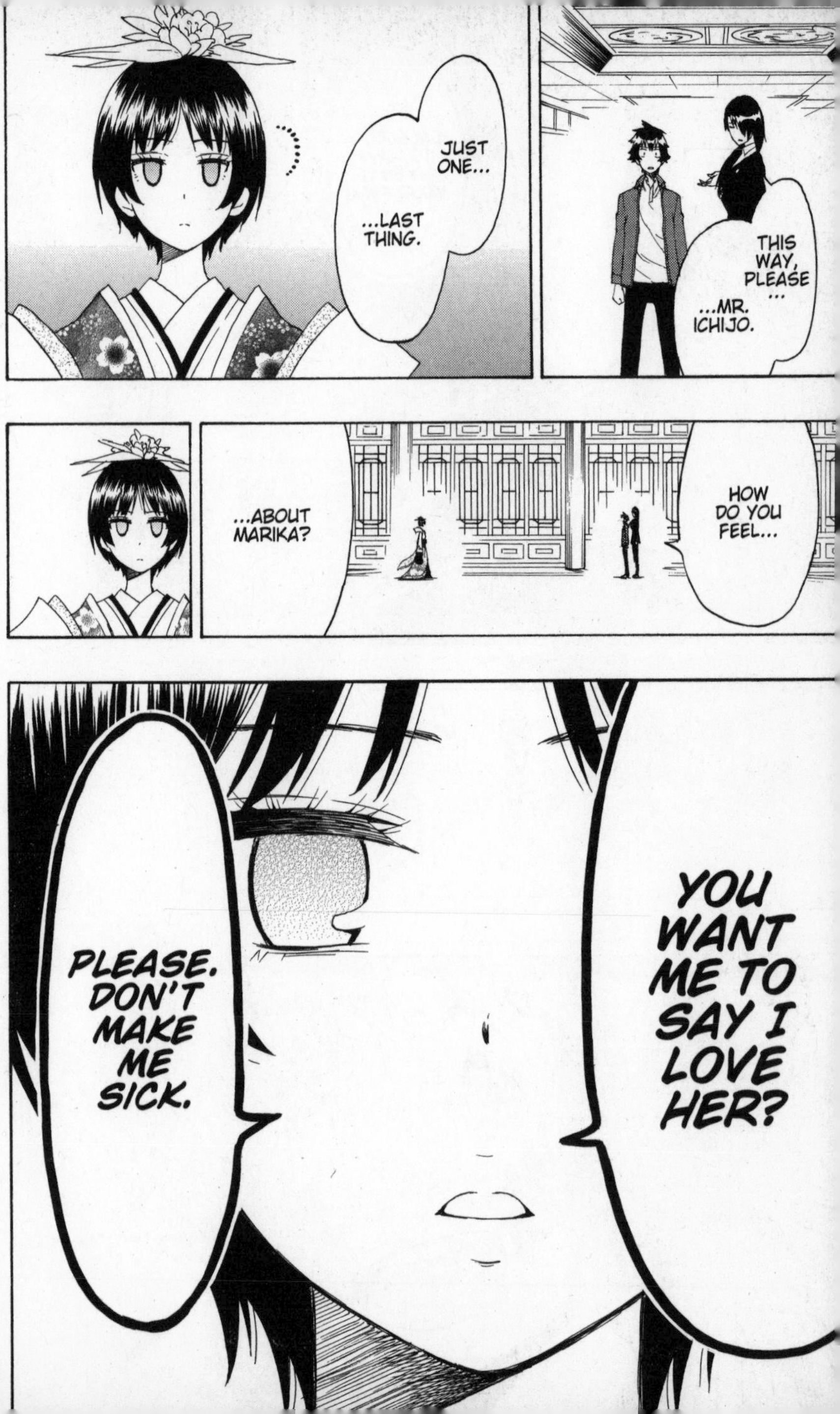
THIS WAY, PLEASE...
...MR. ICHIJO.
JUST ONE...
...LAST THING.
HOW DO YOU FEEL...
...ABOUT MARIKA?
YOU WANT ME TO SAY I LOVE HER?
PLEASE. DON'T MAKE ME SICK.

I'LL GO NOW.

I'M SORRY TO HAVE TAKEN UP YOUR TIME.

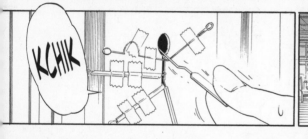

KCHIK

TINK
TINK
TINK

RATTLE!

IT'S OPEN!

Tee hee...
Time to use the special technique I learned in case Raku Dearest is ever kidnapped and locked away...
Marika-style lock picking, Skill #153 of my Perfect Bride Toolkit. ♡

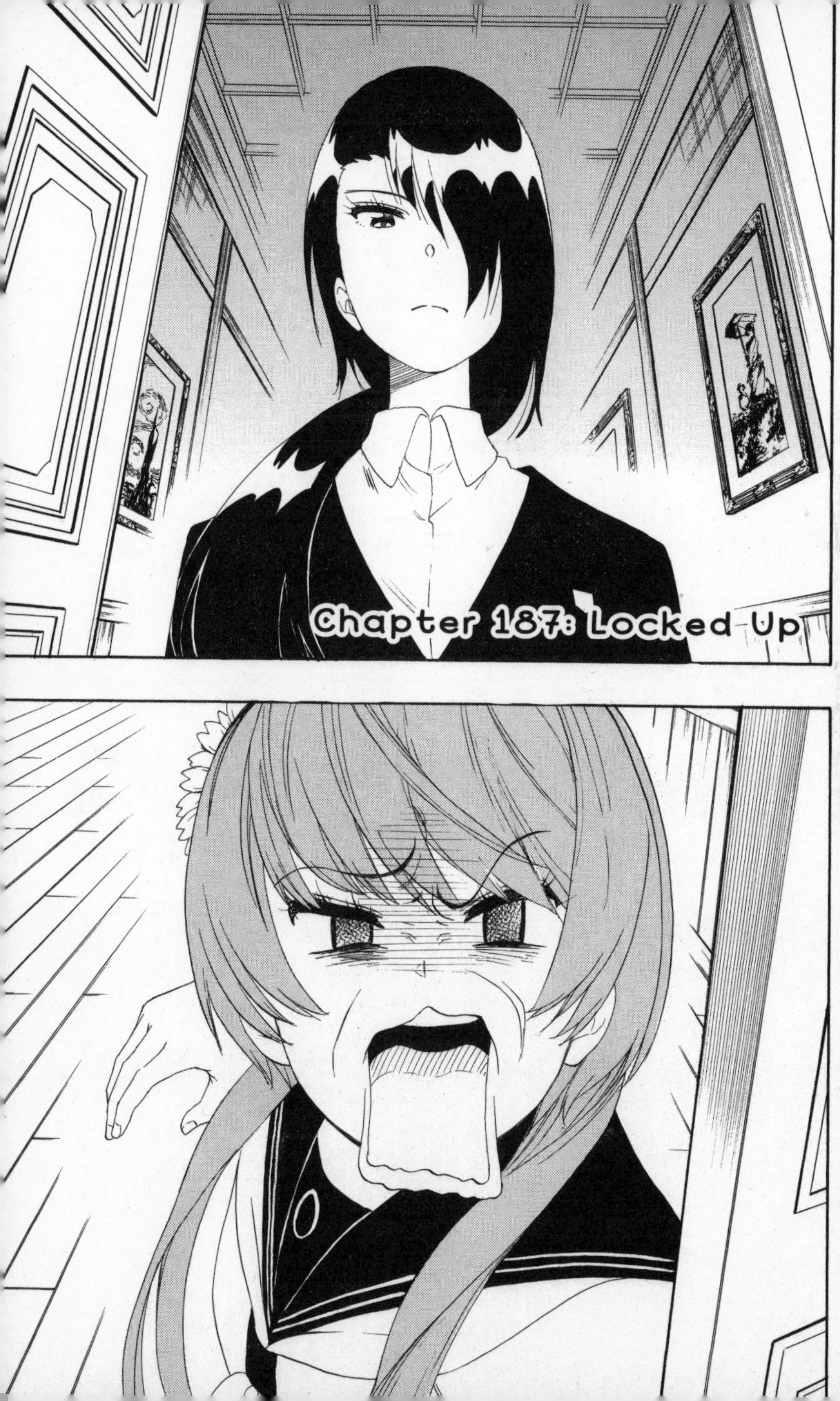
Chapter 187: Locked Up

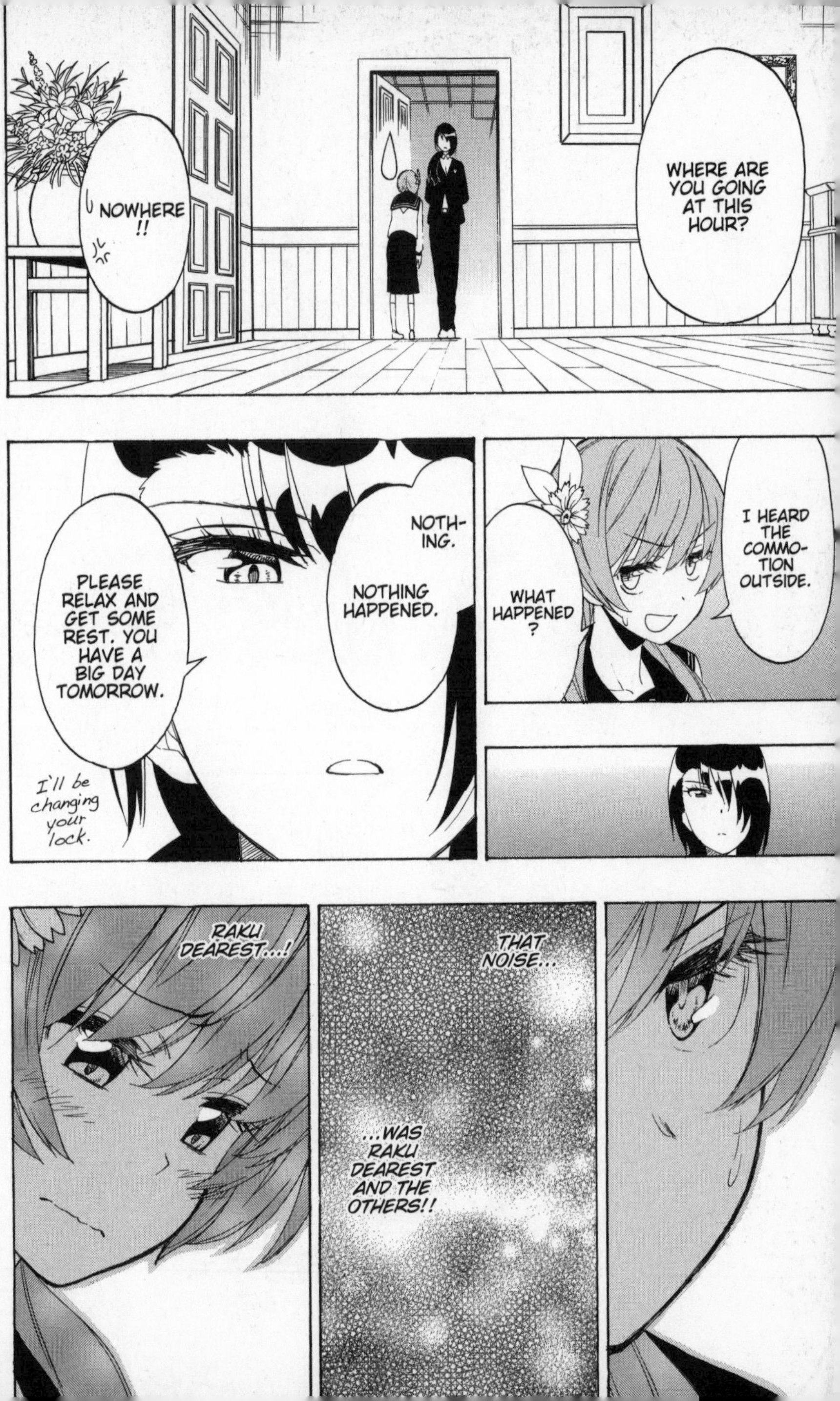
WHERE ARE YOU GOING AT THIS HOUR?
NOWHERE!!
I HEARD THE COMMOTION OUTSIDE.
WHAT HAPPENED?
NOTHING.
NOTHING HAPPENED.
PLEASE RELAX AND GET SOME REST. YOU HAVE A BIG DAY TOMORROW.
I'll be changing your lock.
THAT NOISE...
...WAS RAKU DEAREST AND THE OTHERS!!
RAKU DEAREST...!

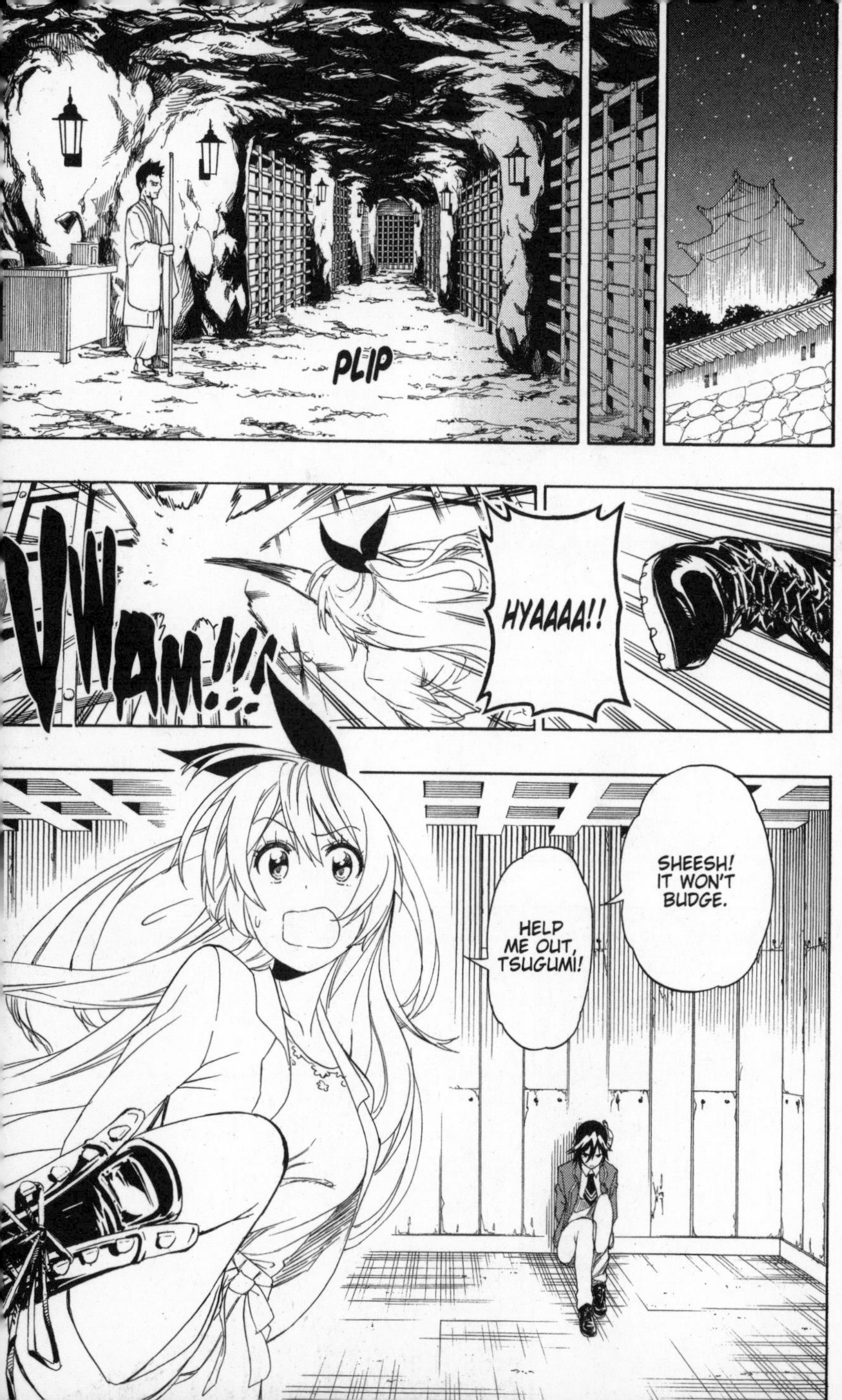
PLIP
HYAAAA!!
WHAM!!!
SHEESH! IT WON'T BUDGE.
HELP ME OUT, TSUGUMI!

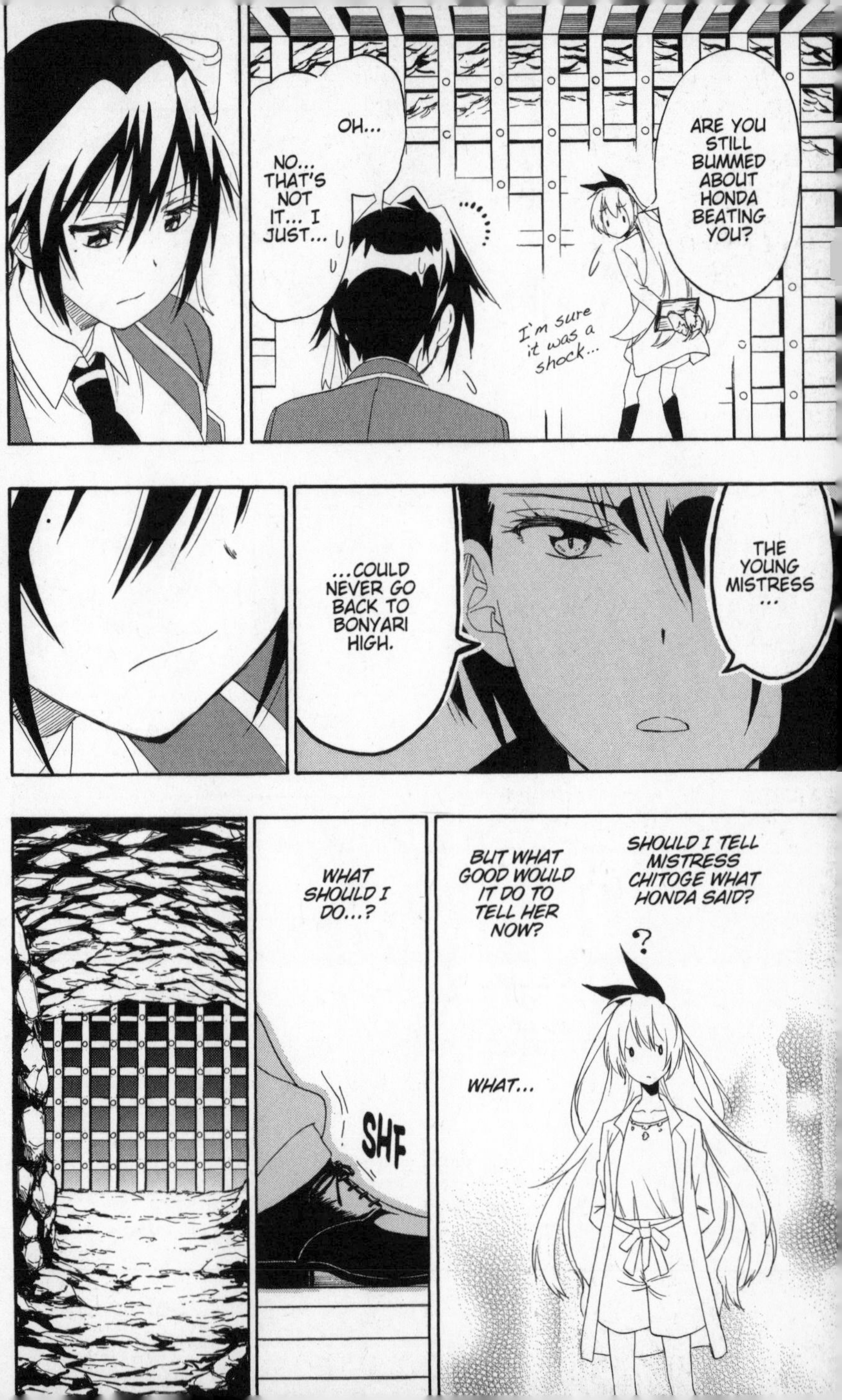
ARE YOU STILL BUMMED ABOUT HONDA BEATING YOU?
I'm sure it was a shock...
...
OH...
NO... THAT'S NOT IT... I JUST...
THE YOUNG MISTRESS ...
...COULD NEVER GO BACK TO BONYARI HIGH.
SHOULD I TELL MISTRESS CHITOGE WHAT HONDA SAID?
BUT WHAT GOOD WOULD IT DO TO TELL HER NOW?
?
WHAT...
WHAT SHOULD I DO...?
SHF

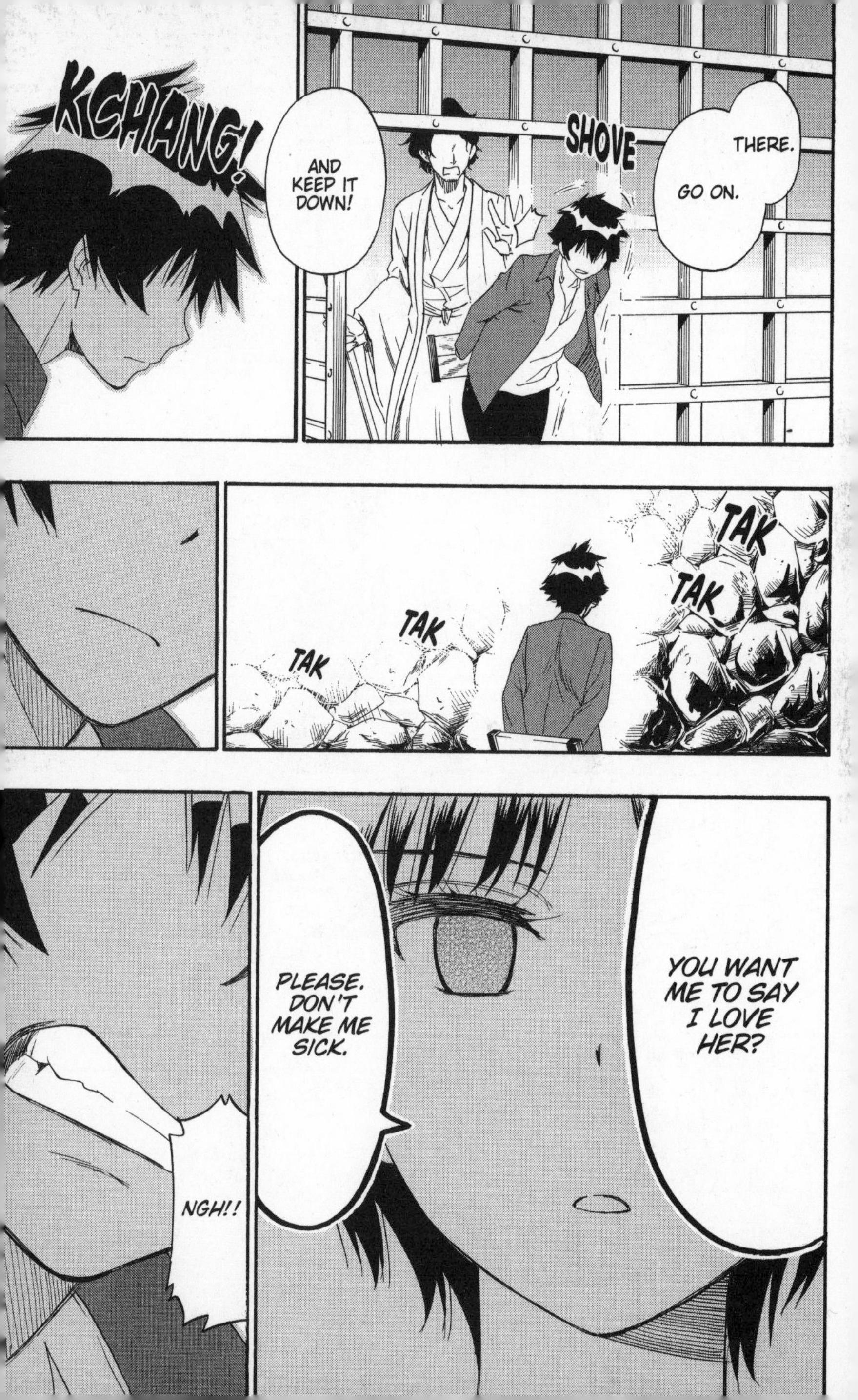
THERE.
GO ON.
SHOVE
AND KEEP IT DOWN!
KCHANG!
TAK
TAK
TAK
TAK
YOU WANT ME TO SAY I LOVE HER?
PLEASE. DON'T MAKE ME SICK.
NGH!!

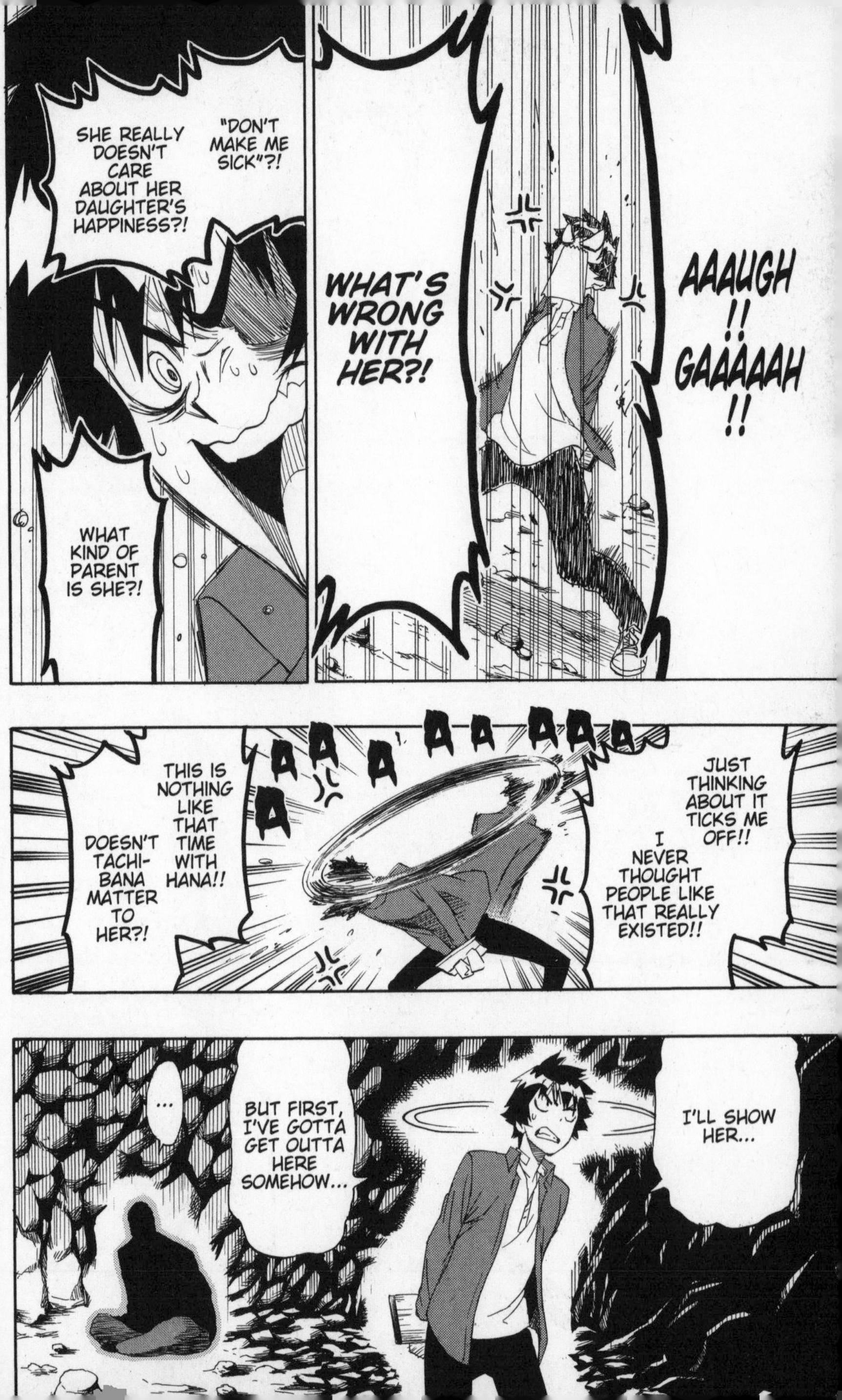
AAAUGH!! GAAAAAH!!
WHAT'S WRONG WITH HER?!
"DON'T MAKE ME SICK"?!
SHE REALLY DOESN'T CARE ABOUT HER DAUGHTER'S HAPPINESS?!
WHAT KIND OF PARENT IS SHE?!
JUST THINKING ABOUT IT TICKS ME OFF!!
I NEVER THOUGHT PEOPLE LIKE THAT REALLY EXISTED!!
AAAAAAAAAAA
THIS IS NOTHING LIKE THAT TIME WITH HANA!!
DOESN'T TACHI-BANA MATTER TO HER?!
I'LL SHOW HER...
BUT FIRST, I'VE GOTTA GET OUTTA HERE SOMEHOW...
...

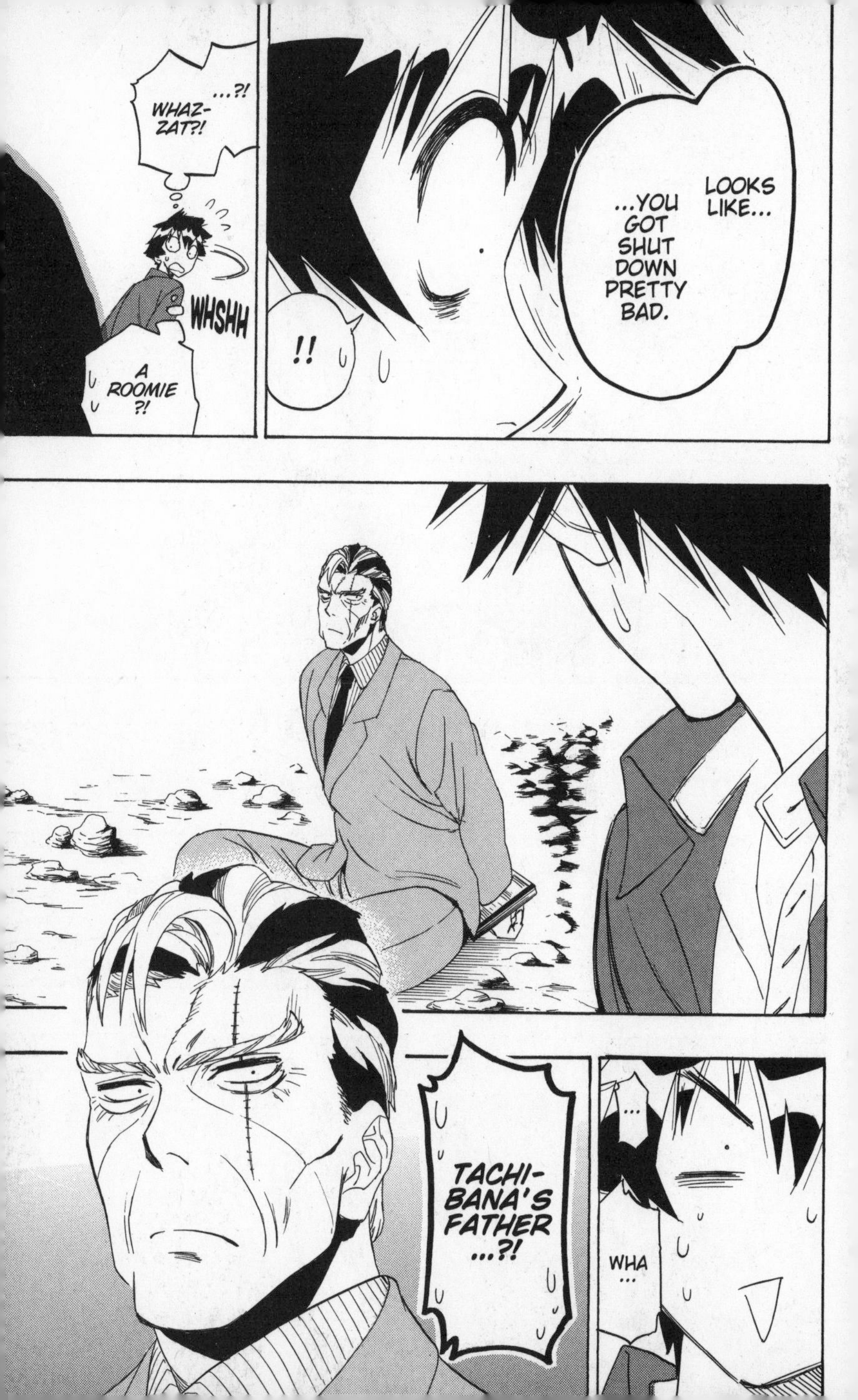
LOOKS LIKE...
...YOU GOT SHUT DOWN PRETTY BAD.
!!
...?!
WHAZ-ZAT?!
WHSHH
A ROOMIE?!
...
WHA...
TACHI-BANA'S FATHER...?!

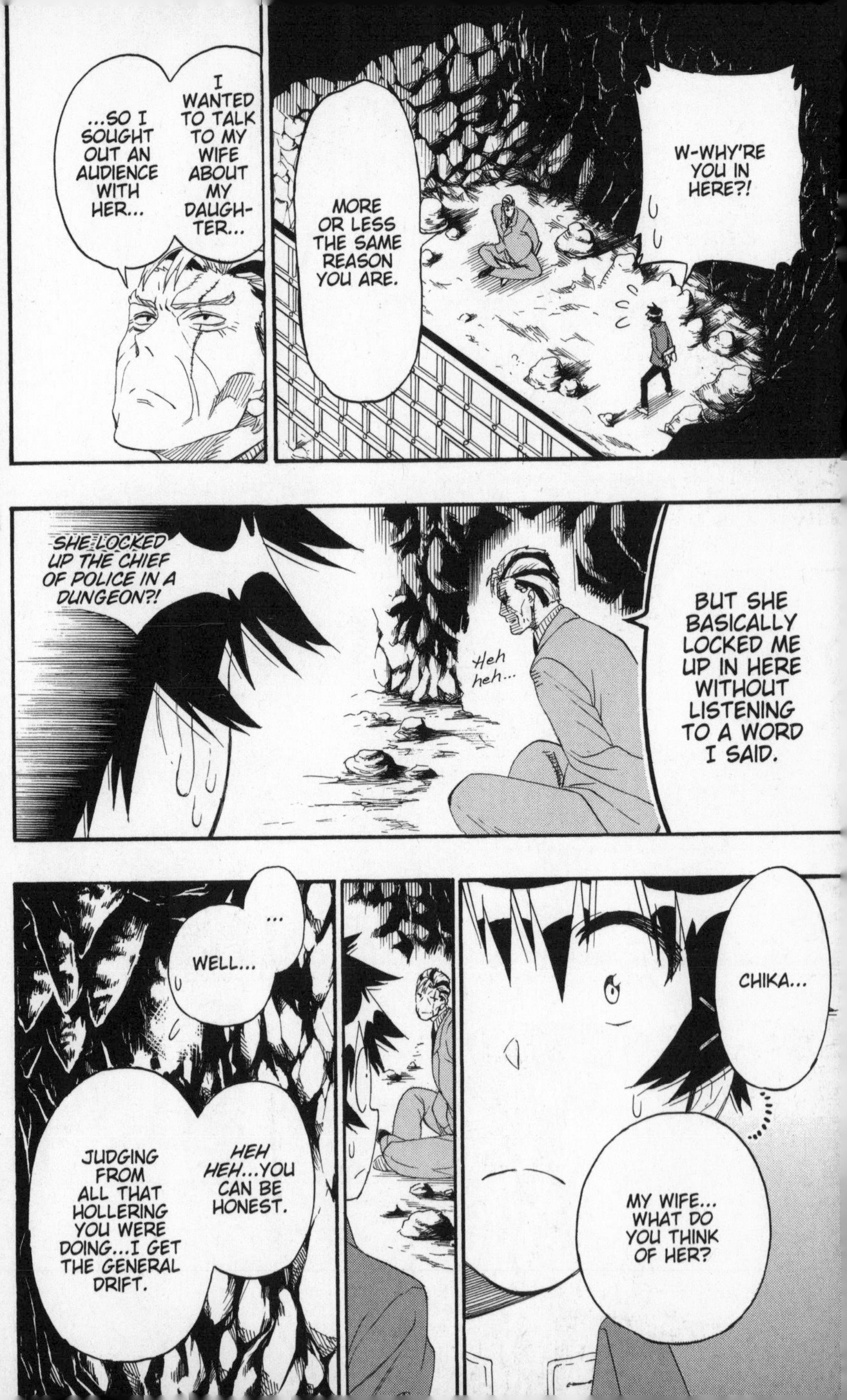
W-WHY'RE YOU IN HERE?!
MORE OR LESS THE SAME REASON YOU ARE.
I WANTED TO TALK TO MY WIFE ABOUT MY DAUGHTER...
...SO I SOUGHT OUT AN AUDIENCE WITH HER...
BUT SHE BASICALLY LOCKED ME UP IN HERE WITHOUT LISTENING TO A WORD I SAID.
Heh heh...
SHE LOCKED UP THE CHIEF OF POLICE IN A DUNGEON?!
CHIKA...
MY WIFE... WHAT DO YOU THINK OF HER?
HEH HEH...YOU CAN BE HONEST.
...
WELL...
JUDGING FROM ALL THAT HOLLERING YOU WERE DOING...I GET THE GENERAL DRIFT.

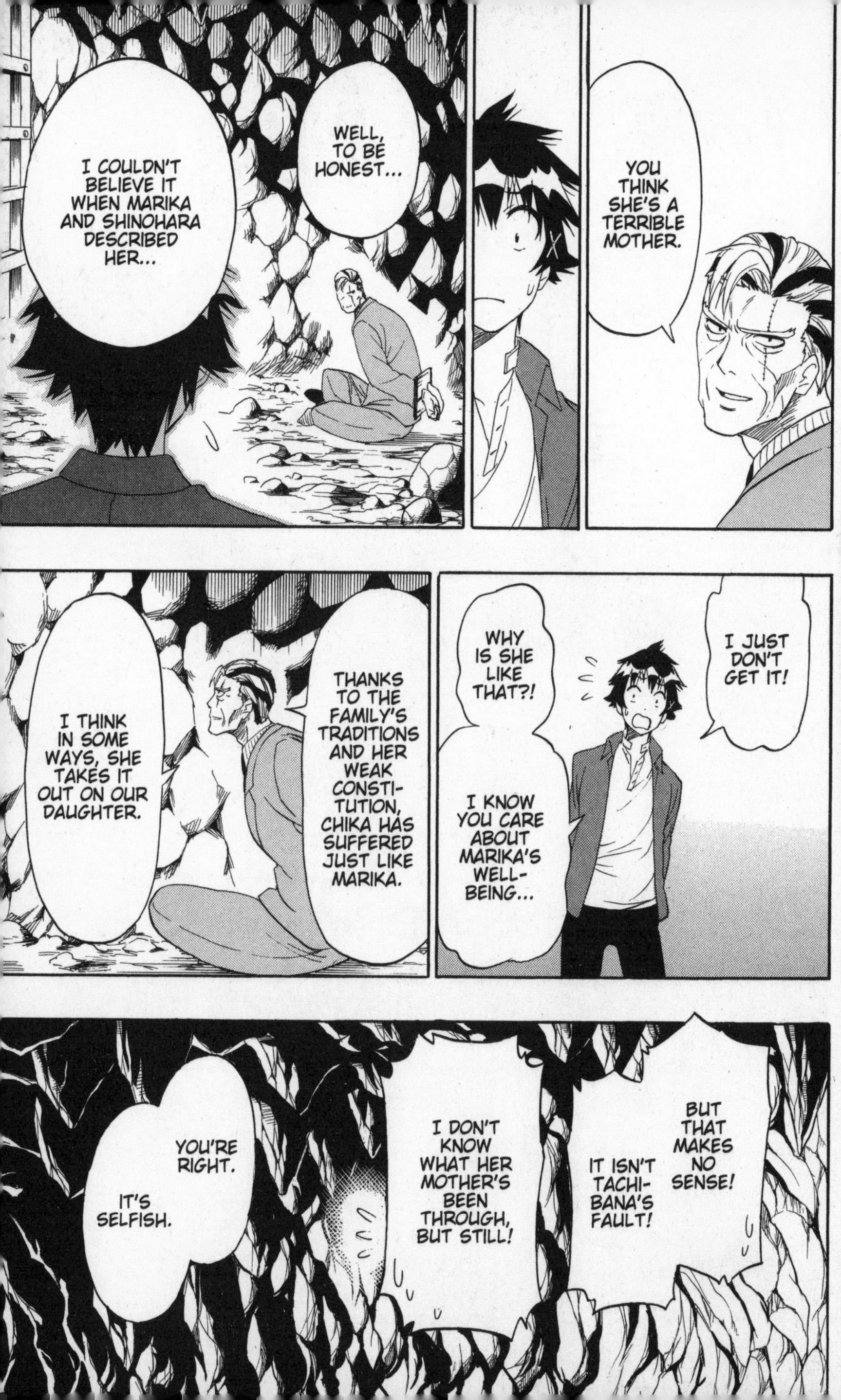
YOU THINK SHE'S A TERRIBLE MOTHER.
WELL, TO BE HONEST...
I COULDN'T BELIEVE IT WHEN MARIKA AND SHINOHARA DESCRIBED HER...
I JUST DON'T GET IT!
WHY IS SHE LIKE THAT?!
I KNOW YOU CARE ABOUT MARIKA'S WELL-BEING...
THANKS TO THE FAMILY'S TRADITIONS AND HER WEAK CONSTI-TUTION, CHIKA HAS SUFFERED JUST LIKE MARIKA.
I THINK IN SOME WAYS, SHE TAKES IT OUT ON OUR DAUGHTER.
BUT THAT MAKES NO SENSE!
IT ISN'T TACHI-BANA'S FAULT!
I DON'T KNOW WHAT HER MOTHER'S BEEN THROUGH, BUT STILL!
YOU'RE RIGHT.
IT'S SELFISH.

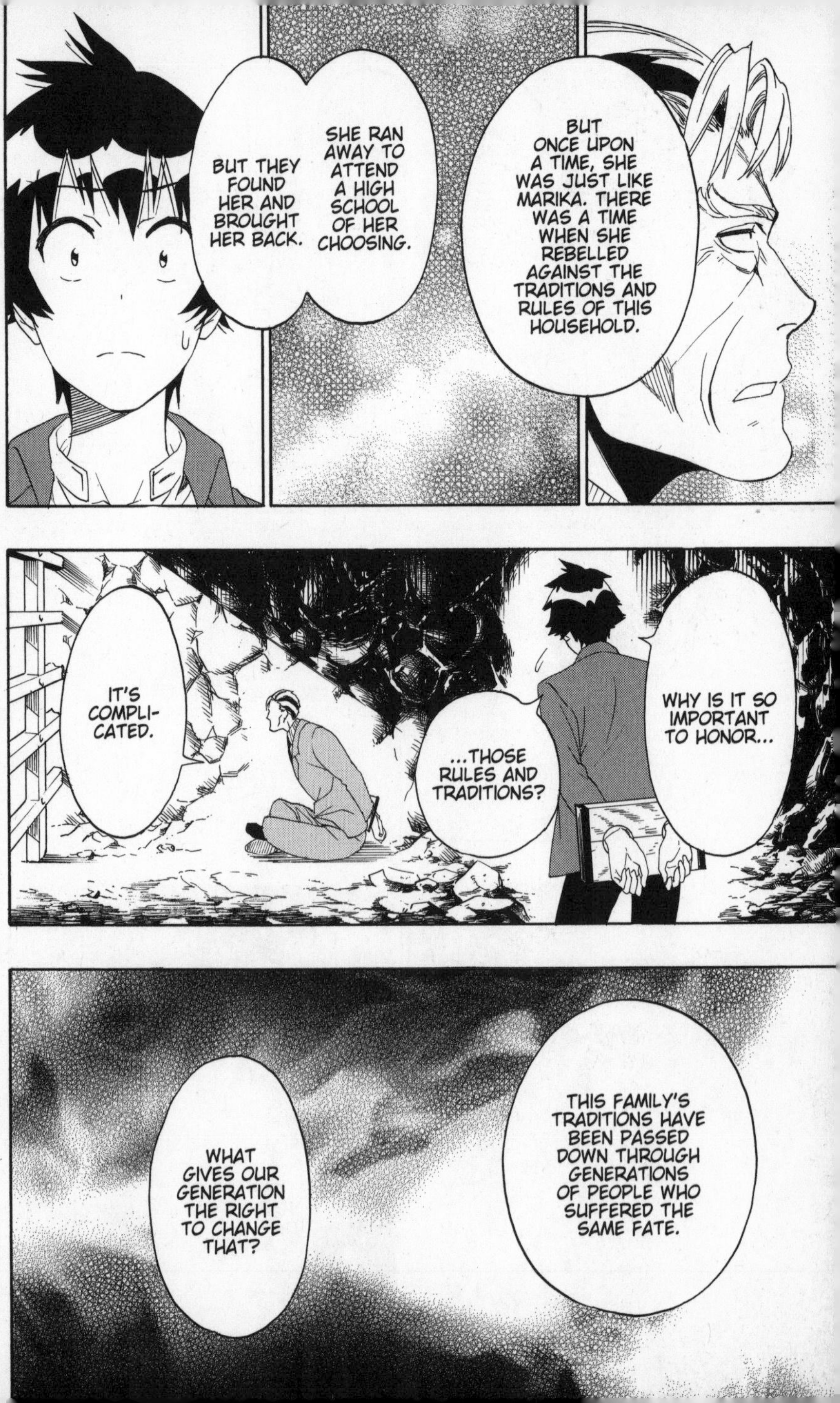
BUT ONCE UPON A TIME, SHE WAS JUST LIKE MARIKA. THERE WAS A TIME WHEN SHE REBELLED AGAINST THE TRADITIONS AND RULES OF THIS HOUSEHOLD.
SHE RAN AWAY TO ATTEND A HIGH SCHOOL OF HER CHOOSING.
BUT THEY FOUND HER AND BROUGHT HER BACK.
WHY IS IT SO IMPORTANT TO HONOR...
...THOSE RULES AND TRADITIONS?
IT'S COMPLI-CATED.
THIS FAMILY'S TRADITIONS HAVE BEEN PASSED DOWN THROUGH GENERATIONS OF PEOPLE WHO SUFFERED THE SAME FATE.
WHAT GIVES OUR GENERATION THE RIGHT TO CHANGE THAT?

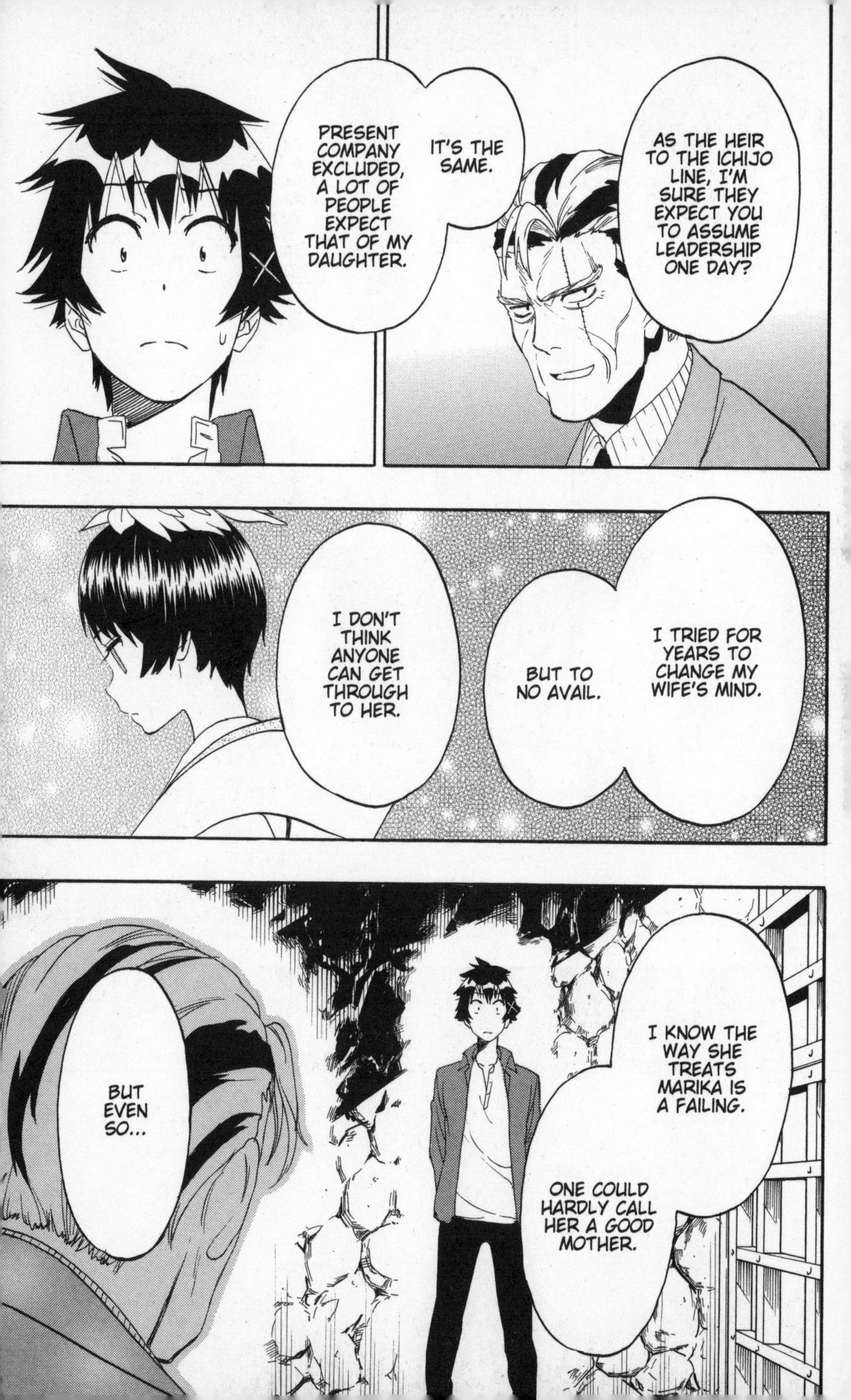
AS THE HEIR TO THE ICHIJO LINE, I'M SURE THEY EXPECT YOU TO ASSUME LEADERSHIP ONE DAY?
IT'S THE SAME.
PRESENT COMPANY EXCLUDED, A LOT OF PEOPLE EXPECT THAT OF MY DAUGHTER.
I TRIED FOR YEARS TO CHANGE MY WIFE'S MIND.
BUT TO NO AVAIL.
I DON'T THINK ANYONE CAN GET THROUGH TO HER.
I KNOW THE WAY SHE TREATS MARIKA IS A FAILING.
ONE COULD HARDLY CALL HER A GOOD MOTHER.
BUT EVEN SO...

...LOVE HER.

I STILL...

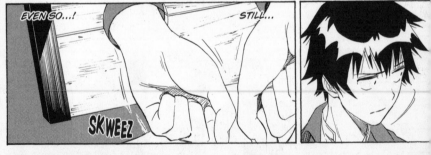

EVEN SO...!

STILL...

SK WEEZ

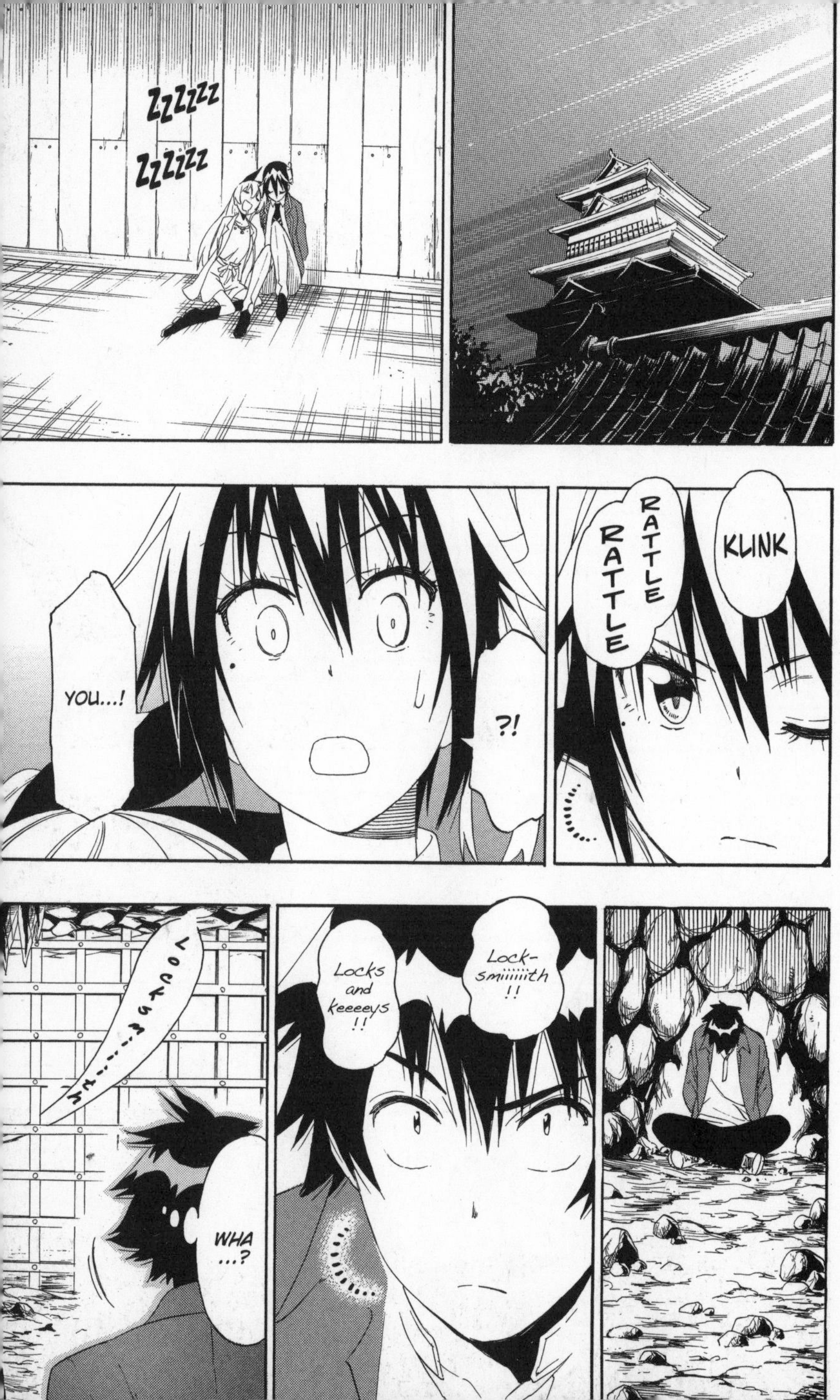
ZZZZZZ
ZZZZZZ
KLINK
RATTLE RATTLE
?!
YOU...!
Lock-smiiiiiith!!
Locks and keeeeys!!
Locksmi......th
WHA...?

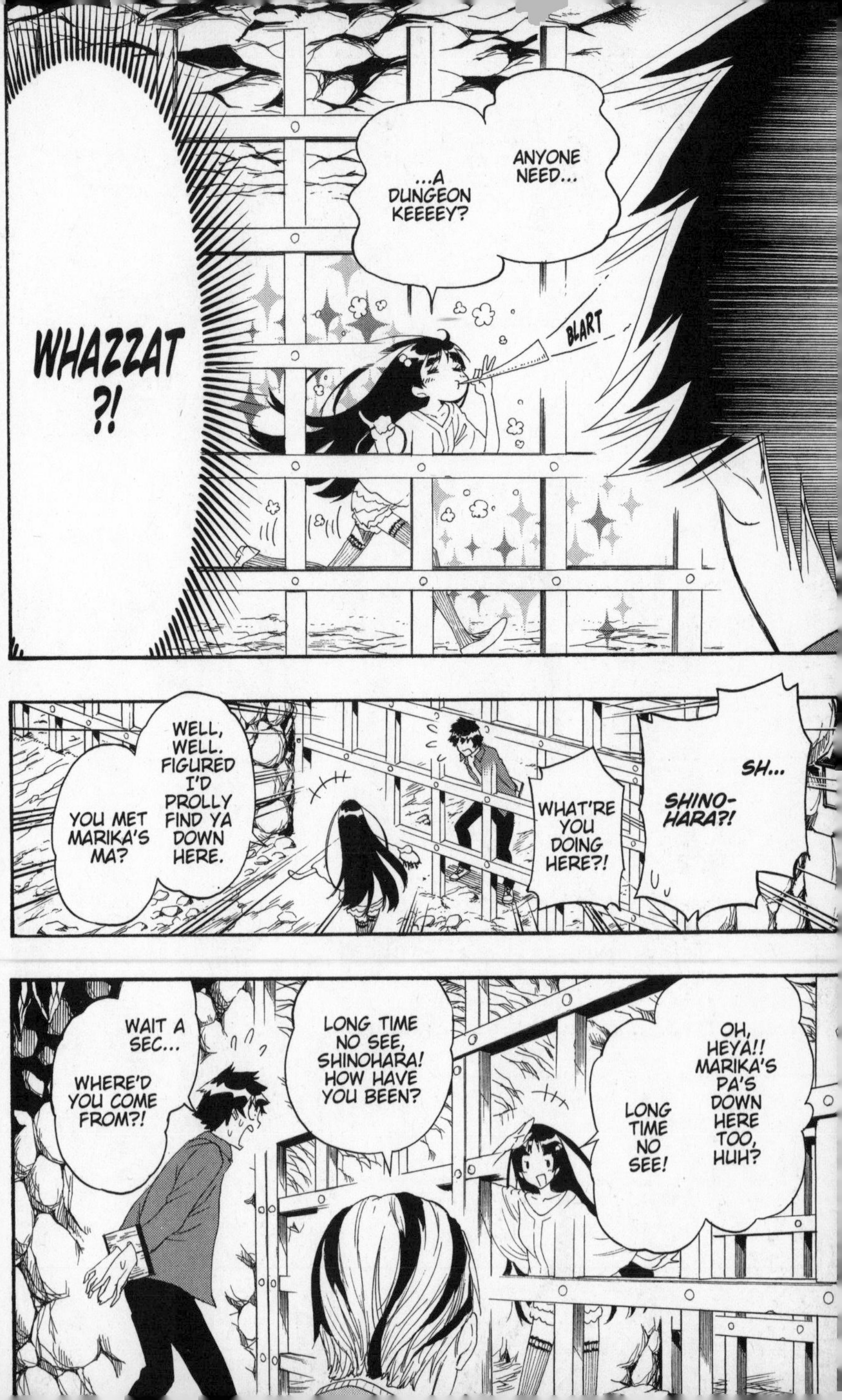

ANYONE NEED...
...A DUNGEON KEEEEY?
BLART
WHAZZAT ?!
SH...
SHINO-HARA?!
WHAT'RE YOU DOING HERE?!
WELL, WELL. FIGURED I'D PROLLY FIND YA DOWN HERE.
YOU MET MARIKA'S MA?
OH, HEYA!! MARIKA'S PA'S DOWN HERE TOO, HUH?
LONG TIME NO SEE!
LONG TIME NO SEE, SHINOHARA! HOW HAVE YOU BEEN?
WAIT A SEC...
WHERE'D YOU COME FROM?!

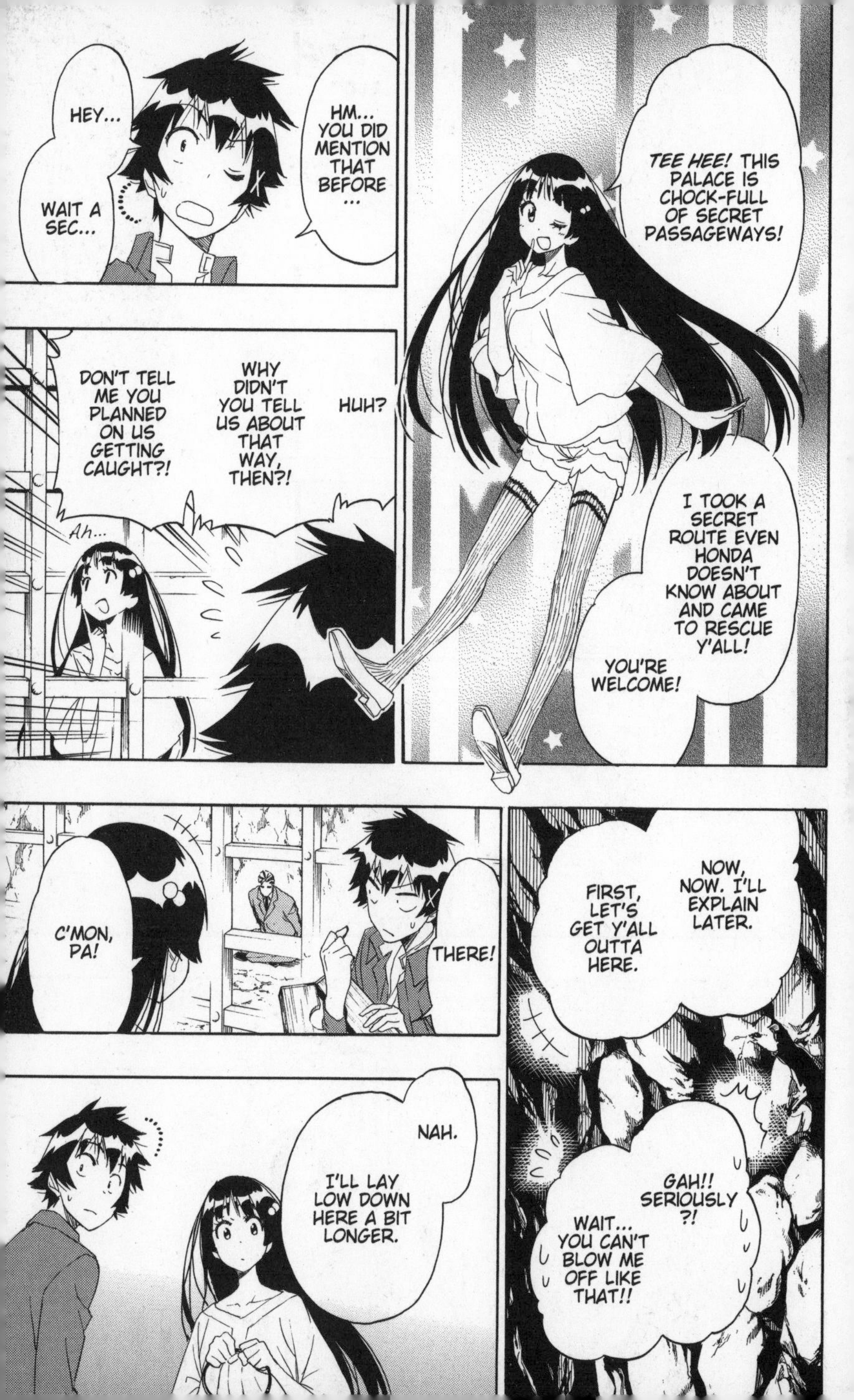
TEE HEE! THIS PALACE IS CHOCK-FULL OF SECRET PASSAGEWAYS!
I TOOK A SECRET ROUTE EVEN HONDA DOESN'T KNOW ABOUT AND CAME TO RESCUE Y'ALL!
YOU'RE WELCOME!
HM... YOU DID MENTION THAT BEFORE...
HEY...
WAIT A SEC...
HUH?
WHY DIDN'T YOU TELL US ABOUT THAT WAY, THEN?!
DON'T TELL ME YOU PLANNED ON US GETTING CAUGHT?!
Ah...
NOW, NOW. I'LL EXPLAIN LATER.
FIRST, LET'S GET Y'ALL OUTTA HERE.
GAH!! SERIOUSLY?!
WAIT... YOU CAN'T BLOW ME OFF LIKE THAT!!
THERE!
C'MON, PA!
NAH.
I'LL LAY LOW DOWN HERE A BIT LONGER.

WHAT DO YOU PLAN TO DO NOW THAT YOU'RE OUT?

ICHIJO...

NOW...

I'M SORRY.

I KNOW IT MIGHT CAUSE A LOT OF TROUBLE FOR YOU, SIR...

BUT I...I...

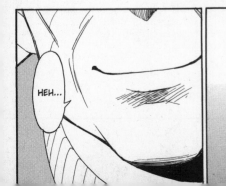

HEH...

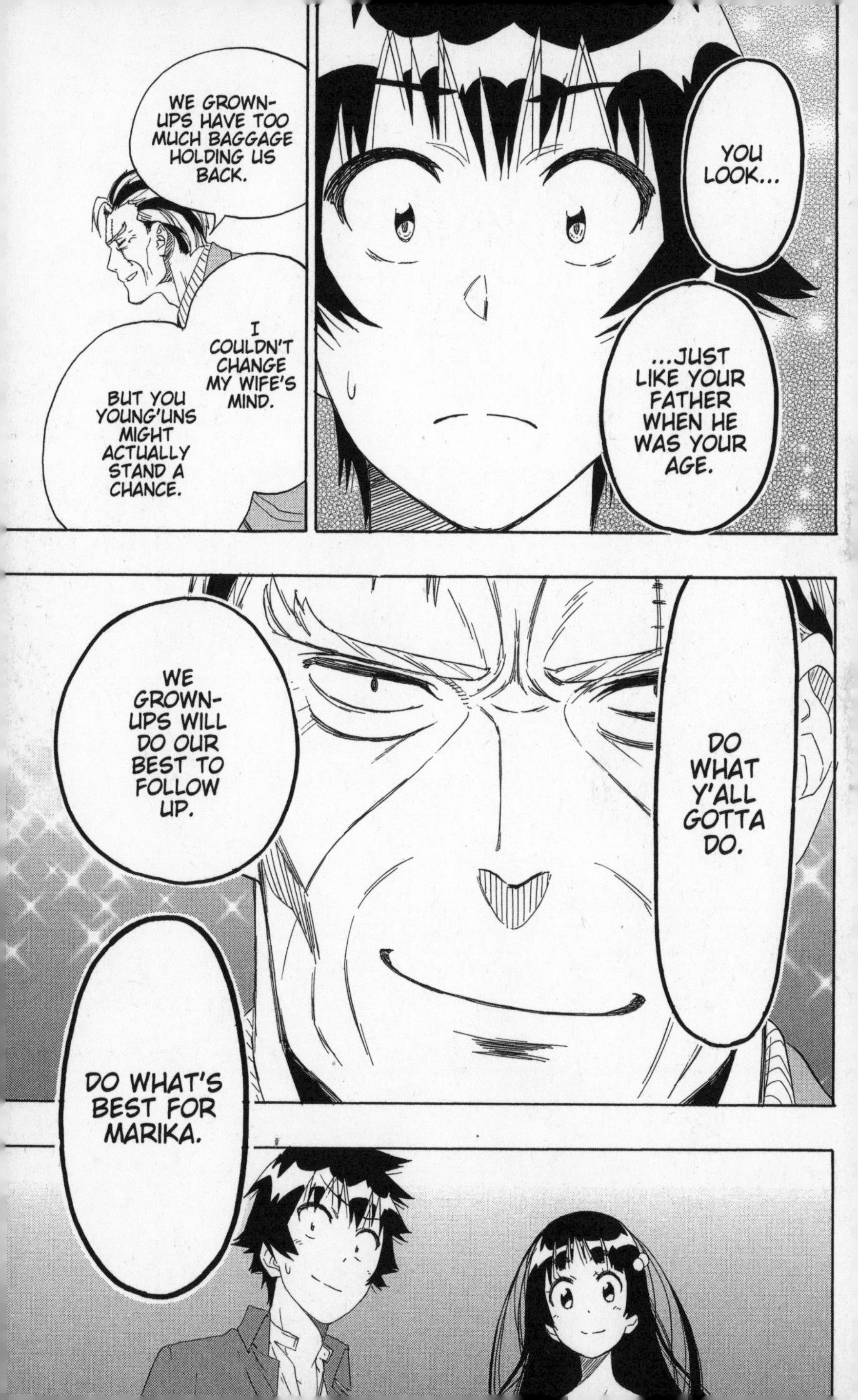
YOU LOOK...
...JUST LIKE YOUR FATHER WHEN HE WAS YOUR AGE.
WE GROWN-UPS HAVE TOO MUCH BAGGAGE HOLDING US BACK.
I COULDN'T CHANGE MY WIFE'S MIND.
BUT YOU YOUNG'UNS MIGHT ACTUALLY STAND A CHANCE.
DO WHAT Y'ALL GOTTA DO.
WE GROWN-UPS WILL DO OUR BEST TO FOLLOW UP.
DO WHAT'S BEST FOR MARIKA.

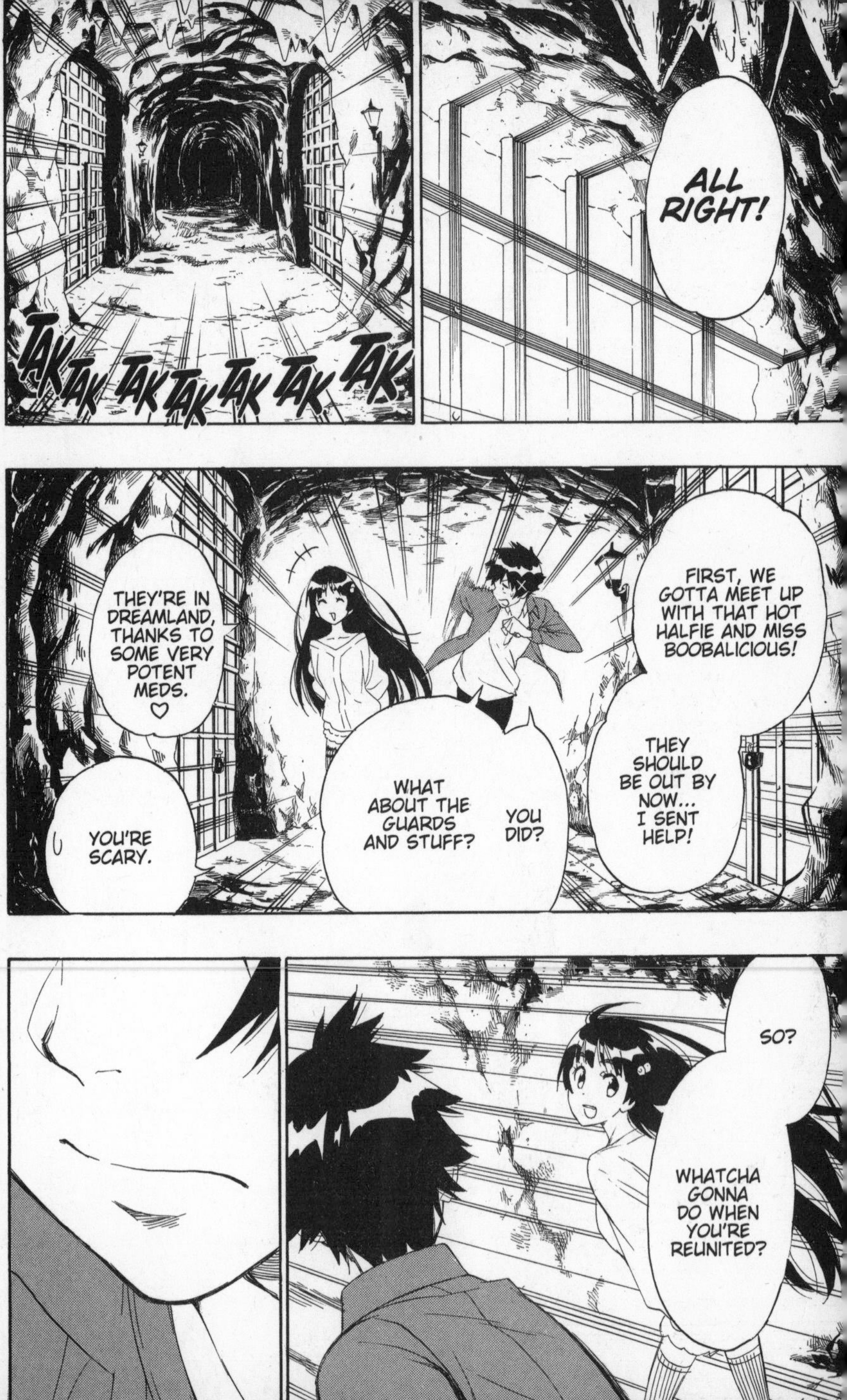
ALL RIGHT!
TAK TAK TAK TAK TAK TAK TAK
FIRST, WE GOTTA MEET UP WITH THAT HOT HALFIE AND MISS BOOBALICIOUS!
THEY SHOULD BE OUT BY NOW... I SENT HELP!
YOU DID?
WHAT ABOUT THE GUARDS AND STUFF?
THEY'RE IN DREAMLAND, THANKS TO SOME VERY POTENT MEDS. ♡
YOU'RE SCARY.
SO?
WHATCHA GONNA DO WHEN YOU'RE REUNITED?

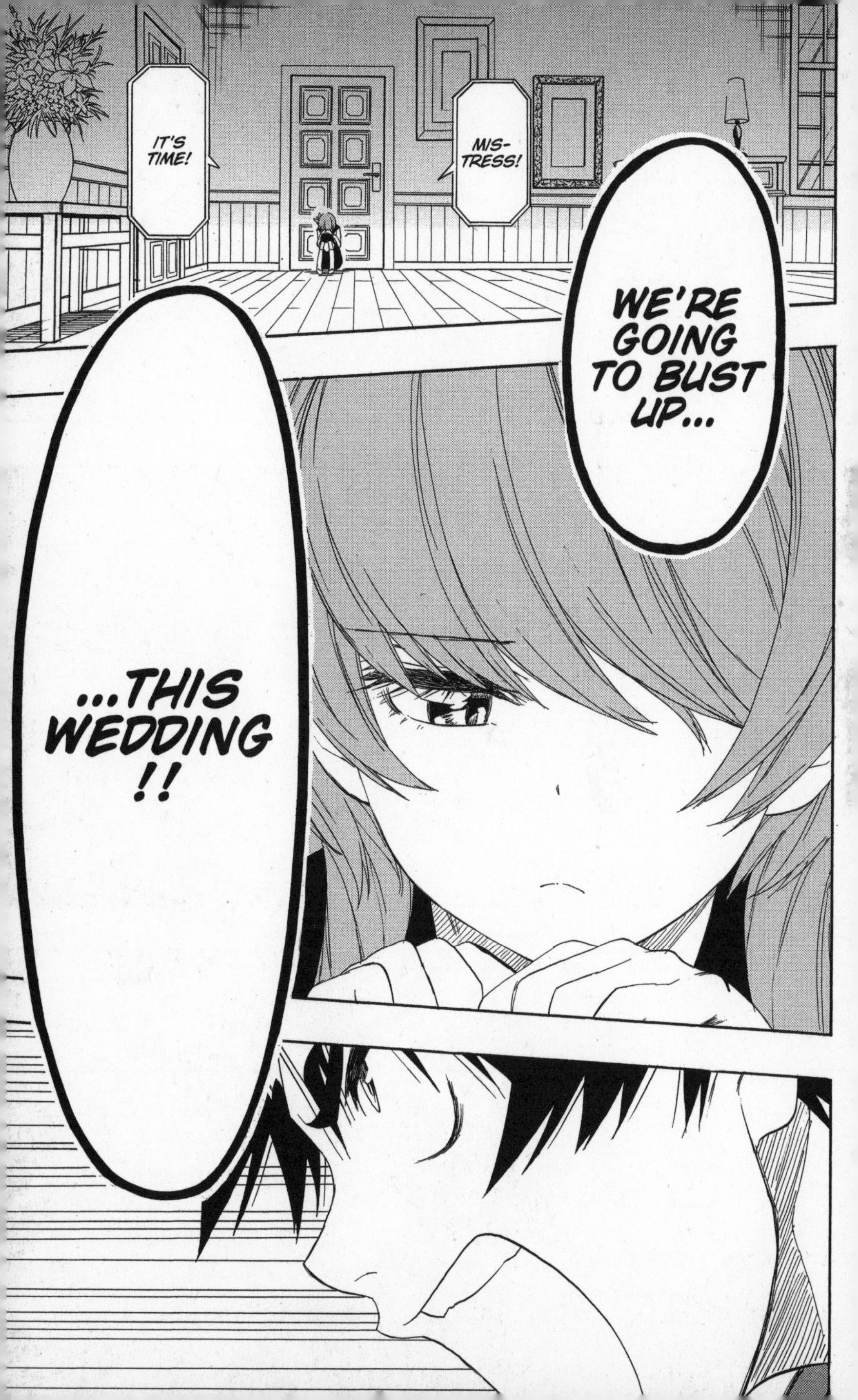
MIS-TRESS!
IT'S TIME!
WE'RE GOING TO BUST UP...
...THIS WEDDING !!

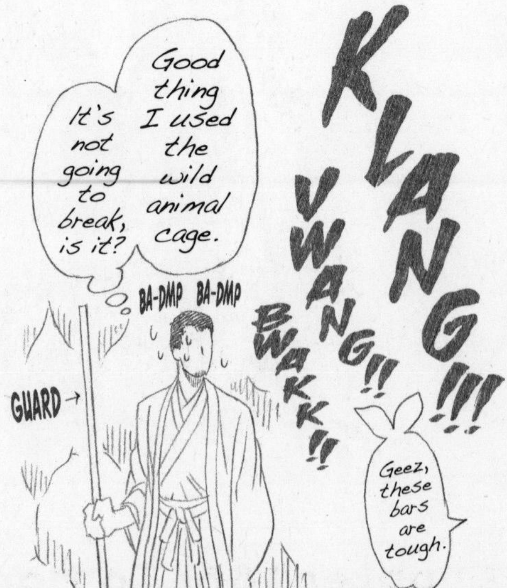
KLANG!!!
VWANG!!
BWAKK!!
Geez, these bars are tough.
Good thing I used the wild animal cage.
It's not going to break, is it?
BA-DMP BA-DMP
GUARD →

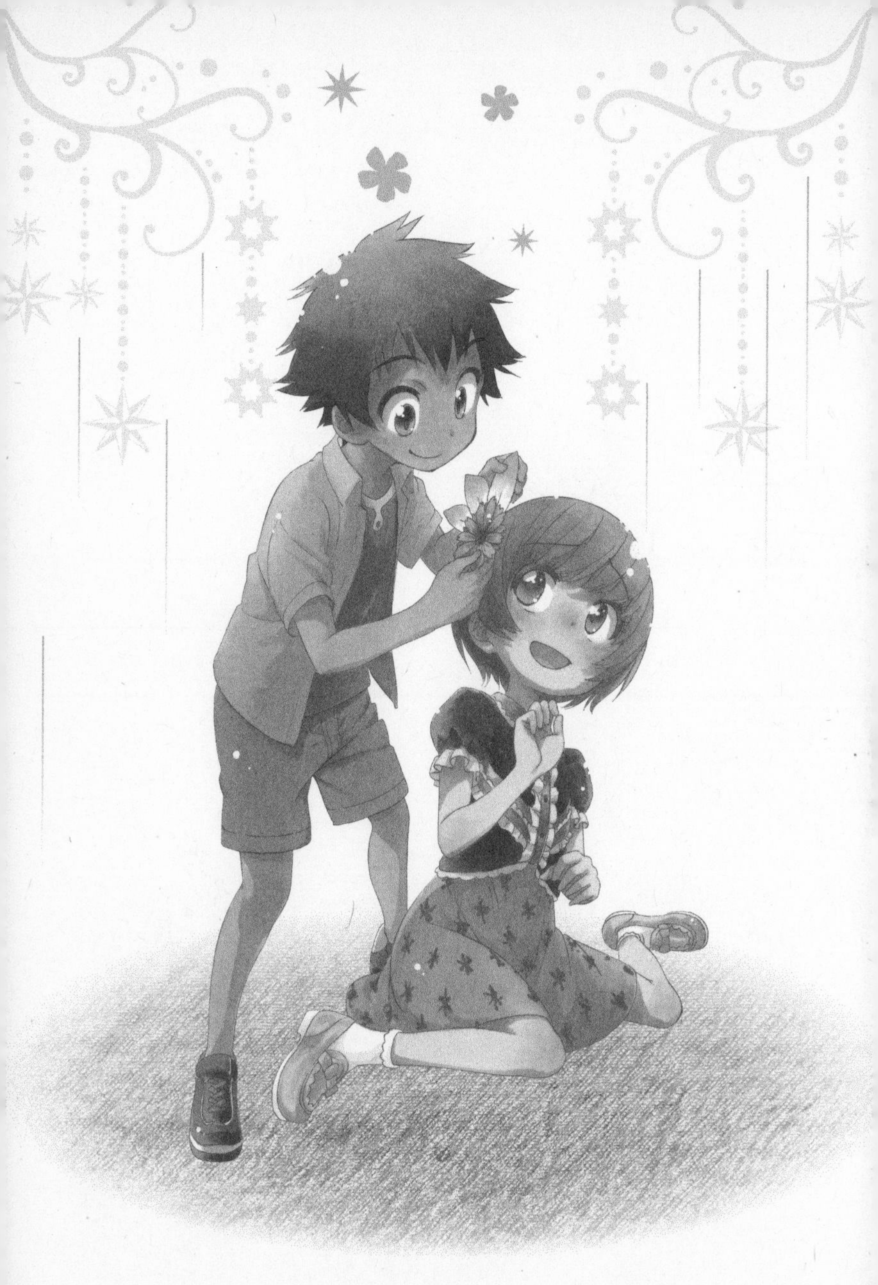

Chapter 188: To Mari

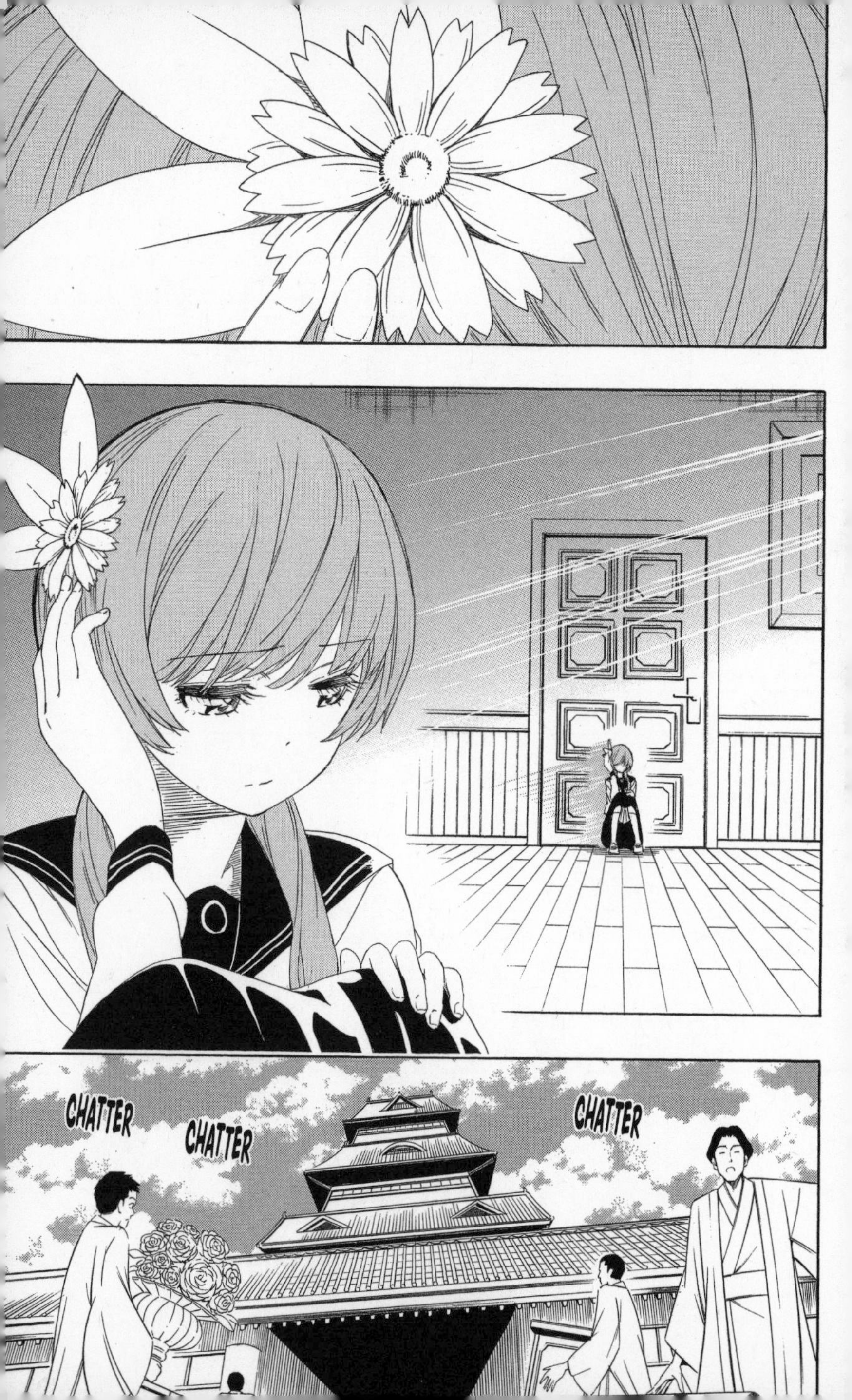
CHATTER
CHATTER
CHATTER

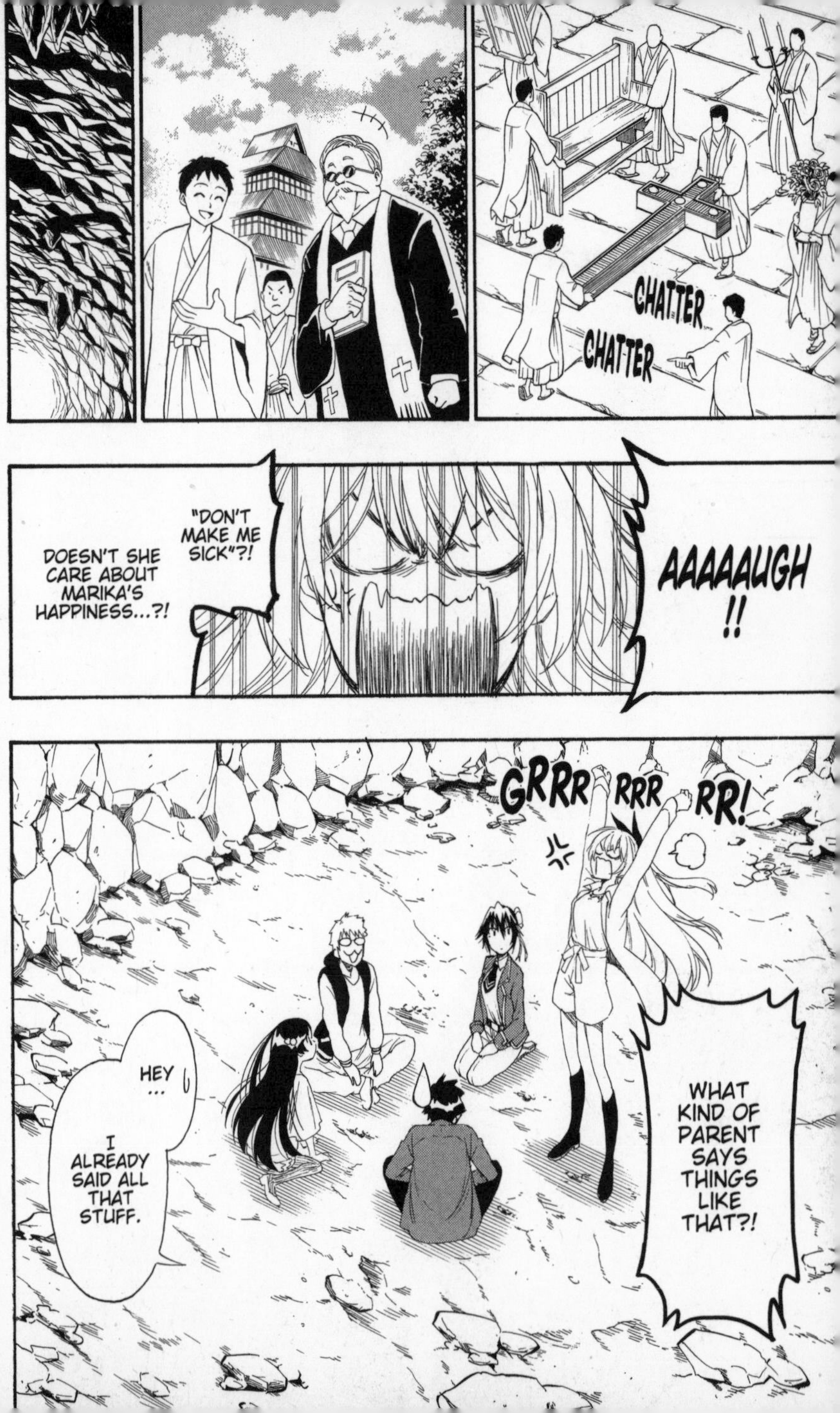

CHATTER
CHATTER
AAAAAUGH!!
"DON'T MAKE ME SICK"?!
DOESN'T SHE CARE ABOUT MARIKA'S HAPPINESS...?!
GRRRRRRRR!
WHAT KIND OF PARENT SAYS THINGS LIKE THAT?!
HEY...
I ALREADY SAID ALL THAT STUFF.

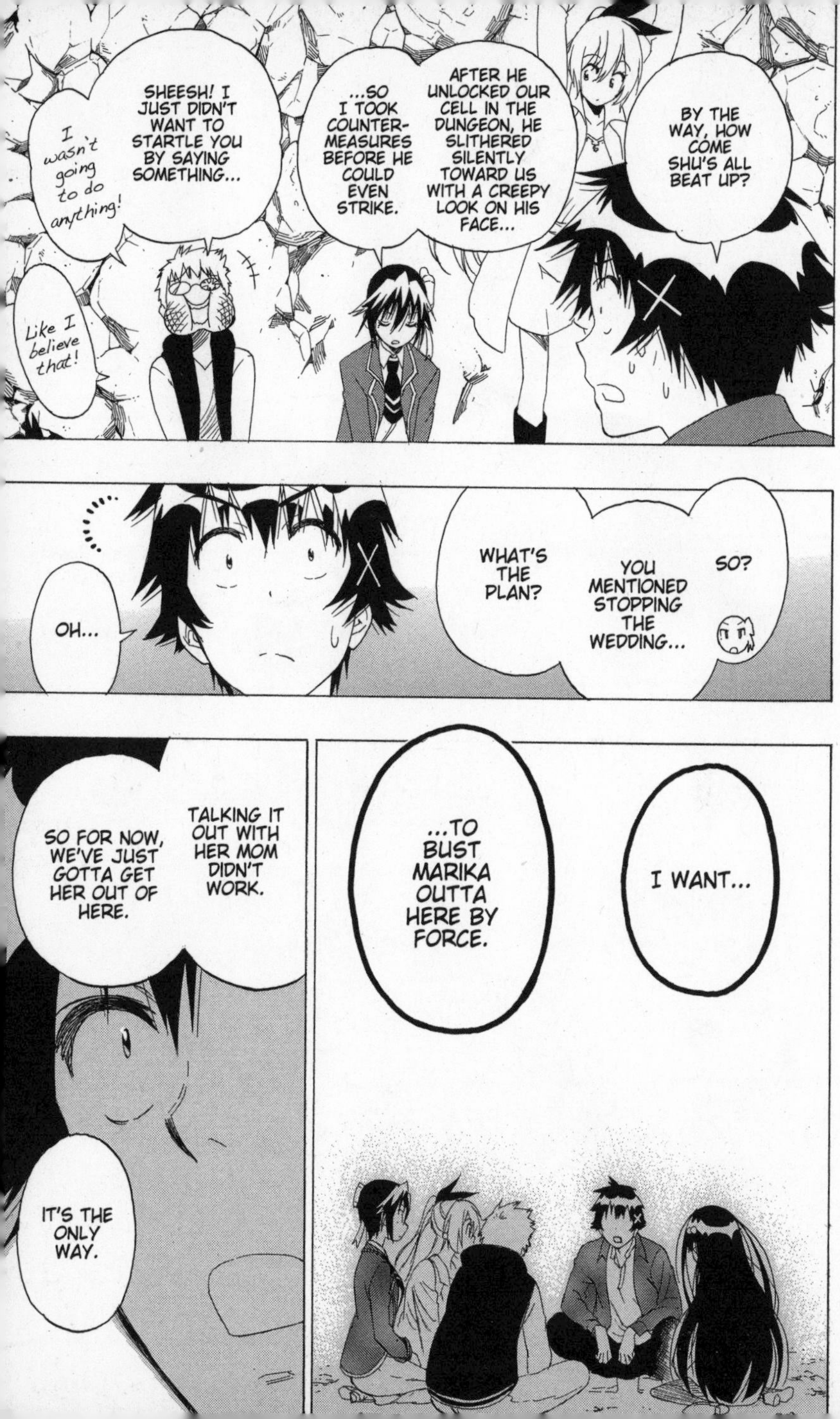
BY THE WAY, HOW COME SHU'S ALL BEAT UP?
AFTER HE UNLOCKED OUR CELL IN THE DUNGEON, HE SLITHERED SILENTLY TOWARD US WITH A CREEPY LOOK ON HIS FACE...
...SO I TOOK COUNTER-MEASURES BEFORE HE COULD EVEN STRIKE.
SHEESH! I JUST DIDN'T WANT TO STARTLE YOU BY SAYING SOMETHING...
I wasn't going to do anything!
Like I believe that!
SO?
YOU MENTIONED STOPPING THE WEDDING...
WHAT'S THE PLAN?
OH...
I WANT...
...TO BUST MARIKA OUTTA HERE BY FORCE.
TALKING IT OUT WITH HER MOM DIDN'T WORK.
SO FOR NOW, WE'VE JUST GOTTA GET HER OUT OF HERE.
IT'S THE ONLY WAY.

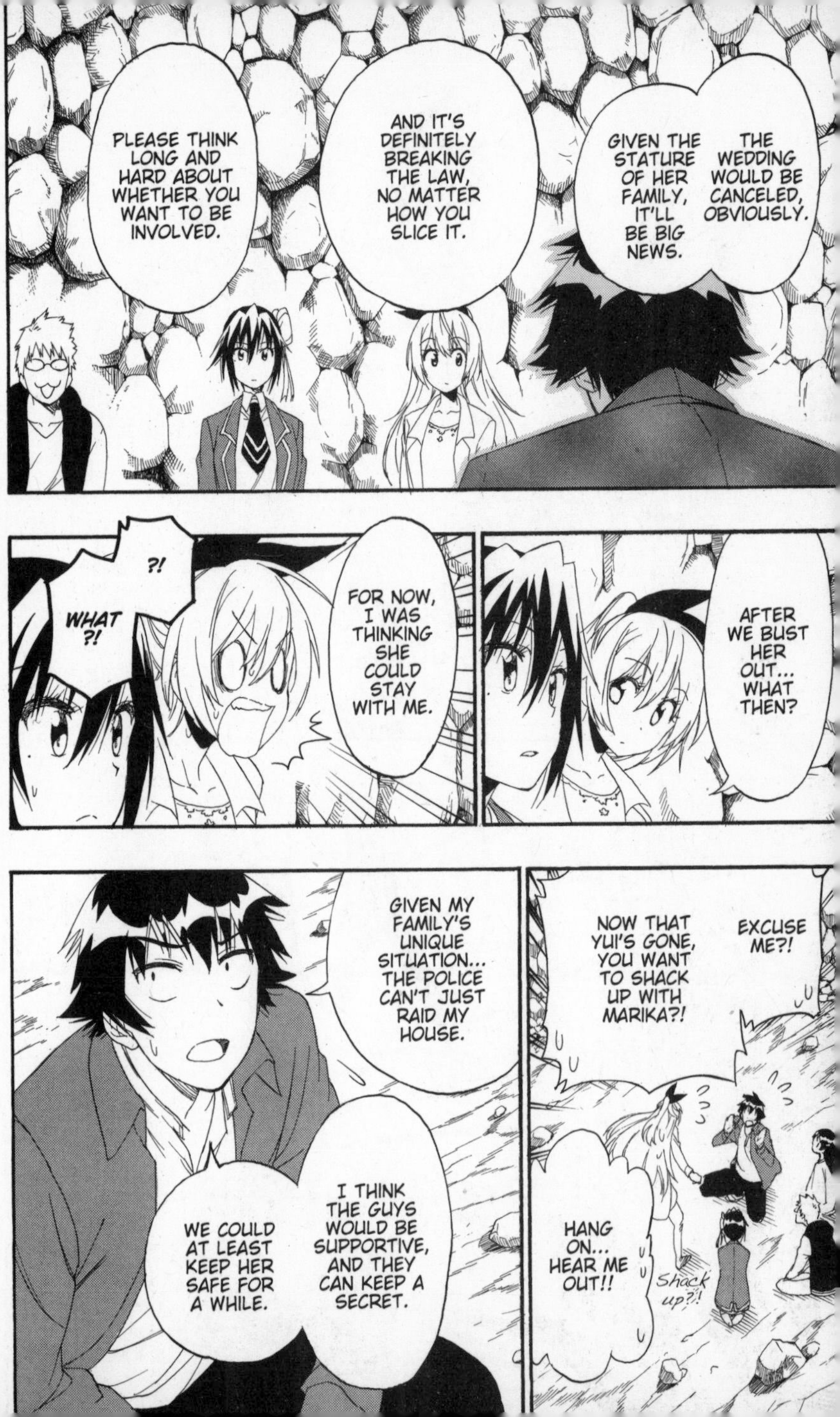
THE WEDDING WOULD BE CANCELED, OBVIOUSLY.
GIVEN THE STATURE OF HER FAMILY, IT'LL BE BIG NEWS.
AND IT'S DEFINITELY BREAKING THE LAW, NO MATTER HOW YOU SLICE IT.
PLEASE THINK LONG AND HARD ABOUT WHETHER YOU WANT TO BE INVOLVED.
AFTER WE BUST HER OUT... WHAT THEN?
FOR NOW, I WAS THINKING SHE COULD STAY WITH ME.
?!
WHAT ?!
EXCUSE ME?!
NOW THAT YUI'S GONE, YOU WANT TO SHACK UP WITH MARIKA?!
HANG ON... HEAR ME OUT!!
Shack up?!
GIVEN MY FAMILY'S UNIQUE SITUATION... THE POLICE CAN'T JUST RAID MY HOUSE.
I THINK THE GUYS WOULD BE SUPPORTIVE, AND THEY CAN KEEP A SECRET.
WE COULD AT LEAST KEEP HER SAFE FOR A WHILE.

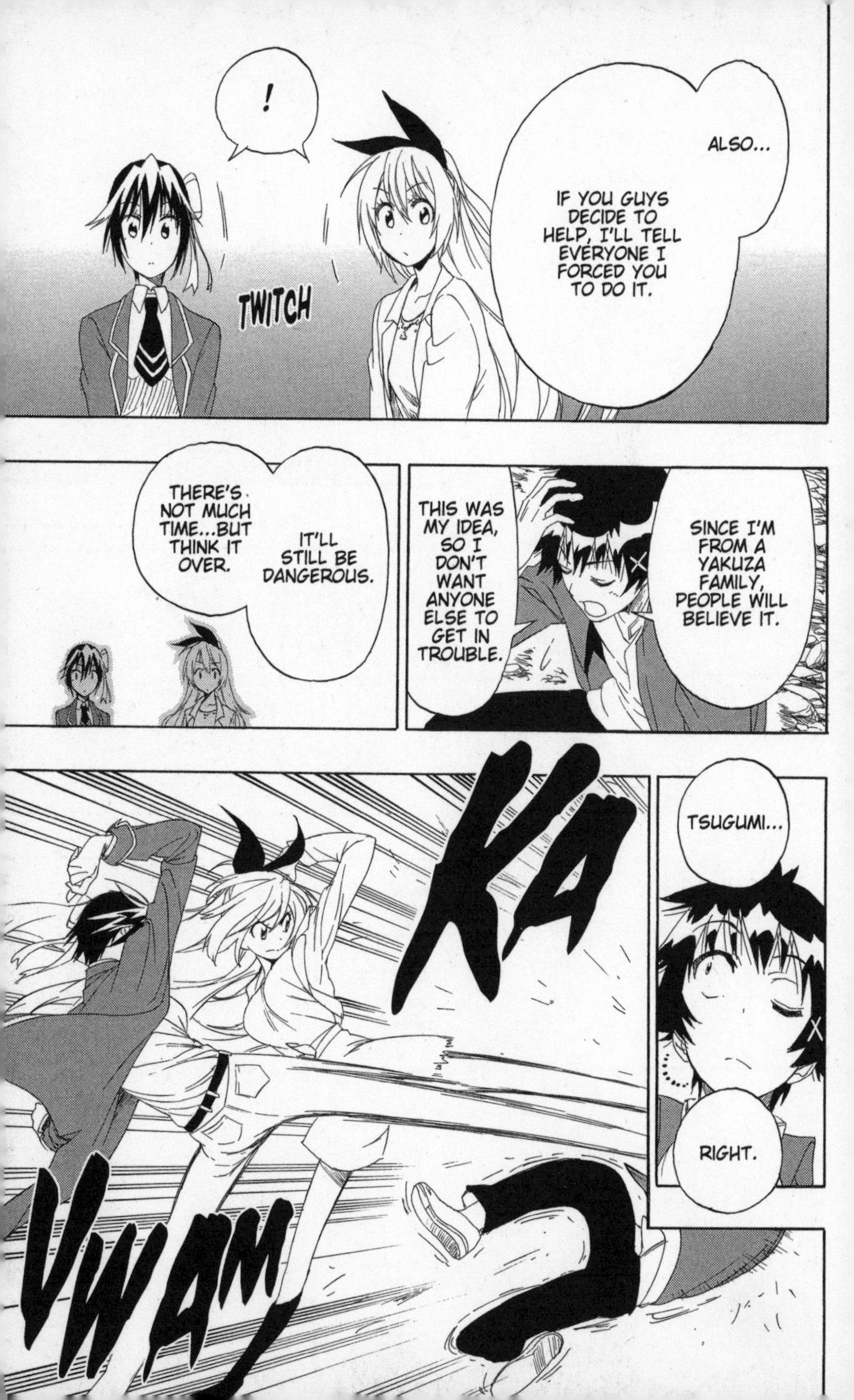
ALSO...
IF YOU GUYS DECIDE TO HELP, I'LL TELL EVERYONE I FORCED YOU TO DO IT.
!
TWITCH
SINCE I'M FROM A YAKUZA FAMILY, PEOPLE WILL BELIEVE IT.
THIS WAS MY IDEA, SO I DON'T WANT ANYONE ELSE TO GET IN TROUBLE.
IT'LL STILL BE DANGEROUS.
THERE'S NOT MUCH TIME...BUT THINK IT OVER.
TSUGUMI...
RIGHT.
KA
VWAM

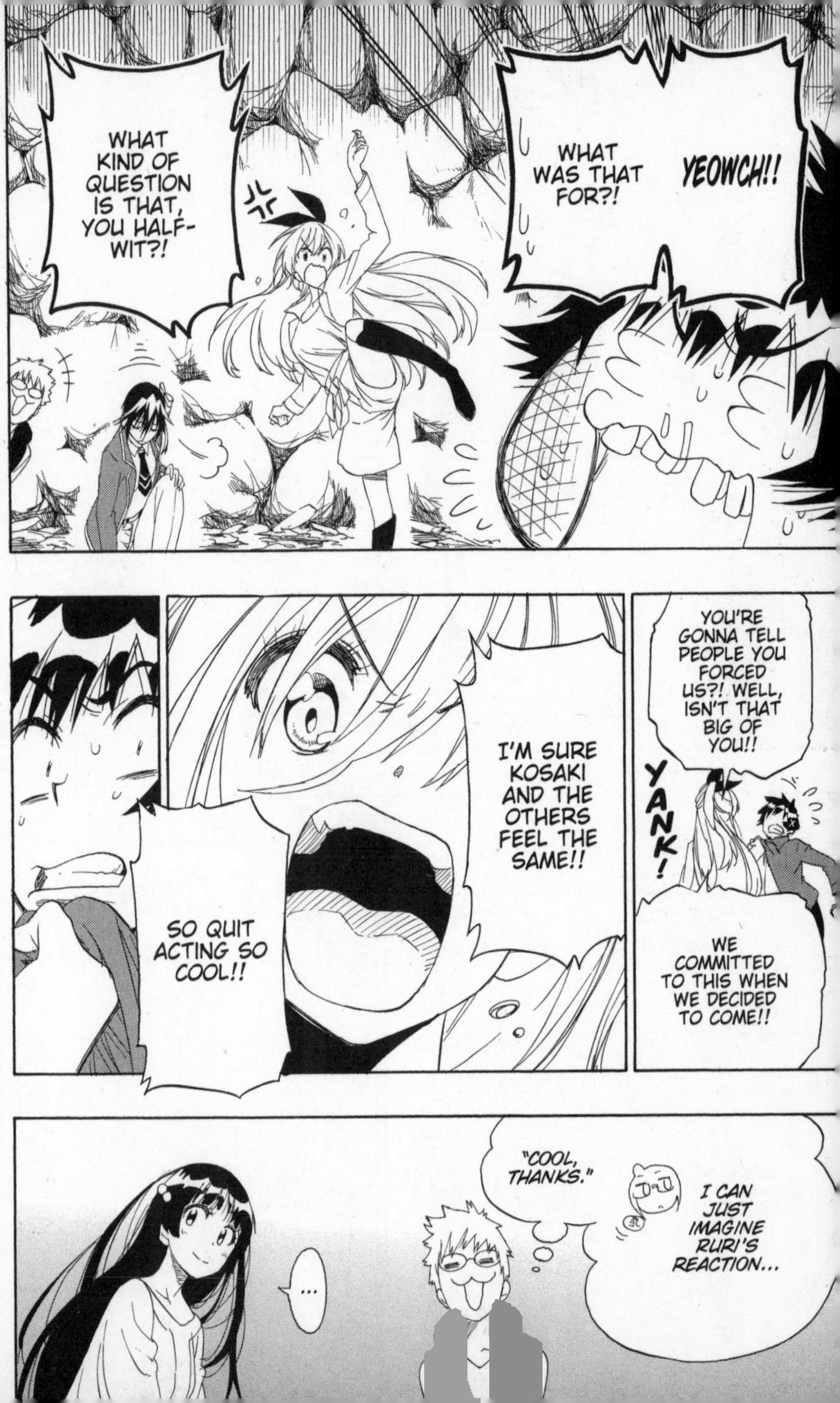
YEOWCH!!
WHAT WAS THAT FOR?!
WHAT KIND OF QUESTION IS THAT, YOU HALF-WIT?!
YOU'RE GONNA TELL PEOPLE YOU FORCED US?! WELL, ISN'T THAT BIG OF YOU!!
YANK!
WE COMMITTED TO THIS WHEN WE DECIDED TO COME!!
I'M SURE KOSAKI AND THE OTHERS FEEL THE SAME!!
SO QUIT ACTING SO COOL!!
I CAN JUST IMAGINE RURI'S REACTION...
"COOL, THANKS."
...

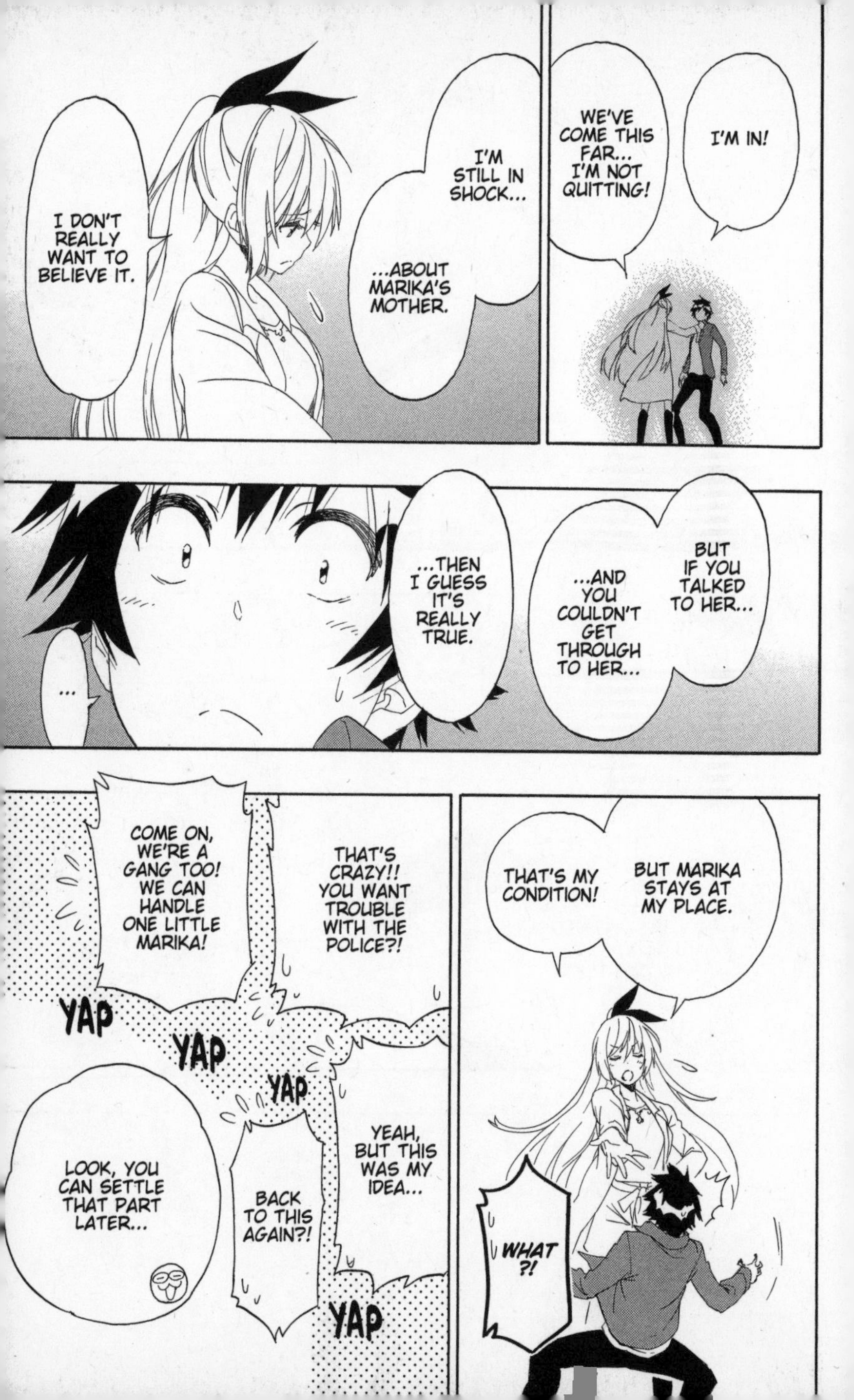
I'M IN!
WE'VE COME THIS FAR... I'M NOT QUITTING!
I'M STILL IN SHOCK...
...ABOUT MARIKA'S MOTHER.
I DON'T REALLY WANT TO BELIEVE IT.
BUT IF YOU TALKED TO HER...
...AND YOU COULDN'T GET THROUGH TO HER...
...THEN I GUESS IT'S REALLY TRUE.
...
BUT MARIKA STAYS AT MY PLACE.
THAT'S MY CONDITION!
WHAT?!
THAT'S CRAZY!! YOU WANT TROUBLE WITH THE POLICE?!
COME ON, WE'RE A GANG TOO! WE CAN HANDLE ONE LITTLE MARIKA!
YAP
YAP
YAP
YEAH, BUT THIS WAS MY IDEA...
BACK TO THIS AGAIN?!
LOOK, YOU CAN SETTLE THAT PART LATER...
YAP

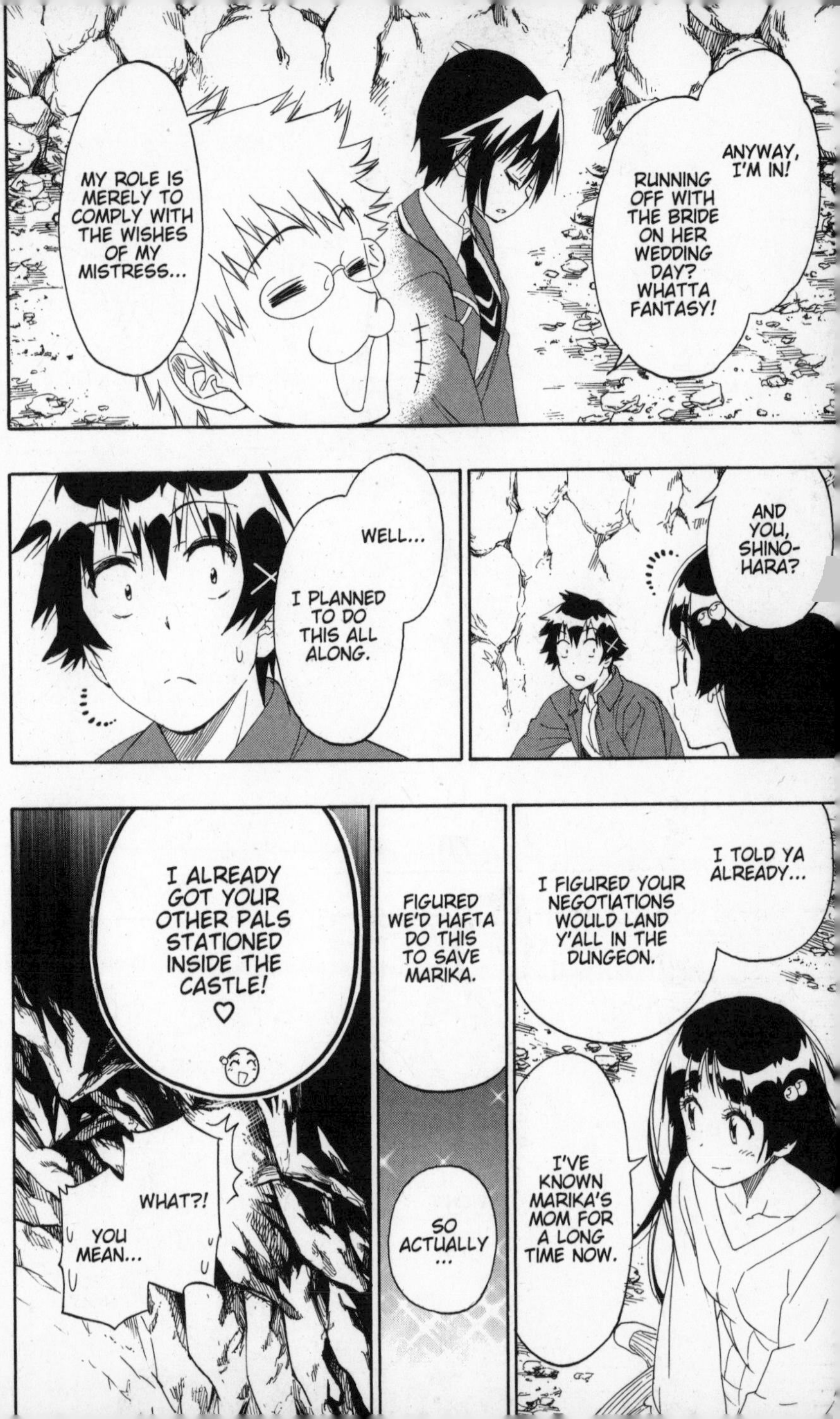
ANYWAY, I'M IN!
RUNNING OFF WITH THE BRIDE ON HER WEDDING DAY? WHATTA FANTASY!
MY ROLE IS MERELY TO COMPLY WITH THE WISHES OF MY MISTRESS...
AND YOU, SHINO-HARA?
WELL...
I PLANNED TO DO THIS ALL ALONG.
I TOLD YA ALREADY...
I FIGURED YOUR NEGOTIATIONS WOULD LAND Y'ALL IN THE DUNGEON.
I'VE KNOWN MARIKA'S MOM FOR A LONG TIME NOW.
FIGURED WE'D HAFTA DO THIS TO SAVE MARIKA.
SO ACTUALLY ...
I ALREADY GOT YOUR OTHER PALS STATIONED INSIDE THE CASTLE! ♡
WHAT?!
YOU MEAN...

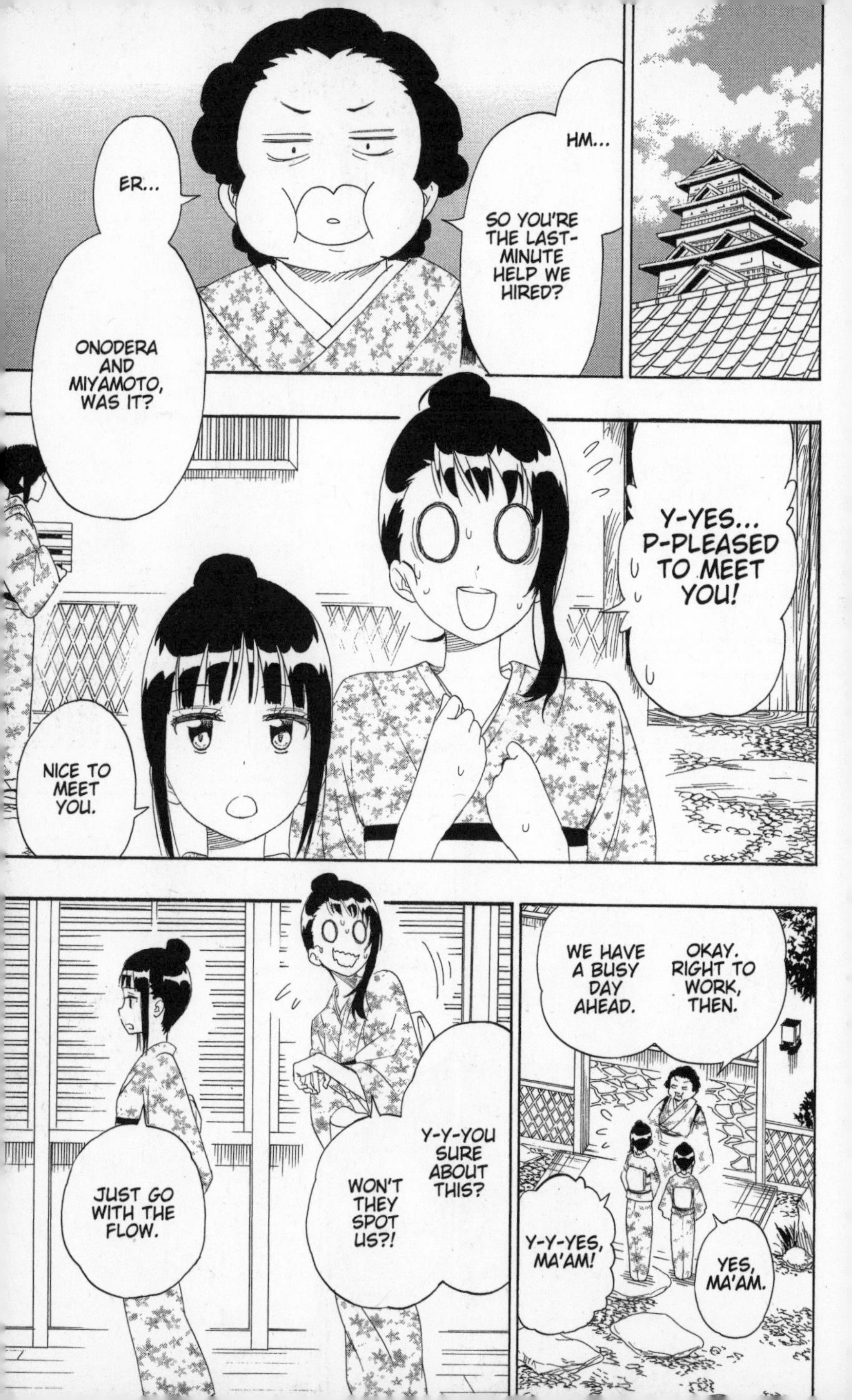
HM...
SO YOU'RE THE LAST-MINUTE HELP WE HIRED?
ER...
ONODERA AND MIYAMOTO, WAS IT?
Y-YES... P-PLEASED TO MEET YOU!
NICE TO MEET YOU.
OKAY. RIGHT TO WORK, THEN.
WE HAVE A BUSY DAY AHEAD.
YES, MA'AM.
Y-Y-YES, MA'AM!
Y-Y-YOU SURE ABOUT THIS?
WON'T THEY SPOT US?!
JUST GO WITH THE FLOW.

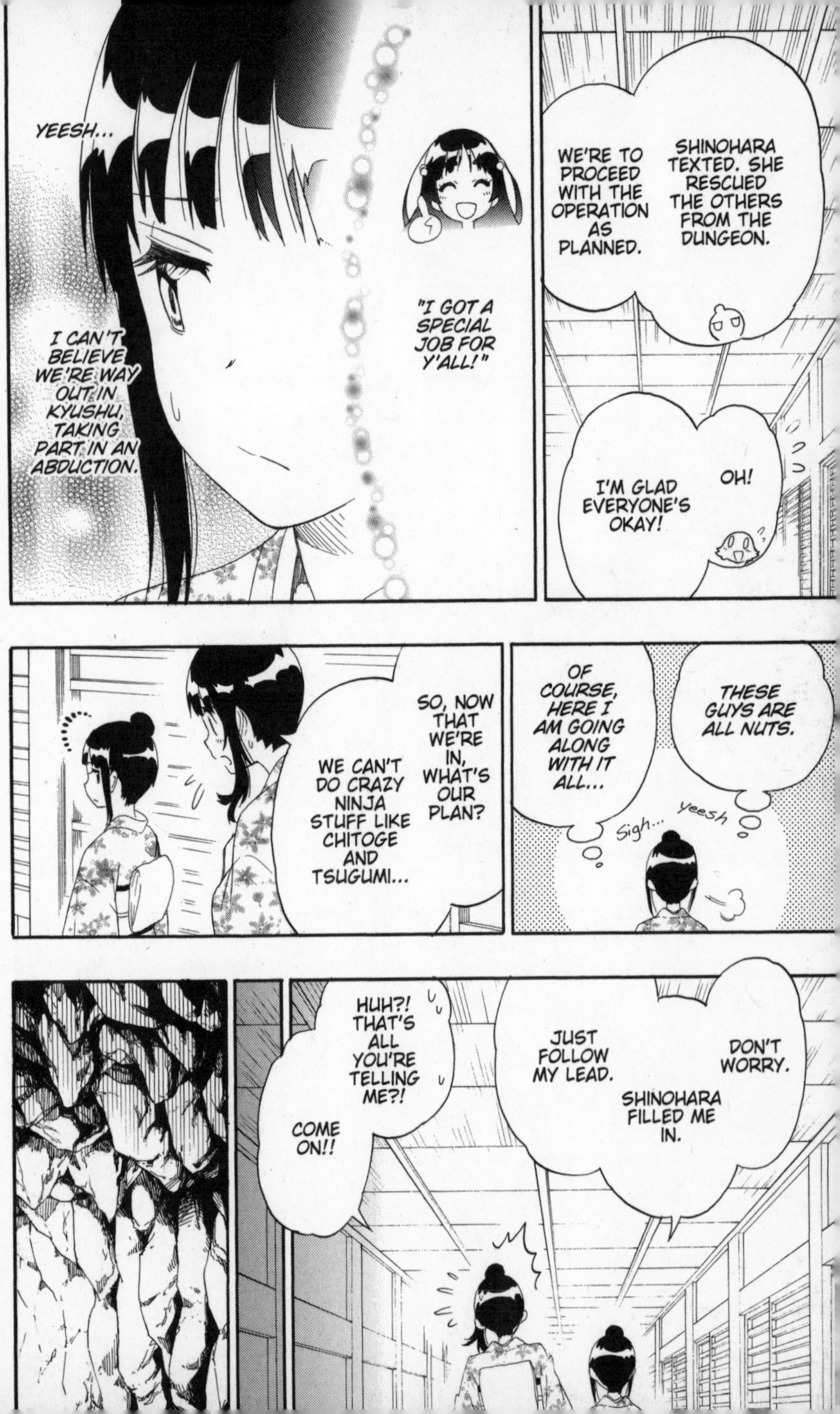
SHINOHARA TEXTED. SHE RESCUED THE OTHERS FROM THE DUNGEON.
WE'RE TO PROCEED WITH THE OPERATION AS PLANNED.
OH!
I'M GLAD EVERYONE'S OKAY!
"I GOT A SPECIAL JOB FOR Y'ALL!"
YEESH...
I CAN'T BELIEVE WE'RE WAY OUT IN KYUSHU, TAKING PART IN AN ABDUCTION.
THESE GUYS ARE ALL NUTS.
OF COURSE, HERE I AM GOING ALONG WITH IT ALL...
yeesh
Sigh...
SO, NOW THAT WE'RE IN, WHAT'S OUR PLAN?
WE CAN'T DO CRAZY NINJA STUFF LIKE CHITOGE AND TSUGUMI...
DON'T WORRY.
SHINOHARA FILLED ME IN.
JUST FOLLOW MY LEAD.
HUH?! THAT'S ALL YOU'RE TELLING ME?!
COME ON!!

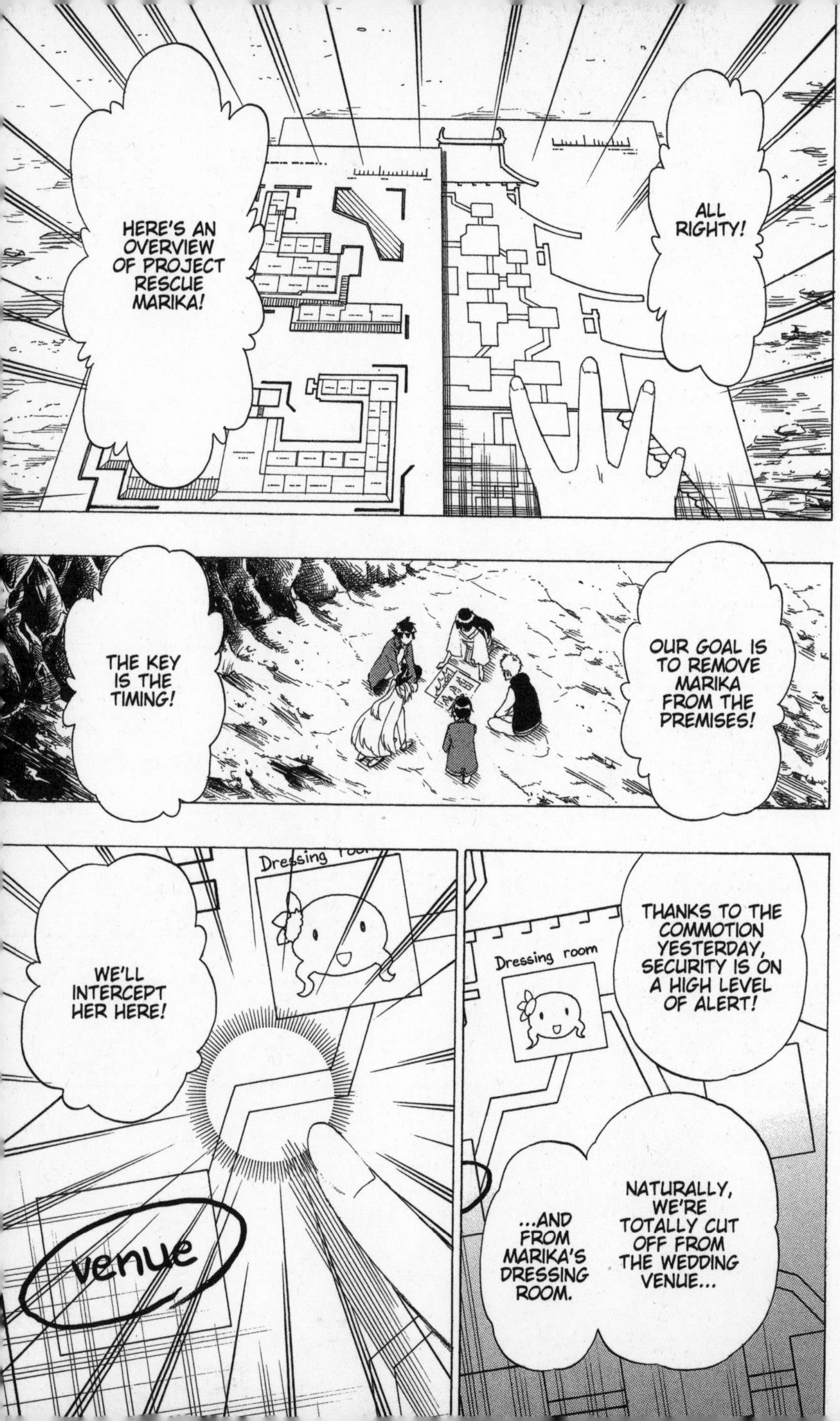
ALL RIGHTY!
HERE'S AN OVERVIEW OF PROJECT RESCUE MARIKA!
OUR GOAL IS TO REMOVE MARIKA FROM THE PREMISES!
THE KEY IS THE TIMING!
THANKS TO THE COMMOTION YESTERDAY, SECURITY IS ON A HIGH LEVEL OF ALERT!
Dressing room
NATURALLY, WE'RE TOTALLY CUT OFF FROM THE WEDDING VENUE...
...AND FROM MARIKA'S DRESSING ROOM.
Dressing
WE'LL INTERCEPT HER HERE!
venue

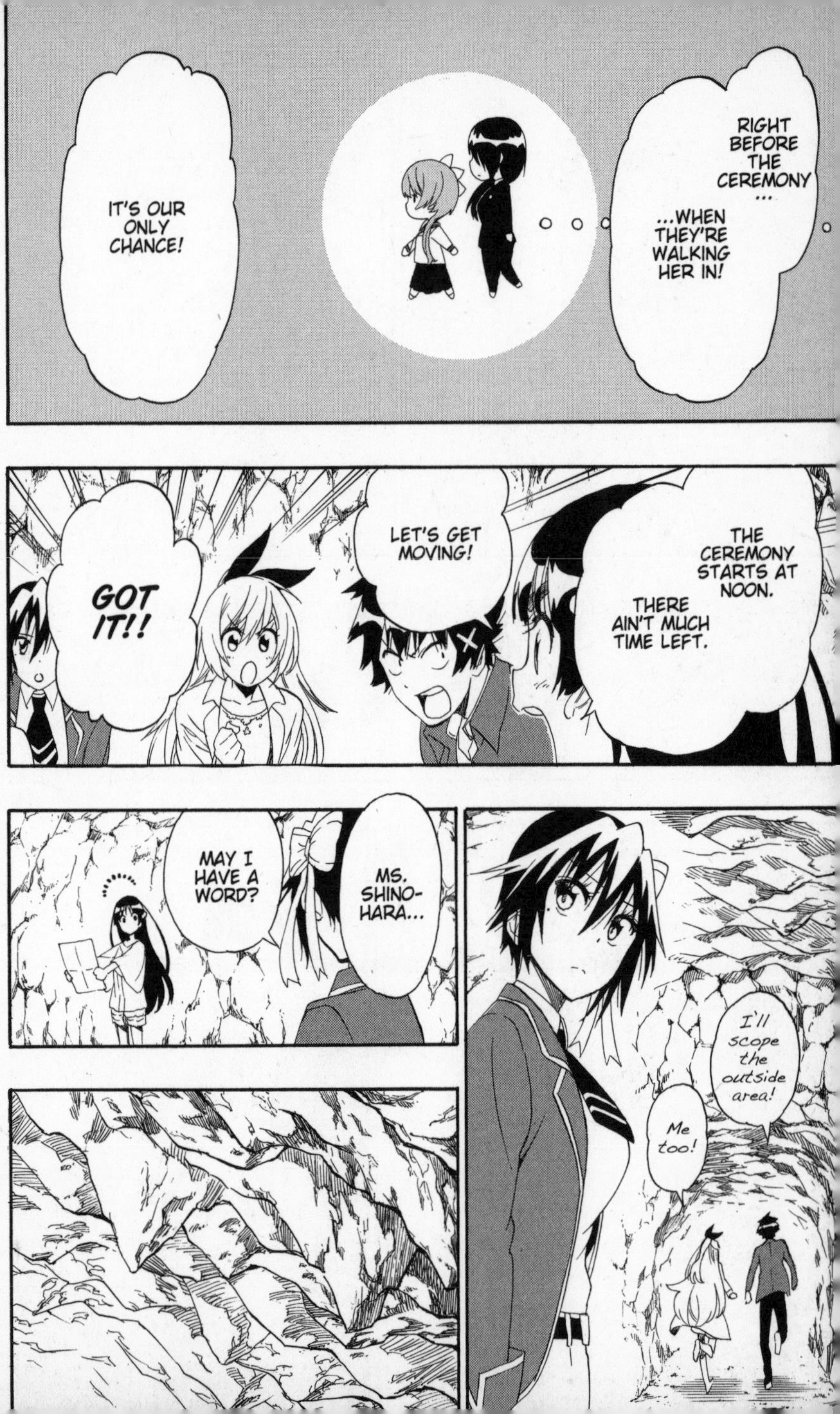
RIGHT BEFORE THE CEREMONY ...
...WHEN THEY'RE WALKING HER IN!
IT'S OUR ONLY CHANCE!
THE CEREMONY STARTS AT NOON.
THERE AIN'T MUCH TIME LEFT.
LET'S GET MOVING!
GOT IT!!
I'll scope the outside area!
Me too!
MS. SHINO-HARA...
MAY I HAVE A WORD?

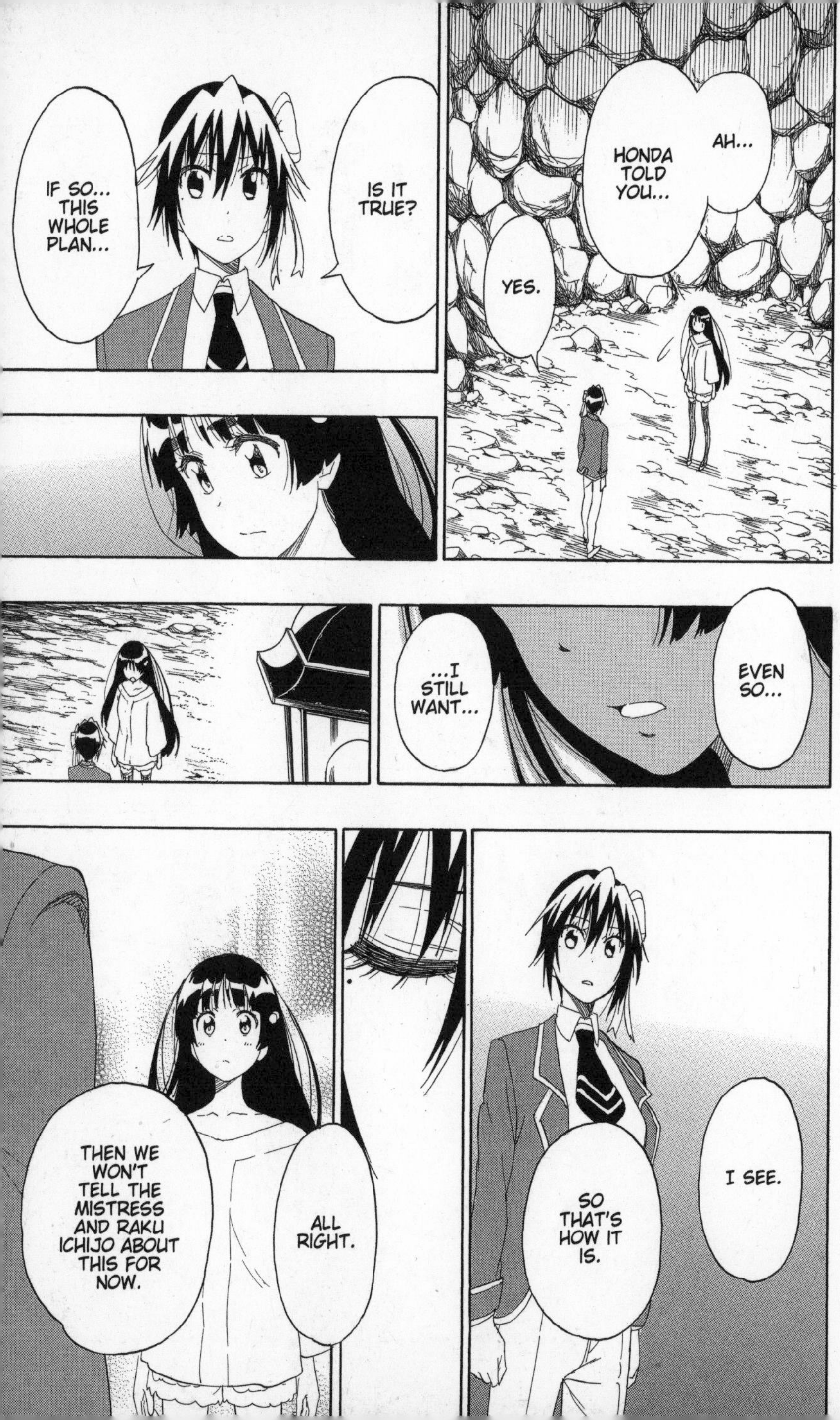
AH...
HONDA TOLD YOU...
YES.
IS IT TRUE?
IF SO... THIS WHOLE PLAN...
EVEN SO...
...I STILL WANT...
I SEE.
SO THAT'S HOW IT IS.
ALL RIGHT.
THEN WE WON'T TELL THE MISTRESS AND RAKU ICHIJO ABOUT THIS FOR NOW.

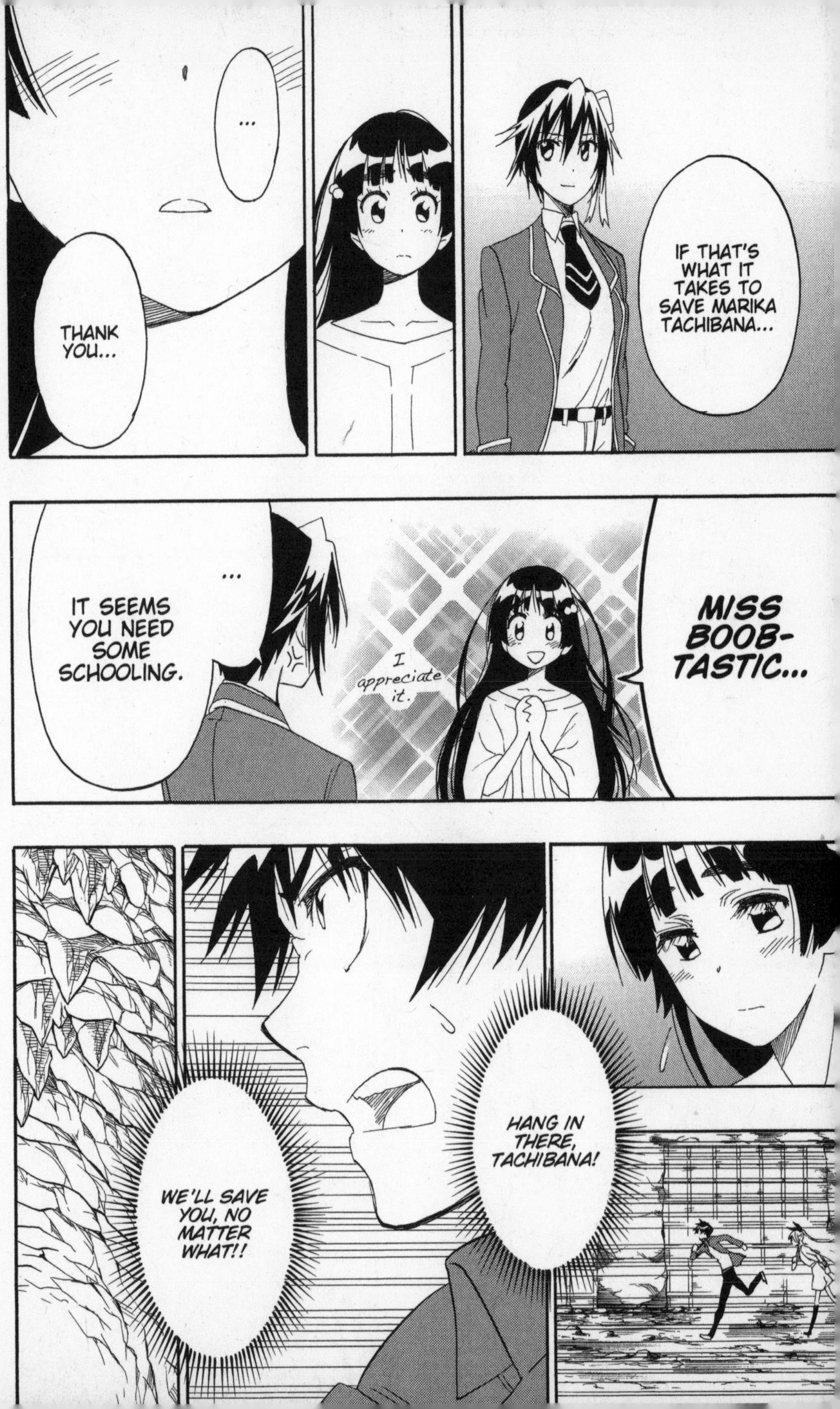
IF THAT'S WHAT IT TAKES TO SAVE MARIKA TACHIBANA...
...
THANK YOU...
MISS BOOB-TASTIC...
I appreciate it.
...
IT SEEMS YOU NEED SOME SCHOOLING.
HANG IN THERE, TACHIBANA!
WE'LL SAVE YOU, NO MATTER WHAT!!

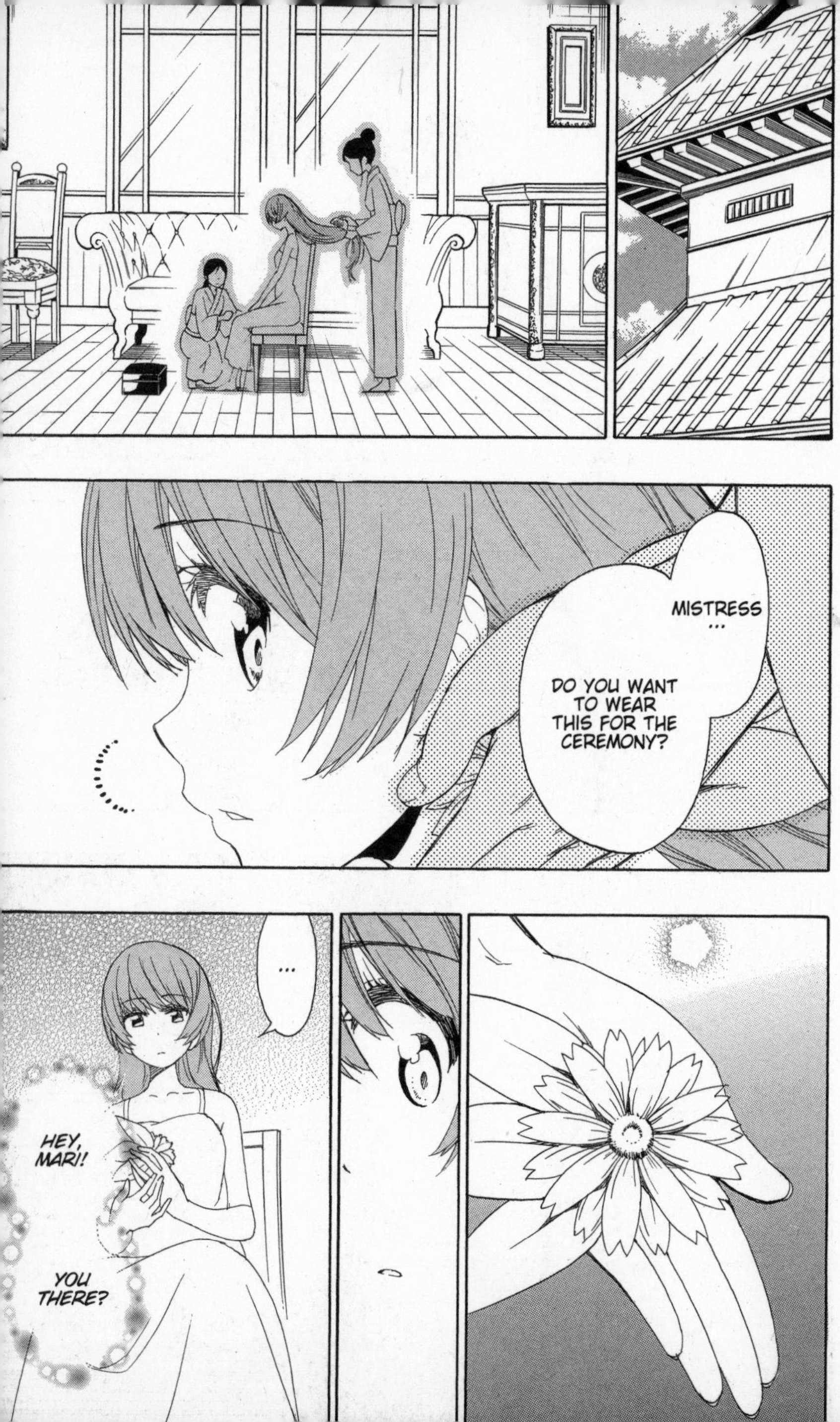
MISTRESS... DO YOU WANT TO WEAR THIS FOR THE CEREMONY?
...
HEY, MARI!
YOU THERE?

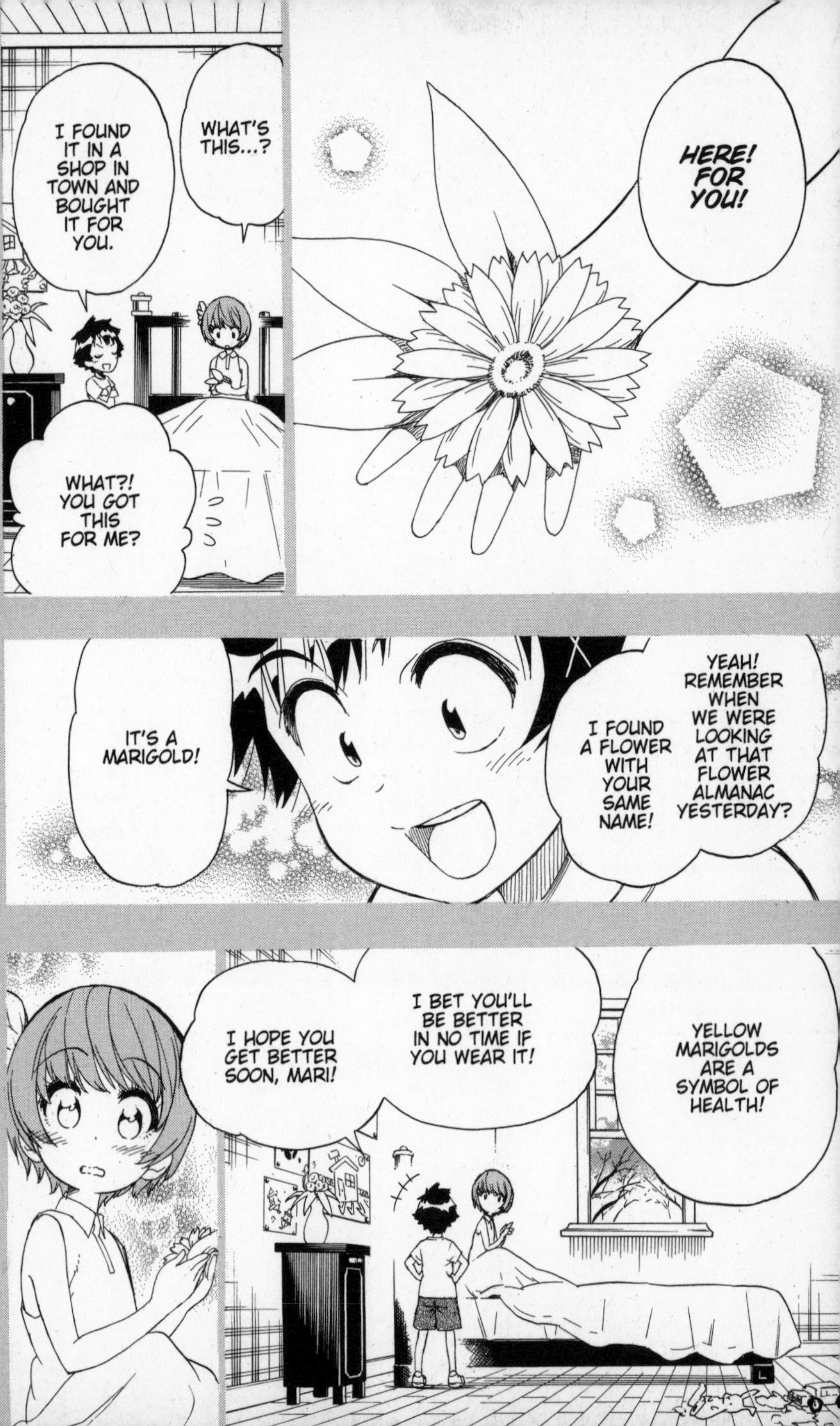
HERE! FOR YOU!
WHAT'S THIS...?
I FOUND IT IN A SHOP IN TOWN AND BOUGHT IT FOR YOU.
WHAT?! YOU GOT THIS FOR ME?
YEAH! REMEMBER WHEN WE WERE LOOKING AT THAT FLOWER ALMANAC YESTERDAY?
I FOUND A FLOWER WITH YOUR SAME NAME!
IT'S A MARIGOLD!
YELLOW MARIGOLDS ARE A SYMBOL OF HEALTH!
I BET YOU'LL BE BETTER IN NO TIME IF YOU WEAR IT!
I HOPE YOU GET BETTER SOON, MARI!

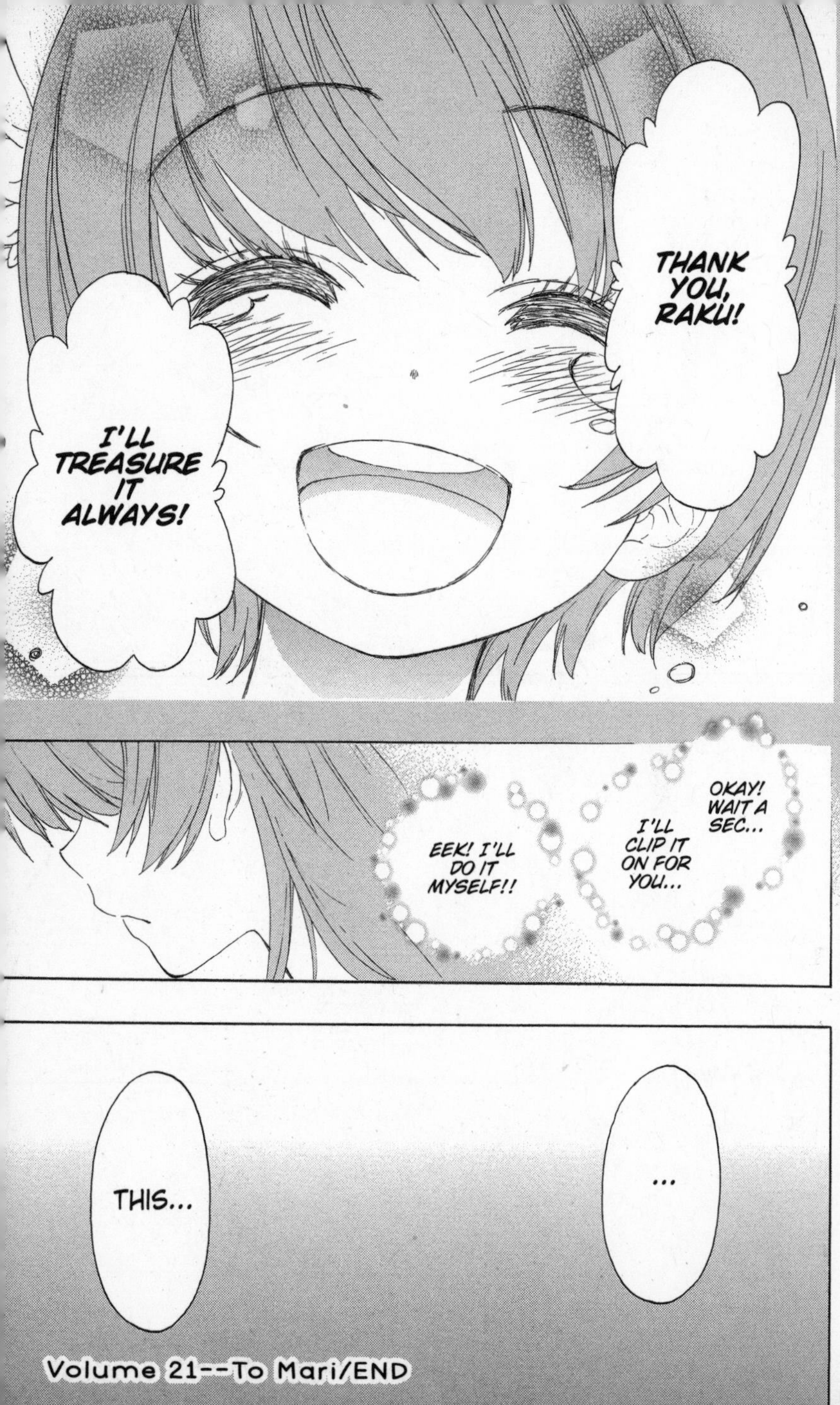
THANK YOU, RAKU!
I'LL TREASURE IT ALWAYS!
OKAY! WAIT A SEC...
I'LL CLIP IT ON FOR YOU...
EEK! I'LL DO IT MYSELF!!
...
THIS...

Volume 21--To Mari/END

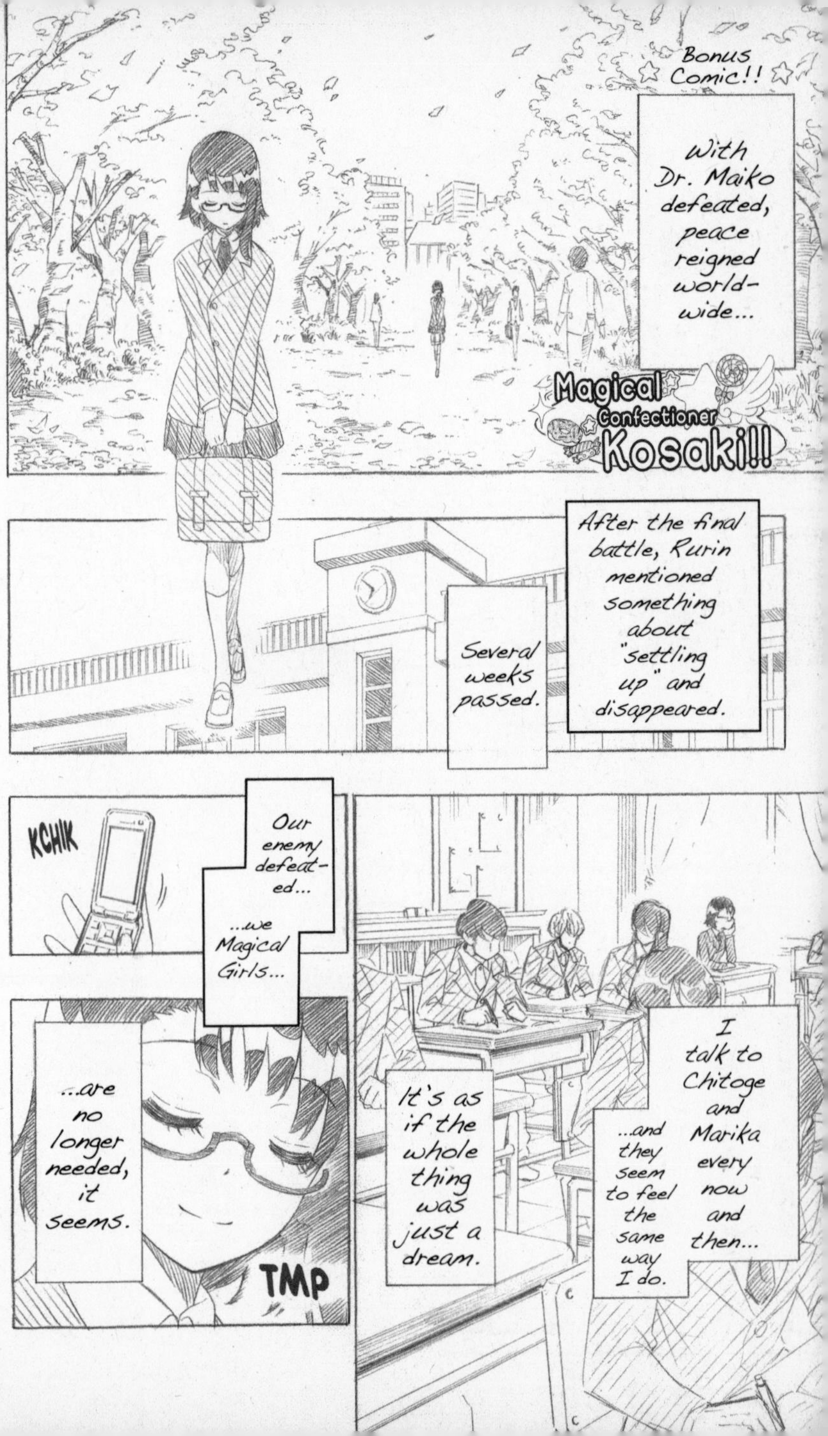
Bonus Comic!!
With Dr. Maiko defeated, peace reigned world-wide...
Magical Confectioner Kosaki!!
After the final battle, Rurin mentioned something about "settling up" and disappeared.
Several weeks passed.
I talk to Chitoge and Marika every now and then...
...and they seem to feel the same way I do.
It's as if the whole thing was just a dream.
Our enemy defeat-ed...
...we Magical Girls...
KCHIK
...are no longer needed, it seems.
TMP

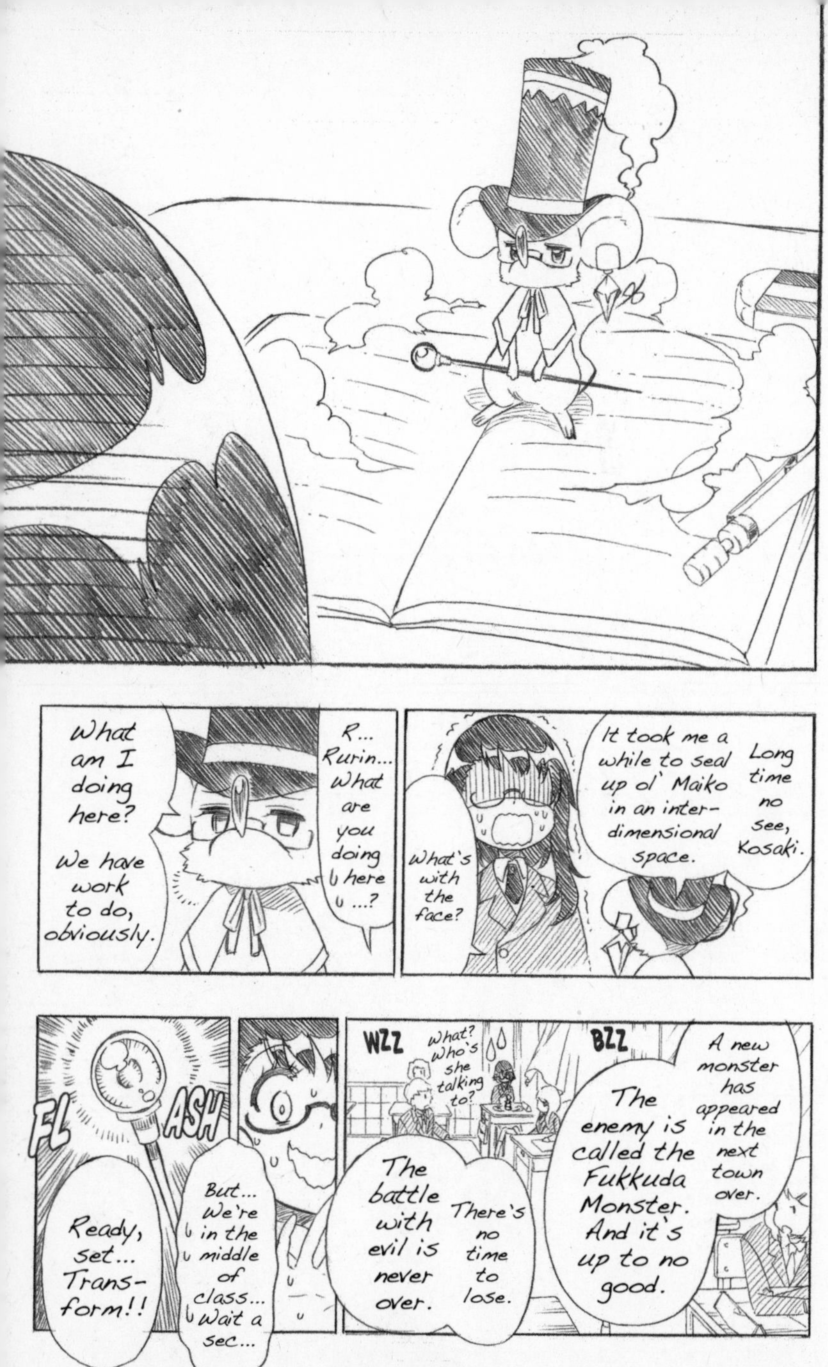
Long time no see, Kosaki.
It took me a while to seal up ol' Maiko in an inter-dimensional space.
What's with the face?
R... Rurin... What are you doing here ...?
What am I doing here?
We have work to do, obviously.
A new monster has appeared in the next town over.
BZZ
The enemy is called the Fukkuda Monster. And it's up to no good.
What? Who's she talking to?
WZZ
There's no time to lose.
The battle with evil is never over.
But... We're in the middle of class... Wait a sec...
FLASH
Ready, set... Transform!!

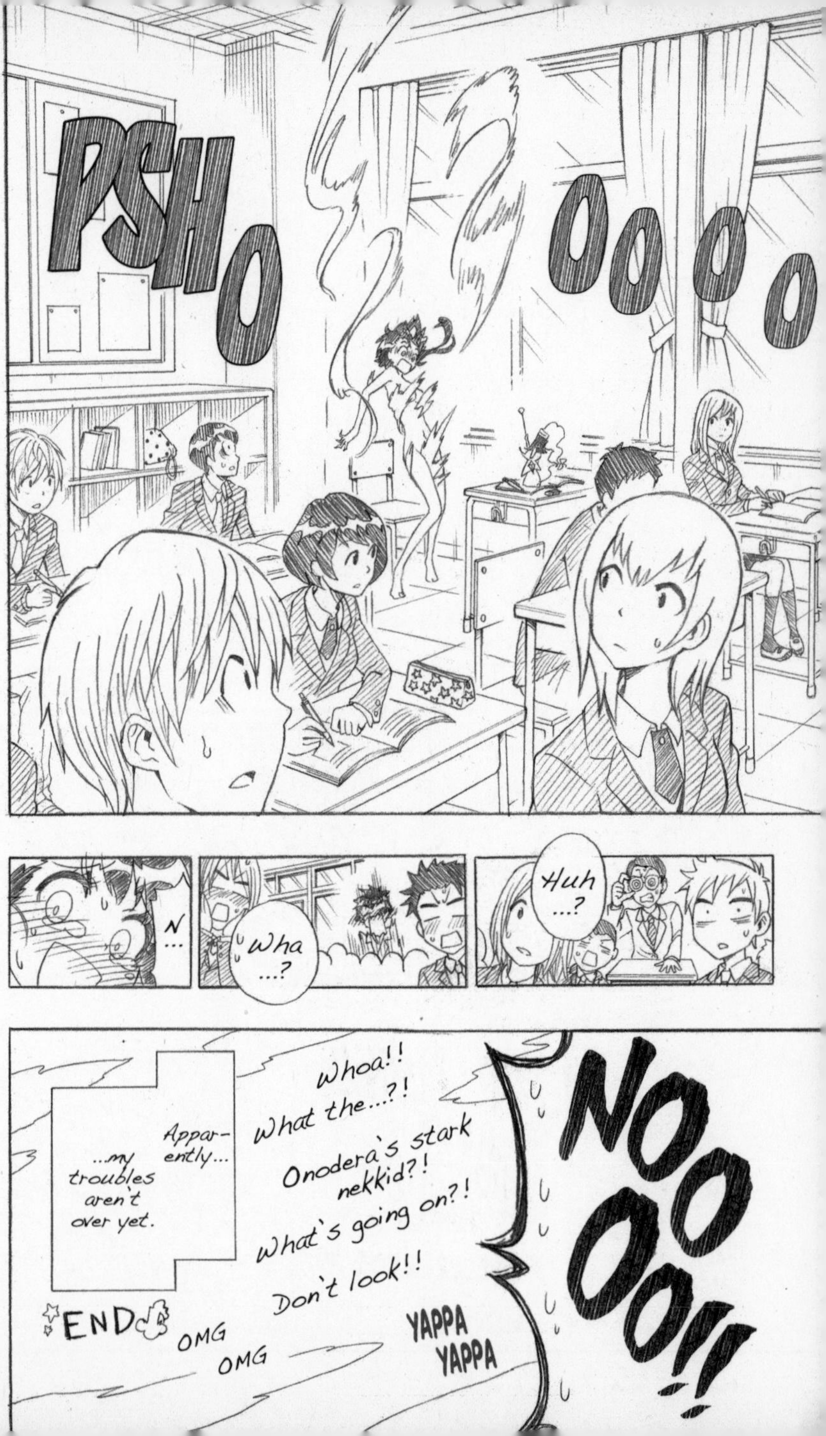
PSHOOOOOO
Huh ...?
Wha ...?
N ...
NOOOOO!!
YAPPA YAPPA
Whoa!!
What the...?!
Onodera's stark nekkid?!
What's going on?!
Don't look!!
OMG OMG
Apparently...
...my troubles aren't over yet.
END

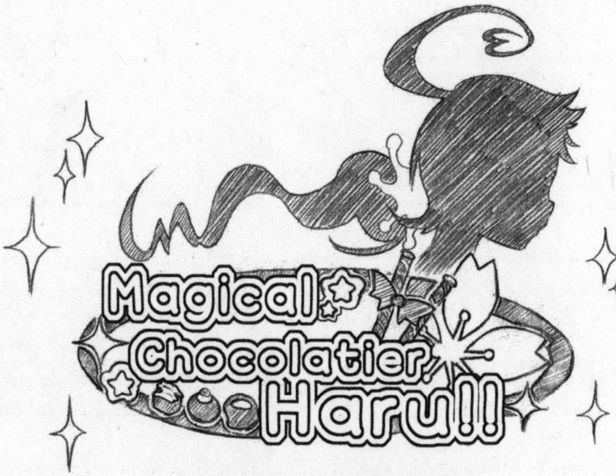
Magical Chocolatier Haru!!

NEXT TIME!!

MAGICAL
CHOCOLATIER
HARU!!

MAYBE...OR MAYBE NOT!

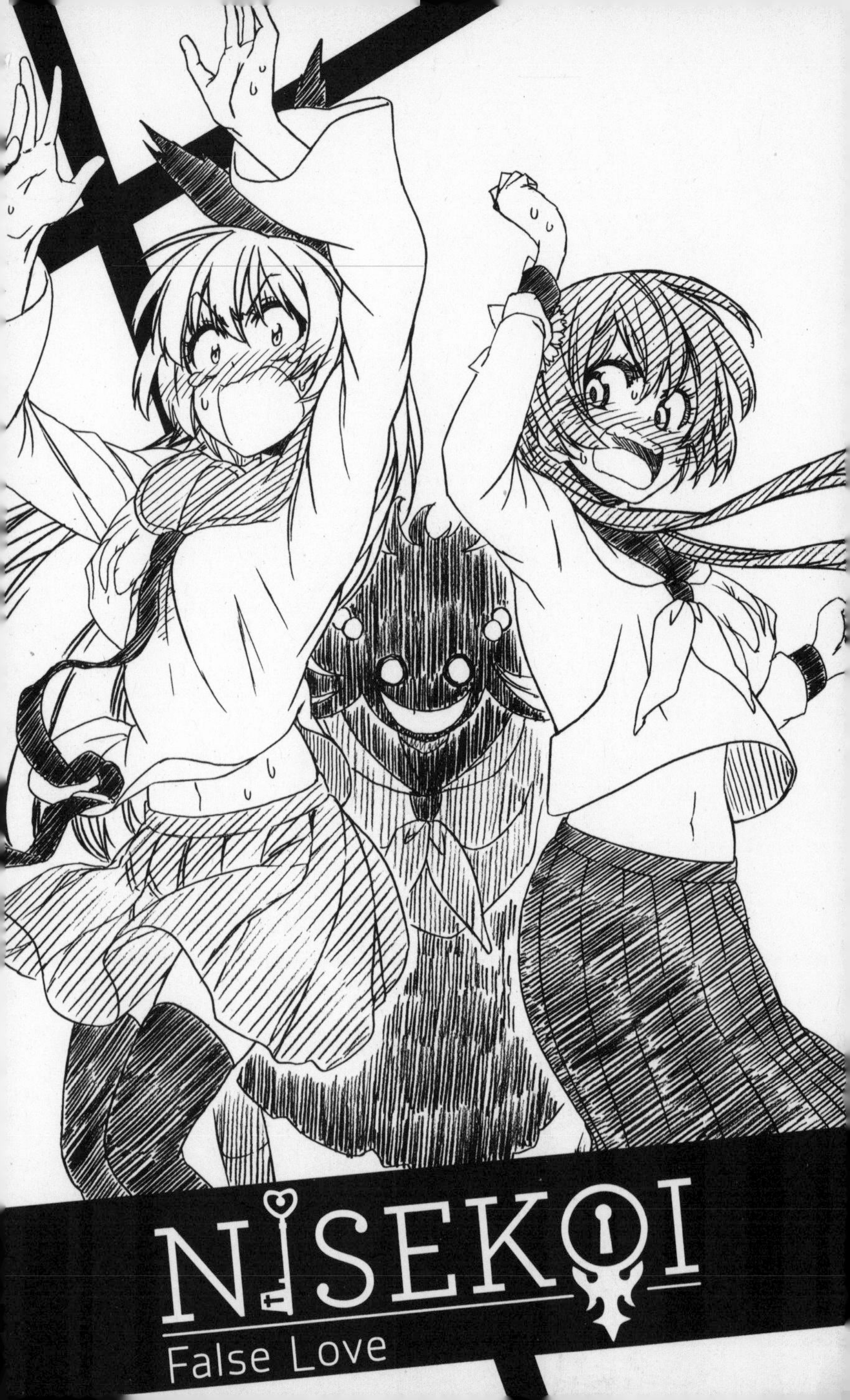
NISEKOI
False Love

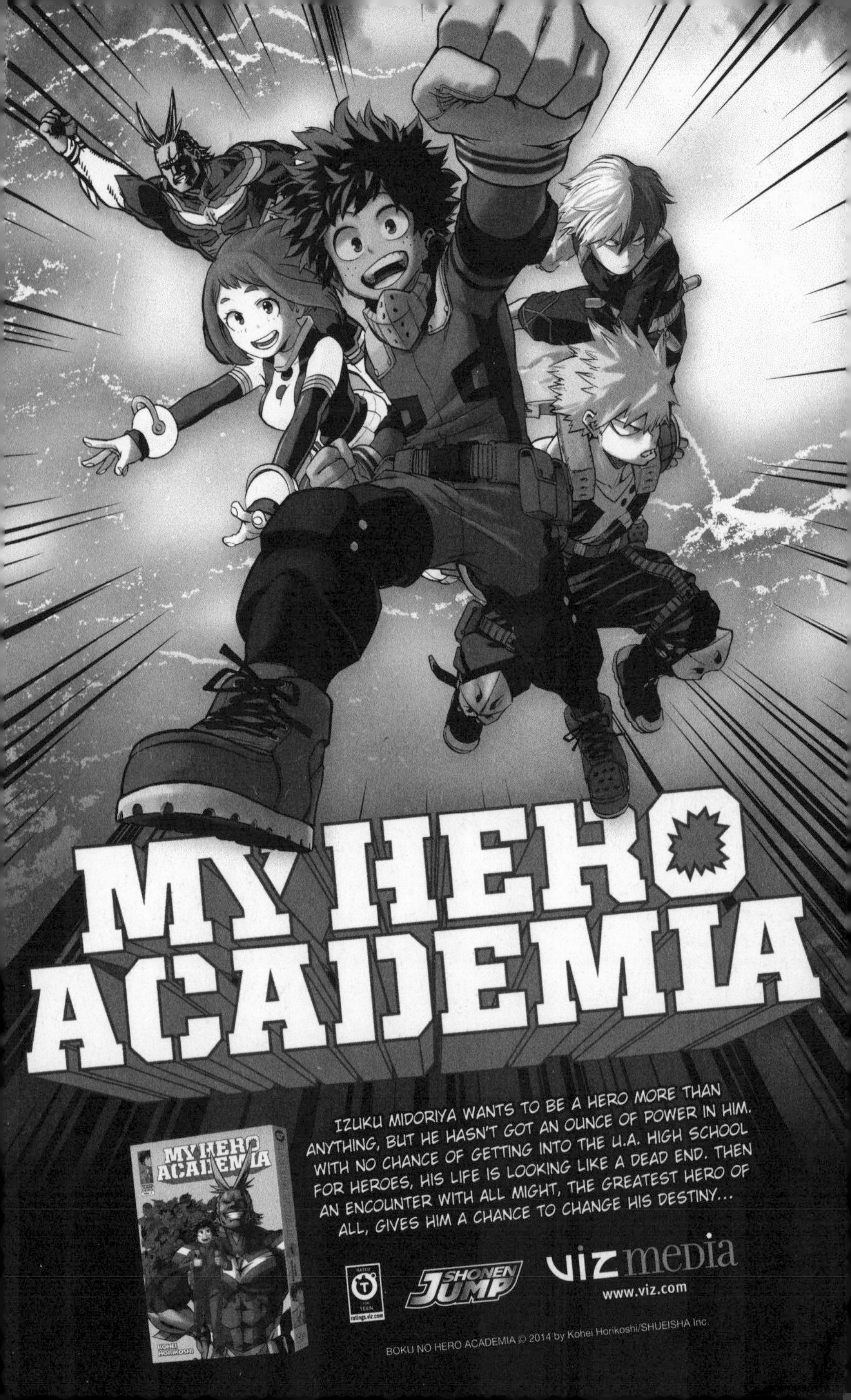
MY HERO ACADEMIA
IZUKU MIDORIYA WANTS TO BE A HERO MORE THAN ANYTHING, BUT HE HASN'T GOT AN OUNCE OF POWER IN HIM. WITH NO CHANCE OF GETTING INTO THE U.A. HIGH SCHOOL FOR HEROES, HIS LIFE IS LOOKING LIKE A DEAD END. THEN AN ENCOUNTER WITH ALL MIGHT, THE GREATEST HERO OF ALL, GIVES HIM A CHANCE TO CHANGE HIS DESTINY…
MY HERO ACADEMIA
KOHEI HORIKOSHI
RATED T FOR TEEN
ratings.viz.com
SHONEN JUMP
viz media
www.viz.com
BOKU NO HERO ACADEMIA © 2014 by Kohei Horikoshi/SHUEISHA Inc.

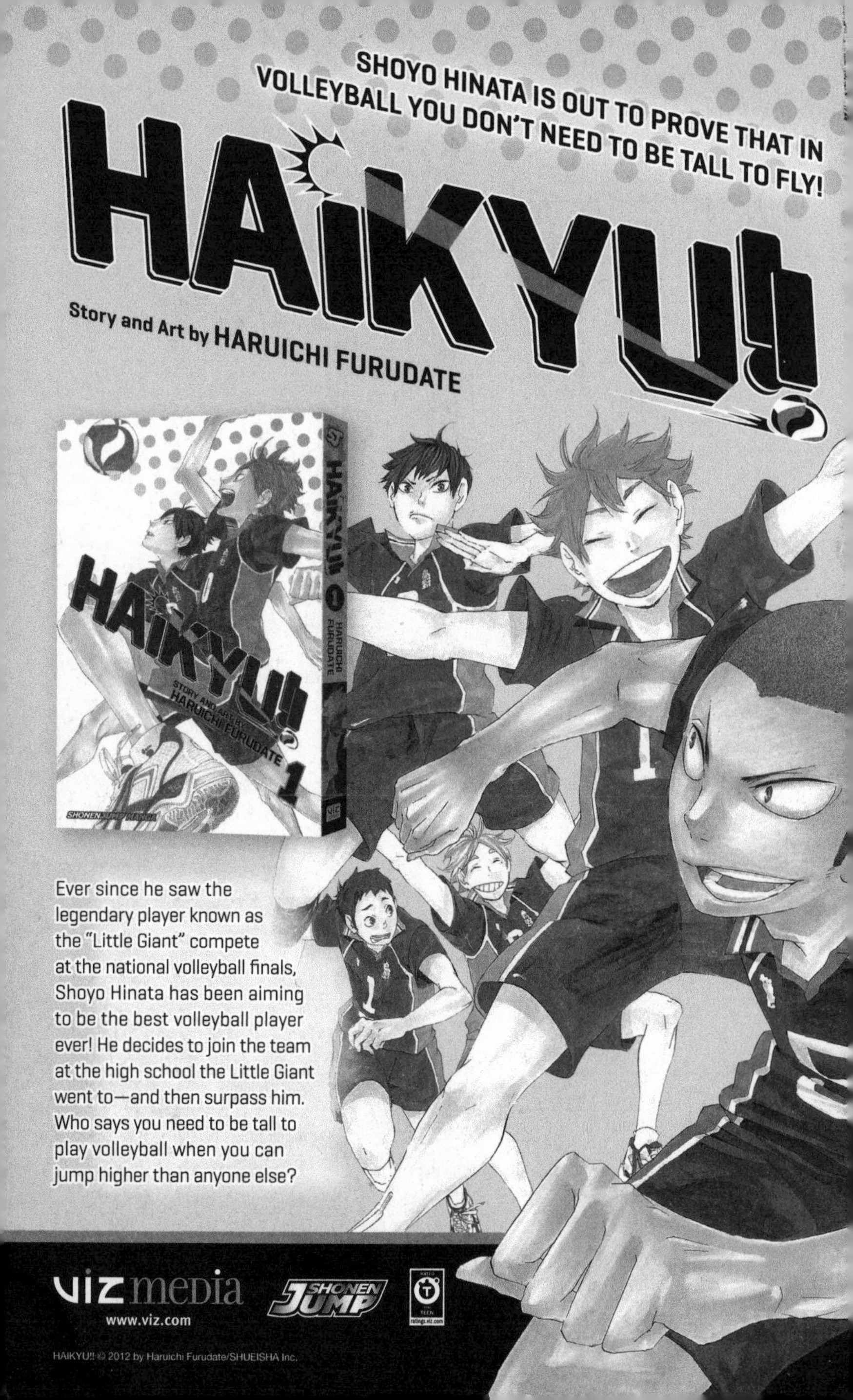
SHOYO HINATA IS OUT TO PROVE THAT IN VOLLEYBALL YOU DON'T NEED TO BE TALL TO FLY!
HAIKYU!!
Story and Art by HARUICHI FURUDATE
HAIKYU!! 1
STORY AND ART BY HARUICHI FURUDATE
SHONEN JUMP MANGA
Ever since he saw the legendary player known as the "Little Giant" compete at the national volleyball finals, Shoyo Hinata has been aiming to be the best volleyball player ever! He decides to join the team at the high school the Little Giant went to—and then surpass him. Who says you need to be tall to play volleyball when you can jump higher than anyone else?
VIZ media
www.viz.com
SHONEN JUMP
RATED T TEEN
ratings.viz.com
HAIKYU!! © 2012 by Haruichi Furudate/SHUEISHA Inc.

You're Reading the WRONG WAY!

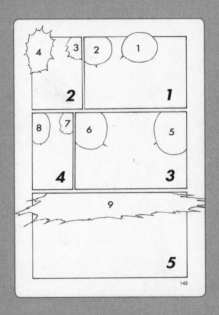

NISEKOI reads from right to left, starting in the upper-right corner. Japanese is read from right to left, meaning that action, sound effects, and ~~rev~~